The Lives of Two Offas

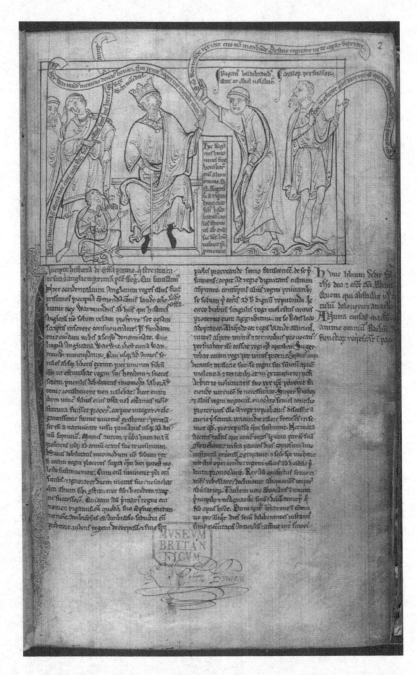

The first page of the thirteenth-century manuscript of The Lives of Two Offas (Vitae Offarum Duorum). *MS Cotton Nero D i, f. 2ʳ © The British Library Board. All Rights Reserved.*

The Lives of Two Offas

Offas

Vitae Offarum Duorum

Introduced, Translated and Edited
by
Michael Swanton

MP
The Medieval Press

The Medieval Press Ltd.,
Curfew Cottage, Church Street, Crediton, Devon EX17 2AQ. UK

www.medievalpress.com

First published in Crediton in 2010
First published in paperback 2011

ISBN 978-0-9566119-0-1 (Hardback)
ISBN 978-0-9566119-1-8 (Paperback)

Typeset in Palatino Linotype

A Note on the Introduction

Recognizing that this volume might be consulted by readers with a wide variety of individual interests, I have made my comments such as might be generally accessible. The 'notes towards' this edition – put to one side with the arrival of new responsibilities during the 1970s – were taken up again only at the point of formal retirement. If the book needs any dedication then it should be to the very many friends and acquaintances who encouraged its eventual publication.

A Note on the Translation

Translation cannot reproduce, or even adequately reflect, the style of an original without departing from its substance to an unacceptable degree. I have tried to present as close a translation as the language will allow without being awkwardly over-literal and with minimum intrusion of the academic voice. In particular I have thought it important not silently to 'improve' the original in places where I felt it to be clumsy, repetitive or obscure.

M.J.S.

Contents

Figures

Introduction I: The Text

It must be admitted at the outset that the twelfth-century Latin *Vitae Offarum Duorum* has little merit as a work of literature. But it is unique and, despite literary and other flaws, offers a variety of insights into early England unavailable elsewhere. Its complete lack of genre and wholesale voracity, of a kind requiring encyclopaedic introductory notes, offers a quarry not only for the literary critic but archaeologist, folklorist and others. It is even possible to extract genuine historical data from the text. However, no fixed boundary between fact and fiction is present at a time when, without means of establishing authenticity, the two were not yet separately significant.[1] Although the general stock of Indo-European imaginative memory focussed in the specific, and most commonly in the political, desires of particular institutions, the impulse of especially the local historian to strip away romantic outer layers of legend to reveal a factual kernel is invariably overconfident. In later times we have been taught to raise a scornful eyebrow at any supposed relationship between the 'real' kings: fourth-century Offa I or eighth-century Offa II and the characters that bear those names in this medieval romance. But our medieval predecessor was not wholly naïve. After all, there were many ways of reading such a text, and the mere fact that something was written in Latin did not necessarily make it 'accurate'.[2] The probably twelfth-century *Deeds of Hereward the Wake* is prefaced with a revealing account of the difficulty of biographical research at this time, having to rely on 'a few loose pages, partly rotten with damp and decayed, and partly damaged by tearing' – while elderly intimates of the real man would fallaciously recount 'the doings of giants and warriors they found in ancient tales along with the true stories.'[3] Even in our own times many a writer has been keen to discover flattering parallels between Queen Elizabeth I and four centuries later her successor the young, post-war Elizabeth II.[4] And indeed, although history rarely repeats itself, it does rhyme a lot.[5]

The creative factor is a major element in the narration of history. With figures and events that have been important to archivists as well as to imaginative writers it is essential to recognise the nature of the irregular interface between record and legend.

---

[1] For an introduction to this issue see S. Fleischman, 'On the representation of history and fiction in the Middle Ages', *History and Theory*, 22 (1983), 278-310.

[2] Thus William of Newburgh, *The History of English Affairs*, ed. and transl. P.G. Walsh and M.J. Kennedy, Warminster, 1988, pp. 28-9.

[3] A text included with Geoffrey Gaimar, *Lestorie des Engles*, ed. T.D. Hardy and C.T. Martin, Rolls Series, 91, London, 1898-99, I, pp. 339-404, transl. M. Swanton in *Medieval Outlaws*, ed. T.H. Ohlgren, Stroud, 1998, pp. 12-60 (pp. 18-20).

[4] E.g. A.L. Rowse, *An Elizabethan Garland*, London, 1954, pp. 144-62; cf. P. Payton, *A.L. Rowse and Cornwall*, Exeter, 2005, pp. 161-3.

[5] An aphorism commonly attributed to Mark Twain, although without evidence.

The authority of any narrative is subject to primordial iconotropy – always liable to penetration and accretion, let alone fictional distortion. Furthermore, as one twelfth-century minstrel points out, 'song can impair the story' (*de la canchon ont corrunpu la geste*).[6] Or perhaps it was merely that propaganda is more to their purpose than poetry. Just as suspicion rather than credulity is preferred in our present-day political stance, so academically we learn to sift misinformation and disinformation presented to us, and consequently are happiest when dealing with very narrowly focussed knowledge in which we are ourselves expert; and any pleasure to be had in mere literary structures – when associated with past data – is felt apostate.[7] Of course in early medieval times history could still properly be regarded as merely one order of *belles lettres*, and not yet a separate science. But it has only ever been the most sober of historians who have allowed dull truth to stand in the way of a good story. Those who seek to restore something authentic but lost will discount all the first part of this text, and be properly sceptical about much of the remainder. Those others who recognise that truth may inhere elsewhere than in trivial actuality will be less concerned with telling true from false than with the value of narrative as a mode of making some sense of the world – providing the consolations of social or moral desire. These are the stories we feel compelled to iterate or invent – the necessary national and personal myths by which we live – typically historicizing alienation of good and evil.[8] Nevertheless, in this text the requirement of the record cynically denies our romantic assumptions, insisting that the simple expectations of folklore are not fulfilled but disrupted. Our tale suggests that it is not always the case that the good queen comes later to take the place of bad (pp. lxxvi-lxxxix)

In a text compiled by men with a taste for antique fables, then supplemented with the oral recollections of old soldiers and finally set in a matrix of archival reference, it is now virtually impossible to unravel the various strands of differing status. No doubt a germ of the historical Offas I and II, give or take romantic exaggeration, lies at the heart of the story – although we might assume a good deal to be fictional.

The chronicle habit is not confined to archival culture; it is articulated no less in what we readily dismiss as 'tradition', folklore' or 'legend'. The creative story-telling instinct exists in parallel with conscious historiography. And just as the tutored historian both builds on and differs from his predecessors, offering either new material or a new perspective on what has been received, the collateral tradition does not merely hand down the received memory of events but, by recycling, elaborating, omitting and inventing, serves a succession of audiences with new interests and expectations. As a society changes, so does its relationship with the past. Certainly the construction of a nation's self-image, and myth – the memory by which that identity is secured – was

---

[6] *La Chevalerie d'Ogier de Danemarche*, 11160, ed. M. Eusebi, Milan, 1963, p. 423.

[7] A convenient example of the scholarly historian's present-day stance comes to hand in R. Abels, 'Alfred and his biographers: images and imagination', in *Writing Medieval Biography 750-1250*, ed. D. Bates, J. Crick and S. Hamilton, Woodbridge, 2006, pp. 61-75.

[8] Cf. L. Passerini, 'Mythbiography in oral history', in *The Myths We Live By*, ed. R. Samuel and P. Thompson, London, 1990, pp. 49-60.

always changing. Significant narration was by no means restricted to a *cadre* of professional entertainers alone but extended to all parts of society, through which both style and substance will have varied. Bede describes how a nervous cow-herd would find some excuse to absent himself upon realising that his turn with the lyre was due.[9] At the same time, when the princely occupants of various ostentatious seventh-century tombs lay in state surrounded by significant items, a prominent place was given to the instrument.[10]

Inevitably we ourselves read and interpret in terms of our own later-developed literary culture those elements of the past that correspond to what presently compels us. But here the very term *litterae* is inappropriate; our surviving text neither necessitates nor supposes the recitation of a written base. The consequence is one of variable forms, constantly interplaying between one another to the point where latter-day scholarship must surrender any question of probability and be exceedingly cautious even in case of possibility. What we have 'picked up somewhere' easily becomes 'common knowledge'. Nowadays, what we have 'read in the newspaper' or 'seen on TV' must surely be true! In this way a *tsunami* easily becomes Noah's Flood.

The *Lives of Two Offas* is fiction interleaved with fact: a kind of romance that offers more than mere entertainment. What it lacks in historical accuracy or chronological perspective, it gains in concrete and dramatic immediacy. It has the lure of celebrity. Never merely proceedings observed, it allows a sense of intimacy with famous men – the history-makers – at critical moments in their lives. We focus on scenes of stress or exhilaration so as to identify the all too human element in decisions affecting the fate of nations. But the figures portrayed here remain two-dimensional Platonically-conceived Romanesque personae engaged in a series of situations that display unmixed motives or emotions. They do not develop fully-realised personalities. Their connecting strand is cause or narrative function rather than psychology.

The St Albans Tradition

The text of *The Two Offas* in its surviving form seems to have been compiled by a cleric attached to the Benedictine abbey at St Albans (Hertfordshire), apparently intending to emphasise the antiquity and regal connections of this institution. We are listening to the voice of one of those cultivated men who found the traditional claims and cults of the place, previously taken for granted, now threatened and disparaged. He has been driven to the task of assembling fragmentary and dispersed information of all kinds

---

[9] Bede, *Ecclesiastical History of the English People*, IV, 24, ed. and transl. B. Colgrave and R.A.B. Mynors, Oxford, 1969, pp. 414-7.

[10] C.L. Wrenn, 'Two Anglo-Saxon harps', in *Studies in Old English Literature in Honor of Arthur G. Brodeur*, ed. S.B. Greenfield, Portland, 1963, pp. 118-28; R.L.S. Bruce-Mitford, *The Sutton Hoo Ship-Burial*, London, 1975-83, III, pp. 611-731; Museum of London, *The Prittlewell Prince*, London, 2004, with full publication awaited.

from unpromising texts in what were rapidly becoming archival curiosities, so as to present a picture of the past which would impress hostile or indifferent newcomers.[11]

In brief, the abbey is said to have been established by Offa II, an eighth-century English king of Mercia (Midland England), in fulfilment of an obligation inherited from his ancestor and namesake, the little-known fourth-century Continental English ruler Offa I. For the purposes of the romance it is supposed that the earlier Offa's family is already established in a Christian Mercia. The genealogies of insular English kings, including Offa II, continued to claim exotic – and even supernatural – ancestry (Fig. 6; Appendix A, pp. 133-4), although how long these names, and which names, were understood by all to be Continental probably varied. Somewhat in the manner of an ancestral romance, our text compares the lives of two dynasts whose careers resemble each other in very many respects, and presents *inter alia* the sensational foundation-myth of St Albans.

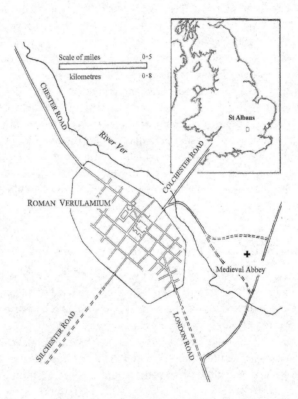

Fig. 1) Location of Roman Verulamium and medieval St Albans abbey.

---

[11] Cf. R.W. Southern, 'Aspects of the European tradition of historical writing: 4, The sense of the past', *Transactions of the Royal Historical Society*, Fifth Series, 23 (1973), 243-63 (pp. 246-49); J. Campbell, 'Some twelfth-century views of the Anglo-Saxon past', in *Essays in Anglo-Saxon History*, London, 1986, pp. 209-28.

Believed to house the bones of the very first national Christian martyr, discovered nearby by King Offa II (pp. 103-8), St Albans abbey had become the premier Benedictine establishment in medieval England, [12] claiming exemption from the jurisdiction of any save the pope (pp. 113-16, 121-4). An exceptionally rich institution and politically influential, it had friends at court and commonly entertained royal visitors it housed in specially-built quarters. Its proximity to the capital, lying less than twenty miles (30 km) from London on the major road north (pp. 117-18), and equipped with stabling for three hundred horses, proved it a centre of affairs. Its facilities provided for men who took pleasure in maintaining a regular knowledge of important people and significant happenings.[13]

Of the pre-Conquest abbey we know relatively little. The formal opinion of the Norman abbots who took over was that their predecessors were *rudes et idiotas*.[14] Stories told how they had been fond of extra-mural activities – too much hunting, too little praying – preferring secular attire, meat-eating and over-friendly relations with neighbouring nuns.[15] Soon all official record of them was simply lost or erased. The last English abbot of St Albans, a friend and tower of strength to Harold Godwinson in 1066,[16] led a robust anti-Norman party in the days afterwards, in consequence of which William the Conqueror seized a good part of the institution's estates, forcing the abbot to flee to Ely, taking Alban's bones with him – or so the men of Ely later claimed.[17]

The new French archbishop of Canterbury, Lanfranc, took the first opportunity to send a reliable man, one Paul of Caen – Lanfanc's own son some would claim – to bring the place to heel. Whether or not, as our text avers,[18] a large number of those originally assembled by Offa II in 793 had been Frankish monks from Bec (pp. 117-18), the arrival of this autocratic Norman from Bec was undoubtedly a shock to the English community he now found at St Albans, leaving no part of their lives untouched. His rule (1077-93) marked a thorough break with past custom.[19] Established members were now excluded from promotion, and almost a century was to pass before there would be another English abbot (p. xxvii). The organisation Paul had been sent to govern must

[12] See generally *The Victoria County History of Hertfordshire*, ed. W. Page, London, 1902-23, II, pp. 483-510, IV, pp. 367-416; also L.F.R. Williams, *History of the Abbey of St. Alban*, London, 1917.

[13] With no want of applicants, it could reject the young Nicholas Breakspear – later the sole English pope – on grounds of insufficient learning; cf. C. Egger, 'The canon regular', in *Adrian IV, The English Pope (1154-1159)*, ed. B. Bolton and A.J. Duggan, Aldershot, 2003, pp. 15-28.

[14] *Gesta Abbatum Monasterii Sancti Albani*, ed. H.T. Riley, Rolls Series, 28, London, 1867-69, I, p. 62; R. Niblett and I. Thompson, *Alban's Buried Towns*, Oxford, 2005, p. 368.

[15] *Gesta Abbatum*, I, p. 11, Niblett and Thompson, pp. 360-61; apparently par for the course in some early communities suggests Bede, *Opera Historica*, ed. C. Plummer, Oxford, 1896, I, pp. 415-16, transl. *English Historical Documents*, I, ed. D. Whitelock, London, 2nd edition, 1979, pp. 804-06.

[16] For the possibility of a pre-Conquest monk's active part in warfare, see *Hereward* in Gaimar, *Lestorie*, Hardy and Martin, pp. 377-78; Swanton, *Medieval Outlaws*, p. 45.

[17] See *Gesta Abbatum*, I, pp. 50-51; by the twelfth century not only Ely, but also places in Denmark and Spain claimed to possess the martyr's bones, I, pp. 12-19, 87-88, Niblett and Thompson, pp. 360, 372.

[18] Inaccurately, inasmuch as Bec in Normandy was not founded until the 1030's.

[19] *Gesta Abbatum*, I, pp. 51-66, Niblett and Thompson, p. 368.

have seemed to him impossibly lax and irregular. We might not be surprised that he should wish to make their diet and dress more frugal than hitherto, forbid conversation in church, cloister and refectory, and during the evening even in hospital or dormitory – imprisoning those who did not comply. Understandable perhaps was his decision to demolish their old church [20] in favour of building anew in the more austere Romanesque fashion then current on the Continent and utilizing much architectural salvage from the now ruined and only vestigially-occupied Roman Verulamium.[21] A formidable construction, vastly exceeding in scale the archbishop's church at Canterbury, it presented striking views from a distance. Harder to bear no doubt was his replacement of their traditional English style of chant with a Norman one and his requirement that their pronunciation of the Latin liturgy change to his own. Together with the old church, he broke up the tombs of his liberal predecessors, scorning to transfer their remains to his new building. And he neglected to secure even the remains of the community's English founder (King Offa II), which in consequence were lost to posterity (pp. xcvii-xi).[22] On the abbey estates Frenchmen replaced English tenants; English benefactors went elsewhere.

Institutionally, as well as nationally, there had been radical change over a remarkably short period. Under foreign rule, that *bloc* of Englishmen who remained at St Albans had good reason to look back to the old days with nostalgia. No doubt a native wish to assert the vernacular status of their community was all the more determined because of recent events. In a long-established, wealthy organization like St Albans, resentment of the incomer must have been considerable and continuous. For, unlike their relatives among the aristocracy who were over-turned and dispossessed within a generation, these monks, steeped in such proofs of original greatness, must have been constantly reminded of the present debasement of their heritage. And these were now the only members of the community who understood the language (English) in which so much of the evidence of the past was preserved. At mid-twelfth-century St Albans, English was still commonly spoken, [23] albeit held cheap by cultivated institutional newcomers.

But the Norman colonials, who came to think of themselves as 'Englanders' long before they spoke the native language, soon became interested in old native stories. Even if the function of accounts such as those of Bevis of Hampton or Guy of Warwick seemed to be more a moral examination of the making of the good king than the

[20] Rather stylish if we may judge from pieces of balustrading incorporated in the north transept: T.P. Smith, *The Anglo-Saxon Churches of Hertfordshire*, Chichester, 1973, pp. 14, 22-23. The Royal Commission on Historical Monuments (England) suggested that they may perhaps be assigned to the time of Offa II, but that needs arguing: *An Inventory of the Historical Monuments in Hertfordshire*, London, 1911, p. 10 and plate facing.

[21] Cf. T.P. Smith, 'Early recycling: the Anglo-Saxon and Norman re-use of Roman bricks' and T. Tatton-Brown, 'The medieval building stones of St Albans Abbey', in M. Henig and P. Lindley, ed. *Alban and St Albans*, Leeds, 2001, pp. 111-17, 118-23.

[22] *Gesta Abbatum*, I, p. 62, Niblett and Thompson, p. 368.

[23] *Gesta Abbatum*, I, p. 99; and perhaps more commonly in all institutions than frequently supposed.

transmission of historical data,[24] it was there they would find their national, if not racial, forefathers.[25] However, witness of a historical revival does not exist solely in the interpretative histories it produced, but in the renewed celebration of national saints, and concern to preserve vernacular literary and scientific texts, together with a wholesale transcription of early charters and legal documents. Now, when even Benedictine institutions were threatened by royal demands, it was more than ever important to demonstrate that the events of 1066 represented no more than a hiccup in history. Easy enough from a twenty-first-century perspective for the critic to recognise elements of cultural continuity across the centuries, but for his twelfth-century counterpart these must have seemed none too apparent. As 'incomers enjoyed the riches and gnawed at the entrails of England and there was no hope of the misery ending,'[26] what was brought into question was its very identity. New writers were driven by a need to demonstrate the existence of a national past. And successfully so; it is rare that the man in the High Street thinks of the Norman Conquest in 1066 as any kind of humiliation for the English but inexplicably as a triumph.

Here at St Albans in Hertfordshire it is understandable that the ancient Mercian traditions should have survived, albeit in the form we have them, despite the cultural parenthesis occasioned by Norman control. In publicizing the story of its foundation, St Albans was no different from other significant monastic houses, such as Abingdon, Ely or Glastonbury, collecting, revising and supplementing archival material accumulated over several centuries. The pattern was one of taking possession of various existing stories of saints and kings, re-locating them on abbey territory, grafting them onto any previous aetiological myth, hopefully omitting contradictions, and presenting all in terms and genre fashionable at the time.

Synopsis of the Text

Since the narrative of the *Vitae* is relatively disorganised, and in consequence any Introduction somewhat piece-meal, here follows a synopsis of the text (*italicised*) together with sufficient information to unscramble what is initially confusing. As presented in the twelfth century, our tale relates the deeds of two early English kings who lived four centuries apart, but who bear the same name. The opening chapter heading (pp. 1-2) makes explicit the resemblance between the two that we might look for. Our story-line supposes, and intends, a dense interrelationship of inexactly parallel

---

[24] Geoffrey Gaimar would provide them with an Anglo-Norman anecdotal history of Britain from its origins to their own times, including passing references to Offa II: *L'Estoire des Engleis*, ed. A. Bell, Oxford, 1960; and, more romantically, Wace recover Celtic legends of Arthur, Guinevere, Merlin and Lear: *Roman de Brut*, ed. J. Weiss, Exeter, 1999.

[25] See generally M.D. Legge, *Anglo-Norman Literature and its Background*, Oxford, 1963, pp. 139-75; W.R.J. Barron, *English Medieval Romance*, London, 1987, pp. 74-85, 217.

[26] William of Malmesbury, *Gesta Regum Anglorum*, ed. and transl. R.A.B. Mynors *et al.*, Oxford, 1998-99, pp. 414-17.

elements, for the full understanding of which we now depend upon unfortunately inadequate information.

Offa I, a pagan who in reality ruled during the fourth or fifth century part of what is now Schleswig-Holstein (see Fig. 4; pp. xxxviii-xliii) is here supposed to have lived in early Mercia, and in a Christianised society. Offa II, his descendant, was an actual ruler of Mercia, 757-96, and a figure of international importance. It is said that Offa I had subjugated the greater part of England (historically the achievement of Offa II), and merely that the later king was very like his predecessor! The *curriculum vitae* of Offa II either did, or is made to, echo various features in the career of his ancestor – or in retrospect in reverse.[27] Then, awkwardly incorporated, there are disproportionate quotations from the genuine archives of Offa II, and clerical concerns with ecclesiastical history in general and of the Abbey of St Albans in particular.

The tale of Offa I is set in the English Midlands (the kingdom of Mercia) and a supposed Christian age (pp. 1-36).

In fact Offa I probably ruled the English people, then pagan and coming from what is now southern Denmark (Angeln) shortly prior to their wholesale migration to settle in the north and midland areas of what would become England (pp. xliii-xlvi). The earlier, together with Scandinavian, versions of the tale (Appendices *passim*), maintain the historical locale (pp. xlvii-l).

Offa, the sole child of an elderly king, has been born disabled; he is blind until the age of seven and mute until later (pp. 1-2).

Such a childhood circumstance has analogues among early literary heroes, and significantly exists as an actual medical condition (pp. liii-liv). Another narrative line understands the father of lumpen Offa to have been a Near Eastern merchant adventurer successfully working in the region (p. l).

Since it is unclear who is to succeed to the throne, another prospective usurper recruits a foreign army. Now Offa, thirty years old, is prompted to speak for the first time, arguing eloquently against this treacherous attempt upon his own family's hold on the throne (pp. 3-6). Taking charge of his father's army, he confronts and defeats the intending invader at a river crossing. Offa takes a leading part in the battle, impulsively rushing across the river and personally slaying individual enemy champions (pp. 7-12).

Scandinavian versions make much of the single combat between champions, often at river locations (pp. lxi-lxii). Cognate material indicates that the river in question was originally the Treene-Eider river system which, together with a monumental dyke, would become the southern frontier of the English nation – with on its southern side the hostile Saxon people (Figs. 7-8; pp. lxv-lxvii).

---

[27] For a ready review of what has been termed 'the Mercian supremacy' see S. Keynes, 'The kingdom of the Mercians in the eighth century', in *Æthelbald and Offa, two Eighth-century kings of Mercia*, ed. D. Hill and M. Worthington, Oxford, 2005, pp. 1-26.

Upon his return to court, Offa is acclaimed a national hero and, in due course, takes the English crown as of right, and reigns commendably (pp. 13-22).

The national frontier is now secure (made implicit in the *vita*; alluded to in the poem *Beowulf*, Appendix C, pp. 141-2; more clearly described in Scandinavian versions which retain a Danish locale, Appendices G and H, pp. 169-72, 179-82).

Hunting in the forest lost and alone, Offa encounters a beautiful Northumbrian princess whom her father, the king of York, has ordered to be abandoned there in retribution for her rejection of his incestuous advances. A hospitable hermit guides them back to Offa's kingdom, where later she becomes his queen (pp. 21-6).

Offa I now features as the male protagonist in the familiar popular 'Constance' folklore narrative formula (pp. lxxvii-lxxix). Neither our text nor Scandinavian analogues name the woman, but the probably eighth-century vernacular poem *Beowulf* calls her Thryth, saying that she had been a difficult woman reformed by her marriage to Offa I (pp. xlix, lxxxiii; Appendix C, pp. 141-2).

The Northumbrian king asks for Mercian help repulsing hostile Scots. Offa agrees, and is away doing just this, when the courier he sends back to Mercia spends the night at York. There the Northumbrian king replaces Offa's official despatches with a forged letter instructing Offa's court to return the queen to the forest where she had been found (pp. 27-32). In the event, she is again given shelter by a hermit; and when Offa turns once more to hunting for consolation, he finds her and all is well (pp. 31-6).

Historically, Northumbria would always prove problematic for the Mercians – a position never in fact overcome even when marriage to Offa II's daughter, the 'peace-weaver' Ælflæd, brought the northern king into line (pp. 85-6, Fig. 25).

Thankful for his wife's restoration, Offa I promises the hermit that in gratitude to God he will found a monastery or restore a wrecked one. However, neither he nor any successor fulfils this pledge, which ultimately devolves upon Offa II (pp. 35-6, 101-2).

The dozen or so generations which occupied the intervening four centuries between Offa I and Offa II, ignored by the text, witnessed the migration of English and Saxons into sub-Roman Britain, their establishment of a variety of regional kingdoms, and eventual Christianisation. A cultural gulf persists between kingdoms of English in the Midlands and North and those of a Saxon character in the South (pp. xl-xliv).

Wynfriđ, the sole child of an elderly member of Offa I's line, has been born disabled: lame, squinting, deaf and dumb. His parents remain optimistic however, reminded of the recovery of their ancestor from a similar condition (pp. 39-40).

Genetically 'imperfect' offspring are in fact more likely the result of elderly parentage (p. liii). Offa I's family had ruled the English frontier kingdom of Mercia intermittently, but by the mid-eighth century his line has no direct claim to the throne. From this point the narrative has entered a historical window where archival records, in addition to oral, are presumably available to the compiler.

The kingdom of Mercia has been seized by the tyrant Beornred, who makes a point of oppressing those of the former royal family. Upon the flight into exile of his parents, one Wynfrið wholly recovers, and so dramatically so that people thereafter refer to him as a second Offa (pp. 41-2).

In 757 a man by the name of Beornred, of uncertain origin, briefly established himself as king of Mercia following the assassination of the powerful Æthelbald, descended from Offa I via a different line from that of Offa II (Fig. 6).

At the head of the loyal Mercian militia, the youthful Offa crushes the tyrant's army, himself in the forefront of battle. Offa's father returns from exile, only to enter the religious life – reminding his son of the monastery yet to be founded. The Mercians receive their new national hero as King Offa II, and he embarks on a lawful and prosperous reign (pp. 43-8).

Beornred ruled for only a few months after the death of Æthelbald, being driven into exile by Prince Offa the same year. Offa II reigns from 757-96 (pp. lxxxix-xcv).

In mainland Europe, at the court of Charlemagne, a young, beautiful but deceitful female member of the Frankish royal family, is guilty of a certain (unspecified) misdeed. In punishment she is cast adrift in a small boat, which washes up on the coast of England. She says her name is Thryth and that she had been condemned for refusing marriage below her rank. Offa's mother recognises her true character but, seduced by her beauty, Offa II impulsively marries her. Their first-born is a son whom they call Ecgfrith (pp. 47-50).

Evidence as to the origin of Offa II's wife Cynethryth is absent, but the marriage of women from high-status families into previously hostile nations is familiar historically and in literature. In our text, whilst redemption of a foreign princess from sexual harassment in her own country offers a further narrative parallel, the outcome is very different in either case. The life of the foreign 'peace-weaver' often proves difficult in practice (pp. lxxvi-lxxxi).

The various Anglo-Saxon kingdoms surrounding Mercia, afraid of Offa II's growing power, form a military alliance and write to two great Continental rulers in turn: Charles (Carloman) and Charles (Charlemagne) asking for help (pp. 49-58). Offa can afford to ignore warnings from Europe, and proceeds to subject all these kingdoms, except for Northumbria, himself taking a leading part in notable battles (pp. 57-66).

Charlemagne and Carloman (both commonly referred to simply as 'Carolus' in contemporary sources, cf. pp. 55-6) were respectively first (technically illegitimate) and second (legitimate) sons of Pepin III and Bertrada of Laon. In 768 at Pepin's death the Franks, as yet with no tradition of primogeniture, divided the west of Europe between these two. Carloman held central and southern provinces such as Burgundy, Provence and Bavaria, while Charlemagne took the outer, sea-bordering provinces such as western Aquitaine, northern France and Frisia.

The ancient antagonism between Englishmen and Saxons persists beyond their migration from Europe and establishment in a number of different regional groupings in Britain (pp. xl-xlvi). *The Anglo-Saxon Chronicles* record significant Mercian battles in Kent at Otford (AD 776) and at Benson in Oxfordshire (AD 779). (Appendix A, pp. 135-6.)

Leaders of the defeated Anglo-Saxon kingdoms flee to seek sanctuary with the wily Welsh king Marmodius (perhaps Meredith, pp. 63-4) who, unable to defeat the Mercians by open means, treacherously attacks under pretext of a truce (pp. 65-6). By mutual agreement the frontier work Offa's Dyke is built but, during the Christmas truce the Welsh refill part of the ditch and attack. Although Offa himself fights bravely, the Mercian army is taken by surprise and temporarily retreats, only to return with particular ferocity (pp. 67-72). Nevertheless, Offa II feels pity for all the dead – just as he is humble in the titles he employs, referring to himself as nothing more than 'King of the Mercians' (pp. 71-4).

Records in respect of Offa II's Welsh wars are minimal (cf. Appendix E, pp. 161-2); but the nature of Mercia's western frontier-work, the ostentatious monumental linear trench-and-bank construction 'Offa's Dyke', is now largely understood (pp. lxix-lxxv).

Offa II seeks to improve relations with the Continental Franks and sends ambassadors to their ruler Charlemagne, who is engaged in military campaigns abroad against both Langobards and Old Saxons. We are given the texts of a series of diplomatic exchanges (pp. 53-80). Anglo-Saxon merchants appear to have been avoiding customs duties under the guise of pilgrims; Charlemagne presents vestments to Anglo-Saxon bishops, and a fine sword and sword-belt to the English king.

The only one of these letters known elsewhere is that, apparently patronising one, describing the prospective Emperor's presentation of a sword to the Englishman, as done to continental subordinates, which probably imputes secondariness (p. lviii).

The senior churchman in England (the Archbishop of Canterbury) appears dangerously close to the Franks so Offa II transfers the primacy to Lichfield, creating a Mercian archbishopric (pp. 79-82).

Upon Offa II's death, and when the current incumbent dies, the former situation is restored (p. xcvi).

The first known Viking intrusion, reconnoitring the land with a view to invasion, is easily repelled by Offa II, who treats prisoners magnanimously (pp. 83-6).

The Anglo-Saxon Chronicle AD 789 tells us that these vikings originated in Hardanger Fjord in Norway (Appendix A, pp. 137-8) and *The Annals of St Neots* that they landed at Portland, Dorset.

The rulers of Anglo-Saxon kingdoms Offa II has defeated are reinstalled as sub-reguli – their position to be endorsed by marriage with Offa's own daughters (pp. 85-6). Queen Thryth dislikes this policy. When King Æthelberht of East Anglia comes to be married, she fails to persuade Offa to have him executed on political grounds, so murders him herself – graphically described. There are miracles associated with the young man's remains, which are accorded saintly treatment. The wicked queen, now estranged, dies a miserable death (pp. 89-100).

There is historical confusion as to the manner of Æthelberht's death (AD 794) and especially as to whether it should be considered the responsibility of Offa himself. Already referred to as 'martyr', Æthelberht would become a significant vernacular saint (pp. lxxxvi-lxxxvii).

Papal legates arrive to affirm the orthodox faith at an ecclesiastical conference assembled at Chelsea. There the Lichfield archbishopric is endorsed and Offa II's son Ecgfrith consecrated king (pp. 99-102).

The Anglo-Saxon Chronicles record a contentious Council (*geflitfullic sinoð*) at Chelsea in 787 (Appendix A, pp. 135-6). The policy of crowning one's son presumably indicates an attempt to ensure the political succession.

No longer distracted by a wicked wife, the mind of a now celibate Offa II turns to his inherited duty to establish a monastery. Praying for divine instruction, he learns that the new monastery is to be established in the name of the national proto-martyr Alban and is given instructions as to the location of that saint's martyrdom and burial – the Roman city of Verulamium, later called 'St Albans' (pp. 101-10). The shrine's original establishment had been inadequate, so a new institution would be established, and Offa II lays the foundation-stone of a new church.

St Alban's earliest shrine seems to have been replaced at the end of the fourth century by a cult-church. The eighth century was witnessing a large-scale increase of monasticism as a way of life, and existing groups of ascetics assembled around a saint's relics were commonly being given over to one of the regular monastic orders – in particular the Benedictine rule favoured by English and Continental rulers (pp. xii-xv, xcvi-xcvii).

To secure special privileges for his institution, both financial and customary, the king undertakes to apply personally to Rome (pp. 109-16). In return, the king inaugurates a regular payment to the 'English hostel' there.

Whether Offa II actually visited Rome himself is extremely uncertain. A supplementary caveat added in one manuscript (Cotton Claudius E iv), points to the possibility of confusion between Offa II and a number of contemporary rulers bearing that name, in particular with a King Offa of Essex who travelled to Rome to become a monk (pp. 125-8). Although a monetary innovator, it is unlikely that his payments to the English hostel at Rome represent the origins of the religious tax called 'Peter's Pence' (pp. xcii-iii, xcix-c).

The physical extent of Offa II's domain is described by way of counties (pp. 119-20). *His titular modesty is reiterated* (pp. 121-2, cf. pp. 71-2); *he introduces the practice of kings being heralded by trumpets* (pp. 121-2); *the gift to St Albans of a royal manor is reiterated* (pp. 121-2, cf. pp. 103-4); *St Albans is to be exempt from 'Peter's Pence', but may collect it from around about for their own purposes; their abbot is to have episcopal rank* (pp. 119-24).

There is included a sequence of summary institutional memoranda compiled from abbey archives.

After four or five years, with almost all the abbey's domestic buildings completed, Offa dies – at a nearby manor many say. He is buried not at St Albans but on the banks of the River Ouse, where his sepulchre is lost during floods (pp. 123-6).

The circumstances of Offa's death are not known from elsewhere, except that a precise date of 29 July 794 is offered by John of Worcester (p. xxxii).

The Manuscripts

The *Vitae Offarum Duorum* is found in three major St Albans manuscripts (British Library MSS Additional 62777, Cotton Claudius E iv and Cotton Nero D i). And there are likely to have been many others (cf. former Gurney MS 119).[28] Each of these presents the same text with no significant discrepancies. The base text printed here is that of Cotton Nero D i. A separate version of the *Life of Offa I* exists in a manuscript from the St Albans cell at Tynemouth, Northumberland (British Library MS Cotton Vitellius A xx).

British Library, Cotton Vitellius A xx, ff. 67^r-70^r.

Badly damaged in the Cotton Library fire of 1731, a quarto vellum book, now 210 x 145 mm, containing 242 folios. It is presently bound up with excerpts from chronicles and a variety of texts of different dates, variously laid out, certain of which relate to places in the north of England, in particular the priory of Tynemouth – technically subordinate to St Albans Abbey, but large and wealthy, with an impressive library.

The *Life of Offa I* occurs on ff. 67^r-70^r, written in a small, thirteenth-century hand. Although the book's mutilated condition does not allow us to more than guess whether this item originally represented the first in this or another volume, the opening page (f. 67^r) bears a note, in a later hand, to the effect that Eadulf (Ralph) de Dunham, prior of Tynemouth (1252-66)[29] had donated this book, presumably to that institution,[30] with the

---

[28] For the immediate situation in the Abbey scriptorium see generally R.M. Thomson, *Manuscripts from St Albans Abbey, 1066-1235*, Woodbridge, 1982.

[29] *Gesta Abbatum*, I, p. 508, also pp. 320-22. D.M. Smith and V.C.M. London, *The Heads of Religious Houses, England and Wales: II, 1216-1377*, Cambridge, 2001, p. 132.

customary anathema on anyone stealing it.[31] The text is laid out in two columns in a rapid hand with plentiful abbreviations and somewhat different wording to that in the lengthier compilation of 'Two Lives'. It has no heading but the later marginal note *Vita Warmundi Regis* suggests that it had been preceded in this or its derivative document with an account of Offa I's perhaps Arab father. Although provided with the occasional rubricated initial, it has no paragraph or other division, and finishes halfway down a recto page, with no suggestion of having continued. The verso of this, and the four next folios, contain a list of St Albans abbots and other institutional memoranda laid out in the same manner; and thereafter the ruling is different.

Although the story-line in this form is the same as that of the other manuscripts, the wording, layout and finish of the copy are sufficient to indicate that the *Life of Offa I* represents an originally separate conceit.

British Library, Additional 62777 (formerly Bute MS 3), ff. 50^r-91^r.

A small, fourteenth-century vellum book, 201 x 130 mm, containing 161 folios. It may have been one of those that at one stage belonged to Sir Henry Spelman (p. xxv) but subsequently went missing.[32] It was probably produced by the St Albans scriptorium in the early fourteenth century and commissioned by Hugh de Eversdone, abbot 1308-1326. The early fourteenth-century hand (a Gothic *textualis rotunda*) which wrote out *The Lives of Two Offas* (ff. 50^r-91^r) continued with a version of Matthew Paris's *Deeds of the Abbots of St Albans* revised and continued to 1308 by Thomas Walsingham, senior scribe 1380-94.[33] A note on the first leaf (f. 1^v) tells us that it had come from the abbot's study – one of a dozen such books surviving from St Albans.[34] Although laid out as a whole, 26 long lines to the page, it was written in a variety of hands up to the sixteenth century. The compilation opens with William's account (p. xxiii) of the Lives of SS Alban and Amphibal (ff. 2^r-34^r), and a tract on the invention and translation of St Alban's remains (ff. 34^r-49^v), and concludes with fourteenth-century legal records relating to St Albans' possessions in the North of England (ff. 158-161).

The first *Life* begins with a rubricated heading and decorated paragraph mark, but is thereafter undivided and without significant decoration of any kind. Individual chapter-headings and decorated initials begin only with the second *Life*, ff. 63^r *et sequ.*

---

[30] Although not listed, *per se*, in the one surviving catalogue: R. Sharpe *et al.*, ed. *English Benedictine Libraries, the Shorter Catalogues*, London, 1996, pp. 588-89.

[31] An extension across the following three pages has been erased.

[32] Cf. L.F.R. Williams, 'William the Chamberlain and Luton Church', *English Historical Review*, 28 (1913), 719-30 (pp. 719-20).

[33] See generally A. Gransden, *Historical Writing in England*, London, 1974-82, II, pp. 118-56.

[34] N.R. Ker, *Medieval Libraries of Great Britain*, 2nd edn, London, 1964, pp. 164-68.

British Library, Cotton Claudius E iv, ff. 84ʳ-97ʳ.

A large, late fourteenth-century vellum book, 435 x 318 mm, containing 171 folios, uniformly ruled. Probably made under the direction of, and perhaps partly in the hand of, Thomas Walsingham. Now bound up with a copy of Thomas Elmham's Chronicle (ff. 2ʳ-32), it formerly opened with f. 34ʳ and contains a variety of texts, including a Brother William's *Life and Invention of St Alban* (ff. 34ʳ-46ʳ) together with Ralph of Dunstable's verse translation (ff. 47ʳ-58ᵛ), an *Invention and Miracles of St Amphibal and his Companions* (ff. 71-83), further accounts of these two saints and a large number of minor administrative and institutional documents, mostly specific to St Albans Abbey.

The Two Offas, found on ff. 84ʳ-97ʳ, is laid out in double columns, not always too carefully. It is given a running title *Gesta Offe I Regis Merciorum* across openings from f. 84ʳ to 87ᵛ, then *Gesta Offe II Regis Merciorum* thereafter. What appears to be the same hand adds on f. 97ʳ a scholarly caveat about attributing deeds of other King Offas to Offa II of Mercia (pp. 125-8). As with Additional 62777, a closely similar hand continues, beginning f. 98ʳ, with the edition of Paris's *Deeds of the Abbots* continued by Walsingham.

Also like MSS Additional 62777 and Nero D i (below), the text of the *Life of Offa I* is undecorated, save for rubricated heading together with opening full border bi-colour floriated paragraph-mark; and thereafter undivided, except for occasional alternate red and blue paragraph marks, whereas the later *Life of Offa II* (f. 87ᵛ *et sequ.*) is accorded regular rubricated chapter-headings and decorated initials. Throughout, however, the text has been closely written in a bold hand, with punctuation often ignored and unnoticed sentence-breaks especially confusing (e.g. pp. 43-4), probably an indication of having been written from dictation.

British Library, Cotton Nero D i, ff. 2ʳ-25ʳ.

A large, mid-thirteenth-century vellum book, 352 x 240 mm, containing 202 folios, ruled in double columns for the greatest part. The opening page bears a marginal note, now partly trimmed away, recording its presentation to St Albans by a dead *frater*[ ]*eus* (perhaps Matthew Paris, the well-known writer, artist and editor, *ob.* 1259 or shortly after – see pp. xxix-xxxi), with a curse on anyone stealing it.[35] The librarian Walsingham (p. xxii) tells us that the monk Matthew 'provided many volumes written in his own and other hands, in which his excellence in both scholarship and painting is clear enough'.[36] This book includes, in a variety of hands, a copy of Paris's *Deeds of the Abbots of St Albans* (ff. 30-69ʳ), cross-referenced (pp. 123-4), as well as a large number of lesser documents pertinent to St Albans Abbey and its possessions.[37]

---

[35] T. D. Hardy, *Descriptive Catalogue of Materials relating to the History of Great Britain and Ireland*, Rolls Series, 26, London, 1862-71, III, pl. I.

[36] Cf. Walsingham, continuing Matthew's *Gesta Abbatum*, II, pp. 394-5.

[37] For a full list of contents see Matthew Paris, *Chronica Majora*, ed. H.R. Luard, Rolls Series, 57, London,

A text of *The Lives of Offas I and II* is the first item in this book, ff. 2ʳ-25ʳ, and is written out in a protogothic hand, either that of the donor or one of his school.[38] The literal errors indicate dictation or copying from a prior text. The mistake of the Old English initial graph *p (wyn)* for *P* in unfamiliar proper names, even that of the chief protagonist, strongly suggests derivation from pre-Conquest written material (p. xxxii).

It was ruled for two columns of text throughout, reserving the upper third of each page for illustrations, similar in layout to a major piece of Matthew's workshop surviving: Trinity College, Dublin, MS 177 (which consists of writings that are partly Matthew's own and partly those of others, and includes, in the course of a French *Vie de Seint Auban*, overlapping content in dealing with Offa II's discovery of the martyr's remains and subsequent construction of St Alban's Abbey.[39]) Here the number of illustrations planned was no less ambitious than that of the Dublin manuscript, but the fact that only a handful at the opening (ff. 2ʳ-4ᵛ) reached any stage of completion suggests that the work was interrupted by death,[40] illness or laid aside because of other commitments. These first drawings are also commonly ascribed to Matthew,[41] and certainly follow his manner, although in a generally less confident hand, roughly inked and lacking his customary tinting (Figs. 14-15). Possibly it was work done under his supervision by an assistant. Only in the first four is draughtsmanship complete; of these only the first two are provided with cartouche-inscriptions; even the frame of the sixth is incomplete, which might intimate despair as to completion of the project.[42] From f. 5ʳ (Fig. 17) onwards, the blank, unframed picture-spaces were subsequently filled with drawings by various fourteenth-century artists – perhaps essaying the manner of the first but less competent and lacking textual cartouches. Rubricated footnotes, partially trimmed away, indicate what their subject should be. Curiously, the upper right-hand space on f. 20ʳ (Fig. 27) had already had to be filled with accidentally omitted text although we know from a manuscript footnote what it had been intended

1872-83, VI, pp. 491-523.

[38] N. Denholm-Young, *Handwriting in England and Wales*, Cardiff, 1954, pp. 51-53; also R. Vaughan, 'The handwriting of Matthew Paris', *Transactions of the Cambridge Bibliographical Society*, 1 (1949-53), 376-94.

[39] N. Morgan, *Early Gothic Manuscripts, I, 1190-1250*, London, 1982, pp. 130-33; M. Otter, *Inventiones: fiction and referentiality in twelfth-century historical writing*, London, 1996, pp. 24-7.

[40] We may imagine a workshop situation similar to that when the elderly children's illustrator Thomas Henry (1879-1963) died leaving drawings for Richmal Crompton's *William and the Witch* incomplete: M. Cadogan and D. Schutte, 'Illustrators', in *The William Companion*, London, 1990, p. 123.

[41] R.W. Chambers, *Six thirteenth century drawings illustrating the story of Offa and of Thryth (Drida)*, London, 1912. There are brief descriptions by M.R. James, 'The drawings of Matthew Paris', *Walpole Society*, 14 (1925-26), 1-26 (pp. 21-24, pls. xxii-vi). Some scholars are doubtful of wholesale attribution, e.g. M. Rickert, *Painting in Britain: the Middle Ages*, 2nd edn, Harmondsworth, 1965, pp. 108-10, 236, n. 75; Morgan, *op. cit.* pp. 134-6. The literature on Matthew's art-work in general is extensive, but in this instance is best begun with S. Lewis, *The Art of Matthew Paris in the Chronica Majora*, Aldershot, 1987, pp. 24-26, *et passim*.

[42] Lewis, *The Art of Matthew Paris*, p. 390; C. Hahn, 'The limits of text and image?: Matthew Paris's final project, the Vitae duorum Offarum, as historical romance', in *Excavating the Medieval Image*, ed. D.S. Areford and N.A. Rowe, Aldershot, 2005, pp. 37-58 (p. 49).

to illustrate (p. 91).[43] The last word of the paragraph was already in place, so this probably represents a simple example of the careless copyist.

The text of the first *Life* that Matthew, or some earlier compiler, has encountered and incorporated, is not presented so as to be visually appreciated as part of the remainder. Apart from an initial heading noting that the second Offa was very like the first, there are no cross-references or forward allusions of any kind. Provision of illustrations was intended to be the same throughout. But so far as the text is concerned, not even section-headings have been invented for the first *Life* to appear in harmony with the second *Life*. As an example of bookwork the link between one and the other is summary to say the least.

In addition, this manuscript includes a host of memoranda and minor documents connected with St Albans in handwriting of various dates until the seventeenth century. The miscellaneous collection of oddments that make up the latter part of the book could well represent the surviving fair copy of a commonplace book to which Matthew relegated material accumulated during local researches so as to make his *Chronica Majora* 'less weighty'; but if so, this copy is incomplete, inasmuch as not all items referred to by him are included.[44]

(Former) Gurney MS 119 16, ff. 96-115.

During the seventeenth century the Revd William Watts (*c.* 1590-1649) says that, in addition to the Cotton Nero and Claudius texts on which he was basing his edition of what he supposed was Matthew Paris's work, he had seen an older manuscript belonging to the prominent antiquary Sir Henry Spelman (*c.* 1564-1641) that was "shorter and more abbreviated" (*brevior sit & contractior*).[45] However, it was not listed as such among the Spelman collection in 1709,[46] and may merely have been on loan to Spelman from his friend and neighbour Sir Robert Cotton, who was notably generous in this manner. In which case Watts's description might well suit MS Cotton Vitellius A xx. Or it may refer to another work altogether. Spelman possessed a series of extracts *ex libro MS Sti Albani de Vitis Offae Regis... et Abbatum...* which in the autumn of 1632 he had his servant John Longford transcribe at Heydon (Norfolk), where Spelman then was,[47] and which may thus have belonged to that house. The transcripts were bound up with a collection of very miscellaneous papers of the sixteenth and seventeenth centuries, but subsequent to the Gurney collection's dispersal in 1936 are untraced.[48]

---

[43] [P]*orro ad aucmentum muliebris tirannidis ... iussit in tesauro recondi precioso, in ecclesia* (pp. 91-2, n. 464). The last sentence of the previous paragraph: *Puella uero regis filia ... uestigia sequeretur* is inserted into the bottom margin of the preceding column.

[44] *Chronica Majora*, Luard, V, p. 229.

[45] W. Watts, ed. *Vitæ duorum Offarum .... Et uiginti trium abbatum Sancti Albani*, London, 1639, p. 2[r].

[46] British Library, MS Harley 7055.

[47] The Royal Commission on Historical Manuscripts, *Twelfth Report*, Appendix 9, London, 1891, p. 158.

[48] The Royal Commission on Historical Manuscripts, *Guide to the Location of Collections described in the Reports and Calendars Series, 1870-1980*, London, 1982, p. 28.

This Edition

The base text used here is that of MS Cotton Nero D i, with significant variants indicated in footnotes. Minor spelling and punctuation differences are noted only incidentally where other features are remarked upon. Manuscript punctuation is expanded only where necessary for the sense, and capitalisation is limited to proper names. Paragraphing in the first *vita* is taken from MS Cotton Claudius E iv. There is none in the other manuscripts.

Authorship

Any question of 'author', or rather compiler, can be nothing other than speculative. All we can be certain of is that the writer of the *Vitae Offarum Duorum* was local to St Albans – and presumably a cleric in view of his knowledge of documents to be found in the abbey collection there (pp. 121-2 *et passim*).[49] But, just as many of those avowing the regular life displayed an active involvement in worldly affairs such as warfare or sexual relations, so they were capable of composing literature for a wide audience, making no distinction between ecclesiastical and secular, learned and popular tastes. Certainly our writer was one with ecclesiastical interests, to judge from his concern with saints, heresies, church proprietorship and the like – occasionally including what might seem trivial and unnecessarily intrusive jurisdictional details.[50] Though not primarily a historian, he is aware that some dates can be very precise when using archival resources (pp. 109-10).

Despite the dismissive attitude of the incoming Norman abbot towards his English predecessors (p. xiii), it would be unreasonable to suppose that pre-Conquest St Albans was a cultural wilderness lacking literary activity. In the late tenth century there were still to be discovered there early Celtic books written in *idioma antiquorum Brittonum*, and a scholar able to translate them. One book included a 'History of Saint Alban' they believed to have been written by contemporaries of the martyr. An elderly monk called Unwona made a translation of this, after which the original manuscript immediately fell to pieces (*in puluerem subito redactam*).[51] Any volume found to give details of idolatrous local customs the monks burned, just as they destroyed the remains of pagan altars in the adjacent Roman city. The topic of their patron saint was naturally a continuing concern.[52] An abbot called Ælfric (*c.* 970-90) was said to have composed a

---

[49] We have no catalogue of the St Albans library, which was probably extensive, J.S. Beddie, 'The ancient classics in the mediaeval libraries', *Speculum*, 5 (1930), 3-20 (p. 4).

[50] Such as remarking the fact that Nottingham looked hierarchically towards York despite lying in Mercia (pp. 119-20).

[51] *Gesta Abbatum*, I, pp. 26-27, Niblett and Thompson, pp. 364-65.

[52] Hardy, *Descriptive Catalogue*, I, nos. 8-31, *et passim*. Also W. McLeod, 'Alban and Amphibal: some extant Lives and a lost Life', *Mediaeval Studies*, 42 (1980), 407-30.

History of the martyr intended for musical setting.[53] And the demand continued. Perhaps motivated by the solemn transference of Alban's remains to a new shrine in 1129, one brother William translated Unwona's work into Latin. William's work may simply have been considered insufficiently stylish, but was subsequently itself rendered into Latin verse by brother Ralph of Dunstable some time about 1190.[54]

The post-Conquest cultural climate at St Albans, as at all institutions, fluctuated, but most abbots encouraged the literary arts.[55] Geoffrey de Gorron (1119-46), a Norman school-master at Dunstable and friend of Christina of Markyate, had composed miracle-plays during the course of his career,[56] was enthusiastic about books and maintained a number of *antiquarii*, one of whom, the English Ralph Gubion,[57] succeeded him (1146-51), attracting artistic men to the abbey. Later the abbacy of the bookish and art-loving, if financially inefficient, Simon (1167-83), another Englishman, must have proved especially encouraging. With a personal interest in calligraphy and finding the scriptorium usually *dissipatum et contemptum*, he brought it back into production, maintaining two or three professional scribes at his own expense and ordaining that in future there should always be one 'special copyist' appointed.[58]

Several St Albans chroniclers are on record. Few of their works survive[59] but we might suppose that local stories and traditions would have interested them. None more so perhaps than those surrounding the man for whom abbey prayers were said several times a day: "May the soul of King Offa rest in peace".[60] A short *gesta* of contemporary affairs seems to have been had in hand by, or for, the abbey's mid-twelfth-century cellarer Adam, well-known for taking women's roles in religious drama and admired enough to be accorded an abbot's burial rites. Matthew Paris later called him 'illiterate' but nevertheless considered Adam's work sufficiently valuable to incorporate into his own.[61]

The author of an anonymous 'Chronicle of England' – perhaps the work of John de Cella (abbot 1195-1214), sometime student at Paris and prior of Wallingford – informs

---

[53] *Gesta Abbatum*, I, p. 32, Niblett and Thompson, p. 366.

[54] *Acta Sanctorum*, ed. J. Bolland, Antwerp, 1707, June IV, pp. 146-59.

[55] See generally C. Jenkins, *The Monastic Chronicler and the Early School of St. Albans*, London, 1922, pp. 23ff.

[56] *Gesta Abbatum*, I, pp. 73, 106. Also D. Knowles *et al.*, *The Heads of Religious Houses, England and Wales: I, 940-1216*, Cambridge, 1972, pp. 66-7.

[57] A popular man, a book-lover, formerly a secular priest in the service of the bishop of Lincoln, then prior of Tynemouth, and unanimously chosen abbot for St Albans, Knowles, *Heads: I*, p. 97, Smith and London, *Heads: II*, p. 131. The name suggests Norman origins, but the *Gesta* is clear that he is English, in some respect or another, I, p. 106.

[58] *Gesta Abbatum*, I, pp. 184, 192.

[59] For the general situation see P. Taylor, 'The early St. Albans endowment and its chroniclers', *Historical Research*, 68 (1995), 119-42 (pp. 123-27).

[60] From the mid thirteenth century at least, said at the end of each canonical hour and at other times, *Gesta Abbatum*, I, p. 394; *Chronica Majora*, V, p. 562, transl. J.A. Giles, *English History from the Year 1235-1273*, London, 1852-54, III, pp. 175-76.

[61] *Gesta Abbatum*, I, p. 121, Niblett and Thompson, p. 373.

us that he is omitting many stories that were told about Offa II because he considers them doubtful or apocryphal.[62] However, he has made notes of them (*in cedulis notauimus*) with the intention of incorporating his conclusions into a larger work as and when he has been able to investigate their veracity.[63] But whether this connects in any way with our text, either in its present or a previous form, we can only guess. Possibly it alludes merely to Offa II's part in the murder of Æthelberht (p. lxxxvii), about which the chronicler confesses his ignorance. It was at this time that St Albans embarked on a phase of overall image-improvement similar to that occurring at many other English monasteries – impressively redesigning the austere public nave of Abbot Paul's church and adding a showpiece frontage in the new Gothic fashion.[64]

From this period historians of national significance are associated with the St Albans facilities: eminently Roger of Wendover and Matthew Paris. Roger had been prior of an outpost at Belvoir but, removed for financial incompetence in 1219, spent his remaining years at St Albans[65] working on the great chronicle he called *flores historiarum*, which he began compiling from the works of many previous worthwhile writers, 'just as flowers of different sorts are gathered from various fields'.[66] These apparently included our *Vitae* or a common or interlinking source. As one would expect, it covers matters of local significance such as the story of Alban and Amphibal and an anti-Pelagian synod at Verulamium (St Albans) under Germanus and Lupus. But he pays little attention to legendary or anecdotal matter, and understandably has nothing to say about Offa I. However, it was clearly convenient to find a wicked woman to whom could be reassigned the sins of Offa II, his institution's reputable founder, notably any responsibility for the murder of Saint Æthelberht (pp. 89-100); but he says nothing of Offa II's Welsh campaigns and turns elsewhere for his account of the king's defeat of the first Viking attack on England, only returning to the story with Offa II's inspired discovery of Alban's remains and the abbey's regal foundation. Matter shared with *The Two Offas* consists in the main of information directly relevant to St Albans.

Roger includes a number of passages very similar to *The Two Offas*. For example, the detail of Offa II's eating nothing for three whole days as a result of his grief at Æthelberht's death he describes in exactly the same way as our text (pp. 97-8), and then, ignoring the next two paragraphs, concludes his sentence by mentioning the king's expedition to East Anglia, just partly in the manner of *The Two Offas* (pp. 99-100). Æthelberht's burial at Hereford is described in almost identical words, although beginning halfway through a paragraph. The account of the penitent Offa II's journey to Rome is often verbally identical, even using one chapter-heading in common (pp.

---

[62] Knowles *et al.*, *Heads: I*, p. 67.

[63] *The Chronicle attributed to John of Wallingford*, ed. R. Vaughan, Camden Miscellany, 3rd S. 90, 1958, pp. xiii, 11, transl. J. Stevenson, *The Church Historians of England*, London, 1854, II, ii, pp. 521-64 (p. 530).

[64] Unfinished for lack of funds; see S. Harrison, 'The thirteenth-century west front of St Albans Abbey', in *Alban and St Albans*, ed. Henig and Lindley, pp. 176-81.

[65] Dying in 1236, *Gesta Abbatum*, I, p. 270.

[66] *Chronica, sive Flores Historiarum*, ed. H.O. Coxe, London, 1841-44, I, p. 3; transl. J.A. Giles, *Flowers of History*, London, 1849, I, p. 2.

109-16). One place where Roger provided a text identical to that of the *Vitae*, but Matthew was to offer significantly different wording, suggests that the previous two had one former source.[67]

The best-known personality from St Albans at this time, Matthew Paris,[68] entered the institution in 1217, dying in 1259. His name suggests French origins, but he may merely have studied there. A frequent traveller in the outside world, he enjoyed the company of high-ranking men and was an intimate of the king. He particularly liked recording events of his own times. When writing about earlier periods, much of what he gives us was edited or abridged from elsewhere, with little or no acknowledgment. It is his 'Deeds of the Abbots of St Albans' (*Gesta Abbatum*), in part deriving from the cellarer Adam (p. xxvii), on which depends much of our knowledge of the early history of the institution.[69] The earlier part of his notable *Chronica Majora* is taken largely from Roger of Wendover's work, although interlarded with his own comments and additions.[70]

A fine calligrapher and skilled draughtsman, he produced many illustrated books for the library, and clearly had been involved with a copy of the *Lives* towards the end of his career, or at his death (pp. xxiv-xxv). Following Roger however, Matthew's Chronicle makes no mention of Offa I save in a genealogy,[71] and refers to major incidents in the life of Offa II, only briefly and *en passant*, although in terms frequently similar to those of the *Vitae*.

The Two Offas has sometimes been assumed Matthew's own composition,[72] but cannot be supposed to have originated with him. It is simply too ramshackle an *omnium gatherum* for the assured author we know Matthew to be. It is not included in any reference to his works made at St Albans after his death,[73] nor does the manuscript copy commonly associated with him (Nero D i) identify it as his work.[74] And romance seems to have been a genre completely outside his normal practice, although he will at times incorporate old and scandalous stories. Folklore is no more important to him than to Roger. He was naturally interested in the founder of his institution. A tract on the invention and translation of St Alban (p. xxii), probably one of Matthew's earliest works, incorporates a long sequence about Offa II similar to that used in his later

---

[67] Cf. p. 40, n. 577.

[68] R. Vaughan, *Matthew Paris*, Cambridge, 1958.

[69] The *Gesta Abbatum Monasterii Sancti Albani*, ed. H.T. Riley, Rolls Series, 28, London, 1867-69.

[70] For the relationship between these two chroniclers see generally F.M. Powicke, 'The compilation of the "Chronica Majora" of Matthew Paris', *Modern Philology*, 38 (1941), 305-17 and the lecture of V.H. Galbraith, *Roger of Wendover and Matthew Paris*, Glasgow, 1944. The place of Matthew in St Albans historiography is well set out in Gransden, I, pp. 356-79.

[71] *Chronica Majora*, Luard, I, p. 343; Roger, *Chronica*, Coxe, I, p. 235, transl. Giles, p. 149.

[72] Following Watts's inclusion of it in his 1639 edition of Matthew's *opus* (p. xxv), notably by L. Theopold, *Kritische Untersuchungen über die Quellen zur angelsæchsischen Geschichte des achten Jahrhunderts*, Lemgo, 1872, pp. 111-28 and Vaughan, pp. 41-48, on the basis that the *Vitae* is unlikely to have been used by Roger.

[73] British Library, MS Nero D vii, f. 51ʳ.

[74] The more significant in view of the reference to a copy of his *Gesta Abbatum* being included in the same manuscript (pp. 123-4).

Chronica Majora, while mentioning an already existing work on Offa: *'plenius in historia de Offa rege scripta continetur'.*[75] This cannot refer to the Nero D i copy of our text if that was among the last of Matthew's handiwork, but possibly to that work the author of the 'Wallingford Chronicle' was intending to write (cf. p. xxviii). A *littérateur* will often talk of a bigger or better book about their hero which is to be found somewhere. It is said in *The Deeds of Hereward*, for example.[76]

Various inadequacies of information and discrepancies of opinion also argue against attribution of the original of our text to Matthew. So generally confident a historian is unlikely, for example, to have muddled the relationship between two such significant Frankish rulers as Carloman and Charlemagne (pp. 51-8),[77] or to have jumbled the succession of bishops at Lichfield (pp. 81-2 *et sequ.*), in the way our text does. He describes the popular name of Offa II's chaplain and confessor differently (pp. 83-4). Even when it comes to straightforwardly archival data, the *Vitae*'s suggestion that early St Albans monks, let alone the earliest, came from Bec in Normandy (pp. 117-18) is wildly inaccurate. Matthew knows that Bec itself was founded only with the 1030s, and that it was rather a question of his own institution having adopted the custom of Bec at some stage.[78] He gives a different account of the origin of 'Peter's Pence'[79] and of the Dane's treatment of St Alban's bones.[80] And, given the encyclopaedic nature of *The Two Offas*, it is perhaps curious that it should contain no hint of Alban's associate Amphibal,[81] the miraculous discovery of whose remains – together with those of his weapon-bearing companions – was believed to have been made nearby in 1178[82] and enthusiastically exploited as a topic at St Albans thereafter, including by Matthew.[83] Our narrator's poorly-written account of a field Offa II is said to have purchased in Flanders (pp. 109-14) is used merely to emphasise the king's wealth, whereas for Roger, and thus Matthew, they are an example of his piety, explicit as to its purpose being to

---

[75] A work 'full of stories written about King Offa', f. 58[v]; or copied thence by a scribe of Matthew's school.

[76] Gaimar, Hardy and Martin, pp. 399-40; Swanton, *Medieval Outlaws*, p. 19.

[77] Understood well enough in the *Chronica Majora*, Luard, I, p. 346 although, as with Roger of Wendover, the existence of the lesser figure receives no more than a line, *Flores Historiarum*, Coxe, I, pp. 239-40, Giles, I, p. 152.

[78] *Historia Anglorum*, ed. F. Madden, Rolls Series, 44, London, 1866-69, I, pp. 24-25. St Albans' post-Conquest abbots came from Caen, which had been a joint-foundation with Bec, and there is evidence that for a short time in the twelfth century St Albans shared the rare cult of St Alexis with Bec, cf. O. Pächt, C.R. Dodwell and F. Wormald, *The St. Albans Psalter*, London, 1960, pp. 131, 135.

[79] *Chronica Majora*, Luard, I, p. 331; Wendover, *Chronica*, Coxe, I, pp. 254-55; Giles, p. 137.

[80] *Gesta Abbatum*, I, pp. 12-13, 35.

[81] The Christian who converted Alban and for whom Alban substituted himself to be killed, but who nevertheless was himself martyred shortly afterwards. Cf. J.S.P. Tatlock, 'St. Amphibalus', *Essays in Criticism* (California), 2S, 4 (1934), 249-57, 268-70.

[82] At Redbourn, where pagan Anglo-Saxon burials may well have been secondary to a cemetery of the Roman period, although no modern excavation has been undertaken.

[83] Notably his compilation Trinity College, Dublin, MS. 177.

provide fodder for needy pilgrims.[84] And their small use of the figure of Cwenthryth is strange in view of the very significant role she plays in our tale.

As for Offa II's alleged journey to Rome, at least one early editor found this suspect. The Claudius E iv manuscript added a paragraph pointing out that it is important not to confuse Offa II of Mercia with an earlier King Offa of Essex or with others (pp. 125-8), not a mistake Matthew made.[85] The East Saxon King Offa, who had owned lands in Mercia and is, perhaps disingenuously presented as the Mercian Offa in an early statement on the foundation and endowment of Evesham Abbey,[86] had abdicated in 708 in order to travel to Rome in company with the then king of Mercia, Coenred, and became a monk.[87] Geoffrey of Wells, writing at much the same time, is similarly concerned that these names should not be confused in a tale of his own.[88]

If Matthew's original authorship of *The Two Offas* is improbable, that is not to say there is nothing of Matthew as an enhancing editor here. This text, as with his writing-up of Roger's *Flores Historiarum* and other of his editions, he seems to have coloured at various points with favourite vocabulary of his own,[89] and probably his is the cross-reference to his *Gesta Abbatum* at the end (pp. 123-4). However, the quotations from Classical poetry, are made direct from their original rather than in the oblique fashion Matthew normally prefers – his customary expression *iuxta illud poeticum* often introducing a merely approximate quotation.[90] He might have been responsible for inserting the few diplomatic letters but, like other chroniclers, himself used only that mentioning Charlemagne's gift to Offa II in 796 of episcopal vestments, and of silk cloaks and a sword and sword-belt of Hunnish workmanship (pp. 77-8).[91]

It is difficult to be conclusive when assessing the works of those who, over a long life-span, not only wrote out much themselves but also dictated a great deal to amanuenses. The issue is also beset by the commonalty of pseudo-scholastic assumptions such as supposing that details used 'in common with' necessarily means 'taken from', or that saying nothing implies 'knows nothing'. The most that can be said

---

[84] Roger, *Chronica*, Coxe, I, p. 255, Giles, I, pp. 162-3; Matthew, *Chronica Majora*, I, pp. 358-59.

[85] *Chronica Majora*, I, pp. 320, 323-24, Giles, pp. 126, 129.

[86] *Cartularium Saxonicum*, ed. W.G. Birch, London, 1885-99, I, pp. 192-95, H.R.P. Finberg, *The Early Charters of the West Midlands*, Leicester, 1961, pp. 181-83.

[87] *Anglo-Saxon Chronicles*, s.a. 709, ed. J. Earle and C. Plummer, Oxford, 1892-99, pp. 40-41; transl. M. Swanton, London, 1996, pp. 40-41; Bede, *Ecclesiastical History*, V, 19, Colgrave and Mynors, pp. 516-17.

[88] Another, otherwise unknown Offa of East Anglia, having no heir is said to have undertaken a pilgrimage to Jerusalem, dying on his return journey: *Corolla Sancti Eadmundi*, ed. F. Hervey, London, 1907, pp. 134-161 (pp. 144-45); cf. Wright, *Cultivation*, pp. 117-120.

[89] For example: *formidolosus, truculenter* (pp. 57, 63, 71; 59, 69, 91). Cf. generally, Vaughan, pp. 47-48.

[90] Thus, for example, for our author's *poeta .. dicens: 'Facilis iactura sepulchri est'* (pp. 125-6), from Virgil's *Aeneid*, II, 646, Matthew (in *Gesta Abbatum*) will offer: *iuxta illud poeticum: 'Levis est iactura sepulcri'*, I, p. 7, and does not go on to use any words from Lucan.

[91] *Monumenta Germaniae Historica, Epistolae Karolini Aevi*, ed. E. Dümmler, Berlin, 1895, II, no. 100, pp. 144-46; *Chronica Majora*, I, pp. 348-49, Giles, p. 153; transl. Whitelock, *English Historical Documents*, I, 2nd edn, pp. 848-49; for the general background to which see B. Solberg, 'Weapon export from the Continent to the Nordic countries in the Carolingian period', *Studien zur Sachsenforschung*, 7 (1991), 241-59.

is that in MS Nero D i Matthew began to produce a handsome volume in his customary fashion, with copies of his own and other books to hand.

One positive hint supports the commonsense assumption that the surviving text has derived, at least in part, from an older written form. At some stage in transmission the early vernacular graph *p* (*wyn*), the phonetic equivalent of modern *w*, has been mistaken for Latin P. Much used until the end of the Anglo-Saxon period, but infrequently thereafter, the *wyn* graph is not uncommonly mistaken by twelfth- and thirteenth-century Continentally-trained copyists for either of the letters P or vernacular *þ* (*thorn*).[92] Thus, for example, the name of Offa II's great-great-grandfather, properly Eawa,[93] is taken as E[a]pa by Henry of Huntingdon, John of Worcester and Matthew.[94] In our text a similar mistake results in the childhood name of Offa II, properly Wynfrið ('Cheerful'), being read as Pynfrið (Penefred) (pp. 41-2).

The details of bishops' jurisdiction given in connection with Offa II's promotion of diocesan Lichfield to metropolitan status in 787 seem to derive from a directory referring to the first quarter of the ninth century. The only time at which the Mercian sees listed were occupied as indicated (pp. 81-2) was 801-14.[95] It was in fact the king's chaplain Hygeberht and not Aldwulf who was elevated metropolitan, the latter succeeding only in 799;[96] five of the other six bishops named did not take office until after Offa's death. A subsequent list (pp. 119-20), drawn upon when summarising the final domain of Offa in general, would appear to refer to the year 869 when bishops' seats at Dunwich and Elmham are still occupied (both ceasing shortly after 870); the diocese of Dorchester-on-Thames has been revived after a two-century break in succession; and it is still possible to speak of bishoprics of Leicester and Lindsey (interrupted respectively in 869 and 875).[97] The Nero D i manuscript may simply have been copying an early list uncritically, but the fact that the fourteenth-century Claudius E iv copyist should jumble the list is understandable.

Archival data incorporated by the compiler includes a number of diplomatic items apparently not surviving otherwise. These consist of: a letter from Offa II to a Welsh King Meredith (pp. 63-4); from an anti-Mercia league seeking an alliance with the overseas Frankish King Carloman (pp. 51-2); an admonitory missive from Carloman's brother Charlemagne to Offa II (pp. 55-8); and subsequent exchanges between Offa II

---

[92] N.R. Ker, *Catalogue of Manuscripts containing Anglo-Saxon*, Oxford, 1957, nos. 14, 28, 120, 345, pp. 12, 40, 156, 424.

[93] Chronicle A, *s.a.a.* 716, 755, Swanton, pp. 42, 50; Appendix A, pp. 133-4.

[94] Henry, Archdeacon of Huntingdon, *Historia Anglorum*, IV, 21, ed. and transl. D. Greenway, Oxford, 1996, pp. 246-47, notes 117-18; John (*alias* Florence) of Worcester, *The Chronicle*, ed. and transl. R.R. Darlington *et al.*, Oxford, 1995-98, II, pp. 198-9; Paris, *Chronica Majora*, I, p. 343.

[95] Matthew seems to have drawn on the same directory, but employed the details rather differently, *Chronica Majora*, I, p. 345, Giles, I, pp. 151-2.

[96] Later William of Malmesbury makes the same mistake: *Gesta Regum*, Mynors *et al.*, I, pp. 122-23, II, pp. 64-65; *Gesta Pontificum Anglorum*, ed. and transl. M. Winterbottom, Oxford, 2007, I, pp. 20-21, 466-67. W.G. Searle, *Anglo-Saxon Bishops, Kings and Nobles*, Cambridge, 1899, pp. 132-33.

[97] Supposing actual synchronicity. For the historical reliability of such data see R.I. Page, 'Anglo-Saxon episcopal lists', *Nottingham Mediaeval Studies*, 9 (1965), 71-95; 10 (1966), 2-24.

and Charlemagne referring to trade and travel (pp. 75-8). But if Charlemagne's reference to himself as already crowned imperial emperor (pp. 57-8) is not a significant political anticipation, at least this detail appears to be the oblique *post quo* emendation of a historian.

Introduction II: The Narrative and its Context

The Lack of Genre

The style and manner of presentation in the story indicates derivation from a wide variety of sources. There has been no obvious attempt to reduce this compilation of different elements to any one genre. If we are not to denounce *The Two Offas* as a mere collection of undeveloped notes, such primitive form as we might choose to recognise is probably as much fortuitous as artistic. Although our narrator reveals clear literary instincts,[98] the result certainly challenges latter-day notions of genre. It is not a talent for, or attraction to, biography he displays; his work cannot be compared with Einhard's *Life* of the Emperor Charlemagne or Asser's of King Alfred.[99] But we are still far from the well-crafted *chanson de geste* telling the success story of the presumed founder of a distinguished dynasty[100] or that in which a son's adventures are not dissimilar to those of his father, with convenient closure in pious withdrawal from the world as pilgrim or hermit.[101] Yet in common with these, its processes demonstrate something of the complex relations between history and romance – the imaginative life actual events can have. *Pari passu*, the compilation is intended to emphasise the antiquity and significance of St Albans Abbey as an institution.

Although our story-teller does not begin 'Once upon a time', clearly what is going to matter will be less the true story than a good story (cf. pp. ix-xi). The tale is acted out within a simple moral matrix – a narration of good and bad acts without analysis of motive; personalities developed solely through an individual's own actions and reactions to those of others. Continuity or coherence is minimal, or improbable, in

---

[98] A useful introduction to which is now provided by R. Martin, '*The Lives of the Offas*: the posthumous reputation of Offa, king of the Mercians', in *Æthelbald and Offa*, pp. 49-54.

[99] *Einhardi Vita Karoli Magni*, ed. O. Holder-Egger, *Monumenta Germaniae Historica, Scriptores rerum Germanicarum*, Hanover, 1911, transl. L. Thorpe, *Two Lives of Charlemagne*, Harmondsworth, 1969; *Asser's Life of King Alfred*, ed. W.H. Stevenson, revd. D. Whitelock, Oxford, 1959, transl. S. Keynes and M. Lapidge, *Alfred the Great*, Harmondsworth, 1983, pp. 65-110.

[100] Cf. M.D. Legge, *Anglo-Norman Literature and its Background*, Oxford, 1963, pp. 139-75.

[101] Cf. generally D.J.A. Ross, 'Old French', in *The Traditions of Heroic and Epic Poetry*, ed. A.T. Hatto, London, 1980-89, I, pp. 79-133.

transactions which are sometimes illogical in time or in terms of cause and effect – interrupted only to be resumed later without any obvious link or transition. Our attention is preoccupied by every part while it lasts, each cut off from the next – separate dramatic moments rather than 'proceedings'. Not always a story, one scene follows another in a series of two-dimensional Romanesque *tableaux*, not dissimilar from the illustration of late Anglo-Saxon manuscripts or wall-hangings in which the framed depiction of occasions presenting statuesque attitudes and symbolic gestures is limited and formulaic.[102] Although the Bayeux Tapestry is the sole-surviving example of the latter medium,[103] perhaps the one we know to have been at Ely Minster portraying the deeds of their patron the tenth-century governor of Essex, Byrhtnoth, would have offered a close model in focussing on the life of a single individual.[104]

From the outset our narrator says that his sources included not merely what had found its way into writing (presumably archival, as well as more creative literature, although he does not distinguish) but importantly oral traditions (pp. 1-2) of a kind twelfth-century historians like Henry of Huntingdon or William of Malmesbury acknowledge drawing upon: 'ballads worn away by the lapse of time, rather than books'.[105] In and around St Albans, the institution's own hundreds of serfs, and any remaining slaves, will have formed a vernacular reservoir of yarns and ballads about ancient English figures. Such stories were no doubt common among the burgher households of next-door Verulam – forty-six of them at the time of the Domesday Survey (though less prosperous than formerly). And probably also at the royal fort of Kingsbury, which survived within the *bloc* of land given by Offa II until bought from the crown in the early eleventh century. Even then the king was concerned that the abbot's plan to level this entire fort should not be carried through, so that at least some memory of royal association with the place would remain.[106] Kingsbury's occupants were the king's tenants and not the abbot's, with whom they were in continual dispute. Squatters remained as late as the mid-twelfth century.[107]

Whereas courtly literature in due course came to execrate the 'Saxon' foe in favour of an Arthurian hero, locally the English clerical community must have retained a considerable affection for stories told of their ancient indigenous patrons – the more so perhaps as a result of the incoming Norman abbot's attitude (see pp. xiii-xv). It is possible that behind this we can ascertain the bemused origins of what would eventually become the distinct genre of 'ancestral romance', but too much is lost from

---

[102] Cf. O. Pächt, *The Rise of Pictorial Narrative in Twelfth-Century England*, Oxford, 1962.

[103] Cf. M. Swanton, 'Gobelen iz Baio: Epicheskoe skazanie ne v stikhakh, no v vyshivke', *Mirovoe Drevo*, 4 (1996), 47-62.

[104] 'A woven hanging depicted with her husband's deeds as a memorial of his virtue', *Liber Eliensis*, II, 63, ed. E.O. Blake, London, 1962, p. 136.

[105] Henry, *Historia Anglorum*, Greenway, pp. 558-59; William, *Gesta Regum*, Mynors et al., I, pp. 224-25.

[106] *Gesta Abbatum*, I, pp. 31-33, Niblett and Thompson, p. 366. J.E.B. Gover et al., *The Place-Names of Hertfordshire*, Cambridge, 1938, pp. 89-90.

[107] *Gesta Abbatum*, I, pp. 121-22, Niblett and Thompson, pp. 373-74.

the record to be able to trace the coherent development of any such native literary tradition across a post-Conquest vernacular hiatus.

The *Life of Offa I* is relatively brief (5,500 words), straightforwardly composed from two major folktale components: (a) the loser makes good, and (b) the innocent but calumniated girl is justified (pp. lxxvii-lxxix). But the formulae are presented together with up-to-date details. We are told of letters – even re-written letters – in a society that was technically illiterate (pp. 27-30). And murdered children are said to be restored to life by the sign of the cross at a time when people were actually still pagan (pp. 31-2).

The availability of one independent version of the *Life of Offa I* (Vitellius A xx) presented *tout court*, and in different layout and somewhat different wording from that incorporated in other manuscripts, strongly suggests a separate existence for that work at an early stage. It seems likely, in any case, that the story of a king living four centuries previously had a separate and earlier origin. Allusions to the figure made by early vernacular poets (see pp. xlvii-l, Appendices B and C, pp. 139-44) indicate that such material had long been circulating in Europe. Nonetheless, creative development has occurred sufficiently late in the day for it to have gained the imaginative colouring it now has, which we might assume then acted as the inspiration for romancing the life of Offa II. The fact that even a Byzantine tale like that of Apollonius of Tyre had found its way into English by the late tenth century indicates an appetite for such things among at least some quarters of Anglo-Saxon society.[108]

In the form of *The Two Offas* we have inherited in Nero D i, it will be found that two English kings, separated by four centuries, who bear the same name – the second intentionally and significantly named after the first – closely resemble each other, having remarkably similar origins and careers. Both lives follow the male-Cinderella or 'zero-to-hero' narrative paradigm canonised by way of innumerable august icons.[109] Both are singularly unpromising children, disregarded or ridiculed by society, but who dramatically respond to a national emergency, take arms, prove victorious and thus return to public acclamation. In both cases their father stands aside in favour of his son who, taking the throne, enjoys a highly successful reign. Both establish notable national frontiers against their people's greatest racial enemy. The first English Offa drives boundaries against Saxons to the south of his kingdom; the second Offa, having overmastered Saxons to the south, fixes his boundary against the western Welsh.

The significant foreign marriage of each is presented in terms of romance, although with very different political outcomes. Both will marry a princess 'found in the wilderness' in flight from persecution in their respective homelands (cf. pp. lxxvi-lxxxi), each of whom is accorded an important, but in the event contrasting, narrative career of her own. The 'Life' of each Offa contains an element of religious closure, as does the whole: the first Offa promising to establish a monastery, and the second Offa

---

[108] *The Old English Apollonius of Tyre*, ed. P. Goolden, Oxford, 1958; transl. M. Swanton, *Anglo-Saxon Prose*, 2nd edn, London, 1993, pp. 234-50.
[109] Thus for example: the Roman emperor Claudius, Albert Einstein, Winston Churchill and many another – although none actually 'rags to riches'.

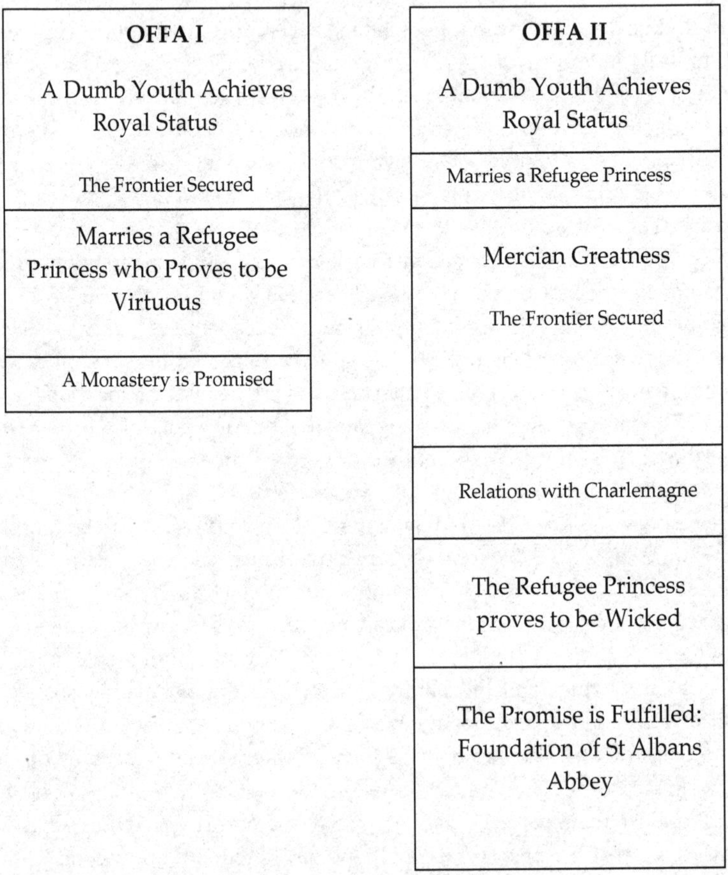

OFFA I	OFFA II
A Dumb Youth Achieves Royal Status	**A Dumb Youth Achieves Royal Status**
The Frontier Secured	Marries a Refugee Princess
Marries a Refugee Princess who Proves to be Virtuous	**Mercian Greatness** The Frontier Secured
A Monastery is Promised	
	Relations with Charlemagne
	The Refugee Princess proves to be Wicked
	The Promise is Fulfilled: Foundation of St Albans Abbey

Fig. 2) Narrative elements in the Vitae Offarum Duorum *(as existing).*

OFFA I	OFFA II
OFFA I A Dumb Youth Achieves Royal Status The Frontier Secured	**OFFA II** A Dumb Youth Achieves Royal Status Marries a Refugee Princess
Marries a Refugee Princess who Proves to be Virtuous	Mercian Greatness The Frontier Secured
A Monastery is Promised	
	The Refugee Princess proves to be Wicked
	The Promise is Fulfilled: A Monastery is founded

Fig. 3) Potential narrative architecture of the Vitae Offarum Duorum *with archival section on Offa II's relations with Charlemagne omitted and that on the foundation of St Albans abbey reduced.*

actually fulfilling his predecessor's vow. Once the audience has been led to recognise parallels between the two 'Lives', the incremental effect is one of expectation, which can be worked with, or perceived, ironically or otherwise (Figs. 2-3).

The *Life* of Offa II may begin with what is a brief reflection of his ancestor's career – the two appear to be very similar – but in practice the transference of formulae between the two figures seems to have proved something of an embarrassment. The account of the first king is relatively limited since, as his twelfth-century fellow-countryman (i.e. Danish) Saxo Grammaticus pointed out, he knew nothing of Offa I's deeds subsequent to his accession, although could only imagine them to have been magnificent and that, if only his contemporaries had been able to write Latin, we should no doubt have been thumbing through countless volumes[110] (Appendix H, pp. 183-4). When applied to Offa II, the folklore formulae occupy little more than one third the wordage they do with Offa I (Fig. 3). Nevertheless the second *Vita* is made well over twice as long, since the compiler of our final version has fallen into the temptation of extensively supplementing the 'tales of old men' (pp. 105-6) by attempting to make relevant whatever to comes to hand. There is added a clumsy assemblage of data culled from existing histories, letters to and from foreign princes available in diplomatic archives, literary references, and a great deal of creative imagination, before the expected point of closure is provided by a well-researched, but over-substantial, tract on the discovery of St Alban's remains and consequent foundation of the Abbey. Such lack of discrimination results in a much less successful overall construction than might have been. Figure 3 illustrates the telling narrative structure for *The Two Offas* that would result if the context of St Albans Abbey could be taken for granted and Offa II's political relations with Europe ignored.

The Kingdoms of Offa I and Offa II

History knows very little of the actual Offa I, save that he was probably ruler of people living in part of what is now southern Denmark: Angeln (Fig. 4) on the eve of their mass-migration to central Britain. Accurate evidence for the dates of any early English king is unavailable, although recourse to the royal pedigree (Appendix A, pp. 133-4) and using the customary genealogical allocation of thirty years per generation would suggest that Offa I flourished in the late fourth or early fifth century.[111] Even this supposes that no generations have been omitted. English dynastic lists are unreliable documents, in their early parts at least. The name of Offa I's father, Wermund, was not unknown in later England. It was used for example of that contemporary of Offa II, the

---

[110] *Gesta Danorum*, IV, 5, ed. J. Olrik and H. Ræder, Copenhagen, 1931-57, p. 100; transl. H.E. Davidson and P. Fisher, *History of the Danes*, Cambridge, 1979-80, I, p. 109.

[111] N.E. Eliason, 'The "Thryth-Offa Digression" in *Beowulf* ', in *Medieval and Linguistic Studies*, ed. J.B. Bessinger and R.P. Creed, London, 1965, pp. 124-38 (pp. 129, 136-37).

late eighth-century bishop of Rochester, while in its cognate form Gurmund, it was used by Guthrum, a ninth-century ruler of Danelaw, in north and midland England.[112]

Offa I's father is elsewhere reported to have had dramatic Near Eastern origins (p. l) as one of the many merchant adventurers who traded arms and slaves within the collapsed or collapsing Roman Empire. Although there seem no reasons to suppose an Arabic origin for the name *per se*,[113] when one's grandfather or great grandfather might have been the war-god Woden, fact, error and myth could not, or would not, be distinguished.[114]

The element of Arab influence on Western culture at this time should not be underestimated. [115] Occupying important posts in both secular and religious life throughout Europe, with commercial communities at the mouths of northern rivers and naval units like that of the Tigris Boatmen at the North Sea end of Hadrian's Wall, the Arab escort was no doubt a familiar figure along the trade-route that Angeln accommodated (see p. lxv). Representing a warrior ideal of fine arms, skill in their use and sheer courage, their employment might have proved no more than practical in the very fluid conditions of the great Migration Age. A number of late Roman emperors are known to have had Middle Eastern or African origins.[116] In the early seventh century disparate Slavs migrating westwards into parts of Eastern Europe now largely vacated by Germani would be brought powerfully together under the sovereignty of a foreign merchant adventurer.[117] However, it was under Offa I's son, the eponymous Angelþeow (Appendix A, pp. 133-4), that the naturalisation of the English people (*Angel-þeod*) in Britain might be referred; as correspondingly the son called Dan would be used to identify Danish rule in the Scandinavian peninsula.[118]

It comes as a surprise to the average present-day 'Englishman' to learn that the English have not always lived in England. And the same would have been true of his twelfth-century predecessor. Only the most scholarly knew from Bede or others that the 'English' (together with Saxons and the like) were in fact tribal immigrants into late Roman Britain during the fifth and sixth centuries from Schleswig-Holstein – what is

---

[112] William of Malmesbury, *Gesta Regum Anglorum*, ed. and transl. R.A.B. Mynors *et al.*, Oxford, 1998-99, I, pp. 184-45.

[113] Personal communication with Professor Rasheed el-Enany.

[114] D.N. Dumville, 'The Anglian collection of royal genealogies and regnal lists', *Anglo-Saxon England*, 5 (1976), 23-50; E. John, 'The point of Woden', *Anglo-Saxon Studies in Archaeology and History*, 5 (1992), 127-34.

[115] See generally W. Ball, *Rome in the East*, London, 2000.

[116] It is worth bearing in mind that of the three dozen or so post-Conquest 'English' sovereigns the majority have been foreign in origin, part of a transnational elite ready to expropriate kingship, J. Goulstone, *An Introduction to English Royal Descents*, Bexleyheath, 1993, pp. 6-7.

[117] The Frank Samo, probably from Sens, Fredegar, *Chronicle*, ed. J.M. Wallace-Hadrill, London, 1960, pp. 39-40, 56-7, 63. See generally R. Latouche, *Les Origines de l'Économie Occidentale (IVe – XIe siécle)*, Paris, 1956, pp. 143-5.

[118] Saxo Grammaticus, IV, 6, Olrik and Ræder, I, p. 100; Davidson and Fisher, I, p. 14, II, pp. 25-6.

now southern Denmark and northern Germany (Fig. 4).[119] Equally, we are nowadays accustomed to think of the pre-Conquest English – King Alfred's nation – as a well-defined, homogenous island race; but these 'Anglo-Saxons' were not a unified people for several centuries.[120] The concept 'Anglo-Saxon' does not properly belong to early England. The word's only certain record in a vernacular context occurs in a tenth-century scholar's seventeen-line exercise in metrical and linguistic ingenuity together with a whole range of Greek and Latin borrowings.[121] It appears to have been a new-fangled expression developed in Continental Carolingian society needing to differentiate the insular ('English') Saxons from those large numbers of their kin who remained on the Continent and who were proving so troublesome to the imperial Charlemagne.[122] Later it is used by the Welshman Asser in the Latin title he gives his patron King Alfred, although not apparently with territorial meaning for he uses simply Mercia (never Anglia) as against Saxonia.[123] Asser's practice may reflect his Frankish Latinity, the customary Anglo-Saxon usage being merely *Rex* (or *Basileus*) *Anglorum* (or *totius Britanniae*).[124] And after Asser, the odd occasion on which 'Anglo-Saxon' is found incorporated into a king's title to denote political union is in post-Conquest copy or forgery.

With the collapse of the Roman Empire, the Germanic immigrants into Britain had come from different parts of Northern Europe. Prior to their settlement, and for some time afterwards, the separate Saxon and English peoples to whom Bede refers[125] were to remain culturally quite distinct, territorially separate and frequently hostile, a fact which survived in vernacular tradition as late as the twelfth century. They spoke different dialects of the Common North-Sea Germanic language. They varied from each other in their style of personal adornment, the distinctive kind of pottery they made and in their very different funerary customs (the English preferring cremation, the Saxons inhumation).[126] On the Continent, Saxons were later rumoured to practise

---

[119] *Ecclesiastical History*, I, 15, Colgrave and Mynors, pp. 50-51; J.N.L. Myres, *The English Settlements*, Oxford, 1986.

[120] See generally: W. Pohl, 'Ethnic names and identities in the British Isles', in *The Anglo-Saxons from the Migration Period to the Eighth Century*, ed. J. Hines, Woodbridge, 1997, pp. 7-40.

[121] Ed. E. v. K. Dobbie, *The Anglo-Saxon Minor Poems*, New York, 1942, pp. xc-ii, 97; F. Holthausen, 'Kleinere altenglischen Dichtungen', *Anglia*, 41 (1917), 400-4 (p. 403).

[122] E.g. Paulus Diaconus, *Historia Langobardorum*, IV, 22, ed. L. Bethmann and G. Waitz, *Monumenta Germaniae Historica, Scriptores rerum Langobardicarum*, Hanover, 1878, p. 124, or *Vita Alcuini*, 18, ed. W. Arndt, *Monumenta Germaniae Historica, Scriptores*, 15, Hanover, 1887, pp. 182-97 (p. 193); cf. W. Levison, *England and the Continent in the Eighth Century*, Oxford, 1946, pp. 92-93.

[123] *Life of King Alfred*, Stevenson, pp. 148-52, Keynes and Lapidge, p. 67 *et passim*.

[124] A survey of usage is given, Stevenson, *Ibid*, pp. 477-52, Keynes and Lapidge, pp. 227-28.

[125] Bede, *Ecclesiastical History*, I, 15, Colgrave and Mynors, pp. 50-51. This is of course a product of its time, looking from hindsight rather than one of synchronous record.

[126] J.N.L. Myres, *Anglo-Saxon Pottery and the Settlement of England*, Oxford, 1969. A simple distribution-map of cremation ritual is available in V.I. Evison, *The Fifth-Century Invasions South of the Thames*, London, 1965, p. 145, although as she points out in 'Distribution maps and England in the first two phases', *Angles, Saxons, and Jutes*, Oxford, 1981, 126-67 (p. 127), there is understood to be an element of mingling prior to migration.

human sacrifice and perhaps cannibalism.[127] Certainly they had distinct political structures; Bede is clear that Continental Saxons were ruled not by kings – the English *principes* and *sub-reguli* with which he was personally familiar – but by a quasi-democratic multiplicity of governors or aldermen (*satrapas plurimos*).[128]

Fig. 4) English homelands in the time of Offa I in modern Denmark and Germany.

The migrant *Seaxe* ('Dagger-Folk')[129] left their relatives living in Continental Saxony between the rivers Eider and Ems to settle scattered around the Channel and Atlantic

[127] *Monumenta Germaniae Historica, Legum*, V, Hanover, 1889, pp. 34-46 (pp. 37-38).

[128] *Ecclesiastical History*, V, 10, Colgrave and Mynors, pp. 480-83. Compare the radical form among the Eruli described by the sixth-century Byzantine Procopius, *History of the Wars*, VI, 14, ed. H.B. Dewing, London, 1914-40, III, pp. 412-43.

[129] The term *seax* is used of the single-edged dagger found in many early warrior-graves, although not exclusively Saxon ones, D.A. Gale, 'The seax', in *Weapons and Warfare in Anglo-Saxon England*, ed. S. Hawkes, Oxford, 1989, pp. 71-83.

coasts of Europe in general, and then in large numbers to southern Britain.[130] Here they would continue to be identified by their racial folk-name. To the marginal wetlands of Essex came those who would now be called 'East Saxons', *East Seaxe,* and towards the south coast in Sussex, the *Suð Seaxe,* further inland along the Thames 'Middle Saxons', *Middel Seaxe,* then Wessex, *West Seaxe* (Fig. 5).

Other Germanic settlers would be identified by their place of settlement rather than racially. The mix of Jutes, Frisians and others who came to occupy the former Roman province of Cantium (*British, 'white', 'chalk') in the furthest southeast were simply the *Cant-ware,* 'Dwellers in Kent'. Close to mainland Europe, their material culture indicates an informed association less with Saxons than with adjacent Franks – whose newly-discovered Christianity they would soon adopt.[131]

The greater part of what was to become 'England' – the Midlands and the North – was settled by the 'English', i.e. Angles, who left their European homeland in such numbers that apparently, as early commentators believed, it remained largely deserted for some considerable time.[132] That was the historical Offa I's country: a then densely-settled district immediately north of the neck of Jutland between the Flensborg and Schlei estuaries (Fig. 4) referred to by classical geographers as *Angulus,* the angle or 'hook' of land from which these *Angli* seem to have derived their name.[133] The original extent of their Continental homeland is not yet clear but seems to have stretched beyond the frontier of modern Angeln.[134] They were separated from adjacent peoples to the north and south by broad uninhabitable zones – heavy clays and infertile sand – a politically desirable circumstance (p. xlvi).[135] Sacrificial bog-sites such as those at Nydam and Ejsbøl probably represented religious *foci* for this Nerthus- or fecundity-worshipping people.[136] The idea that the region remained more or less unoccupied in

---

[130] Still useful is R. von Erckert, ed. *Wanderung und Siedelungen der Germanischen Stämme in Mittel-Europa von der ältesten Zeit bis auf Karl den Grossen,* Berlin, 1901, although modified at points by more recent archaeological evidence.

[131] It is possible that the English might have provided the founding war-leaders of the kingdom. Nennius refers to their presence, *Historia Brittonum,* 37, ed. Lot, Paris, 1934, I, p. 176. Bede refers to Æthelberht and Earconberht of Kent in turn as 'king of the English', *Ecclesiastical History,* I, 32, III, 8, Colgrave and Mynors, pp. 100-11, 236-37.

[132] Bede, *Ecclesiastical History,* I, 15, Colgrave and Mynors, pp. 50-51. For the generally accepted material evidence, see J. Hines, *The Scandinavian Character of Anglian England in the Pre-Viking Period,* Oxford, 1984; and a recent debate as to the racial significance of material data: S. Lucy, *The Anglo-Saxon Way of Death,* Stroud, 2000, pp. 155-86.

[133] W. Laur, 'Angeln und die Angeln in namenkundlicher Sicht', *Jahrbuch Heimatvereins der Landschaft Angeln,* 22 (1958), 46-9.

[134] Second-century Greek geography would allude to English and Suevi further south on the Middle Elbe or Weser, cf. *Die Geographie des Ptolemaeus,* ed. O. Cuntz, Berlin, 1923, pp. 63-4; transl. E.L. Stevenson, *Geography of Claudius Ptolemy,* New York, 1932, p. 64.

[135] H. Jankuhn, 'The Continental home of the English', *Antiquity,* 26 (1952), 14-24; 'Terra... silvis horrida', *Archaeologia Geographica,* 10-11 (1961-63), 19-38; W. Davies and H. Vierck, 'The contexts of Tribal Hidage: social aggregates and settlement patterns', *Frühmittelalterliche Studien,* 8 (1974), 223-93.

[136] Tacitus, *Germania,* 40, ed. M. Winterbottom and R.M. Ogilvie, *Opera Minora,* Oxford, 1975, pp. 57-58, transl. J.B. Rives, Oxford, 1999, pp. 93, 292-94.

consequence of the Migration (*Angulus desertus*) is supported by the fact that some settlement-sites have no great evidence for occupation between 500 and 800 A.D.[137] It may be that, as a result of ecological factors, Angeln was only ever occupied intermittently.[138] As today in various parts of the world, environmental stress of some kind can lead a desperate people to mass emigration – with consequent political tension. The reputation of early Englishmen as seafarers [139] suggests that it might well have been possible for large numbers to move relatively quickly. We must assume that conservative remnants will have remained, if only those who were to maintain the legends utilised in our text in a Scandinavian context (Appendices, F, G and H, pp. 163-84).[140] The fact that the English place-names of the region were so wholly replaced by Danish ones suggests that any remnant was merely residual.[141] Although the name 'Angle' remained sufficiently present to account for Pope Gregory's oral play on the name *c*. 600,[142] these settlers seem generally not to need racial identification like the Saxons but rather, like the mixed people of Kent (*Cantware*), could be categorised simply by way of where they now lived. Just as previously they were 'English' by reason of living in Angeln, so now those who lived along the immediately accessible east coast of Britain that came to be known as 'East England' would be called there merely North folk (*Norð folc*) and South folk (*Suð folc*). Others, north of the Wash, occupying the swamp-lands called by the native British term **lindo* (British, 'pool'), were now 'Lindsey' (*Lindisse*); and then north of the River Humber various 'North-Humbrian' English used group names Deire and Beornice leaning on existing local Brittonic nomenclature. Their ethnic identity they could apparently take for granted. Like their language it was, of course, 'English'. In fact, however, we know that family histories cannot be guaranteed beyond a generation or two, let alone the extent to which they might relate to named individuals.[143] It is this that underlies the close relationship we find between uncle and nephew in early times (e.g. Hygelac and Beowulf) inasmuch as in one's sister's child, unlike one's wife's, the perpetuity of the family blood-line was guaranteed.

[137] Cf. S. Hvass, 'Fem års udgravninger i Vorbasse', *Mark og Montre,* 15 (1979), 27-39; although see M. Gebühr, 'Angulus desertus?', *Studien zur Sachsenforschung,* 11 (1998), 43-85; also S. Jensen, 'Stengården... : the problem of settlement continuity in Later Iron Age Denmark', *Journal of Danish Archaeology,* 1 (1982), 119-25.

[138] Unpopulated from the end of the Bronze Age until the second century: BC: K-H. Willroth, *Untersuchungen zur Besiedlungsgeschichte der Landschaften Angeln und Schwansen,* Neumünster, 1992, pp. 244-444.

[139] Procopius, *History of the Wars,* VIII, 20, Dewing, V, pp. 258-61.

[140] For later settlement see: H. Unverhau, *Untersuchungen zur historischen Entwicklung des Landes zwischen Schlei und Eider im Mittelalter,* Neumünster, 1990, pp. 59-67.

[141] P. Bredsdorff, *Kortlægning og historiske Studier,* Copenhagen, 1973, p. 45, fig. 42.

[142] Supposing this to be authentic, Bede, *Ecclesiastical History,* II, 1, Colgrave and Mynors, pp. 132-35; (*i.e.* young Englishmen had the appearance of angels, and 'Alleluia' should be sung in the land of King Ælle.)

[143] Government-funded DNA investigation (unpublished) from genetic samples in the south of England suggested that 36% of individuals are not procreations of the registered father (Personal Communication).

Fig. 5) Insular Germanic and Celtic kingdoms by the time of Offa II.

To the west of the 'North-' and 'South-folk', across the rich arable and pasture lands of what is now the English Midlands, settled incoming English who determined continually to push any recalcitrant natives (*wealas*)[144] back into the less productive hill-country of present-day 'Wales' (p. lxviii) in order to ensure secure conditions for themselves. These were 'Mercians' (*Mierce*), 'Marchers' or 'Frontier-Folk', and this was Offa II's people. Those they evicted were mainly landowning British aristocrats. It

[144] M.L. Faull, 'The semantic development of Old English *wealh*', *Leeds Studies in English*, NS 8 (1975), 20-44.

seems unlikely that indigenous communities were wholly dispossessed anywhere.[145] A large proportion of the local native population could have been usefully absorbed within a generation or two. But irrespective of whether early Anglo-Saxon kingdoms formed racially homogenous units, displacing native populations wholesale, or were mixed groups dominated by a Germanic élite, [146] all would come to memorise themselves in terms of the esteem in which leading dynasties were held.[147]

The success or otherwise of petty princelings depended on the outcome of the most recent battle against a neighbour – encroaching, or encroached upon. Such men felt that they belonged primarily to a family-group – then to associates and to a people slowly turning into 'nationhood' – interrelationships of social stress and territoriality well known to ethnologists. As late as the ninth century a Mercian 'Tribal Hidage' continues to express the political framework in terms of communities rather than land-holdings,[148] and thus the concept of 'king of the English' (*rex Anglorum*) rather than 'king of England' (*rex Angliae*). Within such a social fabric, membership of a group of comrades (*comitatus*) will have been in no way xenophobic, and 'treason' a matter of personal rather than national concern. Mercenary troops were common. Individual champions, boasting appropriately beast-like names, might trade themselves like international footballers, and be idolised in much the same way. The most famous of Old English literary heroes, the Migration-Age Beowulf, was a Geat living in southern Sweden who performed his exploits on behalf of a Danish king.[149] In Scandinavia in general the most popular tales told seem to have been those of Hunnish, Goth and Burgundian heroes.

We have no way of knowing the stage at which a migrant group might, over generations, come to recognise its place of ultimate arrival – its nationality associated with a notion of 'homeland': stability and concomitant institutions.[150] Most recently it has been territorial frontier that defines a 'country' and hence 'countrymen' in a national sense. Prior to that, with pressure of population low relative to present times and settlement

---

[145] Cf. S. Bassett, 'How the west was won: the Anglo-Saxon takeover of the west midlands', *Anglo-Saxon Studies in Archaeology and History*, 11 (2000), 107-18.

[146] Cf. generally C.J. Scull, 'Approaches to material culture and social dynamics of the Migration Period in eastern England', in *Europe between Late Antiquity and the Middle Ages*, ed. J. Bintliff and H. Hamerow, Oxford, 1995, pp. 71-83; H. Hamerow, 'Migration theory and the Migration period', *Building on the Past*, ed. B. Vyner, London, 1994, pp. 164-77; and 'Wanderungstheorien und die angelsächsische "Identitätskrise"', *Studien zur Sachsenforschung*, 11 (1998), 121-34.

[147] For the difficulties of ethnic definition in general see J. Hines, 'The becoming of the English', *Anglo-Saxon Studies in Archaeology and History*, 7 (1994), 49-59; W. Pohl, 'Ethnic names and identities in the British Isles', in *The Anglo-Saxons from the Migration Period to the Eighth Century*, ed. J. Hines, Woodbridge, 1997, pp. 7-40.

[148] *Cartularium Saxonicum*, I, pp. 414-16; Davies and Vierck, 223-93, and references there cited.

[149] The poem, composed probably in the eighth-century, but recalling fifth-century events – was no doubt supposed by some contemporaries to be factual. For a summary of the evidence see N. Jacobs, 'Anglo-Danish relations, poetic archaism and the date of *Beowulf*', *Poetica* (Tokyo), 8 (1977), 23-43. The parts of the poem at issue will be found in Appendix C, pp. 141-4.

[150] Cf. J. Hines, 'Cultural change and social organisation in early Anglo-Saxon England', in *After Empire. Towards an Ethnology of Europe's Barbarians*, ed. G. Ausenda, Woodbridge, 1995, pp. 75-93.

in terms of focus rather than frontier,[151] people inhabited an elastic area with a fluctuating band of territory between them and their nearest neighbours. Boundaries could afford to be flexible, and it was said that Germanic tribes would lay waste a protective zone around themselves so that it remained as far as possible unsettled.[152]

Nowhere more so than in modern Britain has there been supposed a natural relationship between land and people – to the point where 'England' (country) and 'England' (nation) seemed synonymous. But occupation expressive of ownership is a relatively recent development in European history. During a period of wholesale racial movement, when Germanic peoples especially made their way into and through the one-time components of the now defunct Roman Empire, the concept of fixed territorial boundaries must have been quite exceptional. However, particularly in time of war, and the more so with repeated war, the frontier builds a natural sense of social solidarity and thus national identity – iconic as much as militarily defensive. Both historic Offas (Danish Offa I and Mercian Offa II) were to be remembered for their establishment of secure boundaries against notoriously antagonistic neighbours. In eighth-century England Offa II constructed an impressive rampart against the native Welsh (pp. lxix-lxxv), while in fourth-century Denmark his forebear Offa I had fixed his national boundary against the hostile Saxons to the south on the line of the Treene-Eider waterway (or for our narrator, supposing Offa I to have been a Mercian king, the line of one-or-another River Avon, p. 12). This would have been more of an achievement than we might at first suppose since, however such rivers seem to form natural frontiers for the latter-day map-maker, in practice they made a difficult dividing-line in early times (p. lxiv).

Memories of Offa I

For several generations there survived the legends – perhaps genuine memories – which the immigrants to Britain brought with them from Angeln and Saxony. As Tacitus observed of their first-century predecessors, it was in mnemonic poetry that these peoples' sole species of history existed.[153] But since the function of the early poet was no less to entertain than to report, we cannot regard their work as mere record any more than our own old soldiers' stories are – especially when relayed through poor raconteurs, or those with faulty memories, let alone to a second or third generation.[154]

---

[151] Only some twenty per-cent of the habitable land of Europe was occupied; see W. Müller-Wille, 'Siedlungs-, Wirtschafts- und Bevölkerungsräume im westlichen Mitteleuropa um 500 n. Chr.', *Westfälische Forschungen*, 9 (1956), 5-25 (p. 7).

[152] Caesar, *The Gallic War*, IV, 3 and VI 23, ed. H.J. Edwards, London, 1917, pp. 182-83, 346-49; H. Jankuhn, 'Archäologische Bemerkungen zur Glaubwürdigkeit des Tacitus in der Germania', *Nachrichten der Akademie der Wissenschaften in Göttingen: Philol.-hist. Klasse*, 10 (1966), 409-26.

[153] *Germania*, 2, Winterbottom and Ogilvie, p. 38, Rives, p. 77.

[154] Half of a sample of twenty-first-century youth in the United Kingdom recently mistook Dunkirk for D-day, while a quarter confused events in First and Second World Wars. A well-educated personal

Such remnants of this repertoire to be documented, and then survive, are small. The probably seventh- or eighth-century Old English 'catalogue-poem' we call *Widsith* [155] gives us a tantalising glimpse of a rich legendary lost to us – including the most explicit account we have in Old English of Offa I (Appendix B, pp. 139-40). The narrative voice is that of a minstrel who represents himself as *wid-sið*, 'the Widely-Travelled'. Himself a Saxon, he came from among the group called 'Bog-Folk' (*Myrgings*), [156] living in wetlands south of the Eider (Fig. 4). He had accompanied a young English[157] princess married off to the court of the fourth-century Ostrogoth King Ermanric, and now has a whole variety of tales to tell. Widsith knows about several personalities mentioned by the narrator of *Beowulf*. He manifestly knows about Continental Saxons and nearby Franks, Frisians and English. Now he can tell stories coming from Picts and Irish living on the margins of outermost Britain, or from the Mongol Huns in Eurasia; and further afield yet, about people his audience will scarcely have heard of: Assyrians, Persians, Egyptians and Indians. No doubt such tales will have circulated among visitors to Ermanric's court. Very many of the figures Widsith names are now lost to us, but wherever ascertainable all are historical. No insular Anglo-Saxon references occur – naturally enough since his panorama is that of the antique age of Continental turmoil that preceded the migration to Britain. Although chronologically unreliable, [158] he displays no interest in legendary matter such as gods or dragons.

Following a list of thirty-one rulers' names (lines 18-34), the poet alters his style, turning from a staccato welter of referents to a more expansive mode. This begins with a descriptive account, albeit allusive and brief, of Offa I, primarily remembered as that English ruler who forged a lasting frontier against the Saxons. In a dozen alliterative lines Widsith's audience is told that not even a certain Danish king, whom they know to have been exceptionally spirited, outdid this hero's deeds of valour; but while still a youth, Offa *geslog* ('achieved by blows', 38)[159] the greatest of kingdoms. With a special or particular sword (*ane sweorde*, 41)[160] he fixed the boundary against Widsith's own people at the Eider estuary (*Fifeldor*); afterwards the English (*Engle*) and Suebi (*Swæfe*)

---

acquaintance when speaking occasionally confuses the names of fascist Franco with communist Castro – aphasic merely but momentarily disconcerting!

[155] Ed. K. Malone, *Widsith*, London, 1936; *The Exeter Anthology of Old English Poetry*, ed. B. Muir, 2nd edn, Exeter, 2000, I, pp. 241-46, II, pp. 520-26, transl. S.A.J. Bradley, *Anglo-Saxon Poetry*, 2nd edn, London, 1995, pp. 336-40.

[156] Others under a similar name apparently lived further south by the River Elbe – perhaps the Maurungani of the 'Ravenna Cosmography'. See generally M. Lintzel, 'Myrgingas und Mauringa', in *Beiträge zur Kulturgeographie*, ed. I . Siedentop, Gotha, 1932, pp. 113-22; R.W. Chambers, *Widsith: a Study in Old English Heroic Legend*, Cambridge, 1912, pp. 159-61, 235-6; K. Malone, 'The Myrgingos of *Widsith*', *Modern Language Notes*, 55 (1940), 141-42.

[157] For the woman's origin see K. Malone, 'Ealhhild', *Anglia*, 55 (1931), 266-72.

[158] Claiming to have visited the courts of leaders chronologically as separate as, for example, the Burgundian king Gundaharius (*c.* 411-37) and Attila the Hun (433-53) or the Langobards Audoin (*c.* 546-65) and Alboin (565-73). It would post-date Ermanric up to a couple of centuries.

[159] Cf. Modern English '*sledge*-hammer'.

[160] The semantic field of Old English *an* extends over 'one, only, singular, personal'.

always kept it just as Offa's blow had established it (*geslog*, 44). The ninth-century *Annals of Fulda* repeatedly identify the Eider as that feature which separates off the Saxons.[161] The name *Fifel-dor* derives from *fifel*, 'monster', thus 'monstrous', 'monster-ridden', or perhaps merely 'frightful', and *dor*, 'entrance', 'estuary'.[162] Parallel etymology is probable for Eider (*Egi-dor*), the first element perhaps *egi*, 'fear'.[163] Flowing wide through flooded salt-marsh into the extensive shallow waters of Heligoland Bay and the Frisian Islands, the estuary could well have been dangerous for a variety of reasons. Its character was in particular contrast with that of the near but opposite lengthy shelter of the Baltic Schlei fjord (see Fig. 4, pp. lxiv-lxvii). Except at its estuary, the Treene-Eider is a relatively modest waterway, and presumably awesome only by way of poetic licence. Latterly, however, the name may have had reference not merely to the mouth but to the whole course of the river. Some part of his audience might be familiar with the Continental geography, but where factual data must be transferred by way of mnemonic ballad, details are inevitably, and ironically, subject to literary and linguistic change. Later, given the re-location of our story into the English Midlands, it is natural that an important local river should be identified for the occasion (p. lxii).

Widsith collocates the neighbouring peoples Swæfe and English twice (44 and 61), without prosodic emphasis such as alliteration drawing the names together. Swæfe (Suebi) was the generic name of a large number of tribes, apparently including the Anglii.[164] These Swæfe were settled north of the Eider but west of the Treene, and evidently with distinct gods and customs, but there may well have been a Swæfe element in the movement to Britain.[165]

The fact that Widsith refers to Offa I four times whilst mentioning no other figure more than once – an order of advertisement unusual in Old English poets – could well have had political rather than literary purpose. Circulating in eighth-century England, the account, brief though it is, can only have complimented the hero's descendant Offa II.

[161] *Annales Fuldenses*, ed. F. Kurze, *Monumenta Germaniae Historica, Schriften*, Hanover, 1891, pp. 47, 79, transl. T. Reuter, Manchester, 1992, pp. 39, 71 and note 12.

[162] *Fifel* is commonly associated with water, e.g. *fifel-stream*, *-wæg*, both synonymous with 'ocean', and *fifel-cynn*, a water-monster, cf. *Beowulf*, 104, ed. and transl. M. Swanton, *Beowulf*, Manchester, 1978, pp. 38-39.

[163] R. Much, '*Widsith*: Beiträge zu einem Commentar', *Zeitschrift für deutsches Altertum*, 62 (1925), 113-50 (p. 126); Chambers's note is encyclopaedic: *Widsith*, p. 204, n. 43; and for the relationship between the two names, see F.P. Magoun, 'Fīfeldor and the name of the Eider', *Namn och Bygd*, 28 (1940), 94-114. W. Laur, 'Der Flussname Eider', *Zeitschrift der Gesellschaft für Schleswig-Holsteinische Geschichte*, 87 (1962), 263-71. For alternative river-names in England see Ekwall, pp. xxxiii-xli.

[164] Tacitus, *Germania*, 38-9, Winterbottom and Ogilvie, pp. 56-58, Rives, pp. 282-85. R.L. Reynolds, 'Reconsideration of the history of the Suevi', *Revue Belge de Philologie et d'Histoire*, 35 (1957), 19-47 (pp. 27-31).

[165] E. Ekwall, 'Tribal names in English place-names', *Namn och Bygd*, 41 (1953), 129-77 (pp. 150-51). Their king was Witta, grandson of Woden (*Widsith*, 22) whose own grandsons included Hengest, founder of the Kentish kingdom: Bede, *Ecclesiastical History*, I, 15, Colgrave and Mynors, pp. 50-51.

The place in which the student of English most commonly meets with the pre-Migration figure of Offa I is in the early Old English poem about the adventures of the hero Beowulf in Denmark (Appendix C, pp. 141-4), which, in the form we have it, we may conjecture was produced at Offa II's court – or that of a neighbour. With the recitation of *Beowulf* in the presence of Offa II the reference to his forebear must have been pointed.[166] The awkwardness of its insertion – even given this poet's digressive habit – suggests some such intention. But the thoroughly estimable queen of Offa I represented in our romance (pp. 23-36) could not be more different from the virago pictured by the *Beowulf*-poet. Ostensibly introduced when seeking a contrast to the admirable – discreet, decorous and generous – wife of Beowulf's early patron Hygelac, the poet turns suddenly to tell the story of an overseas princess, Thryth, notoriously cruel and irrational but who, when married to Offa I, became a model wife and mother – a termagant tamed. With a name so very like that of Offa II's actual queen, a covert allusion to some contemporary situation seems very likely (see Appendix C, pp. 141-2).

In our story Offa I's queen is given no name, and unfortunately the name used in *Beowulf* cannot be corroborated from any other source. The half-line in which the name occurs is one of the most difficult passages in the poem, but it seems clear that, as with the valkyrie Þrúþr,[167] the term from which the name of Offa I's queen derived lay in the semantic field of 'severity', if not 'arrogance'.[168] True the element *-ðryð* occurs in a good half of female personal names in the Mercian royal house, but the name of Offa II's historical queen (used for official purposes such as for legal documents or on coinage) was certainly Thryth (see pp. lxxxiv-lxxxv), and the poet's allusion must have raised eyebrows at court. If a commendatory reference to his ancestor and namesake Offa I could do no other than provide an occasion for pleasure on the part of Offa II, by the same token the poet's provision of the name Thryth must implicitly disparage the present queen – whether the result of coincidental fact, creative transference or mere confusion.[169] In any case, some personal appreciation seems inevitable. Offa II's courtiers would know very well whether the story told was familiar, merely varied or really noteworthy, and especially whether or not a fundamental detail such as personal name or reputation was untraditional. Our text, in which the queen of Offa II does indeed prove wicked (pp. lxxxiv-lxxxvii), provides a later framework for the possibility that the reference in *Beowulf* may have had extra-fictional interest.

The material on which the *Life of Offa I* is based must derive ultimately from one or more poems of the kind Widsith and the *Beowulf*-narrator knew – the mnemonic oral record to which Tacitus referred (p. xlvi) – and it was presumably in this shape that English migrating to Britain carried the legend with them. The forms of the names used

---

[166] *A Beowulf Handbook*, ed. R.E. Bjork and J.D. Niles, Exeter, 1997, pp. 13-24 *et passim*.

[167] Cf. H. Damico, 'The valkyrie reflex in Old English literature', in *New Readings on Women in Old English Literature*, ed. H. Damico and A.H. Olsen, Bloomington, Indiana, 1990, pp. 176-90 (pp. 179-81).

[168] K. Malone, 'Hygd', *Modern Language Notes*, 56 (1941), 356-58 (p. 357).

[169] The idea originates with John Earle, 'Beowulf, II,' *The Times*, 29th October, 1885, p. 3, pointing out that such a stance would require a man of sufficient authority – perhaps Offa's new archbishop Hygeberht (see p. xcv).

for Offa I's father and for his enemy's son (Warmund and Sueno pp. 2, 10 *et passim*) are English (or possibly Frisian); although that in itself is no reason why elements in our version should not have been introduced, re-introduced or exchanged as a result of later social traffic with Danelaw – or even in part created anew. Conversely, some have supposed that late Danish versions of the story may have been influenced from England.[170] However, when told as late as the twelfth century by the Danish authors Sweyn Aageson[171] and Saxo Grammaticus,[172] the tale of Offa I remains thoroughly ensconced in Denmark, where Offa I's father Wermund figured as king.

The *Vitae Offarum Duorum* assumes that Offa I's dynasty is already arrived in the English Midlands (although the term 'Mercia' is not employed until the second half of our text, with Offa II, pp. 41-2 *et sequ*.). Offa I's father Wermund is presented as the founder of the city of Warwick – a place-name not certainly recorded before the early tenth century[173] – and as ruler of a long-Christianised nation, where there exist monasteries already deteriorated which a king, historically pagan, could be supposed to restore or found anew (pp. 35-6).

In recounting the story of early Britain, the English poet Laȝamon [*c.* 1200] draws on a probably vernacular tradition telling us that, just as it was the British leader Vortigern who introduced the Saxons to southern Britain, so it was Gurmund (Wermund) – Offa's father – who brought about the English immigration into Britain. An Arab warrior-adventurer, he has given his inherited kingdom away, wishing to possess none he has not conquered for himself. Now, from a base in Ireland, with militia thought to be recruited from throughout the Near East, he is employed by the Saxons as a mercenary leader to help them conquer Britain. This he successfully does, but subsequently hands it over to the English – not yet emigrated. He himself is then said to depart[174] (Appendix, D, pp. 145-60). There is no mention of a son. Laȝamon makes a point of differentiating between Saxons and English, the former now virtually disappearing in his chronicle while the latter are presented in an increasingly positive light.[175] The Frenchman Wace, although also familiar with the story of Wermund's exploits and Arab origin,[176] was happy to think English and Saxons one and the same.[177]

---

[170] Cf. I.M. Boberg, 'Die Sage von Vermund und Uffe', *Acta Philologica Scandinavica*, 16 (1942), 129-57.

[171] Sweyn Aageson's Chronicle, *Scriptores Minores Historiae Danicae*, ed. M.C. Gertz, Copenhagen, 1917-20, I, pp. 94-174 (pp. 98-105), transl. E. Christiansen, *The Works of Sven Aggesen*, London, 1992, pp. 50-54. Appendix G, pp. 165-72.

[172] Appendix H, pp. 173-83.

[173] When fortified by the governor of Mercia as one of a line of anti-Danish strongholds: *Anglo-Saxon Chronicles*, C, *s.a.* 914, D, *s.a.* 915, Swanton, pp. 98-99; J.E.B. Gover *et al.*, *The Place-Names of Warwickshire*, Cambridge, 1936, pp. 259-60. Also see F.T. Wainwright, 'Æthelflæd Lady of the Mercians', in *The Anglo-Saxons*, ed. P. Clemoes, London, 1959, pp. 53-69.

[174] *Brut or Hystoria Brutonum*, ed. W.R.J. Barron and S.C. Weinberg, London, 1995, pp. 742-55.

[175] Cf. F. Le Saux, *Layamon's Brut: the Poem and its Sources*, Woodbridge, 1989, pp. 174-75. I.J. Kirby, 'Angles and Saxons in Laȝamon's Brut', *Studia Neophilologica*, 36 (1964), 51-62.

[176] *Roman de Brut*, ed. J. Weiss, Exeter, 1999, pp. 30-31, 336-43.

[177] 1196-7, 13637-48, Weiss, pp. 30-31, 342-43.

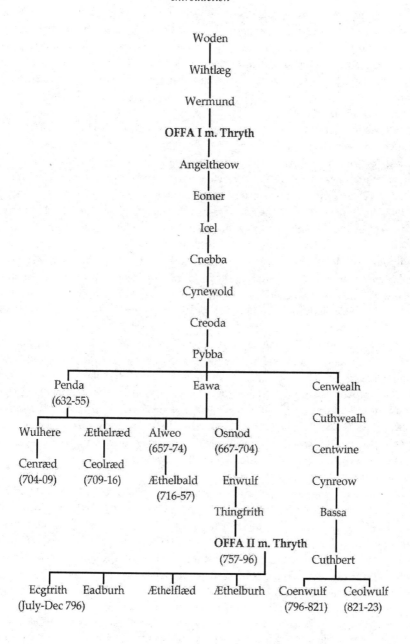

Fig. 6) Family Relationship between the two Offas. Reigns in brackets when known.

The Danish tradition represents the father of the historical Offa I as an elderly man, at the end of his long and prosperous reign, subject to invasion from north Germany – i.e. by Saxons says Saxo Grammaticus and by Teutons say Sweyn Aageson and the thirteenth-century *Annals of Ryd* (Appendices F, G, H, pp. 163-76). In the English Midlands locale of our text it is an internal aggressor and would-be usurper who threatens the throne (pp. 1-4). In neither instance do we expect the boy to have any hope of inheritance.

In the subsequent case of the Mercian Offa II the throne belonged not to his father but an elderly relative, the long-reigning Æthelbald. When in 757 he was 'treacherously murdered' one night by his own bodyguards (*a suis tutoribus*) this usurpation is more likely to have been the result of internal ambition than external invasion insofar as we know.[178] The usurper Beornred, who was probably one of the assassins' party,[179] was now an imminent threat to the hero's family. Little enough is recorded about this man, although he was apparently well-enough known for an English historian like Matthew Paris to use his behaviour as a convenient parallel for Harold Godwinson's despotism. [180] Reading between the lines of the Continuator of Bede, Offa II's subsequent take-over – conquering the Mercian kingdom 'with sword and bloodshed' – was not easy.[181] The benefit of strong, even ruthless, kingship in an unstable world where commonplace violence and treason were evident, was reflected, and perhaps exaggerated, in fiction (cf. pp. 71-2).

As told by the *Vitae Offarum Duorum* as well as the early Danish chroniclers, Offa I had been the only son of an elderly king, but considered quite incapable of succeeding to the throne (pp. 1-2). The name by which he was called had the fundamental sense of Latin 'lump' or 'abortion'. Details vary between versions, but for our text he is sightless until the age of seven and mute until thirty. None of the Danish sources speak of the boy's blindness, but rather that of his elderly father. For the *Annals of Ryd* Offa I is said merely to have refused to speak between the ages of seven and thirty (Appendix F, pp. 163-4). Sweyn Aageson specifies that this was from a time of national disgrace until the age of thirty (Appendix G, pp. 165-6).

A folk-hero's pre-pubescent years are commonly said to be clouded by some defect – inactive and ostracised, living typically in kitchen or cowshed, from which lowly condition he will emerge only when the right time comes. Childhood problems experienced will be exaggerated or even invented in order to make later achievements seem the more remarkable. Our text presents no reason for Offa I's sad childhood condition. But Scandinavian sources make the issue a question of wilful taciturnity rather than mere physical disability (Appendices F, G, H, pp. 163-76). Elective (or

---

[178]Although Roger of Wendover was in no doubt; he says that Æthelbald died in 755 fighting against invading West Saxons in the heart of Mercia at Seckington (Warwickshire), *Chronica*, ed. Coxe, I, p. 233, Giles, I, p. 148.

[179] As much seems to be implied by the Continuator of Bede, *Ecclesiastical History, s.a.* 757, Colgrave and Mynors, pp. 574-75.

[180] Matthew Paris, *Historia Anglorum*, Madden, I, p. 8.

[181] *Loc. cit.* in n. 179.

selective) speech-suppression and or blindness not infrequently occurs as a type of traumatic stress-disorder known among soldiery, especially territorial units whose members perform military and civilian roles closely together, and also among children, especially male infants,[182] who experience the wilful violence of warfare at first hand.[183] Whether victim or witness of extreme events – which cannot have been unusual in the always uncertain and frequently dramatic circumstances of 'heroic society' – the child can experience intense personality problems: rendered speechless or exhibiting other dissociative states. Loss of all five senses is possible, but most commonly speech-disorders with occasional loss of vision. Cases consequent upon disease like rubella in a pregnant woman may go unrecognised in the infant for months or even years after birth.[184]

Not necessarily the result of personal trauma associated with birth or early life, however, a condition such as Childhood Disintegrative Disorder exhibits similar autistic symptoms,[185] characteristically delay in, or total lack of, the development of speech. This, together with a marked impairment of non-verbal communicative comportment such as: eye-to-eye gaze, facial expression, body postures and gestures regulating social interaction, all results in a general failure to develop peer relationships. Subsequent adolescence is characterised by reduced self-esteem, withdrawal and apathy, often denounced as malingering and – militarily significant – defective control of temper, especially towards strangers. [186] Often these symptoms wane as the child grows and the nervous system matures. But the individual may remain wholly literal – unable, for example, to appreciate metaphors – and of limited empathy, capable of arbitrary marriage or able cold-bloodedly to kill without emotion. The condition is occasionally associated with exceptional arithmetical ability, appropriate to the deployment of militia, particular battle strategies, engineering construction, monetary reform and the like.

For Sweyn, the young Offa is not represented as physically unpromising, but associated with products of kitchen and cellar – a narrative characteristic of the male Cinderella. He has declined to speak from the age of seven onwards due to shame at the conduct of fellow countrymen encountering and killing an enemy leader two-against-one – a national disgrace comparable with the present-day supposed 'rule of

---

[182] Female infants subject to similar experiences are said to exhibit greater core stability than the male, generally continuing to look around and speak.

[183] For the ancient association of Mars not only with warfare but also speech – and other body defects – and their care see Ptolemy, *Tetrabiblos*, III, 12, ed. F.E. Robbins, Cambridge, Mass., 1940, pp. 322-7.

[184] Cf. A. Ghidini and L. Lynch, 'Prenatal diagnosis and significance of fetal infections', *Western Journal of Medicine*, 159 (1993), 366-73 (p. 370).

[185] A useful summary account is available in G.C. Davison *et al.*, *Abnormal Psychology*, 9th edn, New York, 2004, pp. 506-11. Further: L. Kannner, 'Autistic disturbances of affective contact', *Nervous Child*, 2 (1943), 217-50.

[186] The literature is extensive and difficult; a good beginning may be made with: *Anxiety Disorders in Children and Adolescents*, ed. J.S. March, New York, 1995, especially: H. Leonard and S. Dow, 'Selective Mutism', pp. 235-50; L. Amaya-Jackson and J.S. March, 'Posttraumatic Stress Disorder', pp. 276-300, and the references there cited.

war' forbidding the use of chemical weapons (Appendix G, pp. 165-6, 171-2).[187] Different from what we might assume to have been the hurly-burly of a battlefield in practise, perhaps it contravened some heroic notion of 'fair play': the expectation of a champion, on challenging the opponent to single combat, to be met by a single man alone. We learn from Saxo that the two responsible were in fact Offa I's brothers-in-law (Appendices H, pp. 173-4, cf. F, pp. 163-4). The boy's early condition, dumb and considered a simpleton, is not imputed to this dishonour; nevertheless, he is aware of the standing reproach to his nation which will only be made good by his own subsequent exploit in killing two enemy champions at once, himself single-handed (pp. lix-lxiii, 9-10).

In practice, instinctive shame does not come upon an infant until exhibited to him from elsewhere. Children noticing the attitudes of friends and relatives, and thus modifying their self-concept, are characteristically subject to such personality disorders from about the age of ten.[188] Although devastating, such hysterical stress is not irreversible and sometimes cured by later circumstances – recovery of sight less likely than of speech – although with no explicit evidence for reversal being due to social shock of the kind referred to in our romance.

Whether factual or legendary in Offa I's case, the theme of a Germanic hero's tardy development is familiar. The honourable and courageous Beowulf had long been despised by his people, firmly believed to be dull and feeble;[189] the heroes Starkaðr and Hálfdan are ridiculed for taciturnity in their youth; King Hjörvarðr's son Helgi is tall and handsome but habitually mute (*þögull*), and it is only with the shock of a valkyrie greeting him by name does he begin to speak.[190] Analogues occur in a wide sweep from ancient times to the present day, from Classical to Celtic worlds: the Greek Croesus's son provoked into speech only when about to see his father slain by an invading Persian; the Irish prince Labraidh Móen, struck dumb at being made to eat his father's heart by a usurper although later recovering when accidentally struck during a game and eventually returning to take the kingdom for himself.[191]

In the *Vitae Offarum Duorum* it is the urgent circumstance of a usurper's threat that prompts dramatic recovery in the case of both Offa I and Offa II (pp. 3-6, 41-2). It is in the midst of the assembly that Offa I suddenly begins to speak out for the first time in his life. Now the focus of attention, the young man is accepted as leader of the English army. Although without any reference to his people's previous discredit, the fact that

---

[187] Hereward, the eleventh-century English guerrilla opponent of the Conqueror, is also said to regard it shameful to fight two against one: Gaimar, Hardy and Martin, pp. 398-99; Swanton, *Medieval Outlaws*, p. 56.

[188] P. Costanzo *et al.*, 'Social Development', in *Anxiety Disorders in Children*, ed. March, pp. 82-108 (p. 99).

[189] *Beowulf*, 2183-8, Swanton, pp. 138-39.

[190] *Edda: die Lieder des Codex Regius*, ed. G. Neckel, rev. H. Kuhn, Heidelberg, 1962, I, p. 142; transl. H.A. Bellows, *The Poetic Edda*, New York, 1923, I, p. 276.

[191] Herodotus, I, 85, ed. A.D. Godley, London, 1920-25, I, pp. 106-09; cf. G.H. Gerould, 'Offa and Labhraidh Maen', *Modern Language Notes*, 17 (1902), 201-3. See generally L. Bragg, 'Telling silence: alingualism in Old Icelandic myth, legend, and saga', *Journal of Indo-European Studies*, 32 (2004), 267-98.

he personally confronts and butchers two of the enemy champions in single combat – taking on two at once – is perhaps to be associated with the redress of national disgrace spoken of in the Scandinavian tradition. Thereafter Offa I rules both his own people and the Saxons, succeeding to the throne during his father's lifetime (pp. 15-16); a kind of dynastic asseveration unparalleled until the time when Offa II has his only son Ecgfrith anointed king ten years prior to his own death (pp. 101-2).

Our text seems explicit as to Offa I being thirty years old at the time of his success, and thirty-four shortly after his father's death (pp. 1-2, 21-2). Saxo mentions no age, but both Sweyn Aageson and the *Annals of Ryd* agree with *The Two Offas* as to the age of thirty (Appendices G, pp. 165-6, F, pp. 163-4). This is scarcely the heroic youngster a modern audience might have expected from Widsith's term *cnihtwesende* (Appendix B, pp. 139-40), or apparently represented in the Nero MS drawings (Figs. 14-17) – our understanding of 'juvenile' having become increasingly young over the centuries. Thirty years being the characteristic generative period (p. xxxviii), this might represent a natural age for the acknowledgement of ability in a dynastic line of succession. For the Roman Emperor Tiberius certainly, no man should need counseling beyond this age.[192]

If we should we seek a more dramatically youthful hero – a mere teenager – then there may have been a misunderstanding of the Anglo-Saxon poetic convention *þritig missera* (thirty half-years), i.e. fifteen years old.[193] This was noted as the age of majority for Anglo-Saxon youths in the seventh century according to Archbishop Theodore,[194] appropriate for marriage and military service. So far, the youngest male yet to be found buried with a sword appears to have been of that age.[195] Boyhood (*pueritia*) might be reckoned to cease with the attainment of youth (*adolescentia*) at fifteen, and then young manhood (*iuventus*) at thirty.[196] Offa I is spoken of as *iuvenis* more frequently than *adolescens*. All versions make much of the lad's big build and, according to Saxo, even his father's body-armour was insufficiently large or strong enough for him (Appendix H, pp. 179-80).

In the *Vitae*, the father on whose behalf the future Offa I is to act formally presents his new champion with an indicative sword (pp. 5-6), desirable examples of which we know derived from the East (pp. xxxi, 77-8). For both Sweyn Aageson and Saxo the

---

[192] Tacitus, *Annals*, VI, 46, ed. J. Jackson, Cambridge, Mass., 1951, pp. 236-7.

[193] J. Bosworth and T.N. Toller, *An Anglo-Saxon Dictionary*, Oxford, 1898, p. 692. Also in general early Germanic usage, cf. R. Cleasby and G. Vigfusson, *An Icelandic-English Dictionary*, 2nd edn, Oxford, 1957, p. 431; J. de Vries, *Altnordisches Etymologisches Wörterbuch*, Leiden, 1962, p. 389; J. Grimm, *Deutsche Mythologie*, Göttingen, 1844, pp. 716-7.

[194] A.W. Haddan and W. Stubbs, *Councils and Ecclesiastical Documents*, Oxford, 1869-78, III, pp. 173-213 (p. 201), transl. J.T. McNeill and H.M. Gamer, *Medieval Handbooks of Penance*, New York, 1938, pp. 182-215.

[195] A sword of less than usual substance in this instance, but in an unusually well-constructed sepulchre, and together with a whetstone clutched in his left hand a medallion bearing an image of the man-eating monster associated with power over death: D.R.J. Perkins and S.C. Hawkes, 'The Thanet gas pipeline phases I and II, 1982', *Archaeologia Cantiana*, 101 (1984), 83-114 (pp. 91-2, 95, 102-07).

[196] Cf. A. Hofmeister, 'Puer, iuvenis, senex', in *Papsttum und Kaisertum*, ed. A. Brackmann, Munich, 1926, pp. 287-316.

weapon is a uniquely historical one disinterred from an ancestor's grave (Appendices G and H, pp. 169-70, 179-80). This gains narrative direction if, as seems likely, burial together with weapons might reflect not necessarily one's own heroic ability but rather the warrior-status of one's family – ethnically, socially and perhaps ideologically defined.[197] Given the majority of fighting men equipped merely with spear and shield, the sword is a powerful symbol of executive heroism. It accompanied aristocrats like those buried at seventh-century Sutton Hoo and Prittlewell, or in Frankish royal tombs at Cologne or St Denis,[198] and there are echoes of this tradition in later times. In the narrative template the significant sword is commonly said to have been taken from a noble ancestor's grave, although the place of the hero's own burial may not be known.

In practice not all weapons are found buried with their first owners. A scabbard might bear fittings that spanned a hundred years, while the worn condition of a scabbard-mouth will suggest considerable usage.[199] Some were probably brought from abroad. Certain swords having the symbolic ring removed from the hilt may indicate a change of owner – if not change in status of owner.[200] Much is made of the sword, in both fiction and reality – with good reason. It is not merely the weapon itself which is of considerable value – spoken of in the same breath as estates endowed[201]– but also the jewellery decorating its trappings: sheath and belt. Handed down within families,[202] this weapon is often given an individual name – a custom clearly considered no more grotesque than present-day naming of a nuclear submarine. In the eleventh-century Old French epic told about the slaughter of the Frankish rear-guard by Saracens at Roncevaux in 778, several prominent warriors wield named swords, and on either side the name of the leader's weapon is taken up as a battle-cry.[203] In early English literature Waldere's sword that had been made by the legendary smith Weland and had previously belonged to Goth notables, is named Mimming.[204] Beowulf carries into different exploits two such weapons – Hrunting and Nægling – although in the event, both fail the hero, fine though they are.[205] No name is given to Offa I's sword in our text,

---

[197] For sociological considerations see H. Härke, '"Warrior graves"? The background of the Anglo-Saxon weapon burial rite', *Past and Present*, 126 (1990), 22-43.

[198] Bruce-Mitford, *The Sutton Hoo Ship-Burial*, II, pp. 273-309; Museum of London, *The Prittlewell Prince*, London, 2004. J. Werner, 'Frankish royal tombs in the cathedrals of Cologne and Saint-Denis', *Antiquity*, 38 (1964), 201-16.

[199] V.I. Evison, *The Fifth-Century Invasions South of the Thames*, London, 1965, pp. 32-32, 51; S.C. Hawkes and R.I. Page, 'Swords and runes in south-east England', *Antiquaries Journal*, 47 (1967), 1-26.

[200] V.I. Evison, 'The Dover ring-sword and other ring-swords and beads', *Archaeologia*, 101 (1967), 63-118.

[201] It is with the presentation of a sword that the young Beowulf was described receiving his ancestral estates: *Beowulf*, 2190-96, Swanton, pp. 138-39.

[202] A 'sword which belonged to King Offa' was in turn bequeathed by Prince Æthelstan to his brother Edmund in the eleventh century, mentioning several swords to be variously inherited: *Anglo-Saxon Wills*, ed. D. Whitelock, Cambridge, 1930, pp. 56-61.

[203] *The Song of Roland*, 2508-10, 3145-8, ed. G.J. Brault, London, 1978, II, pp. 152-53, 190-03.

[204] *Waldere*, 2-4, ed. F. Norman, London, 1933, pp. 32, 35, Bradley, p. 511.

[205] *Beowulf*, 1455-91, 1519-33, 1659-60, 1807-12, 2499-509, 2680-87, Swanton, pp. 102-07, 112-13, 120-21, 152-55, 162-63.

but for Saxo it is Skrep (Old Norse, 'Swish') – which his father extravagantly had buried, thinking there was no-one worthy of inheriting it (Appendix H, pp. 179-80). Sweyn Aageson gives it no name but describes it having to be dug out from a grave-mound, presumably that of a predecessor (Appendix G, pp. 169-70).[206] The fact that valuable items like swords buried in early Anglo-Saxon graves would be carefully wrapped in cloth, may indicate an awareness of a possible need for retrieval. This might gain particular significance if we can believe that a Germanic warrior's weapons were ideally that part of his property which should not be inherited but accompany him to the grave. The arrival of Christian culture with the seventh century might also have brought immunity from any curse associated with robbing the pagan dead.

Saxo emphasises not only Offa I's personal strength but his weapon's cutting power. When Wermund the sword-giver asks which part of the enemy's body had been struck, he is told that his son had cleft the man's entire body (Appendix H, pp. 181-2). There is nothing quite so wholesale in our text (pp. 9-10), but this is not dissimilar to the seventh-century historical account of Theodoric slaying the Ostrogoth Odovacar in 493 with a blow that cut from collarbone to hip.[207] Skeletons from some early Scandinavian war-graves give evidence of wounds perhaps inflicted as a result of *berserkr* frenzy.[208]

Champion Personalities

For many people, the hero is prototypical, a paradigmatic figure defining social values. Typically the offspring of exotic parentage,[209] s/he represents a simulacrum of those impulses we cannot implement in ourselves; the cult of celebrity releases an enthusiasm for mortal excellence otherwise unrealised. The iconic presentation of a present-day sports star or TV dance personality is not dissimilar.

In this story Offa II, like his ancestor, was also a late developer – said to be physically sub-standard – crippled by defective sight, speech and hearing (pp. 39-42). The condition (p. liii) might not perhaps have been entirely unexpected, if, as a genetic predisposition, the lad was recognisably a throwback.

We are told that his parents called him Wynfrið, 'Cheerful' (pp. 39-42), a name no doubt given to many a child,[210] but especially pointed in view of the boy's condition,

---

[206] Blades protected in scabbards might well remain in good condition. Practical work at the Musée de Nancy together with the late Albert France-Lanord in 1963 indicated that, when restored, a pattern-welded sword of this date remains usable at the present time!

[207] John of Antioch, *Fragmenta Historicorum Græcorum*, ed. C. Müller, Paris, 1841-74, V, p. 29.

[208] B.E. Ingelmark, 'The skeletons', in B. Thordeman *et al.*, *Armour from the Battle of Wisby, 1361*, Stockholm, 1939-40, I, pp. 149-209, *passim*; A. France-Lanord, 'La fabrication des épées damassées aux époques mérovingienne et carolingienne', *Le Pays Gaumais*, 10 (1949), 19-45.

[209] F.R. Somerset (Lord Raglan), *The Hero*, London, 1936, *passim*.

[210] This had been the birth-name of Boniface before missionary work on the Continent led to its Latinization: *Vitae Sancti Bonifatii*, ed. W. Levison, *Monumenta Germaniae Historica, Scriptores rerum Germanicarum*, 57, Hanover, 1905, pp. 19, 29 *et passim*.

representing affectionate pleasantry of a kind not absent today.[211] His name was formally altered to Offa only when the similarity with his prominent ancestor finally came to be publicly recognised (pp. 41-2). The parents are optimistic in view of the famous change in life of their predecessor, and vow that, if restored to health, their son will fulfil the notoriously long-delayed pledge to build a monastery (pp. 41-2). Association between the two Offas was all the more emphatic inasmuch as it was not yet customary for dynasties to repeat their personal names as it would later become in medieval Europe.

Such an actual phase of adolescent apathy or lethargy may have been ironically recalled in later years. In a document said to have been signed by Offa II in the year of his accession he refers to himself as 'a child by nature' (*indolis puer*), which might represent candour rather than the modesty our story emphasises (pp. 71-2, 121-2). As so often, the sole copy of this document to survive was made some three centuries later, and may simply represent local tradition.[212] When we hear of Charlemagne addressing Offa (his elder by some twenty years) as 'young man' (*iuuentus*) it is probably in terms of implicit belittlement rather than a flattering allusion to any self-image the king may have promoted (pp. 57-8). Implicit of much the same superiority-inferiority in their relationship was probably the sword we hear of Charlemagne later sending the English king – significantly the weapon presented to one from whom the donor would tacitly, if not explicitly, anticipate some form of service (pp. 5-6, 77-8).[213]

Genetically predisposed, it is a fact that physical and psychological disorders of the kind both Offas suffered tend to run in families,[214] although ten or twelve generations would be a lengthy term for no other incidence to be remarked. However, as told, the two children both remain unseeing, unhearing and silent until a dramatic turning-point, when they are stimulated into heroic action by rousing events and resulting expectations of themselves. Each youth appears strong, handsome and eloquent, with mental deficiency apparently no longer an issue.[215] Such an exceptional restitution and its consequences may well be thought of as a somewhat extravagant rite of passage involved in becoming a fully-qualified adult member of society.[216] Commonly

---

[211] Cf. the colloquial address 'Sunshine', *Supplement to the Oxford English Dictionary*, Oxford, 1972-86, IV, Se-Z, p. 631.

[212] *Cartularium Saxonicum*, no. 183, I, p. 261.

[213] Cf. *Beowulf*, 2884-90, Swanton, pp. 172-3. Not investigated by H.E. Davidson in the excellent general account of *The Sword in Anglo-Saxon England*, Oxford, 1962.

[214] M.A. Riddle *et al.*, 'Obsessive compulsive disorder in children and adolescents: phenomenology and family history', *Journal of the American Academy of Child and Adolescent Psychiatry*, 29 (1990), 766-72; C.G. Last *et al.*, 'Anxiety disorders in children and their families', *Archives of General Psychiatry*, 48 (10) (1991), 928-34.

[215] Although such a disguise is not unknown, cf. H.R.E. Davidson, 'The hero as a fool: the northern Hamlet', in *The Hero in Tradition and Folklore*, ed. Davidson, London, 1984, pp. 30-45.

[216] Cf. J. de Vries, *Heroic Song and Heroic Legend*, London, 1963, pp. 220-01. Of course the notion of dramatic access to loquacity can occur at any level. It is reported, presumably by the man himself, that the distinguished seventh-century poet Cædmon only felt able to hold forth subsequent to his traumatic experience in the cowshed (Bede, *Ecclesiastical History*, IV, 24, Colgrave and Mynors, pp. 414-19).

symbolised by sprinkling water, ring-giving or similar dramaturgic act, in most narratives it marks a change of status in the protagonist, formative at a fundamental level. Although all too easily dismissed as merely part of the romance imagination along with dragons, virgin births and the like, the phenomenon described is not actually impossible. Many a latter-day celebrity has experienced a childhood unhappy or disadvantaged in some way, and not improbably that is what underlies this motif.

Success for the male Cinderella[217] is achievable in pre-feudal society when high status was still accessible to those of modest origins, albeit invariably through brutal avenues. Less feasible in feudal times, the 'zero-to-hero' narrative is assigned to the field of fairy-tale or folklore until once more realisable with democracy. In this formula, for whatever reason the poor schmuck gets no respect: a failure at school, passed over for promotion or ignored by women, until something dramatic – the 'beneficent catastrophe' – occurs (e.g. epidemic, economic crash or total war) that, instead of destroying what is left of his status and self-esteem, paradoxically results in public recognition of him as the embodiment of unshakeable self-assurance.[218]

Whereas most such individuals as these spend their early life being persuaded to control and direct their aggressive drive into socially-approved channels, this previously introverted champion's temperament would be released uncontrolled in the direction of violent action: an exceptional personality whose belligerent attitudes develop into successful heroic leadership.[219] The plot in which our heroes figure as the protagonist strings together a number of folktale motifs and fairy-tale elements readily understood worldwide and open to a variety of critical interpretations.[220]

The potential hero's vocation comes suddenly – he is called to an exceptionally difficult task: to confront a monster in its lair, marauding giant, or alien military threat. For both Offas it is this last. The sensational moment of recovery and lasting recognition comes with their rescuing the nation from usurpation, the dramatic opposition and defeat of a dangerous enemy. Both young men are depicted prominent in the vanguard of battle, specifically seeking out leaders of the enemy force (pp. 7-12, 43-4, 59-60). What must always have been the literary ideal, the personal confrontation of opposing leaders, may not have been unfamiliar in reality: the hero's vizored helmet looking to neither side but sternly frontward.

---

[217] Compare Old High German *äscherling*, *aschenbrödel*, Old Norse *askefis*, *kolbítr*. Cinderella is acknowledged beautiful, but socially and materially disadvantaged; Offa, although both handsome and materially well-endowed, is nevertheless handicapped to the point of being considered stupid – perhaps Frog-Prince rather than Ugly Duckling. It is the theme of a large number of narratives, supremely that of the baby born in a stable going on to become king of heaven.

[218] Cf. e.g. De Vries, pp. 214-29; J. Campbell, *The Hero with a Thousand Faces*, Princeton, NJ., 1949, pp. 325-6. In practice many a significant statesman, author or inventor had been a school-room failure, although the fact is rarely recalled in *Who's Who*.

[219] The vocabulary can be confusing. An attempt to define the 'heroic' insofar as it applies to England at this period was made in 'Heroes, heroism and heroic literature', *Essays and Studies*, NS 30 (1977), 1-21.

[220] Of the kind listed by Raglan, *The Hero*, chapters 16-18; Campbell, pp. 321-56, *passim*.

The robust government required by heroic society meant that in principle it must be shameful for a leader to be surpassed in valour; in any case, it seems to have been conventional for members of a war-band (*comitatus*) to ascribe their individual deeds to its commander.[221] Idealised fiction easily concealed and transformed the sordid proclivity for mutual extermination confessed by the heroic but dismal facts of the late tenth-century verse *Battle of Maldon*. As depicted at Maldon oral defiance being all on one side falls curiously flat. There the critical weapon proves not the leader's expensive sword but the cheap, levelling missile of a man-at-arms; cowards flee and it is admitted that the former boasts of comrades were insincere; the nobleman Byrhtnoth meets his death early, unceremoniously, and merely at the hand of an anonymous *ceorl*.[222] We are accustomed rather to the projection of that which we would like to believe, whether or not we know it to be true, of Agincourt, the Somme or skies over London.

And then, of course, life invariably strives to imitate art. When armies of many thousands might take the field, to be slaughtered at random, there was the possibility, in fiction at least, of early Germanic commanders executing their missions at the risk of merely one or two champion lives. In ancient times Diodorus of Sicily said of the north-Europeans that, when formed up for battle, it is their custom:

> to step out in front of the line and to challenge the most valiant men from among their opponents to single combat, brandishing their weapons in front of them to terrify their adversaries. And when any man accepts the challenge to battle, they then break forth into a song of praise of the valiant deeds of ancestors and in boast of their own high achievements, all the while reviling and belittling their opponent and, in a word, trying by such talk to strip him of his bold spirit before the combat.[223]

It was certainly considered possible to test the likely outcome of an entire battle on the result of a sample contest – belief in a notion of the individual as representative of the whole, *pars pro toto*,[224] no doubt assessing the nature of their opponents' disposition

---

[221] Tacitus, *Germania*, 14.1, Winterbottom and Ogilvie, p. 44, Rives, pp. 82-83. An aspect of the systematic anonymity of the individual to be found in gang or mob conduct, cf. R.H. Turner and L.M. Killian, *Collective Behavior*, Englewood Cliffs, NJ., 1972, pp. 12-16. Thus in *Beowulf* Hygelac can be described as the slayer of King Ongentheow, although elsewhere in the poem this is acknowledged to have been the work of Wulf and Eofor: 1968-70, 2484-89, 2957-98; Swanton, pp. 128-29, 152-53, 174-77.

[222] Ed. D.G. Scragg, Oxford, 1981, p. 61, transl. Bradley, *Anglo-Saxon Poetry*, pp. 518-28; see M. Swanton, *English Poetry before Chaucer*, Exeter, 2002, pp. 182-88.

[223] *Bibliotheca Historica*, ed. C.H. Oldfather *et al.*, London, 1933-67, III, pp. 172-73 (v. 29). A little later Tacitus says of the early Germani that they chanted the praise of heroes as they advanced into battle, *Germania*, 3, Winterbottom and Ogilvie, pp. 38-39, Rives, p. 78; also Ammianus Marcellinus, *Rerum Gestarum Historia*, XVI, 12.43, ed. J.C. Rolfe, London, 1935-40, pp. 286-89; and Vegetius, *Epitoma Rei Militaris*, III, 18, ed. M.D. Reeve, Oxford, 2004, pp. 101-02.

[224] *Germania*, 10, Winterbottom and Ogilvie, pp. 42-43, Rives, p. 81. Procopius records one such in 583 between the Goth Valaris and Roman Artabazes (VII, 4, Dewing, IV, pp. 186-91); Paul the Deacon one between a Langobard and Assipitti, *Historia Langobardorum*, I, 12, ed. Bethmann and Waitz, pp. 46, 53-54,

and armoury rather than seeking a mere omen. Those whose champions lost were by no means obliged to come to terms.

The champion individuals, emerging from better-nourished parts of society, were naturally taller, capable of the powerful over-shoulder slashing stroke – *sweord-geswing* or *sweord-slege* – for which the northern sword at this date was designed rather than for thrusting delivery.[225] A great number of such fatal blows were received by the head.[226] Such fighting techniques as those used between the Swede Ongentheow and Beowulf's fellow countrymen Eofor and Wulf is often described as a lengthy exchange of exhausting alternate blows, a literary response to the natural rhythm of parried blow and counter-blow *en face*. [227] The significance of the custom and its outcome would presumably be appreciated in formal literary terms. It offers dramatic possibilities, allowing us to concentrate on the actions of the major figures; any subordinates are remitted to the periphery, or omitted altogether in favour of a bold narrative tempo.

Fighting at close quarters allowed for verbal exchange – invariably vilification (pp. 9-10) – to form a significant part of any combat on foot.[228] The social significance and physical strength of one's enemy might be readily acknowledged since death was best undergone defying a worthy enemy. For merely domestic encounters, a verbal combatant like the orator Unferth ('Discord' or 'Antagonism') whom Beowulf met at the Danish court might be retained to provide a test of mettle for visiting notables. [229] But this need not necessarily lead to physical violence any more than Parliamentary front-bench badinage does.

Even military champions set to oppose each other, especially if mercenaries, might have no more reason for personal animosity than present-day professional boxers.[230] The eventual ceremonialisation of single combat was inevitable. The individual glorification of contestants is what lies behind the development of tournament and judicial duel, played according to elaborate rules.

transl. W.D. Foulke, *History of the Langobards*, Philadelphia, 1907, pp. 20-21; Gregory of Tours, another between a Vandal and Swæf *c*. 410, *Historiae Francorum*, II, 2, *Monumenta Germaniae Historica, Scriptores rerum Merovingicarum*, I (i), ed. W. Arndt and B. Krusch, Hanover, 1885, p. 39, transl. L. Thorpe, *The History of the Franks*, Harmondsworth, 1974, pp. 106-7.

[225] P. Hill and L. Thompson, 'The swords of the Saxon cemetery at Mitcham', *Surrey Archaeological Collections*, 90 (2003), 147-61 (p. 158).

[226] Cf. S.J. Wenham, 'Anatomical interpretation of Anglo-Saxon weapon injuries', in *Weapons and Warfare*, Hawkes, pp. 123-39.

[227] *Beowulf*, 2961-81, Swanton, pp. 176-77. Saxo Grammaticus tells of a large number of duels; but the *locus classicus* is the description given in *Kormáks Saga*, X, ed. E.Ó. Sveinsson, *Íslenzk Fornrit*, VIII, Reykjavík, 1939, pp. 236-39; transl. W.G. Collingwood, *The Life and Death of Cormac the Skald*, Ulverston, 1902, pp. 65-68.

[228] Later medieval literature provides plentiful examples of such 'flyting'; see generally: W. Parks, *Verbal Dueling in Heroic Narrative*, Princeton, NJ, 1990; M. Bax, 'Rules for ritual challenges: a speech convention among medieval knights', *Journal of Pragmatics*, 5 (1981), 423-44.

[229] *Beowulf*, 499-528, Swanton, pp. 58-59.

[230] An apparently sporting relationship exists between two such champions described in *Þorsteins Þáttr Stangarhǫggs*, ed. J. Jóhannesson, *Austfirðinga Sǫgur*, Reykjavík, 1950, pp. 67-79, transl. E. Magnússon and W. Morris, *The Tale of Thorstein Staff-smitten*, Cambridge, Ont., 2000, pp. 6-7.

Offa I's significant confrontation is set at the very point – the line of a river – that will be memorialised as the major achievement of his career: the establishment of a lasting national frontier. Where this part of the story retains an historical provenance, as with the Danish chroniclers, the river is specified as the Eider and the enemy to its southern side the Saxon (pp. xlvii-xlviii, 8). When transferred to an English midlands environment however there can be no reference to the particularised location of the Scandinavian tradition, although the major narrative features are present: a significant combat between notables witnessed from a distance by their respective armies – an honour-killing in this case, the outcome revoking what had been considered a stain on his people's character (p. liv). In the *Vitae* the river in question is referred to merely as the 'Avon' (p. 12), a native Celtic word that might apply to any river of consequence during the Germanic settlement of Britain (*abonā*, 'river').[231] The word survived to identify several major rivers, and there will have been others to which the name is no longer applied. Some still have notable shifting mudflats like those where the Wiltshire-Somerset-Gloucestershire river debouches into the Severn, thought to be passable by those of heroic temperament – or hard pressed.[232] Such shallows could be strategically obstructed, given sufficient numbers of sharp stakes. [233]

In our tale after the two sides have fought themselves to a standstill, Offa I, who has already fought bravely and is wounded, impulsively rushes towards the two hostile sons of the would-be usurper and, in full view of the two separated armies, alone slays both of them (pp. 9-10). The remainder of the enemy, now in despair, are either butchered or flee in large numbers, many of them being drowned in the river. In the dramatization offered in twelfth-century Scandinavian versions the riverine confrontation is constricted to an islet in the River Eider, still known in the thirteenth-century as 'Kings-combat' (Appendix F, pp. 163-4), while a large audience watches from the banks on either side. [234] It exemplifies a familiar Old Norse 'islet-going' (*hólmganga*), a fight between individuals conducted according to custom and rule that survived at least to the eleventh century and beyond. In this an islet rendezvous is secure, allowing neither protagonist to escape; and it protects the duel's symmetry, isolated from interfering partisans or any more formal sequence of alternate

[231] E. Ekwall, *English River-Names*, Oxford, 1928, pp. 20-23.

[232] Considerable areas of salt-marsh here were not drained until the seventeenth century. Notoriously dangerous tidal estuaries of this kind are exemplified by the four-mile (6 km) wide mouth of the River Nene (The Wash) where the royal baggage-train succumbed in 1216. W. St J. Hope, 'The loss of King John's baggage train', *Archaeologia*, 60 (1907), 93-110.

[233] A.N. Jørgensen, 'Sea defence in Denmark AD 200-1300', in *Military Aspects of Scandinavian Society in a European Perspective, AD 1-1300*, ed. A.N. Jørgensen and B.L. Clausen, Copenhagen, 1997, pp. 200-09 (Fig. 1).

[234] Saxo provides no specific nomenclature; Sweyn affirms the name of the river but does not specify the islet (Appendix G, pp. 169-70). The *Annals of Ryd* says simply that Offa single-handed fought against both the Teutonic king and their leading champion together and slew them both (Appendix F, pp. 163-4).

retribution.[235] Ultimately the term for riverine or lacustrine 'islet' would come to denote any demarcated cockpit.

Germanic warriors from areas like the lower Rhine were renowned for their ability to swim powerful rivers whilst wearing full armour.[236] The epitaph of the second-century Batavian trooper Soranus refers to his crossing the Danube in full armour whilst firing arrows – a historic feat not dissimilar to those in which an armour-clad Beowulf is described swimming in the ocean bearing weapons, or later after defeat in Frisia, visualised taking to the water carrying with him large quantities of salvaged armour.[237] In our text it is the defeated leader's weight of arms that causes him to drown when retreating (pp. 11-12).

Historically the Danish Offa I's dash through the Eider estuary is credible in practice given low tide on this broadest of sea-bays. Less so perhaps in terms of Widsith's 'monstrous entrance' (Appendix B, pp. 139-40, cf. pp. xlvii-xlviii). However, in narrative assessment, our hero's achievement is that he undertakes boldly to tackle what lesser men would not – in this case that mythical river a mile wide but found by him to be only a few inches deep. The image of the mounted champion leading his men into battle, is in practise improbable. The majority of horses reared in Germania might be considered too small to be used as cavalry mounts – short and stocky, typically only four and a half feet (1.35 m) at the shoulder[238] – especially impracticable in view of the lengthy, over-arm Germanic sword-blade.

Although represented in our text as spontaneous, Offa I's exploit seems to reflect an arranged encounter, indifferently expressed rather than misunderstood. To later medieval people this incident must have evoked the procedure of trial-by-combat most common in treason trials, in which challenger and defendant fought not by means of champions but in their own person – appealing to the judgement of God. And victory being conferred by God, the defeated can be deemed unquestionably vicious. But to what extent this would have been recognised by an early English audience is uncertain. Whilst references to the practise of judicial combat are present in the earliest law codes of most Continental Germanic peoples,[239] it is found in no surviving Anglo-Saxon code.[240] There are, probably unreliable, reports of such a combat between historical

---

[235] K. Maurer, *Altisländisches Strafrecht und Gerichtwesen*, Leipzig, 1910, pp. 694-711. Further see F. Wagner, 'L'organisation du combat singulier au moyen âge dans les états Scandinaves', *Revue de Synthèse Historique*, 56 (1936), 41-60.

[236] Cassius Dio, *Roman History*, ed. H.B. Foster, transl. E. Cary, London, 1914-27, VIII, pp. 442-43.

[237] T. Mommsen, *Inscriptiones Britanniae Latinarum*, III i, Berlin, 1873, p. 462; *Beowulf*, 506-81, 2359-62, Swanton, pp. 58-61, 146-47.

[238] S. Bökönyi, 'Data on Iron Age horses of Central and Eastern Europe', *Bulletin of The American School of Prehistoric Research*, 25 (1968), 1-71 (pp. 47-49).

[239] References to many Continental Germanic peoples are cited by R. Bartlett, *Trial by Fire and Water: The Medieval Judicial Ordeal*, Oxford, 1986, pp. 115-6 *et passim*.

[240] For the notion of victory in divine hands cf. the Old English verse fragment *Waldere*, Norman, pp. 36-38; Bradley, pp. 511-12; M. Ashdown, 'The single combat in certain cycles of English and Scandinavian tradition and romance', *Modern Language Review*, 17 (1922), 113-30; M.W. Bloomfield, 'Beowulf,

kings: Edmund 'Ironside' and the Dane Cnut, coming together on an islet in the Severn in 1016, the victor's prize to be the other's kingdom.[241] The motif is certainly common in the kind of Continental fiction introduced by post-Conquest society. Laȝamon has his King Arthur confront the king of France alone on an islet in the River Seine, the starving citizens of Paris clambering onto roofs to witness the outcome.[242]

The fact that in our account of Offa I's encounter the river location which gives occasion for heroism is not yet ceremonialised in any sense perhaps suggests an early date (pp. 7-12). But whether or not this significant combat originated with the kind of arena-encounter visualised in Scandinavian tradition or in the manner of our narrator's more instantly exciting picture, the prince's deed is explained as compensating for that previous shameful incident which had seen his nation unfairly attack a Saxon enemy king two against one (pp. liii-iv).

National Frontiers

The mighty flood across which Offa I's army initially faced its enemy, although not yet a frontier in itself, provided a natural location for conflict. Many a historical battle took place at major river-crossings: for example Offa II's own at Otford on the Darent in 776 and Benson on the Thames in 779 (pp. 59-62; cf. Appendix A, pp. 135-6). It forms a strategic point of engagement between armies – both a practical and political focus of aggression. In practise waterways made for difficult 'frontiers' at this time. It was the river-system that provided important passageways for Migration-Age population-movements and continued to represent major avenues of traffic for peoples settled either side. Additionally, land-drainage issues would be problematic for centuries (witness the fate of Offa II's sepulchre, pp. 123-4). Whilst a market town might owe its origin to a significant bridging-place, in general a river-bank was unsuitable for early individual settlements, which were sited on slopes away from marshy flood-plains.

For the pre-Migration seafaring English of Offa I's world the location of his long-remembered victory was of particular significance inasmuch as the Treene-Eider river system formed part of one of the major crossroads of European trade: north/south by way of what would later be called the *Herepath* ('Army road') and, of greater significance, east/west from the Middle East via Slavic lands and the Baltic to where this river-system meanders for a hundred or so miles (some 180 km) from east to west across what is now the province of Schleswig, winding continuously through swamps

Byrhtnoth, and the judgment of God: trial by combat in Anglo-Saxon England', *Speculum*, 44 (1969), 545-59 (p. 550 *et passim*).

[241] Dramatic accounts are given by Henry of Huntingdon, *Historia Anglorum*, VI, 13, Greenway, pp. 360-61, and Walter Map, *De Nugis Curialium*, V, 4, ed. M.R. James, revd. C.N.L. Brooke and R.A.B. Mynors, Oxford, 1983, pp. 424-27; William of Malmesbury has Cnut reject the suggestion as unworthy a man of his strength, *Gesta Regum*, Mynors et al., pp. 316-19. The *Anglo-Saxon Chronicles* say rather that this was the occasion of an amicable conference, Swanton, pp. 152-53.

[242] *Brut*, Barron and Weinberg, pp. 610-13.

leading down to the North Frisian islands of the North Sea and points beyond, including the British Isles. At the head of the lengthy Schlei inlet connecting eastwards into the Baltic lay the, now drowned, mart of Hedeby (Old Schleswig).[243] Later, together with the military and mercantile ambitions of King Godfred (*ob.* 810), this trading centre would grow rapidly into a town, minting its own coins, and eventually becoming the seat of a bishop. Godfred strengthened its defences and re-located merchants from the rival Slavic mart at Reric. Visits are recorded from ninth-century England and from Araby,[244] and Adam of Bremen comments that from this sea-port ships were sent not only to Slavic lands but beyond, even to 'Greece' – i.e. the Byzantine Empire.[245]

From Hedeby a short nine-mile (15 km) porterage through the Reide ('travel') meadows brought goods and ships to the Treene-Eider with its estuary, providing convenient passage for travellers between the Baltic and the North Sea that avoided the dangerous circumnavigation of Jutland (Figs. 4 and 7). Commanding the flow of trade, and consequently wealth, between Eastern and Western worlds along this particular route lay an immense travelling earthen rampart (dyke). Subsequently when Danes came to occupy this region now deserted by the English, the great dyke, continuously modified, was referred to as 'Danevirke' (The Danish-Work). Like the Antonine Dyke in Roman Britain, running across the narrow waist of land between estuaries of Forth and Clyde,[246] it was of major military significance, as it would remain to later Denmark. The developed system was to prove an important feature of local defences into historical times, first against marauding Saxons and then Carolingian Franks whose armies, having annexed Saxony, would embark on a series of campaigns against what had become 'Denmark'. In the later nineteenth century it formed an important line against the newly-founded state of Germany, and was sufficiently critical for strategic openings to be made during the course of World War II.[247]

The Danevirke was reinforced and developed at many different times, becoming in places fifteen feet (5 m) high and forty yards (35 m) wide, fronted by a trench fifteen feet (5 m) wide and six feet (1.8 m) deep. A ninth-century Frankish annalist who describes it as broken by merely a single gate through which (the horse-drawn wagons of) merchantmen could pass, attributes the whole to their current enemy King

---

[243] H. Jankuhn, *Haithabu. Ein Handelsplatz der Wikingerzeit*, 8th edn., Neumünster, 1986.

[244] *The Old English Orosius*, ed. J. Bately, Early English Text Society, Supplementary Series 6 (1980), pp. lxi-ii, 16; transl. Swanton, *Prose*, pp. 65-66; the 'Travel Book' of Ibrahim ibn Jakub, c. 975, incl. in H. Birkeland, *Nordens historie i middelalderen etter arabiske kilder*, Oslo, 1954; G. Jacob, *Arabische Berichte von Gesandten an germanische Fürstenhöfe aus dem 9. und 10. Jahrhundert*, Berlin, 1927.

[245] Then presumably with porterage via the River Volga to the Caspian Sea. Adam of Bremen, *Gesta Hammaburgensis Ecclesiae Pontificum*, IV, I, ed. B. Schmeidler, *Scriptores rerum Germanicarum*, Hanover, 1917, p. 228; transl. F.J. Tschan, *History of the Archbishops of Hamburg-Bremen*, New York, 1959, revd. edn, 2002, p. 187.

[246] D.J. Breeze, 'The Antonine Wall', in *Glasgow, the Antonine Wall and Argyll*, ed. H. Swain and P. Ottaway, London, 2007, pp. 11-18.

[247] H.H. Andersen, H.J. Madsen and O. Voss, *Danevirke*, Copenhagen, 1976.

Godfred,[248] but that was merely a time when reinforcement and extension took place.[249] No less than nine separate developments modified both its plan and profile.

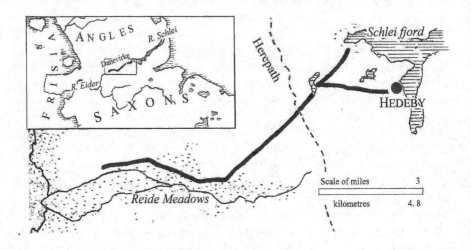

Fig. 7) Location of Danevirke in Offa II's time.

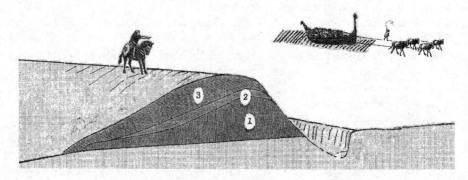

Fig. 8) Schematic profile of Danevirke in Offa II's time.

But at any stage the engineering facilities required by this feature would have seemed primitive enough particularly in the eyes of Eastern merchants, military men and others with many millennia of sophisticated survey and constructional skills behind them. A timber palisade frontage affords dendrochronological evidence for one

[248] *Annales Regni Francorum*, ed. F. Kurze, *Monumenta Germaniae Historica, Scriptores rerum Germanicarum*, Hanover, 1895, p. 126, transl. B.W. Scholz, *Carolingian Chronicles*, Ann Arbor, 1970, pp. 88-89. The position of the gate is not yet identified.

[249] See generally H. Jankuhn, 'Karl der Grosse und der Norden', in *Karl der Grosse, Lebenswerk und Nachleben*, ed. W. Braunfels, Düsseldorf, 1965-8, I, pp. 699-707. H. Jankuhn, *Die Wehranlagen der Wikingerzeit zwischen Schlei und Treene*, Neumünster, 1937.

major rubble enlargement beginning from 737 AD – i.e. during the reign of Offa II's notable Mercian predecessor Æthelbald.[250] The Danevirke in place at the time of Offa II was to be some four-and-a half miles (7 km) long, with a shallow U-section ditch six feet (1.8 m) deep and fifteen feet (5 m) wide with a seven feet (2 m) high bank, its entire profile, including the berm, stretching across some twenty-five yards (22 m).

Whilst work on subsequent developments inevitably disturbed any recoverable data from previous times, excavated sections indicate that prior to 737 there had been at least three phases (see Fig. 8), any one of which might be ascribed to the age of Offa I; certainly something was in place for medieval opinion to link with his story. Uncertainty as to which name a monument of this kind should be attributed was not unknown. Even the scholarly historian Bede lapses when, in referring to the linear earthwork the Romans had dug to advance Hadrian's Wall against the Scots, he speaks only of the provincial governor Julius Severus (in fact already transferred to troublesome Judea), without any mention of his successor the Algerian Quintus Lollius, under whom it was made, or the emperor Antoninus 'Pius' who ordered it to be made.[251]

Just as in pre-Migration Europe the Saxons had been broadly separated from English to the north by the Eider and from Franks to the west by the River Rhine, so now it came about that in their new homelands it was the middle and upper Thames that were later to significantly separate Saxon and Englishman. By the time of *The Two Offas*'s compilation, rivers were long understood to be boundaries as well as commercial avenues. What had initially provided ready passage and access to the hinterland, subsequently could, with jealous colonization, become easily recognised territorial limits, and consequent *loci* of hostility.

By the seventh century most Germanic groups who had settled in Britain enjoyed broadly-understood frontiers. But for one significant people there was, as yet, no such satisfaction – to whom the importance of frontier, or lack of it, was of such overriding concern that it gave them a name – known specifically, and simply, as *Mierce*, Mercians, 'Frontiersmen' (p. xliv). Surrounded by debatable land on all sides, the total lack of secure border in any direction gave rise to constant concern. These midland men must have felt themselves particularly vulnerable. On every side were discontents: probable enemies – yet also potential subordinates. Mercia under stress grew vigorous.

They knew themselves separate from any kind of Saxon to the south, trans-Humbrian English to the north and a variety of *Northfolc* and *Southfolc* in 'East Anglia' at their back.[252] But most significantly, against their western front were those whom

---

[250] H. Erlenkeuser, 'Neue C14-datierungen zum Danewerk', in H.H. Andersen, *Danevirke og Kovirke*, Aarhus, 1998, pp. 189-201.

[251] *Ecclesiastical History*, I, 5, 12; V, 24, Colgrave and Mynors, pp. 26-7, 42-5, 562-3. And cf. Wat's Dyke, pp. lxxiv-xxv.

[252] By now – whatever the racial complexity of the actual settlement – the relative stability of the population is probably marked by those regional dialects which linguistic analysis of the earliest vernacular texts indicates.

they referred to simply as 'the foreigners', *wealas*, 'Wales'.[253] Englishmen living at this last point of the western advance called themselves *Mægonsætan*, 'Dwellers at the Edge', or perhaps 'Those Occupying Tough Places'.[254] From the Dee to the north and Severn to the south, the mountainous country that reached as far as the Irish Sea (Fig. 9) was inhabited by those linguistically, culturally and racially different neighbours, with whom British ruling families had found asylum when ousted from their hereditary estates. Here the fractious groups of small *wealisc* principalities that today form Wales were still as divided as the Germanic settlers themselves, and being no less reluctant to accept any hierachy among themselves, would not be brought together for some three centuries.[255] A certain Marmodius (perhaps Meredith[256] of Dyfed, South Wales, who died in 796, the same year as Offa II) is the only Welsh king mentioned by name in our text (pp. 61-70). During much of the seventh century relations between the Welsh kingdoms and Mercia had been relatively peaceful in consequence of a common need for defence against inroads from Northumbria. Only after the decisive Mercian victory over the Northumbrians at the battle on the River Trent in 679 were the Welsh to be considered the more dangerous.[257] Here it was the kingdom of Powys that represented the major military threat. The twelfth-century Welsh chronicle *Brut y Tywysogyon* mentions bloody raids, and their retributions, throughout the eighth century (Appendix E, pp. 161-2).

The Mercians' expropriations included not only large areas of forest and swamp,[258] but also the rich arable and meadow land that had been occupied and cultivated for centuries by the British whom they now dominated. It seems clear that, by the end of the seventh century, what are now Cheshire, Shropshire and part of Herefordshire had fallen to Mercia. This loss – a clear entity as seen from the west, and probably still worked in part by its original labour-force – must have provoked great resentment amongst its ousted aristocrats. And from out of the mountainous interior of Wales there would inevitably emerge indigenous guerrillas, especially where ridge-ways following the natural east-west orientation of the topography provided an easy route

---

[253] Not dissimilar would be the term 'Ab-origine' as used by nineteenth-century English settlers for those native to the colonies.

[254] Old English *gemære*, 'limit, termination'; cf. *Mægon-folc, -heap*. See generally P. Sims-Williams, *Religion and Literature in Western England, 600-800*, Cambridge, 1990, pp. 16-53.

[255] And then only briefly under Gruffydd ap Llywelyn (1057-63). See generally W. Davis, 'Celtic kingships in the early Middle Ages', in *Kings and Kingship in Medieval Europe*, ed A.T. Duggan, London, 1993, pp. 101-24.

[256] Certainty is impossible since at this stage the territories were ultimately partible and dynasties unestablished, cf. P.C. Bartrum, ed. *Early Welsh Genealogical Tracts*, Cardiff, 1966. The name is found more frequently among tenth- and eleventh-century Welsh kings.

[257] See generally J.E. Lloyd, *A History of Wales*, 3rd edn, London, 1939, I, pp. 162-202; T.M. Charles-Edwards, 'Wales and Mercia, 613-918', in *Mercia: an Anglo-Saxon Kingdom in Europe*, ed. M.P. Brown and C.A. Farr, London, 2001, pp. 89-105.

[258] Itself often productive like Ely, 'eel-country', P.H. Reaney, *The Place-Names of Cambridgeshire and the Isle of Ely*, Cambridge, 1943, p. 214.

for the hill men into the heart of Mercia,[259] which possessed no natural line of defence hereabouts.

The middle one of those monumental linear earthworks that are today commonly called 'Offa's Dyke'[260] runs for sixty or seventy miles (100 or 115 km) from Rushock Hill near Kington (Herefordshire) northwards to Llanfynydd near Wrexham (Denbighshire), except for a length along the River Severn in Montgomeryshire (Fig. 9). It separated Mercia from Powys, the Welsh kingdom with which eighth-century Mercia was continuously at war, and was presumably constructed during either a period of urgent need or one of negotiated peace. Our text tells us that work was begun by common consent during the Christmas truce of 775 (pp. 67-70); although one version of the Welsh *Chronicle of the Princes* identifies the summer of 784, after a year's campaigning, as the season for the Dyke's construction,[261] and excavations suggest that, in part at least, it was dug at a period of low rainfall. It is certainly reasonable to suppose that construction was preceded by an over-winter marking-out stage – an issue of mature rather than urgent military defensiveness, set out in one season and completed in the next.[262] To north and south of this, those short intermittent sections of earthwork that drew lines against the Welsh kingdoms of Gwynedd and Gwent are uncoordinated and of different design. Less aggressive kingdoms here meant less urgent concern. Indeed, the people of North Wales, who remained vulnerable to Northumbria, were relatively friendly towards Offa II, and in any case already provided against by Wat's Dyke (pp. lxxiii-lxxv).

A work of ostentatious definition rather than conquest, this was to be Offa II's most lasting achievement – the establishment of an effective geographical demarcation between England and Wales that remains not markedly dissimilar to the present day.[263] Like the dike cut across the 'debatable lands' between English and Scots in 1552, or the British anti-*blitzkrieg* 'stop-lines' created across different parts of England at the beginning of World War II,[264] it represented as much a political statement as a purely defensive one, and was sufficiently demanding a commission to suggest that on this front at least Mercia acknowledged a long-term limit to its expansion. The fact that the Welshmen of Powys finally both halted Mercian colonisation and won back

[259] For those unfamiliar with the country, C.F. Fox, *The Personality of Britain; its influence on inhabitant and invader in prehistoric and early historic times*, Cardiff, 1932, remains useful.

[260] C. Fox, *Offa's Dyke. A Field Survey of the Western Frontier-Works of Mercia in the Seventh and Eighth Centuries A.D.*, London, 2nd edn, London, 1955. Best now read in conjunction with reports of field-work and excavations described by D. Hill and M. Worthington, *Offa's Dyke: History and Guide*, Stroud, 2003, pp. 47-172.

[261] *Brut y Tywysogion*, ed. J.W. Ab Ithel, Rolls Series 17, London, 1860, pp. 8-9. Appendix E, pp. 161-2.

[262] M. Worthington, 'The Offa's Dyke project', *Archaeology in Wales*, 25 (1985), 9-10. D.H. Hill considers construction in relation to the agricultural calendar: 'The construction of Offa's Dyke', *Antiquaries Journal*, 65 (1985), 140-42.

[263] Fox, *Offa's Dyke*, p. 291, Fig. 121.

[264] Royal Commission on the Ancient and Historical Monuments of Scotland, *Eastern Dumfriesshire*, Edinburgh, 1997, p. 47, Fig. 42; M. Osborne, *Defending Britain: Twentieth-century Military Structures in the Landscape*, Stroud, 2004, pp. 44-70.

considerable areas was celebrated on the so-called Pillar of Eliseg, a granite cross-shaft a mile or two west of the of the Dyke near Llangollen, Denbighshire. The inscription on this tells us that it was erected by King Cyngen to commemorate his great-grandfather who, during a campaign of nine years, had recovered territory previously conquered by the English and 'made into a sword-land by fire' (*IN GLADIO SUO PARTA IN IGNE*).[265] The fact that Cyngen died in 854 suggests that Eliseg and Offa II were contemporaries in the mid- to late eighth century.

Subsequent forays, including that of 796, in which Mercian forces would be defeated at the lowest crossing-point on the River Clwyd, three miles (5 km) west of the Dyke, should probably be regarded as punitive or controlling campaigns rather than indications of further territorial ambition. In any case, hereafter Mercia was to be more concerned with Viking attacks from across the North Sea (pp. 83-6).

Variations in profile through its length may reflect a degree of personal control by individual foremen or gangmasters, but Offa II's Dyke seems sufficiently uniform in conception and design to suggest overall planning and organization by a single mind. The defensive cross-section consists of a deep U- or V-shaped ditch on the Welsh side, the spoil from which was piled up on the English side, and sometimes supplemented from other sources, to create the rampart: a steep turf bank continuing the cant of the ditch towards a flat top and gently-sloping rear. Although for long stretches the bank is now eroded and the trench silted up, the total distance from bottom to top typically remains twenty feet (6 m). The rampart averaged twelve feet (3.5 m) in height and twenty (6 m) wide, fronted by a trench seven feet (2 m) deep and twenty feet (6 m) across, so as to occupy an overall width of some thirty yards (27 m). Whether the rampart was supplemented by some further defensive structure, like the timber palisade found on part of the contemporary Danevirke (pp. lxv-lxvii), we do not know.

The line represents a continuous vantage-point providing effective views both east as well as west. But, although including a number of tactically strong points, without watchtowers or other associated fortifications it cannot have been permanently garrisoned in the manner of the Antonine Dyke, and was probably safeguarded by way of occasional patrols,[266] perhaps seasonal, and signallers.[267] Presumably contingent scrub or other obstruction to view would be cleared and, when informed by watchmen or intelligence, any hostile approaches might be held by sallies from the east. Half-a-dozen well-placed signal beacons in Mercian territory would allow a *levée-en-masse* to be summoned at need. The names of a number of settlements a short distance to the

---

[265] V.E. Nash-Williams, *The Early Christian Monuments of Wales*, Cardiff, 1950, pp. 123-24; J.D. Bu'Lock, 'Vortigern and the Pillar of Eliseg', *Antiquity*, 34 (1960), 49-53; N. Edwards, 'Re-thinking the Pillar of Eliseg', *Antiquaries Journal*, 89 (2009), 143-77 (pp. 161-3, 171-3).

[266] Roughly estimated: foot-patrols composed of ten men tramping at four miles (6 km) per-hour and set to provide a reconnaissance of any given stretch every two hours would require more than three hundred men to man the entire length of Offfa II's frontier at one time. Maintenance through the hours of darkness would prove an added factor; numbers might be reduced if mounted – unlikely at this date. Cf. Hill and Worthington, p. 126.

[267] Cf. D.J. Woolliscroft, *Roman Military Signalling*, Stroud, 2001, pp. 21-30 *et passim*.

east of the Dyke include elements such as –*byrig*/*burh* or –*wardine*, indicative of fortification; and, as late as the ninth century, certain estates like Blockley (Gloucestershire) seem to have been responsible for maintaining a 'wales' troop/patrol (*wealh-færeld*) apparently under a distinguishable sheriff (*wealh-gerefa*)[268] – perhaps a form of Home Guard or Territorial unit.

So remarkable an enterprise could scarcely have been undertaken, let alone completed, except by a man with considerable imagination, resources and power of organization. Whereas the Danevirke, with the advantage of significant water-inlets either end, need be constructed over no more than eight miles (13 km), a project which we might imagine being completed within a relatively short time, the trench-and-rampart which is Offa II's Dyke, drawn across remote and often rough countryside (Fig. 9), was a massive physical and administrative undertaking on an unprecedented scale, requiring conscription of a very substantial labour-force, among whom *wealas* could very well have formed a large part.[269] If not made during peacetime or a period of diplomatic understanding, the engineers and labourers at work must have been augmented by large military contingents.

This earthwork's location in the landscape as a whole reveals intimate local knowledge and expert surveying skills. It is said that Charlemagne was obliged to abandon work on a similar large-scale project in 793, having been misled by 'self-styled experts'.[270] Offa II's Dyke, lying largely along the 400 ft (120 m) contour,[271] is topographically sophisticated, using natural barriers such as rivers or ravines where practicable, avoiding or overcoming problems such as drainage so that no stretch should become waterlogged. It forms a strategic rampart, broadly aligned north-south facing present-day Wales and providing a wide visual command over foreign territory to the west for the greater part of its length. The trench is on the western side of the rampart and where the line of an escarpment or cliff is followed, this also faces west.

When in the mid-eleventh century the Welsh under Gruffydd ap Llywelyn were again a danger, it was said that any Welshman found crossing the Dyke in possession of a weapon should have a limb cut off.[272] Originally, however, no precise racial division was intended: Welsh kings continued to make grants of borderland estates to

---

[268] *Cartularium Saxonicum*, nos. 488-89, II, pp. 89-90; *Anglo-Saxon Chronicles*, A, *s.a.* 897, Swanton, p. 91, n. 13. Whether this referred to an English frontier-force, to Welsh allies or to mercenaries otherwise unprovisioned, is unclear. No comparison can be drawn with the origins of latter-day regiments such as the Coldstream Guards or King's Own Scottish Borderers.

[269] Cf. generally T. Reuter, 'The recruitment of armies in the early Middle Ages: what can we know?', in *Military Aspects*, ed. Jørgensen and Clausen, 32-37 (p. 33).

[270] A massive ditch intended to link Rivers Main and Danube: *Annales Regni Francorum*, Kurze, p. 93; Scholz, pp. 71-2.

[271] One spectacular stretch around Clun Forest north of Knighton the Dyke climbs to almost one and a half thousand feet (400 m) on Llanfair Hill. For the altitude in general, see Fox, *Offa's Dyke*, fig. 121.

[272] John of Salisbury, *Policraticus*, VI, 6, ed. C.C.J. Webb, Oxford, 1909, II, pp. 19-20; transl. C.J. Nederman, *The Frivolities of Courtiers*, Cambridge, 1990, p. 114. Walter Map refers rather to the loss of a foot: *De Nugis Curialium*, II, 17, James *et al.*, pp. 166-9.

their own bishops as late as the ninth century;[273] Offa's Dyke did not separate ecclesiastical jurisdiction; it even bisects some parishes.[274] Place-names show that English communities persisted on the one side and Welsh on the other.[275] But it is rarely the fact that economic zones correspond conveniently with 'national' ones. We might compare the history of Israeli settlements in Palestine through the twentieth century, at some times friendly, at others exceptionally hostile.[276]

As with Danevirke (pp. lxv-lxvii), it seems likely that Offa II's intervention would serve a mercantile as much as military function. It effectively separated the highland economy of the Welsh mountains from the English Midlands. Sight of the six hundred and fifty foot (200 m) contour gave Mercians control of the required yearly movement by herds and people down the natural lines of communication in the region: the ridge-ways that provided drove-roads along gently sloping routes between seasonal cold and warm grazing. And with that contour also roughly demarcating the western limit of intensive arable farming at the time, critical access to lowland agricultural markets was easily interrupted.[277]

Whether or not the rampart was militarily defensible in itself, our text describes the Dyke as a point of conflict between Offa and the Welsh in 775 – and its ditch as convenient for mass graves (pp. 73-4). Down in the valleys stretches of swamp or dense oak forest, if not cleared, could represent ideal guerrilla terrain, or cover for the small number of troops needed overnight to fill a trench of this type sufficiently rapidly to allow passage to a large native force. In narrative romance terms however (pp. 65-70), we might have expected just such chaotic reversal of order to come at the time of the Feast of Fools governed by a 'lord of misrule' that is drawn into the peaceful so-called 'Days of Christmas' which lie between Christmas Day on 25th December and Epiphany Eve (Twelfth Night, 5th January) when it was celebrated that three wise men had come to visit the Christ-child.[278] Whether pagan 'Saturnalia' or Christian 'Christmas', this ancient mid-winter light-festival is traditionally a twelve-day period of feasting and revelry, games of forfeit, disguise and the like, best kept indoors, inasmuch as outside there raged The Wild Hunt across northern skies, led by Woden or the Devil, and werewolves and trolls appeared in large numbers.[279]

---

[273] Finberg, *Early Charters*, nos. 7, 81, pp. 32, 49.

[274] D. Brook, 'The Early Christian church east and west of Offa's Dyke', in *The Early Church in Wales and the West*, ed. N. Edwards and A. Lane, Oxford, 1992, pp. 77-89; W. Davies, *Patterns of Power in Early Wales*, Oxford, 1990, pp. 62-4.

[275] B.G. Charles, *Non-Celtic Place-Names in Wales*, London, 1938, pp. xxii-xxxi; A.H. Smith, *The Place-Names of Gloucestershire*, Cambridge, 1964-5, IV, pp. 25-30, 216 and end-map. Also M. Gelling, 'Why aren't we speaking Welsh?', *Anglo-Saxon Studies in Archaeology and History*, 6 (1993), 51-56.

[276] I. Pappe, *A History of Modern Palestine: One Land, Two Peoples*, Cambridge, 2004, pp. 109-16.

[277] A detailed survey of the social significance of separate stretches of the dyke is provided by S.C. Stanford, *The Archaeology of the Welsh Marches*, London, 1980, pp. 186-98.

[278] Cf Matthew I-XII. For such mid-winter folk-festivals in general see E.K. Chambers, *The Mediaeval Stage*, Oxford, 1903, I, pp. 228-335, II, pp. 290-306.

[279] C. Lindahl *et al.*, ed. *Medieval Folklore*, Oxford, 2002, pp. 432-3.

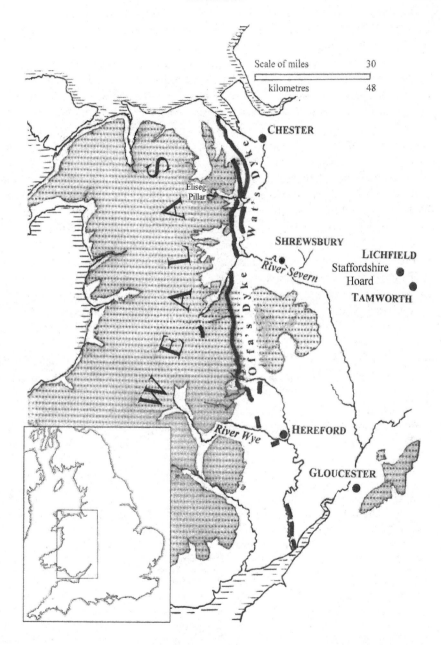

Fig. 9) Welsh Marches in the time of Offa II. The location of Offa II's Dyke and Wat's Dyke in relation to 600 ft contour.

Quite apart from the Continental Danevirke and north British Antonine Dyke (pp. lxv-lxvii), Offa II's undertaking had not been wholly unprecedented,[280] even on site. A number of short ramparts, perhaps provisional or experimental demarcations, already existed along the central sector – close to the vulnerable centre of Mercia, with Offa II's major residence at Tamworth and religious centre at Lichfield. Five had been dug across ridge-ways leading from the central Welsh massif along which the hill-men had always moved towards the Midlands on pastoral business, for trade – or to war. Another three were aligned across the heads of fertile valleys. Although controlling traffic westwards into the Mercian heartlands, these seem less like formal state frontiers than previous attempts to protect isolated communities, and only of local significance. They are what we might expect to characterise debatable land prior to consolidation, and perhaps appropriate to the seventh century when Mercians began to exploit country west of the middle reaches of the Severn. But their distribution to both east and west of Offa II's frontier implies formation over a considerable period of time.[281]

Significantly, the forty-mile (65 km) length of 'Wat's Dyke' that runs along the edge of the Cheshire Plain from near Maesbury on the River Vrynwy to Greenfield on the Dee estuary (Fig. 9) is very similar to Offa II's Dyke, although its shorter length and more easterly situation represent a prior phase of Mercian expansion – radiocarbon dates merely testifying construction some time later than the sixth century.[282] Two or three place-names such as Bryn Offa and Llwyn Offa indicate its early association by the Welsh with one Offa or another,[283] but presumably once the 'Dyke thesis' was attached to the name of Offa II, it might well attract additional otherwise unconnected elements, exercising the imagination of early story-tellers no less than the practice of latter-day archaeologists. When in the ninth century King Alfred's Welsh biographer Asser is happy to tell us that Offa II's rampart ran 'right from sea to sea' (*de mari usque mare*)[284] he is probably drawing on mere rhetoric – similar to the literary *cliché* used by

---

[280] See generally P. Squatriti, 'Digging ditches in Early Medieval Europe', *Past and Present*, 176 (2002), 11-65.

[281] Archaeological dating of such cross-valley embankments varies from the mid-sixth to eighth centuries, cf. R. Hankinson and A. Caseldine, 'Short dykes in Powys and their origins', *Archaeological Journal*, 163 (2006), 264-69.

[282] H.R. Hannaford, *Archaeological Excavations on Wat's Dyke*, Shrewsbury, 1998; 'An excavation on Wat's Dyke at Mile Oak, Oswestry, Shropshire', *Transactions of the Shropshire Archaeological and Historical Society*, 73 (1998), 1-7, p. 5. Corroboration awaits further finds: K. Nurse, 'New dating for Wat's Dyke', *History Today*, 49.8 (1999), 3-4.

[283] Fox, pp. 225-75, *passim*. The association apparently persisted in local tradition into the nineteenth century: D. Hill, 'Offa's and Wat's Dykes – some exploratory work on the frontier between Celt and Saxon', in *Anglo-Saxon Settlement and Landscape*, ed. T. Rowley, Oxford, 1974, pp. 102-07.

[284] *Life of King Alfred*, Stevenson, p. 12; Keynes and Lapidge, p. 71. One version of the Welsh *Brut* is more explicit: it was in consequence of a devastating South Welsh incursion in summer 787 that Offa had "the dyke – to this day called Offa's Dyke (*Glawd Offa*) – made as a boundary between him and Wales, to enable him the more easily to withstand the attack of his enemies; and it extends from one sea to the other, from the south near Bristol, to the north above Flint, between the monastery of Basingwerk and Coleshill", Appendix E, pp. 161-2.

Bede of the Antonine Dyke.[285] A similar expression would be used by the author of the *Annales Regni Francorum* to describe Danevirke (p. lxvi), which at that time in fact extended for less than a quarter of the critical width of Jutland.

Walter Map in the twelfth century speaks of a certain mercenary Vandal warrior named Wade (*Gado*) as having been a powerful friend of that Offa who was builder of 'the dyke which still bears the king's name'.[286] Coming to England, he meets with a teenage Offa who had confined the Welsh and taken to wife a daughter of the Emperor of Rome (Charlemagne) – a marriage which, says Map, turned to grief. Wade then helps Offa resist a subsequent attack by Frankish (*Roman*) forces from the Continent. Other story-tellers would place the figure of Wade in Fairyland.[287] The personal name was not unknown to the early English,[288] although there is no obvious figure we can certainly identify in this. The narrator of *Widsith* refers to a certain Wada as ruler of the Hælsings – a Germanic tribe but whose location is the subject of some debate.[289] Perhaps, like Wansdyke in Cambridgeshire, the two Grim's Ditches in Oxfordshire and others in various places through southern England called after the pagan war-god Woden, *alias* Grim, Wat's Dyke was attributed to a mythical builder.[290] Woden, Germanic god of death and thus connected particularly with war, was favoured by warrior leaders especially. And, included among our protagonists' notable ancestors, no doubt a common topic of the sort of tale later wilfully destroyed at St Albans (p. xxvi).

Offa's Dyke remains an impressive feature in the landscape. So substantial a monument commemorating so great a king, the *ealdan dic* ('ancient rampart') was naturally used as a notable landmark for centuries.[291] Offa II's project was clearly a signal undertaking. At a time when 'nation' was not yet synonymous with territory (cf. pp. xlv-xlvi), the notion of a permanent frontier was just taking hold among these people and must have been striking both in terms of political stability and the sense of 'national' identity it defined. But, looking back from the thirteenth-century it would

---

[285] *Ecclesiastical History*, I, 5, V, 24, Colgrave and Mynors, pp. 26-27, 562-63.

[286] *De Nugis Curialium*, II, 17, James *et al.*, pp. 166-75.

[287] See *Fasciculus Morum*, ed. S. Wenzel, Pennsylvania, 1989, pp. 578-9. Chambers, *Widsith*, pp. 95-100, discusses the mythological origins; also R.M. Wilson, *The Lost Literature of Medieval England*, London, 1952, pp. 16-19.

[288] W.G. Searle, *Onomasticon Anglo-Saxonicum*, Cambridge, 1897, pp. 472-73.

[289] Line 22, Malone, pp. 153-54, 193-94; Chambers, *Widsith*, pp. 108-09, 194.

[290] Linear earthworks bridging the open gaps between natural obstacles such as swamp or forest, and attributed dates ranging between the Migrations and the seventh century. For the problems see: C. Fox, 'Dykes', *Antiquity*, 3 (1929), 135-54; T.C. Lethbridge, 'The riddle of the Dykes', *Proceedings of the Cambridge Antiquarian Society*, 51 (1958), 1-5; A. and C. Fox, 'Wansdyke reconsidered', *The Archaeological Journal*, 115 (1958), 1-45; J.N.L. Myres, 'Wansdyke and the origin of Wessex', in *Essays in British History*, ed. H.R. Trevor-Roper, London, 1964, pp. 1-27.

[291] In the tenth century at Tidenham, Gloucestershire: *Cartularium Saxonicum*, III, p. 212, and as late as the thirteenth century at Rhiston, Shropshire (Public Record Office, MS B 3063); Fox, *Offa's Dyke*, pp. 1, 217, note 2.

have seemed natural enough, and our compiler feels he need do no more than provide antiquarian explanation.

Refugee Queens

The two young Offas have had matching careers – so very similar for the latter to have been deliberately renamed after the former. Unpromising as children – they have received exactly comparable calls to heroism and then to kingship, enjoying correspondingly successful reigns, both establishing unusually secure national frontiers. The analogy continues. Each marries a prominent woman who is in flight from sexual harassment in her own country. A sympathetic, charitable engagement, this is the very opposite of the diplomatic, peace-weaving marriage – typically *de haute en bas* – which neither of these powerful rulers would require. But these wives are to prove very different from each other in character and, as a result, from here onwards the stories diverge in every respect.

In twelfth-century Denmark, Offa I's historical homeland where stories about him lived on, Saxo Grammaticus mentions that Offa I's father had arranged the marriage of his autistic son to the daughter of a governor of Schleswig in the hope that this might better Offa's hopes of succeeding to the throne, but can take the story no further than his accession (Appendix H, pp. 183-4, xxxviii). In our version, however, the lad's marriage takes place only after he has secured the throne, and then by way of involving Offa I in a common folklore narrative formula. Although with no suggestion that we are here entering the 'otherworld', our hero finds his beautiful princess whilst out hunting one day in the forest.[292] With the story-line set in England, she is said to be a Northumbrian, although given no name. The name Thryth given her by the *Beowulf*-poet probably has intrusive, extra-textual, political implications (p. xlix). She declares herself deserted, starving and left as prey to wild beasts in consequence of having rejected incestuous advances from her father the king – a common enough Indo-European narrative motif.[293] Intercourse with a daughter as in the case of the post-Roman British leader Vortigern, (considered part of his generally wicked character by Nennius[294]), was a desperate measure not unknown among the sixteen percent of couples normally finding themselves to be sterile, although commonly resulting in

---

[292] The folktale maiden is typically encountered lost in a forest. The general formula was examined by A.B. Gough, *The Constance Saga*, Berlin, 1902, presupposing an 'English' folktale. It is whilst out hunting that the historical West Country *thegn* Eadric 'the Wild' (cf. *Anglo-Saxon Chronicles*, *s.a.* 1067, Swanton, p. 201, n. 13), was said to have encountered a glamorous fairy and, falling instantly in love, married her and taken her to William II's court: Walter Map, *De Nugis Curialium*, II, 12, James *et al.*, pp. 154-59.

[293] S. Stefanović, 'Ein beitrag zur angelsächsischen Offa-sage', *Anglia*, 35 (1912), 483-525; M. Schlauch, *Chaucer's Constance and Accused Queens*, New York, 1927, pp. 35-46 *et passim*. A useful introduction to the subject of incest remains R. Fox, *Kinship and Marriage*, Harmondsworth, 1967, pp. 54-76.

[294] Nennius, *Historia Brittonum*, 39, Lot, p. 178.

autistic offspring.[295] In an early patriarchal society there will have been those who thought the refusal of a father's wishes, regardless of what they were, *per se* wicked. And certainly the figure described by the *Beowulf*-poet was none too free with her favours (Appendix C, pp. 141-2). Nevertheless, it is as an innocent girl that she is given sanctuary by Offa I, and later married to him, with resulting children (pp. 21-6).

Offa II's beautiful princess – a foreign girl – is discovered washed up on the shoreline. She introduces herself as Frankish royalty, and says, at this stage, that her name is Thryth – like that of Offa I's queen. Although a relative of the great Charlemagne himself (Map goes so far as to say his daughter, p. lxxv),[296] she had been condemned to exposure upon the ocean, set adrift in a small boat without sail or steerage, by Frankish magnates whose proposals of marriage she had rejected. Although characteristically a romance penalty visited on women for immorality,[297] this is not an altogether fictional feature inasmuch as historic examples of such punishment are known.[298] Whilst his parents recognise her character, the young Offa II is ensnared by the girl's beauty and, without seeking advice, marries her, and there are ensuing offspring (pp. 47-50).

This large element in the Offa I *vita* broadly corresponds with a folklore formula of which there are two common versions. In one, the catastrophe suffered by a princess is brought about as vengeance by her incestuous foreign father; in another, it is brought about by her new mother-in-law – often employing the mechanism of a falsified letter – wishing to be rid of her son's wife. For our narrator, however, it is the princess's father who both initiates her suffering and then furthers it by means of the fraudulent document (pp. 21-30).

As told so far, explicitly in the Life of Offa I and gestured towards in the Life of Offa II, these two apparently innocent, merely maligned, women join with a host of other calumniated wives in a familiar narrative formula which recurs throughout medieval Europe and the Middle East.[299] This retails the adversities suffered by a beautiful heroine who, although totally guiltless, is persecuted either by an unsympathetic father,

---

[295] M.G.R. Hull *et al.*, 'Population study of causes, treatment, and outcome of infertility', *British Medical Journal*, 291 (1985), 1693-97.

[296] For the significance of a connection to Charlemagne, Holy Roman Emperor, see G. Spiegel, *Romancing the Past*, Berkeley, California, 1993, p. 95.

[297] In the case of *Emaré* who, unrecognised, arouses the passion of her father which when rejected results in her exposure in a small boat, only to drift onto a foreign land and wed its ruler; ed. E. Rickert, Early English Text Society, Extra Series, 99 (1908), pp. 8-15.

[298] Apparently for final judgement to be left to the will of God, cf. M.E. Byrne, 'On the punishment of sending adrift', *Eriu*, 11 (1932), 97-102. For an example imposed on a jealous royal huntsman, see Roger of Wendover, *Chronica*, Coxe, I, pp. 306-7, Giles, I, pp. 194-5. William of Malmesbury gives a dramatic account of a similar penalty imposed by King Æthelstan on his brother Edwin, although acknowledging his information to derive from oral rather than scholarly history, *Gesta Regum*, Mynors *et al.*, I, pp. 224-27, II, p. 127.

[299] For the literary general types with cognate folktales, see A.B. Gough, *The Constance Saga*, Palaestra 23, Berlin, 1902; E. Rickert, 'The Old English Offa Saga', *Modern Philology*, 2 (1904-05), 29-76; 321-76 (pp. 356ff.); J. Schick, 'Die Urquelle der Offa-Konstanze-Sage', in *Britannica, Max Förster, zum ...*, Leipzig, 1929, pp. 31-56.

envious step-mother, malevolent mother-in-law, jealous sister or rejected lover, and endures such ordeals as exile, loss of her children, imprisonment or servitude; but whose afflictions eventually come to an end when, after the defeat of her enemy, she is restored to her husband and family with her character completely exonerated. In England the story of Constance was told in prototypical form by the Anglo-Norman Somersetshire chronicler Nicholas Trivet,[300] but is best known from Chaucer's *Man of Law's Tale*.[301] As with our text, both of these set it in wild, remote Northumbria and identify the king in question as king of York (Ælle of Deira, 560-88), the pagan king who figures in Bede's story of the first missionaries to England (p. xliii).

In this narrative formula the significance of the heroine's suffering lies in the fact that it is entirely undeserved, and the plot is one of her endurance in adversity – without vilifying those responsible. Resulting from accusations of unacceptable behaviour, in reality deriving from her resistance to an unwelcome suitor, the primary threat is one of lechery – often incest. Certainly at a time when patrilineal rights did not necessarily prevail over the matrilineal, the daughter was one who, if not diplomatically traded, might be kept close to ensure at least endogamous political security.[302] With the suitor rejected, the initial threat is replaced by one of exclusion from society, realised either by compulsory expulsion or voluntary flight. And whereas the ocean or forest offers an arena for reported male heroism – typically a confrontation with monsters – it provided for the female protagonist only an occasion of fearful isolation and peril: one threat exchanged for another.[303]

The plight of Offa I's queen was due to her rejected father (pp. 23-4). (In the case of Offa II, her mother-in-law will be hostile (pp. 49-50) – a familiar figure in fiction, the over-possessive mother resenting another woman taking the time and affection of her son,[304] although in this case we have known from the beginning that the mother-in-law is a good woman who only has the interests of her son at heart.) There follows a no less formulaic condemnation by the misled husband. Seemingly saved by her marriage, a subsequent threat to the life of Offa I's queen occurs as a result of the accusation or contrivance of a malicious relative during her husband's absence. The formula

---

[300] Ed. and transl. E. Brock in *Originals and Analogues of some of Chaucer's Canterbury Tales*, ed. F.J. Furnivall *et al.*, London, 1872-88, pp. 1-53, 221-50.

[301] *The Canterbury Tales*, ed. F.N. Robinson, transl. D. Wright, *The Canterbury Tales*. Oxford, 1986, I, pp. 266-329.

[302] For the ultimately political impulse of this motif, see Schlauch, *Chaucer's Constance*, pp. 40-47.

[303] Cf. L.C. Ramsey, *Chivalric Romances: Popular Literature in Medieval England*, Bloomington, Indiana, 1983, pp. 176-77. For the role of aristocratic women in this society see generally M.J. Enright, *Lady with a Mead Cup*, Dublin, 1996.

[304] She commonly assumes all those hostile characteristics conventionally associated with the 'wicked stepmother' figure: D. Noy, 'Wicked stepmothers in Roman society and imagination', *Journal of Family History*, 16 (1991), 345-61. Particularly common in fairy tales where a child is portrayed as victim, such as 'Cinderella', 'Snow White' or 'Hansel and Gretel': M. Dainton, 'The myths and misconceptions of the stepmother identity', *Family Relations*, 42 (1993), 93-98; L.V. Salwen, 'The myth of the Wicked Stepmother', *Women and Therapy*, 10 (1990), 117-25.

frequently features letters that are intercepted and falsified[305] (pp. 27-30), a 'beneficial catastrophe' leading to the woman's further disadvantage but which does not go uncompensated – the conclusion of the story usually a reunion of the family and the reaffirmation of love and of community.

Why a legend of this Constance type should have become attached to Offa I's queen remains a matter of speculation – except that it will clothe the king with greater heroic glamour. It is not found in the Scandinavian tradition and has the air of later addition. An arguably amalgamated formula, if used here, would suggest secondary development.[306] It was perhaps merely a matter of narrative convenience, providing both story-material and foil for the second queen. However, the career of Offa II's wife as described is entirely different. She may have formulaic origins similar to those of Offa I's queen, but now follows a wholly alternate, and less commendable track. She is revealed to have a character just like that ascribed to the Thryth referred to by the *Beowulf*-poet (p. xlix, Appendix C, pp. 141-2).

In practice it is unlikely for a woman to have been encountered romantically in the circumstances described – our hero personally rescuing her – let alone espoused impulsively. Usually most royal marriages were carefully considered eventualities, arranged with a view to political advantage. In the *Beowulf*-allusion Offa I has received Thryth – a foreign, perhaps Saxon, princess – as a diplomatic gift sent by her father as a 'peace-weaving' gesture towards the king of the English.[307]

The term 'peace-weaver' (*freoðuwebbe*) is used in early English for the woman thus consigned to a potentially, or actually, hostile foreigner in the hope of actively promoting greater amity between two peoples.[308] For example, having defeated in battle the rulers of Northumbria and Wessex, Offa II attempts to secure a peaceful future by having these now subordinate kings marry his own daughters (pp. 85-6). Present-day presumption of romantic choice in respect of carnal relationships reckons despatch unseen to an arbitrary marriage distasteful. Yet the *Beowulf*-poet speaks of the great affection (*heahlufan*) that Thryth found for the king to whom she has been given. And the arranged exogamy considered appropriate to European royalty until relatively recently was never represented to the public as entirely loveless. In early England such matters were taken seriously. A pagan king of Mercia will invade Wessex and depose its ruler for divorcing the sister he had sent him.[309] When Anglo-Frankish negotiations between Offa II and Charlemagne broke down regarding inter-marriage between their

---

[305] The Letter motif is commonly preceded by an Incestuous Father figure, as here, while a Malevolent Mother-in-law is often responsible for falsifying the letter: Schlauch, pp. 23-37, 46-7, 52-3, 76-83.

[306] A. H. Krappe, 'The Offa-Constance legend', *Anglia*, 61 (1937), 361-9; S. Stefanović, 'Zur Offa-Thryðo-Episode im *Beowulf*', *Englische Studien*, 69 (1934), 15-31.

[307] According to the Scandinavian tradition, daughter of Freawine and sister of those responsible for the dishonourable two-against-one incident (see p. liv).

[308] Although see L.J. Sklute, '*Freoðuwebbe* in Old English poetry', in *New Readings on Women*, ed. Damico and Olsen, pp. 204-10; generally C. Cessford, 'Exogamous marriages between Anglo-Saxons and Britons in seventh century northern Britain', *Anglo-Saxon Studies in Archaeology and History*, 9 (1996), 49-52.

[309] Bede, *Ecclesiastical History*, III, 7, Colgrave and Mynors, pp. 232-35.

offspring,[310] the two nations promptly took economic sanctions against each other – closing their ports to the other's trade[311] – in which act the literary eye might well recognise sexual symbolism.

Ideally, those generously despatched to 'weave peace' with counsel and affection might do so to the point of producing a common heir. Nevertheless, the peace-weaver is frequently represented as a pitiable figure – the politically-arranged marriages alluded to in literature generally understood to be unsuccessful, if not overwhelmingly tragic, ones.[312]

The foreign queen must have had to overcome an initial barrier of distrust, perhaps based on fear that she would contrive to hand the nation's resources, if not the nation itself, over to her relatives. Ironically the 'peace-weaver's' major problem is that she is, by definition, an alien, from a hostile nation, and therefore inevitably suspect. No doubt the woman looks different, if only as regards apparel or hairstyle. The mere fact of being on different ground, might result in sufficient nervousness to bring about an uncivil air – frightened perhaps but frightening certainly; and coming from a privileged background she will have domestic expectations that may, or may not, be met. If she speaks the local language at all, it is probably only with difficulty – and certainly with an unfamiliar accent. To those already unsympathetic, the foreigner's manner of speech may well seem constantly over-excited or ill-tempered – when not just broodingly silent.

Dislike of the 'peace-weaving' outsider will be strongest among those who have most to lose from any disturbance of their circle – those *comites* disappointed of any hopes for their own daughters. In 697 the peace-weaving Northumbrian princess Osthryth, now Queen of Mercia, is said to have been killed by her own Mercian nobles.[313] Under normal circumstances, endogamous rather than exogamous marriage might be considered best practice for a king – marriage not with daughters of neighbouring princes but with those of distinguished men from among his most influential supporters. Indeed, should the foreigner's relatives ever fall from power the 'peace-weaver' could herself prove a political encumbrance.

---

[310] According to one Frankish source (*Gesta Sanctorum Patrum Fontanellensis Coenobii*, ed. F. Lohier and R.P.J. Laporte, Paris, 1936, pp. 86-7, transl. P.D. King, *Charlemagne: Translated Sources*, Kendal, 1987, p. 334), Charlemagne's proposal that his eldest son should marry one of Offa's daughters, Bertha, was agreed on condition that in return Charlemagne's daughter Bertha is betrothed to Offa II's son Ecgfrith, now co-king – which Charlemagne refused. Einhard tells us that Charlemagne was devoted to his various daughters and did not wish any of them to marry at all: Holder-Egger, pp. 24-5, Thorpe, pp. 74-75. See J.L. Nelson, 'Did Charlemagne have a private life?', in *Writing Medieval Biography*, ed. Bates *et al.*, pp. 15-28 (p. 21).

[311] Cf. Alcuin, *Epistolae Karolini Aevi*, II, Dümmler, pp. 32-33; transl. S. Allott, *Alcuin of York*, York, 1974, p. 43.

[312] For the role of peace-weaver in general, see J. Chance, *Woman as Hero in Old English Literature*, Syracuse, NY, 1986, pp. 1-11; C. Fee, '*Beag & beaghroden*: women, treasure and the language of social structure in *Beowulf*', *Neuphilologische Mitteilungen*, 97 (1996), 285-94. It is an emotional situation explored by Mai Zetterling in the film *Frieda*, director Basil Dearden, 1947.

[313] Bede, *Ecclesiastical History*, V, 24, Colgrave and Mynors, pp. 564-5.

The reverence of Germanic society for the intuitive insight of womenfolk is well known,[314] but any interference in domestic politics will be bitterly resented, triggering all kinds of accusation, true or false. Given the intensely personal character of local dynastic rule, the part that could be played by women close to the throne was a not inconsiderable factor in the politics of this period.[315] Even her violent influence requires merely forethought rather than physical strength. At its very simplest, the social role of a noble hostess personally passing bowls to those present offered unrivalled access to any in attendance.

Evil and Innocent Queens

Offa II's mother soon realises that there will have been some good reason for her daughter-in-law's exile. Her son has married an arrogant hussy (pp. 49-50). Indeed, Queen Thryth proves to be a proud, greedy and devious woman, who plots against the royal policy and eventually meets with a violent death (pp. 89-100).

Some individuals, of either sex, given even token authority become arrogant. But that treachery which in the male is commonly excused as *Realpolitik* seems decidedly shocking when found in the female – and all the more so when linked with personal beauty. It is so entirely contrary to that other archetype of grace and affection which society expected.[316] Whether in bed or at table, wealthy women easily found surreptitious ways to exercise influence in matters of state.[317] And perhaps more publicly. In *Beowulf* one widowed queen is represented as being in a position herself to offer the throne to a nephew, thinking him more suited than her own son to 'treasury and government'.[318] It is as if the throne with all its rights was regarded very much like ordinary family property, although in practice the majority of *comites* would have to consent. *Beowulf*'s fictional queen is easily outdone in reality by the widow of one West Saxon king, who simply kept the throne for herself, superintending *sub-reguli*, for a

---

[314] Cf. F.C. Robinson, 'The prescient woman in Old English literature', in *Philologia Anglica*, ed. K. Oshitari *et al.*, Tokyo, 1988, pp. 241-50.

[315] Cf. *Beowulf*, 612-65, 1162-1232, 2016-24, Swanton, pp. 62-67, 88-93, 130-31.

[316] Much as, for example, public opinion seems to find female crime more shocking than male, and female alcoholism more surprising than that among men (although in the United Kingdom at the present time 50-100% more women than men die annually of alcohol poisoning).

[317] The Frankish Swiss monk Notker 'Stammerer' tells us how Hildigard, Charlemagne's Swabian second queen, could 'sway the emperor's resolute mind by soft caresses in the female fashion', *Monachus Sangallensis, De Gestis Karoli Imperatoris*, ed. G.H. Pertz, *Monumenta Germaniae Historica, Scriptores*, 2, Hanover, 1829, p. 732; transl. L. Thorpe, *Two Lives of Charlemagne*, Harmondsworth, 1969, p. 97. Cf. J. Ferrante, 'Public postures and private maneuvers: roles medieval women play', in *Women and Power in the Middle Ages*, ed. M. Erler and M. Kowaleski, Athens, Georgia, 1988, pp. 213-29.

[318] *Beowulf*, 2369-79, Swanton, pp. 146-49.

year after her husband's untimely death – although her role not acknowledged by the northern monk Bede.[319]

The spirited nature of certain women could well result in military confrontation. Procopius has heard of a northern war *c.* 550 brought about in consequence of an English princess being jilted in favour of her intended's Frankish stepmother in order to ensure the succession, at which the princess invades the neighbouring land with a fleet and large army, insisting that the man be captured alive so that they may return to their previous arrangement.[320] Germanic women went to the front themselves primarily to encourage their men-folk.[321] A small number of early English women seem to have taken weapons with them to the grave,[322] but only when skeletal remains are found showing undeniable indications of battle-wounds will it be clear whether these accompaniments denoted practical use rather than status or temperament.[323] Nevertheless, the war-spirit seems to reside in some women no less than men. The destructive valkyrie (*wælcyrge*: 'chooser of the slain'), is female[324] and it is not the monster Grendel but Grendel's mother who destroys Beowulf's weapons.[325] Saxo refers to several warrior-women by name, a number of who come from Hedeby.[326] Rich ground for the *littérateur*, and that which to one seems merely sordid may be seen by another in the light of romantic adventure. When Attila the Hun died in 453, at least two accounts of the event became current. The prosaic – perhaps merely cynical – explanation was that the elderly man had died from bursting a blood-vessel whilst with his latest Germanic concubine.[327] The other version – and certainly that preferred by the Germanic poets of north and west – was that he had been bloodily murdered,

---

[319] *Anglo-Saxon Chronicles, s.a.* 672, Swanton, pp. 34-35; cf. Bede, *Ecclesiastical History*, IV, 12, Colgrave and Mynors, pp. 368-69.

[320] *History of the Wars*, VIII, 20, Dewing, V, pp. 254-65.

[321] Tacitus, *Germania*, 8, Winterbottom and Ogilvie, pp. 142-43, Rives, pp. 80, 152-3; cf. Caesar, *Gallic War*, I, 50-51, Edwards, pp. 82-83. D.J. Shepherd, 'The elusive warrior maiden tradition: bearing weapons in Anglo-Saxon society', in *Ancient Warfare*, ed. J. Carman and A. Harding, Stroud, 1999, pp. 219-43.

[322] S. Lucy, 'Housewives, warriors and slaves? Sex and gender in Anglo-Saxon burials', in *Invisible People and Processes*, ed. J. Moore and E. Scott, London, 1997, pp. 150-68; N. Stoodley, *The Spindle and the Spear*, Oxford, 1999, pp. 29-30.

[323] A-S. Gräslund, 'Is there any evidence of powerful women in Late Iron Age Svealand?', in *Völker an Nord- und Ostsee und die Franken* , ed. U. von Freeden *et al.*, Bonn, 1999, pp. 91-98.

[324] C.J. Clover, 'Maiden warriors and other sons', *Journal of English and Germanic Philology*, 85 (1986), 35-49; 'Regardless of sex: men, women, and power in early Northern Europe', *Speculum*, 68 (1993), 363-87.

[325] *Beowulf*, 1519-28, 1605-17, 1659-68, Swanton, pp. 106-115. An up-to-date appreciation of the figure is essayed by C. Alfano, 'The issue of feminine monstrosity: a re-evaluation of Grendel's mother', *Comitatus*, 23 (1992), 1-16.

[326] *Gesta Danorum*, II, 1, IV, 10, VII, 6, VIII, 2, Olrik and Ræder, I, pp. 214-5; Davidson and Fisher, I, pp. 42, 211, 238-9, 280, II, pp. 40, 71.

[327] Jordanes, *Getica*, ed. T. Mommsen, *Monumenta Germaniae Historica, Auctores Antiquissimi*, 5 (1), Berlin, 1882, pp. 123-24, transl. C.C. Mierow, *The Gothic History of Jordanes*, Cambridge, 1915, p. 123.

dramatically stabbed by the supposedly 'peace-weaving' girl in revenge for Attila's own treacherous murder of her two brothers.[328]

Commonly such women are represented as sexually aggressive, exploiting libido as a factor of power politics. The Biblical story of Judith would provide one approved model, picturing a rich and beautiful widow in control of events, able to use her erotic talent violently to remove a military threat to her nation, assassinating an unsuspecting enemy leader.[329] Nevertheless, when retold for a Christian Anglo-Saxon audience, the moral gulf between male and female protagonists is emphasised. The character of the enemy is irredeemably blackened, the immodesty of the heroine downplayed, and perfidious aspects of her behaviour ignored.[330] Removed from the scene of the leader's feast, it even sets aside her complicity in his drunkenness. Both innocent and fearsome, her ability to act like a man is divinely inspired, her action more heroic than pornographic. [331] Rendered powerless less by lust than inebriation, the enemy is significantly beheaded with his own weapon. Although, by the twelfth century, clergy were once more deeply wary of the malicious potential in womankind as a whole, this particular aspect of female conduct is rarely advertised, and we might wait until the twentieth century for its explicit artistic depiction.[332]

Offa I's wife as represented by the *Beowulf*-poet has not been encountered by chance, as here in our text, but instead sent overseas to be married to 'the grateful champion' at her father's bidding. A fiercely unapproachable woman – over gender-sensitive, finding the masculine gaze particularly disturbing, she contrives to have put to death any man who upsets her in this way. Her disagreeable quality is on a par with Grendel's mother, the only other unwomanly female in the poem. Vain and violent, and initially displaying a casual contempt for men,[333] one could choose to see here a reflection of the familiar folktale topic of the proud maiden who sets her suitors severe tests, with death as the penalty for failure.[334] But upon marriage to a man of Offa I's stature, this fearsome virago is said to have changed her character completely,

---

[328] Marcellinus Comes, *Chronica*, ed. J.P. Migne, *Patrologia Latina*, Paris, 1844-64, 51, col. 929. *Atlakviða*, ed P.K. Dronke, *The Poetic Edda*, Oxford, 1969-97, I, pp. 10-12; *The Saga of the Volsungs*, ed. R.G. Finch, London, 1965, p. 73.

[329] Judith XII-XVI.

[330] *Judith*, ed. M. Griffith, Exeter, 1997, pp. 47-61, transl. Bradley, *Anglo-Saxon Poetry*, pp. 495-504; cf. M. Swanton, 'Die altenglische Judith: Weiblicher Held oder frauliche Heldin', in *Heldensage und Heldendichtung im Germanischen*, ed. H. Beck, Berlin, 1988, pp. 289-304. Also generally H. Magennis, '"No sex please, we're Anglo-Saxons"? Attitudes to sexuality in Old English prose and poetry', *Leeds Studies in English*, NS 26 (1995), 1-27 (pp. 12-13).

[331] M. Dockray-Miller, 'The masculine queen of *Beowulf*', *Women and Language*, 21 (1998), 31-8.

[332] For example, Picasso's caricature of ecstatic hatred in 'Woman with Stiletto', Musée Picasso, Paris, nos. 136, 1135, *Picasso's Picassos*, London, 1981, pp. 23, 89.

[333] Thus G.R. Overing, *Language, Sign, and Gender in Beowulf*, Carbondale, Illinois, 1990, pp. 102-03.

[334] Eormenðryð, founding mother of the Mercian royal house, who married Wihtlæg son of Woden (Appendix A, pp. 133-4), was said by Saxo to have proffered the same, by proxy, to the Danish Hamlet, *Gesta Danorum*, V, 2, Olrik and Ræder, pp. 91-2, Davidson and Fisher, I, pp. 97-101, II, p. 65. See generally S. Thompson, *Motif-Index of Folk-Literature*, revd edn, Bloomington, Indiana, 1966, III, pp. 398-408.

transformed by the love and guidance of a good husband into a model wife and queen – a 'taming of the shrew' motif found extensively through northern literature.[335] In contrast, the unnamed woman that our story presents as Offa I's queen is throughout an exemplary, and incidentally beautiful, maiden, model of the 'Constance' type (p. lxxix). A hermit who comes to know her will tell her that "although a woman, you are not womanish" (pp. 35-6) – although by 'womanish' the contemporary cleric might as well have meant 'murdering' and 'dangerous' as much as 'passive' and 'accepting'.

Surprisingly little is known about Offa II's historical wife Cynethryth.[336] If she had derived from an alternate branch of the Mercian royal line it would be valuable to Offa in cementing his own claim more firmly.[337] The date of their marriage is unknown. The English churchman Alcuin, writing from Charlemagne's court in 786-87 to Cynethryth's son Ecgfrith, speaks of her approvingly as a model of piety, compassion and charity in general, and elsewhere says that he would have written her a personal letter of advice, if only her preoccupation with regal business left her time to read it.[338] But Alcuin's perspective would not necessarily have been that of those at home. There, where it seems clear that it was her career that created a whole Mercian tradition of female power,[339] it is easy enough to understand the fame she enjoyed.

The conduct of one of her daughters, Eadburh, was said to have resembled that of Cynethryth herself. Upon marriage to the king of Wessex, she began to execrate powerful men and, if she could not have them done away with by her husband, to poison them herself – accidentally killing her husband that way, at which point she fled to the Frankish court becoming an abbess until expelled for lack of chastity.[340] Cynethryth certainly appears to have been at one with her husband's appetite for majesty. Her name appears on charters;[341] and – uniquely in western Europe – she was the first, and last, Anglo-Saxon queen to see coins minted in her own name and bearing her own portrait like an ancient Classical empress: the bust in profile on the obverse, while the reverse bore CYNEÐRYÐ REGINA in circumspection around an MI for M[ERCI]I (Fig. 11).[342] Similar coinage for Irene, Empress of Byzantium, was being struck in the

---

[335] For two powerful examples see J.L. Nelson, 'Queens as Jezebels: the careers of Brunhild and Balthild in Merovingian history', in *Medieval Women*, ed. D. Baker, Oxford, 1978, pp. 31-77.

[336] Variants of this name such as Cwenðryð are assembled by H. Suchier, 'Ueber die Sage von Offa und Þryðo', *Beiträge zur Geschichte der deutschen Sprache und Literatur*, 4 (1877), 500-21 (pp. 507-09).

[337] P. Stafford, 'Political women in Mercia, eighth to early tenth centuries', in *Mercia*, Brown and Farr, pp. 35-49 (p. 36).

[338] *Epistolae Karolini Aevi*, II, Dümmler, pp. 104-06, Allott, pp. 48-49.

[339] Stafford, 'Political women', *passim*.

[340] Thus Richard of Cirencester, *Speculum Historiale*, ed. J.E.B. Mayor, Rolls Series, 30, 1863-69, I, pp. 260-61; the Welsh nationalist Asser supposes her character inherited from her oppressor father, *Life of Alfred*, Stevenson, pp. 12-14, Keynes and Lapidge, pp. 71-72.

[341] *Cartularium Saxonicum*, no. 259, I, p. 362; see Levison, *England and the Continent*, p. 8, n. 1.

[342] C.E. Blunt, 'The coinage of Offa', in *Anglo-Saxon Coins*, ed. R.H.M. Dolley, London, 1961, pp. 39-62 (46-47 *et passim*); G. Williams, 'Mercian coinage and authority', in *Mercia*, Brown and Farr, pp. 210-28 (pp. 216-7), fig. 15.1; A. Gannon, *The Iconography of Early Anglo-Saxon Coinage*, Oxford, 2003, pp. 40-41. Also D. Chick, 'The coinage of Offa in the light of recent discoveries', in *Æthelbald and Offa*, pp. 111-22.

780s, but that may well post-date that of Cynethryth.[343] Some coins had Offa II's portrait on the obverse together with Cynethryth's name on the reverse. No doubt all of this would offend conservative figures at court. In our story it is acknowledged from the moment of her arrival that she is deceitful, and in fact guilty of the unspecified crime that had led to her exile (pp. 47-8). She is contemptuous and uses angry and excitable words, typical of her people (pp. 49-50). It is not long before she is causing trouble – setting what are intriguingly described as 'female mouse-traps' for her husband's counsellors (pp. 89-90). A twelfth-century readership might well recall the *Sheila na gig* cult-figure so frequently found displaying her vulva on the exterior of churches of that date.[344]

The fact that Thryth has presented herself as a blood relative of Charlemagne (pp. 47-8) is particularly pointed in view of his known reluctance to send the women of his household to serve as wives in the Mercian court (p. lxxx). She later refers to herself as 'Petronilla' (pp. 49-50) – the name of a daughter of the Apostle Peter, who when pressed to marry by the pagan king Flaccus had starved herself to death[345] – a virgin saint who found many votaries at Charlemagne's court. The Emperor regarded her as a personal patroness and of the treaties he concluded with the pope. In 757 her remains had been transferred to an early imperial mausoleum adjacent to St Peter's; this became the 'Chapel of St Petronilla' and subsequently the burial place for French kings.[346]

By-names were frequently used at Charlemagne's court, those of his women relatives 'entering religion' often adopting the name of an early virgin martyr – a practice followed by at least one among Offa's daughters.[347] As their counsellor Alcuin pointed out, the idea had been approved by Jesus.[348] But as used here, its effect is at least potentially ironic (etymologically *petronilla* = 'little rock'), although what we are to make of the reference will depend on our current turn of mind. We are told first of her deceitful nature and then that she says her name is Ðryþ ('Force, Power, Strength');[349] by which she might falsely offer herself as a god-sent opportunity for the young Offa II to continue his career in remarkable parallel with that of his own namesake and ancestor by marrying a woman with not merely the same immediate history but even the same name – if we may rely on the *Beowulf*-poet's information (p. xlix). However,

---

[343] S. Zipperer, 'Coins and Currency – Offa of Mercia and his Frankish neighbours', in *Völker* ... , ed. von Freeden *et al.*, pp. 121-27. P. Grierson and M. Blackburn, *Medieval European Coinage*, I, Cambridge, 1986, pp. 279-80.

[344] J. Andersen, *The Witch on the Wall: Medieval erotic sculpture in the British Isles*, Copenhagen, 1977; A. Weir and J. Jerman, *Images of Lust*, London, 1986.

[345] H. Delehaye, *Sanctus*, Brussels, 1927, pp. 118-20. The legend is accessible in *The Minor Poems of Lydgate*, ed. H.N. MacCracken, Early English Text Society, Extra Series, 107, Oxford, 1911, pp. 154-59.

[346] R. McKitterick, 'The illusion of royal power in the Carolingian Annals', *English Historical Review*, 115 (2000), 1-20 (pp. 12-13).

[347] Offa II's daughter Æthelburh is addressed by Alcuin as Eugenia: *Epistolae Karolini Aevi*, II, Dümmler, nos. 36, 300, pp. 77-8, 458-9, Allott, nos. 44-45, pp. 56-57.

[348] *Epistolae Karolini Aevi*, II, Dümmler, no. 241, pp. 386-87, Allott, no. 86, p. 100.

[349] For the Germanic use of the name see E. Förstemann, *Altdeutsches Namenbuch*, Bonn, 1900-16, I, cols 421-7.

the audience of our present *Vitae Offarum Duorum* must have been expected to appreciate the point without the need to labour it since this text nowhere hints at the name of Offa I's queen. Charlemagne's daughter Bertha used the same by-name, but whether or not Cynethryth's employment of the name here implies an attempt to fraudulently pass herself off as daughter of the Frankish ruler is a further matter.

Whatever Cynethryth's personal reputation may have become in certain quarters, her name cannot have been obnoxious *per se*, even locally. Offa II's more or less immediate successor Coenwulf[350] had his only daughter christened Cwenthryth.[351] However, it is not impossible that some of the ill-will or misunderstanding the earlier individual had attracted was transferred to the later name. When Cynethryth was abbess of Offa II's foundation at Winchcombe (p. xcvii), and was involved in a long territorial dispute with the archbishopric of Canterbury,[352] rumours circulating suggested that she had contrived the murder of her saintly seven-year old brother in the vicinity of the disputed estates.[353]

For our story-teller, and many another later, the climax of Queen Cynethryth's evil career will come with her part in the death of St Æthelberht. Her wishes to have her first two daughters married off overseas (to the detriment of Mercia, says our narrator, pp. 89-90) had been flouted by the king's counsellors. And then it is decided that her third and last daughter is to be given as 'peace-weaver' to Æthelberht, the devout teenage ruler of East Anglia. We know nothing of his background, but according to the earliest account of his martyrdom he had succeeded to kingship in 793 and, approaching fifteen, is required by his magnates to find a wife.[354] His presentation at the Mercian court enrages the queen who now takes matters into her own hands (pp. 89-92). Separated from the band of warlike companions that characteristically accompanied men of status,[355] the naïve young man accepts his putative mother-in-law's invitation into her apartment, and there falls into the trap carefully prepared for

---

[350] From a collateral dynasty, the anointed Ecgfrith (Fig. 6, p. li) having survived his father by only a month or two.

[351] Another Cynethryth was queen of King Wiglaf of Mercia (827-40). Later St Dunstan's mother was to be called the same, *Memorials of Saint Dunstan*, ed. W. Stubbs, Rolls Series, 63, London, 1874, p. 6, *et passim*.

[352] Only resolved at the Conference at Clovesho, *Councils and Ecclesiastical Documents*, Haddan and Stubbs, III, pp. 596-601.

[353] For the story see *Three Eleventh-Century Anglo-Latin Saints' Lives*, ed. R.C. Love, Oxford, 1996, pp. lxxxix-cxxxix, 49-89; S. Sharp, 'Æthelberht, king and martyr: the development of a legend', in *Æthelbald and Offa*, pp. 59-63. For the cult see A. Thacker, 'Kings, saints and monasteries in pre-Viking Mercia', *Midland History*, 10 (1985), 1-25 (pp. 8-12); C. Cubitt, 'Sites and sanctity: revising the cult of murdered and martyred Anglo-Saxon royal saints', *Early Medieval Europe*, 9 (2000), 53-83 (pp. 75-77). An abbess – formerly queen – Ricthryth, is described by Roger of Wendover as ending her days together with a shower of blood from heaven in 787: *Chronica*, ed. Coxe, I, p. 246, Giles, p. 156.

[354] We learn elsewhere that their first choice – of an otherwise unknown south British princess – had been disappointed: M.R. James, 'Two Lives of St. Ethelbert, king and martyr', *English Historical Review*, 32 (1917) 214-44 (p. 224).

[355] Tacitus speaks of a *comitatus*, p. lx, n. 221.

him – smothered with pillows in a pit (pp. 91-6). It is typically a pit, sometimes explicitly a cesspit, in which a narrative victim dies.[356]

The common belief of early historians was that it was the king himself who had been responsible for the man's death, agreeing with *The Anglo-Saxon Chronicles'* explicit statement that in 792 [794] 'Offa ordered Æthelberht's head to be struck off' (Appendix A, pp. 137-8).[357] According to the early twelfth-century *Passio Sancti Athelberhti*, Æthelberht did not even enter the king's presence, but was assassinated by a disaffected East Englishman called Winberht, engaged for the purpose by Offa II who, after talking with Thryth, had become suspicious of his guest.[358]

The fundamentally reciprocal nature of heroic society that might regard the despatch of any given ruler as thoroughly excusable – indeed, a duty not uncommonly undertaken by the *comites* – would in due course pass. But any distinction between 'murder' and 'execution' is presumably dependent on political stance or moral hindsight. It was perhaps in consideration of this incident that William of Malmesbury later declared of Offa II: 'When I consider his achievements I do not know whether to praise or condemn.'[359]

The fifteenth-century antiquarian William Worcestre tells us that Winberht did not carry out this deed until fifteen years after Cynethryth's plot, on 20th May 794.[360] But for those associated with St Albans it would certainly be convenient to argue that although their founder may have given 'the loathsome command', this was only because persuaded to do so by his wicked queen.[361] This is much as Einhard would blame the evil Fastrada's influence for leading Charlemagne into taking actions contrary to his good nature.[362] The picture painted by our text completely exonerates Offa II from any complicity in so nefarious an act. He banishes the guilty woman from his marriage-bed and condemns her to penitential sequestration awaiting a miserable death.[363] No talk here of her position as abbess of Cookham.[364] At the same time Offa II promptly sends an army to secure East Anglia for himself (pp. 99-100), an outcome arguably already acknowledged by the putative marriage-alliance.

---

[356] For example, the youthful martyr King Edmund of East Anglia (855-69), with whose tale that of Æthelberht may have coalesced: cf. Henry of Huntingdon, *Historia Anglorum*, Greenway, pp. 360-61; and Walter Map, *De Nugis Curialium*, James *et al.*, pp. 430-31. Cf. C.E. Wright, *The Cultivation of Saga in Anglo-Saxon England*, Edinburgh, 1939, pp. 198-203.

[357] For example, *The Chronicle of Æthelweard*, ed. A. Campbell, London, 1962, pp. 27-28.

[358] James, 'Two Lives of St. Ethelbert', pp. 228, 239-40.

[359] *Gesta Regum*, 86, Mynors *et al.*, I, pp. 120-21; 'murdered without good reason' William says, 'a wicked plot against his daughter's suitor': *Gesta Pontificum*, Winterbottom, I, pp. 462-63.

[360] *Itineraries*, ed. J.H. Harvey, Oxford, 1969, pp. 328-29.

[361] Cf. John (*alias* Florence) of Worcester, Darlington *et al.*, *s.a.* 793, II, pp. 224-25.

[362] Holder-Egger, p. 26, Thorpe, p. 76.

[363] Eventually thrown into a cesspit of her own (pp. 97-100); for the appropriateness of which cf. Psalms VII.15.

[364] Cf. J. Story, *Carolingian Connections: Anglo-Saxon England and Carolingian Francia*, Aldershot, 2003, pp. 181-84.

Coinage of Offa II and Cynethryth

Fig. 10) Silver penny of Offa II, obverse with head and inscription: + OFFA REX + (left), reverse with moneyer's name (right).

Fig. 11) Silver penny of Queen Cynethryth, obverse with head and moneyer's name (left), reverse with inscription: + CYNEÐRYÐ REGINA (right).

Fig. 12) Offa II's copy of Caliph al-Mansur's gold dinar of 774, obverse with 'OFFA REX' (left) upside down in relation to the original cufic inscription (right).

Until the point of marriage, the tales of the two Offas had run broadly in parallel, after which their scenarios diverge. There are adventures ahead for both, but while the more recent king has entered historiography, the story of the earlier king continues in legendary mode. However, because the fourth or fifth-century Danish Offa I now fictionally exists in a 'Mercian' setting, his romance is given a political environment appreciable in terms which might be more appropriate to the circumstances of the historically Mercian Offa II. He is depicted as a powerful man to whom neighbouring rulers commonly look for arbitration. The king of Northumbria, now at war with the Scots, offers to subject himself to Offa I in return for support (pp. 27-8). Both we, and apparently also Offa I, have forgotten that this is the immoral king whose daughter Offa had saved and wed. Nevertheless, the double-dyed villain has provided an opportunity for Mercian aggression. Offa I mounts a successful campaign against the remote north. However, the courier he sends back to Mercia rests overnight at his Northumbrian ally's court and, while asleep, his despatches are altered so as to instruct Offa I's magnates to consign the queen to the forest where she had formerly been found. Although puzzled, they carry out what are believed to be Offa's instructions. Upon the victorious king's return, he is shocked to find no wife. For consolation (if not mere displacement activity) he once more turns to hunting in the forest,[365] and once more discovers her (pp. 33-6) – again in the safe-keeping of a hermit – a familiar figure in romance narratives as: dispenser of hospitality to the stranger, defender of the weak, confessor and counsellor to the knight.[366] Acknowledging that he owes his family's restitution to the grace of God, Offa I vows to found a monastery or restore a ruined one (pp. 35-6). In the event, that notion lapses and the obligation subsequently descends unfulfilled through several generations until the time of Offa II.

Nothing is made of the dynastic succession save to say that in consequence of neglecting their obligation, the family had ceased to enjoy the favour of the nobility (pp. 39-40). We are not told whether Offa II is potential heir to the Mercian throne. The irregular nature of warfare society meant that any notion of direct descent was inevitably tenuous, subject to the vagaries of conflict and sickness. Although certainly related to the royal family, he cannot boast direct descent from a king (Pybba) for several generations (Fig. 6, Appendix A, pp. 133-4).

With this somewhat artless transition the compiler embarks on the second *Life*.

Offa of Mercia: Regal Image

Probably the close resemblance of the early part of Offa II's life to that of his namesake is wilful invention. It is a common phenomenon that, once a historic figure is recognised as notable, the name can attract to it a variety of stories that are clearly

---

[365] A common metaphor of venery for the erotic quest, cf generally M. Thiébaux, *The Stag of Love: the Chase in Medieval Literature,* Ithaca, New York, 1974.

[366] C.P. Weaver, *The Hermit in English Literature from the Beginnings to 1660,* Nashville, Tennessee, 1924.

legendary. The history of Offa II no doubt continued to be informed by the oral tradition – those kinds of "old men's stories" (pp. 105-6) which fleshed out the story of Offa I. In fact the author of 'John de Cella's Chronicle' hesitates to incorporate everything he has heard about Offa II until he has had a chance to research further (pp. xxvii-iii). And a codicil in the Claudius manuscript of the *Vitae Offarum* (p. xxiii) explicitly warns against the errors that might result from careless research (pp. 125-8), although it is unclear as to whether this should be regarded as an indication of the scribe's doubt as to the reliability or otherwise of his data as a whole.

As our narrator now turns his attention to major events of Offa II's rule, he can refer to the books and lesser documents which he tells us were at that time kept at St Albans (pp. 123-4). And we are sometimes in a position to corroborate his version from alternative sources. However, the plethora of available material tempting him to forsake the parallel track of ideal romance in favour of archival reality results in an accumulation of superfluous information. We are given a basic chronicle of wars not only against various kingdoms of the Heptarchy, and against Wales, but also against invading Danes (pp. 83-6). The abbey archives would provide a host of relatively minor administrative notes: correspondence with foreign princes, details of transferring ecclesiastical dioceses, most of it clumsily listed. An account of Offa purchasing a field while on a journey to Rome (pp. 111-2) is an apparently unwarranted digression of no significance to the narrative and of only limited interest in itself. Although adding an air of authenticity, it seems that nothing is too trivial to be included. Nevertheless, the work ultimately returns to *schema*, properly concluding with a tract on the eventual 'foundation' of the long-promised abbey (pp. 115-20).

Despite our text's undoubted literary and other flaws, it builds the picture of a successful forty-year reign worth notice. Offa II was the most powerful of the English kings before Alfred – a strong personality who, by the time of his death, dominated directly or indirectly the whole of Anglo-Saxon England. The first English ruler to carry any weight abroad, he was on comparatively good terms with Charlemagne and the pope.

Mercian expansion was not new with Offa II, but an inevitable factor of circumstances (pp. xliv-xlvi). Those whom Offa invades – the previously independent kingdoms of Northumbria, East Anglia, Wessex, Sussex and Kent – form a temporary alliance which seeks help from the rulers of the powerful Continental Franks, in whose interest the continuing division of the insular kingdoms clearly lay. We are told that the anti-Offa league appeal initially to Carloman (768-71) for help, although improbably in fact since that man's current concern lay rather in inland Europe, and in any case there was no reason for the military reputation he is supposed in our text.[367] Nothing coming of him, they turn then to Charlemagne, who by 771 governed the whole Frankish realm (pp. 49-56). His brother, we are given to understand, has died from an apoplectic fit or

---

[367] Perhaps transferred from another Carloman such as the Frankish king *ob.* 884 AD about whom heroic tales circulated: E.L. Dümmler, *Geschichte des ostfränkischen Reiches*, Leipzig, 1887-88, I, p. 238. Carloman was the name of several members of the Frankish royal family.

of poison while returning victorious from an anti-Saxon campaign (pp. 53-6), for which we have no evidence. The Frankish chronicler Einhard ascribes Carloman's death to nothing more heroic than 'a certain illness', but then he had no wish to talk-up somebody who had been no friend of his own personal patron Charlemagne.[368] The texts of various diplomatic exchanges with Offa II are cited at length (pp. 75-80), and the one we know from alternate sources (p. 78) is quoted in the manner of other English chronicles except for minor graphic and suchlike differences. As portrayed by our narrator, Offa II and Charlemagne negotiate as equals – even allies.

Although ignored in *The Anglo-Saxon Chronicles*, political relations between the two are emphasised by later chroniclers.[369] The rumour in Rome that the Englishman has suggested to Charlemagne that the current pope be ousted in favour of a Frankish cleric may well be true.[370] Offa II's Mercia is clearly to be reckoned with. Certainly he can afford to shrug off mere epistolary admonition from abroad. His foreign intelligence is good. He knows that in fact these Frankish rulers have quite enough troubles with Continental Saxons and Langobards to contemplate the logistics of cross-Channel hostilities (pp. 57-8).[371] Offa II proceeded to crush first East Anglia (pp. 53-4) then Kent (pp. 59-60), himself playing a heroic role in battle at Otford (776);[372] before going on to defeat the kings of Northumbria, Wessex and Sussex at Benson (779),[373] whereupon they flee to find sanctuary among the Welsh (pp. 61-4).

Now the most serious threat to Offa II's kingdom was to come from across the North Sea – ironically from that part of Europe whence came his own ancestors and the historical Offa I. English forces were easily able to repulse a small reconnoitring company from just three great ships (pp. 83-6). But such reports of early success would prove over-confident. Millions (*milia immo milium milia*) were to die as, during the course of the next hundred years, the Danes came to colonise just that part of Britain originally settled by the English now known as Danelaw (*Danelagh*).[374] The English race of Offa was to all intents no longer a political power – that passed to Saxon Wessex. But the fact that Saxon kings would be called nothing other than kings of 'England' and

---

[368] On the death of the twenty-year old Carloman in 771, his sovereignty was absorbed into that of Charlemagne: Einhard, Holder-Egger, p. 6, Thorpe, pp. 57-8.

[369] E.g. William of Malmesbury, *Gesta Regum*, Mynors *et al.*, I, 91-94, pp. 134-37; Roger of Wendover, *Chronica*, Coxe, I, 240-2, Giles, p. 153; whether this reflects actual parity may be questioned, cf. J. Nelson, 'Carolingian contacts', in *Mercia*, Brown and Farr, pp. 126-43 (139-43); generally J.M. Wallace-Hadrill, 'Charlemagne and England', in *Karl der Grosse*, Braunfels, I, pp. 683-98.

[370] *Circa* 784; robustly denied by Charlemagne: *Epistolae Merowingici et Karolini Aevi*, Berlin, 1892, I, pp. 629-30.

[371] Charlemagne's sole period of peace with the Old Saxons was the seven years 786-92. Cf. J. Hines, 'The conversion of the Old Saxons', in D.H. Green and F. Siegmund, ed. *The Continental Saxons from the Migration Period to the Tenth Century*, Woodbridge, 2003, pp. 299-328.

[372] Although considered a brilliant military victory in our text, the political success of this battle is questioned by F.M. Stenton, *Anglo-Saxon England*, Oxford, 3rd edn, 1971, p. 207.

[373] *The Anglo-Saxon Chronicles* speak merely of the king of Wessex, Cynewulf (Appendix A, pp. 135-6); understandable perhaps since the battlefield Benson lies on the Thames in Oxfordshire.

[374] See generally C. Hart, *The Danelaw*, London, 1992.

their entire people and its language 'English',[375] must have been in no small measure
due to the significance of Offa II.

The adoption of Christianity by early English kingship had inevitably strained its
'heroic' terms of reference. Once it was discovered that the new faith involved practical
corollaries in the conduct of affairs, many a ruler, unable to come to terms with the
quandary, themselves retired to monastic seclusion or disappeared as 'pilgrims
towards love of God' (*peregrini pro amore deo*). But others, like Offa II, recognised the
political advantage of Church support, as well as the provision of a ready-fashioned
secretariat to serve their increasing administrative requirements. Reciprocal privileges
might result from the lustre of a special relationship. The theory of government
bestowed by God would allow Offa II to grant conquered lands 'in the name of Jesus
Christ... through whom sovereigns reign and divide the kingdoms of the earth'.[376]
Governorship *dei gratia* 'by grace of God' meant that now, theoretically at least, King
Offa II was irremovable by any earthly authority.[377] It implies the independence of
monarchical power from popular will, and conversely the sinfulness of disobedience to
one considered *vicarius dei*, Christ's substitute on earth. In 787 Offa II had his only son
Ecgfrith, apparently now 15, crowned king while his father was still alive – consecrated
(*gehalgod*) in a manner previously allowed only to bishops – hopefully securing the
rights of lineal succession for his dynasty in the eyes of future kingmakers, when no
son had succeeded his father to the Mercian throne for some time (Appendix A, pp.
135-6).[378] Ironically, Ecgfrith was to live for only four or five months after his father's
death, whereupon Mercian government turned elsewhere. However, the central
ceremonial thrust of the developing coronation *ordines* of the following century is a
repeated insistence upon the people's necessary subordination to a ruler made distinct
in kind from themselves by anointment.[379] The Mercian law-code, now lost, must have
embodied what were no longer the ancient customs of the community but the wishes
of its ruler, reflecting a new 'regal' identity for the Germanic war-leader, the sacredness
of both his person and his enactments.[380]

Also there was famous monetary reform: a systematic common currency replacing
the former *sceat* coinage of irregular local design with a new uniform silver *penig* – the
use of Offa II's name and often his head in profile making it clear to whose authority

---

[375] *King Alfred's West Saxon Version of Gregory's Pastoral Care*, ed. H. Sweet, Early English Text Society, Old
Series, 45, 50, London, 1871-72, pp. 2-9.

[376] *Cartularium Saxonicum*, nos. 213, 214, I, pp. 300-03, *et passim*.

[377] From 764 onwards, *Cartularium Saxonicum*, no. 195, I, p. 276; *Councils and Ecclesiastical Documents*,
Haddan and Stubbs, III, pp. 483-4.

[378] For the background to this practice see Levison, *England and the Continent*, pp. 115-19. Offa II will have
heard that Charlemagne had had his own two sons anointed kings in Rome by the pope a year or two
previously: *Annales Regni Francorum*, Kurze, *s.a.* 781, p. 61; Scholz, p. 59.

[379] M.J. Swanton, *Crisis and Development in Germanic Society*, Göppingen, 1982, pp. 61-81; also Story,
Carolingian Connections, pp. 261-72.

[380] P. Wormald, 'In search of King Offa's "law-code"', in *Legal Culture in the Early Medieval West: Law as
Text, Image and Experience*, London, 1999, pp. 201-23.

that mintage was now subject[381] – to remain a standard style until the thirteenth century. Its size and weight remained consistent with Continental coinage during the eighth century, demonstrating significant trading links, whilst copies of the Arab gold *dinar* – facilitating trade with the Islamic world – might differ from the original merely by adding OFFA REX (Fig. 12).[382] Serving a propagandistic as well as economic function, the new coinage had obvious socio-political implications; and it was produced possibly in very large numbers.[383] Among designs used by Offa II, those displaying a diademed bust clearly echo those of Roman emperors. It is at one with Offa II's custom of being heralded by clarions – six-foot long trumpets capable of only a limited scale but suitable for announcements and ceremonial purposes,[384] imparting an air of dramatic sovereignty probably not seen since Classical times (pp. 121-2). The affectation of 'Romanitas' was clear enough, if not explicitly declared like that of his Continental contemporary, and makes all the more pointed our text's repeated emphasis on the man's personal modesty (pp. 71-4 *et passim*). Although titular self-aggrandisement was no doubt encouraged by clerical staff, it is said here that Offa II never called himself other than 'King of the Mercians', albeit *dei dono* (cf. pp. 71-2, 121-2). There is no evidence elsewhere that broader descriptions of him such as *patria Anglorum* or *decus Brittanniae* were titles directly claimed.[385] Indeed, it appears that in some later legal documents referring to kings, bishops and noblemen, his name is so well known that no title at all need be used.[386] However, the version we are given of Offa II's letter when writing to the Welsh employs the term 'Emperor (*basileus*) of Mercians' about himself (pp. 63-4). And when, shortly after his death, we find the term 'Emperor (*imperator*) of the Mercians' used of Offa II's son and successor Ecgfrith,[387] it is still about three years before Charlemagne's imperial coronation (on Christmas Day 800) and the European ruler's adoption of the title 'Emperor' in practice. Where here the text of Charles's letters already employs such titles (pp. 57-8) it presumably derives from late transcripts of those letters.

---

[381] Probably using ancient Roman models. Charlemagne's reforms closely followed those of Offa II, and his moneyers apparently copy some of Offa's designs, Blunt, p. 42; P. Grierson, 'Money and coinage under Charlemagne', in *Karl der Grosse*, Braunfels, I, pp. 501-36 (pp. 507, 510-11).

[382] Blunt, pp. 50-51, pl. iv, 5.

[383] P. Grierson, 'Carolingian Europe and the Arabs', *Revue Belge de Philologie et d'Histoire*, 32 (1954), 1059-74 (pp. 1067-68); cf. 'Some aspects of the coinage of Offa', *Numismatic Circular*, 71 (1963), 223-25, and references there cited.

[384] Cf. *er ek læt blása*, Snorri Sturluson, *Heimskringla*, ed. B. Athalbjarnarson, Reykjavík, 1941-45, II, p. 59, transl. E. Monsen and A.H. Smith, Cambridge, 1932, p. 250.

[385] None of the surviving documents referring to him in this way is a strictly contemporary copy; cf. generally B.A.E. Yorke, 'The vocabulary of Anglo-Saxon overlordship', *Anglo-Studies in Archaeology and History*, 2 (1981), 171-200 (pp. 186-8); A. Scharer, 'Die Intitulationes der angelsächsischen Könige im 7. und 8. Jahrhundert', *Intitulatio III*, ed. H. Wolfram and A. Scharer, Vienna, 1988, pp. 9-74 (pp. 63-70).

[386] *Anglo-Saxon Writs*, ed. F.E. Harmer, Manchester, 1952, pp. 345-46.

[387] *Cartularium Saxonicum*, no. 289, I, p. 400; but this appears to be the sole recorded example and may represent semantic inexactitude in the use of an unusual term, cf. Levison, *England and the Continent*, pp. 121-25.

Fig. 13) Bishoprics and Archbishoprics at the death of Offa II.

This new concept of kingship resulted in a general augmentation of, if not the titles, then the stuff of dignity. The king's position now demands the majesty of possession, gathering both territorial and material wealth to his person – a persona identified with nation rather than _folc_ as formerly. The progressive association of regal authority with that of God results in, or perhaps precedes, a correlative detachment of the king from his people. The traditional social cohesion depending on personal respect is no longer adequate; obedience is required. With administration both legal and territorial increasingly centred in the king's hands, _folc-land_ changes to royal demesne and consequently the older *comitatus* into landed nobility, with the English free peasant (*ceorl*) subordinate as described in the *Rectitudines*.[388] Offa II seems happy to take away the estates of certain monasteries, to all intents and purposes suppressing them, in order to transfer their lands to his lay followers.[389] Presumably this recognised the need for manpower and suchlike resources to be centralised in face of the present Viking threat (pp. 83-6). But shortly a fully-fledged feudal state would exist. And this our tale's authors – and their audience – would take for granted; they knew no other.

Recognising the potential threat of a political Church, Charlemagne constantly resisted his clergy's encouragement to add to the number of Frankish archbishoprics. However, in England the situation was rather different. There, reflecting the original missionary centres, government of the Church from earliest times had been divided into two archiepiscopal provinces: that of York, administratively responsible for the north, and that of Canterbury[390] responsible for the south of England. Mercia had hitherto lacked such ecclesiastical status. Now, following heated dispute at the Church conference where Ecgfrith was consecrated, Offa II, who was later renowned for interfering in church provincial administration, creating or coalescing dioceses on his own initiative,[391] caused Mercia to be created an archiepiscopal province in itself, carved out of that of Canterbury.[392] Its archbishop would be seated in the cathedral at Lichfield and advertised by the construction of fine new buildings to adorn the long-sanctified shrine of Saint Chad.[393] To Lichfield was now transferred over half the provincial remit of Canterbury – lengthily, unnecessarily and inaccurately, detailed by our narrator (pp. 79-82). This move freed every diocese lying north of the Thames, except for London's, from the political influence of Canterbury – located within hostile Kent and suspiciously close to the Carolingian Continent. Jænberht the Archbishop of Canterbury had (we are told, pp. 81-2) been encouraging Charlemagne to invade – a familiar enough kind of political excuse to justify antagonism towards a third party. Although the ecclesiastical primacy of Canterbury was hereafter no more than nominal, when Jænberht died five years later in 792, he was replaced by a Mercian candidate more amenable to Offa II and consecrated by Hygeberht of Lichfield.[394] In our text it seems understood also that the ecclesiastical primacy of Canterbury passed to Lichfield (pp. 81-2). But in any case, although according to our narrator's sources this state of affairs had been agreed by Jænberht quite voluntarily (pp. 101-2), it was to last only

---

[388] *Die Gesetze der Angelsachsen*, ed. F. Liebermann, Halle, 1898-1916, I, pp. 444-53.

[389] R.P. Abels, *Lordship and Military Obligation in Anglo-Saxon England*, London, 1988, pp. 52-57.

[390] Intended for London, the major city in the south (Bede, *Ecclesiastical History*, I, 29, Colgrave and Mynors, pp. 104-07), it was transferred shortly afterwards.

[391] Thus William of Malmesbury, *Gesta Regum*, Mynors *et al.*, pp. 122-23; *Gesta Pontificum*, Winterbottom, I, pp. 18-21.

[392] Approved by the pope (Adrian, 772-95) in 788: H. Tillmann, *Die päpstlichen Legaten in England bis ... 1218*, Bonn, 1926, pp. 156-58. See generally J.W. Lamb, *The Archbishopric of Lichfield (787-803)*, London, 1964.

[393] Evidence is assembled in W. Rodwell *et al.*, 'The Lichfield angel', *Antiquaries Journal*, 88 (2008), 48-108.

[394] The Lincolnshire abbot Æthelheard, supported by Alcuin: *Epistolae Karolini Aevi*, II, ed. Dümmler, pp. 189-91, transl. Whitelock, *English Historical Documents*, I, pp. 856-61.

some dozen years when, with the death of Hygeberht *c.* 803 and Offa II now gone, the traditional suzerainty of Canterbury would be restored whilst Lichfield returned to its former subordinate diocesan status.

Pledge Fulfilled: St Albans Abbey

An account of the long-postponed foundation of a religious institution provides the narrative compilation with its expected end – another event which links the two Offas but for which there is no parallel in the first part, except anticipation. The tract seems clearly to derive from a different source to what has gone before, but the continuous layout of the major manuscript indicates that it was now intended to be attached.

Alban was the earliest Christian martyr recorded from Britain, and the earliest certain martyr in Western Europe.[395] He had been executed at or near the Roman city of Verulamium (subsequently 'St Albans',[396] Hertfordshire), probably during or shortly after [397] the visit of Constantius Chlorus (husband to British Elene) to the city in 297 – by then one of the largest in the country, its site now more or less deserted.[398] The shrine that typically arose at the place of an early martyr's execution or over their grave, usually lay beyond the walls of Roman cities and therefore in places ill-suited to regular congregational worship (cf. pp. 105-10). At Verulamium the shrine was possibly replaced at the end of the fourth century by a cult-church – perhaps monastic – at a time when monastic communities were rare anywhere in Europe.[399] Continuity of this kind from simple Roman or Celtic shrine to major medieval church is found nowhere else in Britain.[400] The Glastonbury monks, discovering 'an ancient church built by no human hand', would bravely claim foundation by disciples of Christ, possession of the Holy Grail and patronage of King Arthur.[401] At St Albans, however, an

---

[395] But for this status cf J.K. Knight, 'Britain's other martyrs', in *Alban and St Albans*, ed. Henig and Lindley, pp. 38-44.

[396] First recorded as a place-name in the tenth century, Gover *et al.*, *Place-Names of Hertfordshire*, pp. 86-87; there are parallels elsewhere, such as St Ives or St Neots (Huntingdonshire). Matthew Paris says that the place was earlier known as Holmhurst: *Gesta Abbatum*, I, p. 18, Niblett and Thompson, pp. 361-62.

[397] Bede, drawing on an earlier *Passio Albani*, assumes the former (*Ecclesiastical History*, I, 7, Colgrave and Mynors, pp. 28-35); but see: J. Morris, 'The date of Saint Alban', *Hertfordshire Archaeology*, 1 (1968), 1-8; G.R. Stephens, 'A note on the martyrdom of St Alban', *Ibid.*, 9 (1983-6), 20-21. M. Henig, 'Religion and art in St Alban's city', in *Alban and St Albans*, ed. Henig and Lindley, pp. 13-29 (24-25).

[398] J. Wacher, *The Towns of Roman Britain*, 2nd edn, London, 1995, pp. 214-41.

[399] Variously sought: outside the south (London) gate to Watling Street, I.E. Anthony, 'Excavations in Verulam Hills Field, St Albans, 1963-4', *Hertfordshire Archaeology*, 1 (1968), 9-50 (pp. 49-50); within the city walls, R. Niblett, *Verulamium*, Stroud, 2001, pp. 136-7, fig. 71; and at or near where the medieval abbey was established, M. Biddle and B. Kjølbye-Biddle, 'The origins of St Albans Abbey: Romano-British cemetery and Anglo-Saxon monastery', in *Alban and St Albans*, ed. Henig and Lindley, pp. 45-77.

[400] Although comparable with those over the graves of Asclinus and Pamphilius at Cologne or of Mallosus and Viktor at Xanten, cf. C.A.R. Radford, 'The archaeological background on the Continent', in *Christianity in Britain 300-700*, ed. M.W. Barley and R.P.C. Hanson, Leicester, 1968, pp. 19-36 (pp. 32-33).

[401] John of Glastonbury, *The Chronicle of Glastonbury Abbey*, ed. J.P. Carley, Woodbridge, 1985, pp. 16-55.

institution that could so easily have asserted its foundation by Alban himself, merely associates its origin with the supposed discovery of that saint's remains by an eighth-century English king, Offa II. The probable existence of an earlier monastic community on the site is certainly ignored by our text, as is the pagan English invaders' destruction of the British church referred to by Roger of Wendover.[402]

Offa II's discharge of the debt he owes the memory of his forebear Offa I has been long postponed by his unhappy marriage. But now, no longer distracted by Thryth, the celibate king's mind turns to this 'heavy obligation' (pp. 101-2). In fact, the dramatic decision with which our narrator provides the king is unlikely to have been quite so unrehearsed as it is represented. His family does not seem to have been wholly negligent in respect of its inherited pledge. In 780 Offa II refers to the church of Bredon monastery (Worcestershire) as one erected by 'my grandfather Eanwulf';[403] and a document from Pope Adrian I (772-95) associates Offa II not merely with St Albans but 'all the numerous monasteries built and legally acquired, established and dedicated to your protector St Peter'.[404] Ironically, it is only the name of 'your wife Cynethryth' that remains in the sole surviving copy of this.[405] The list of specific houses is gone, but candidates for them are clear. Near to Bredon, which was inherited, he founded a nunnery in 787 at Winchcombe,[406] location of a royal fort and mausoleum;[407] and in 781 an already extant house at Bath was acquired from the bishop of Worcester which he was later thought to have founded.[408] And no doubt there were others. The name of Offa II was clearly sufficiently desirable to cite for St Peter's, Westminster, to claim him as an early patron.[409] Strict evidence for their origins is not markedly less than that for St Albans where this story of foundation by Offa II is unsupported by any archival evidence – surviving charter or suchlike – which is perhaps surprising from such a significant institution.[410]

---

[402] *Flores Historiarum*, Coxe, I, pp. 91, 253, Giles, I, p. 161.

[403] *Cartularium Saxonicum*, nos. 234, 236, I, pp. 326, 329-330; also Finberg, *Early Charters*, no. 42, pp. 40-41.

[404] See generally Sims-Williams, *Religion and Literature*, pp. 154-68, *passim*.

[405] *Liber Diurnus Romanorum Pontificum*, ed. T. von Sickel, Vienna, 1889, no. 241, pp. 122-23. Generally Levison, *England and the Continent*, pp. 29-31; C. Cubitt, *Anglo-Saxon Church Councils, c. 650-c. 850*, Leicester, 1995, p. 226; Stafford, 'Political women', pp. 40-41.

[406] F. Liebermann, ed. *Ungedruckte Anglo-Normannische Geschichtsquellen*, Strassburg, 1879, p. 19; but see Cubitt, *Anglo-Saxon Church Councils*, p. 284. For Offa II's interest in nunneries, see B. Yorke, *Nunneries and the Anglo-Saxon Royal Houses*, London, 2003, pp. 53-54 *et passim*.

[407] S.R. Bassett, 'A probable Mercian royal mausoleum at Winchcombe, Gloucestershire', *Antiquaries Journal*, 65 (1985), 82-100; J. Haslam, 'Market and fortress in England in the reign of Offa', *World Archaeology*, 19 (1987-8), 76-93 (pp. 83-86).

[408] *Cartularium Saxonicum*, no. 241, I, p. 335, transl. Whitelock, *English Historical Documents*, I, p. 506; William of Malmesbury is in no doubt that he had founded it, *Gesta Pontificum*, Winterbottom, I, pp. 306-07. There was almost certainly change of some kind at Bath, whether material or institutional.

[409] B.W. Scholz, 'Sulcard of Westminster: *Prologus ...*', *Traditio*, 20 (1964), 59-91 (p. 66).

[410] Cf. J. Crick, 'Offa, Ælfric and the refoundation of St Albans', in *Alban and St Albans*, ed. Henig and Lindley, pp. 78-84.

It was while Offa II was staying at the ancient Roman resort of Bath (Somerset),[411] we are told, that divine inspiration indicates the whereabouts of St Alban's burial (pp. 103-4), which is where Offa II will build the long-promised monastery. The remains of the martyr were apparently still at Verulamium when visited by Germanus in 429,[412] but seem to have been afterwards lost (pp. 103-6). By the eighth century the authenticity of any skeletal identification must be doubtful. Outside the walls of this ancient city large inhumation cemeteries existed and bones were to be found easily enough quite irrespective of any local information or tradition.

The pledge descending from Offa I to Offa II has been to found, or to restore, a monastic church (pp. 35-42, 45-6, 101-2) and the latter was very probably the case. Certainly medieval tradition suggests that King Offa had *repayred*, rather than instituted, the monastery of St Albans.[413] By his time there was very probably already in existence a fine church commemorating the saint (pp. 105-6) – no doubt constructed with masonry coming from the ruins of Roman Verulamium.[414] But the historical fact was insufficiently dramatic and provided no immediate narrative opportunity. Offa II's miraculous location of Alban's remains was later variously described as both a 'discovery' (*inventio*) and a 'transference' (*translatio*), without distinguishing between original discovery and later transference from earthen grave to shrine.[415] Until 1129 the occasion was celebrated on 1st August and thereafter on the 2nd – supposedly to avoid conflicting with a Feast of St Peter (pp. 119-22), although no doubt celebration of the ancient Lammas customs was no less an issue.[416]

This translation of St Alban – merely relics perhaps – is recorded in one late manuscript of *The Anglo-Saxon Chronicles* as having been in 793,[417] in which year a provincial Church conference attended by Offa II and Archbishop Hygeberht evidentially met at Verulamium acknowledging the event.[418] The fact that Offa II then laid the foundation-stone of a church (pp. 117-18) need not imply the construction of an entire monastery afresh as suggested a little later on the page, although subsequently the expression 'from the foundations' is used (pp. 123-4). It may represent no more than the re-housing of Alban's shrine in an improved building. However, almost

---

[411] For Bath's strategic importance to Offa, see H. Edwards, *The Charters of the Early West Saxon Kingdom*, Oxford, 1988, pp. 226-7.

[412] Bede, *Ecclesiastical History*, I, 18, Colgrave and Mynors, pp. 58-61. E.A. Thompson, *Saint Germanus of Auxerre and the End of Roman Britain*, Woodbridge, 1984, pp. 49-50.

[413] *The Kalendre of the Newe Legende of Englande*, ed. M. Görlach, Heidelberg, 1994, p. 54.

[414] Bede describes it as having been 'built of wonderful workmanship, worthy memorial of his martyrdom', *Ecclesiastical History*, I, 7, Colgrave and Mynors, pp. 34-35.

[415] W. Levison, 'St. Alban and St. Albans', *Antiquity*, 15 (1941), 337-59 (pp. 350-52).

[416] *Gesta Abbatum*, I, p. 85. R. Hutton, *The Stations of the Sun: a history of the ritual year in Britain*, Oxford, 1996, pp. 330-31.

[417] F.P. Magoun, '*Annales Domitiani Latini*, an edition', *Mediaeval Studies* (Toronto), 9 (1947), 235-95 (p. 254), Swanton, p. 56, n. 6. The present site of that burial awaits discovery; it is not, as once supposed, behind the high altar of the abbey, M. Biddle and B. Kjølbye-Biddle, 'St Albans', *Current Archaeology*, 11 (1990-93), 412-3.

[418] J.D. Mansi *et al.*, ed. *Sacrorum Conciliorum, Nova Collectio*, Florence, 1767, cols 861-2.

certainly finding the place served by an irregular group of secular clergy such as were general in the earliest Church, and possibly a joint male-female community of a kind familiar in England,[419] there was installed a more systematised group of monks. It is accompanied by the thought that, if something was not done properly first time, one must do it again (pp. 109-10). Throughout Europe, this period was witnessing a large-scale increase of monasticism as a way of life, and existing groups of ascetics who had assembled around a saint's shrine were commonly being given over to one of the regular monastic orders – in particular the Benedictine rule favoured by Offa II and Charlemagne.[420] Some of those introduced to the new monastery here are specifically, although inaccurately, said to have come from the Frankish Benedictine monastery at Bec in Normandy (pp. 117-18). In fact Le Bec itself was not founded until 1039, although eventually it was to have close links with the post-Conquest English Church, hold extensive estates in England and provide two future archbishops of Canterbury: Lanfranc and Anselm.

With affairs of Church and state increasingly interdependent, splendid new foundations were privileged by gifts, immunities and favours of all kinds.[421] Our narrator tells us that Offa II made a personal visit to the pope to secure the special exemptions his new foundation is to enjoy (pp. 109-16), although it is surprising that so significant an event should have escaped more general notice.[422] At this time the pilgrimage to Rome was a common enough undertaking in the lives of wealthy men and women for political and socio-cultural as well as religious purposes,[423] and one medieval editor of our text seems to think this reference merely mistaken for a different King Offa altogether (pp. 125-8, cf. p. xxxi). Or it may perhaps be a convenient romance formula excited by the misrepresentation of some unimproved statement like that of the Anglo-Saxon Chronicler's bald: 'In 794 [796] Pope Adrian and King Offa passed away' (794. *Her Adrianus papa ond Offa cining forðferden*).[424]

Anglo-Saxon visitors to Rome commonly frequented the so-called *schola Saxonum* or *Angelcynnes scolu*, a colony of Anglo-Saxon ecclesiastics, tradesmen and such-like adjacent to St Peter's (similar to others of Langobards, Franks and Frisians) which they

[419] Bede, *Ecclesiastical History*, Colgrave and Mynors, pp. 327, n. 3, 356, n. 1, 420, n. 2.

[420] Cf. S. Keynes, 'A lost cartulary of St Albans Abbey', *Anglo-Saxon England*, 22 (1993), 255-79.

[421] Although, with heavy editing, reconstitution and forgery rife, the authenticity of many an institutional claim is questionable, J. Crick, *op. cit.* p. cxvi, and J. Sayers, 'Papal privileges for St Albans Abbey and its dependencies', in *The Study of Medieval Records*, ed. D.A. Bullough and R.L. Storey, Oxford, 1971, pp. 57-84.

[422] The Douce manuscript of Roger of Wendover's *Chronica* also alludes to this, but probably merely another detail taken from our text: *Flores Historiarum*, Coxe, I, p. 254-6, Giles, I, pp. 162-4. See generally S. Matthews, 'Legends of Offa: the journey to Rome', in *Æthelbald and Offa*, pp. 55-58.

[423] B. Colgrave, 'Pilgrimages to Rome in the seventh and eighth centuries', in *Studies in Language, Literature, and Culture of the Middle Ages and Later*, ed. A.B. Atwood and A.A. Hill, Austin, Texas, 1969, pp. 156-72.

[424] Eds cit., p. 56; Appendix A, pp. 137-8. The chronicler's metaphorical use of the verb *forðferden* to mean 'passed away/died' was only part of a generous semantic field that included 'travelled', 'processed', 'proceeded' and 'passed by'.

referred to as their 'fortress' (*burh*, now the 'Borgo').[425] Offa II is said to have become the benefactor of what was a flourishing community; but whether this can be regarded as the origin of the regular Rome tax (*Romscot*), later 'hearth-tax' or 'Peter's Pence', as our text [426] maintains (pp. 115-16), is uncertain. The first clear records of an ecclesiastical levy raised on behalf of Rome begin with Alfred in the 880s. [427] Nevertheless it was about this time that Offa II began to make large annual payments to Rome – nominally for the relief of the poor and the maintenance of church lights: a thank-offering to St Peter for the various victories granted to him.[428] It is quite clear to our narrator that St Albans Abbey was to be exempt from any such tax themselves, but might collect it locally for their own use.[429]

As first abbot of his new institution the king appointed one Willegod, a man who had been present at the discovery of Alban's remains. A relative of Offa II, he is said to be of royal descent like many of his successors in the post. We know little more of him, save that he died only a few months after the king – ostensibly a divine punishment for neglecting to secure the king's body. [430]

A cluster of place-names to the south of Lichfield like Wednesbury and Wednesfield attests the existence of a formerly flourishing pagan cult significant to his ancestors;[431] but when in 796 Offa II himself died we are told just a dozen miles (20 km) north of St Albans at the manor of Offley (Offa's Clearing or Wood),[432] he might have expected greater acknowledgement from his notable foundation (pp. 123-6).

Willegod's apparent disregard of the king's remains might be construed as a deliberate insult at a time when what happened to bones (we are at St Alban's) was important in terms of future reputation: how a life is evaluated by one's contemporaries and subsequent visitors. Instead of entombment at St Alban's abbey, where their founder could have been provided with a magnificent sepulchre appropriate to him, the king's body is buried in a manorial chapel – perhaps at Oakley – near a well-endowed religious house at Bedford then under the jurisdiction of a certain Cynethryth (perhaps the king's widow)[433] and which held relics of the martyred

[425] W.J. Moore, *The Saxon Pilgrims to Rome and the Schola Saxonum*, Fribourg, 1937, pp. 90-125; Levison, *England and the Continent*, pp. 40-41. Said to have been built largely of wood, it was to be badly damaged by fire in 817, *Anglo-Saxon Chronicles, s.a.* 816, Swanton, pp. 60-61.

[426] Together with Henry of Huntingdon, *Historia Anglorum*, Greenway, pp. 246-47.

[427] R.H.M. Dolley, 'The so-called piedforts of Alfred the Great', *Numismatic Chronicle*, 6th S. 14 (1954), 76-92. See generally W.E. Lunt, *Financial relations of the Papacy with England to 1327*, Cambridge, Mass., 1939, pp. 1-30.

[428] Thus Pope Leo III writing to the king's successor Coenwulf: *Epistolae Karolini Aevi*, ed. Dümmler, II, no. 127, pp. 188-89, transl. Whitelock, *English Historical Documents*, I, no. 205, pp. 861-2.

[429] Cf. Roger of Wendover, *Chronica*, I, p. 258, Giles, pp. 164-5.

[430] *Gesta Abbatum*, I, pp. 4-8, Niblett and Thompson, p. 360.

[431] M. Gelling, *Signposts to the Past*, London, 1978, pp. 158, 160-1, fig. 11.

[432] Gover, *Place-Names of Hertfordshire*, p. 19.

[433] Cubitt, *Anglo-Saxon Church Councils*, p. 226.

Æthelberht.[434] However, on the banks of the River Ouse, the area is susceptible to powerful floods, and soon after the abbacy of Paul at St Albans (pp. xiii-xiv) this chapel was lost together with Offa II's tomb itself (pp. 123-6). Early river bathers sometimes reported seeing the appearance of a sepulchre in the depths of the water, but no-one who deliberately set out to look could ever find the dead king.[435] So in the event, as typically with heroes, Offa II has no known grave – no more than Offa I.[436] Although archaeologically disappointing, the *ubi sunt* motif makes for a powerful literary conclusion: the most impressive of men reduced to less than dust.

[434] D.W. Rollason, 'Lists of saints' resting-places in Anglo-Saxon England', *Anglo-Saxon England*, 7 (1978), 61-93 (p. 90).

[435] Roger of Wendover, *Chronica*, I, pp. 261-62, Giles, I, 166-67.

[436] Matthew draws a parallel with the biblical leader and lawgiver Moses, *Gesta Abbatum*, I, p. 7, but for us there are plentiful distinguished parallels, from Hereward the Wake to Genghis Khan.

The Lives of Two Offas

Offas

Vitae Offarum Duorum

Vitae Offarum Duorum

[2ʳ]¹ *Incipit historia de Offa primo qui strenuitate sua sibi Anglie maximam partem subegit. Cui simillimus fuit secundus Offa.²*

Inter occidentalium Anglorum reges illustrissimos, precipua commendacionis laude celebratur rex Warmundus, ab hiis qui historias Anglorum non solum relatu proferre, set eciam scriptis inserere consueuerant. Is fundator erat cuiusdam urbis a se ipso denominate, que lingua Anglicana Warwic,³ id est curia Warmundi, nuncupatur. Qui usque ad annos seniles absque liberis extitit, preter unicum filium; quem, ut estimabat, regni sui heredem et successorem, puerilis debilitatis incomodo laborantem, constituere non ualebat.⁴ Licet enim idem unicus filius eius, Offa uel Offanus⁵ nomine, statura fuisset procerus, corpore integer, et elegantissime forme iuuenis existeret, permansit tamen a natiuitate uisu priuatus usque ad annum septimum. Mutus, autem et uerba humana non proferens usque ad annum etatis sue tricesimum. Huius debilitatis incomodum non solum rex, set eciam regni proceres, supra quam dici potest moleste sustinuerunt.

Cum enim imineret patri etas senilis, et ignoraret diem mortis sue, nesciebat quem alium sibi constitueret sibi⁶ heredem, et regni successorem. Quidam autem primarius regni, cui nomen Riganus, cum quodam suo complice Mitunno nomine, ambiciosus cum ambicioso, seductor cum proditore, uidens regem decrepitum, et sine spe prolis procreande senio fatiscentem, de se presumens, cepit ad regie dignitatis culmen aspirare, contemptis aliis regni primatibus,⁷ se solum pre ceteris ad hoc dignum reputando.⁸ Iccirco⁹ diebus singulis regi molestus nimis, proterue eum aggreditur, ut se heredis loco adoptaret. Aliquando cor regis blande alliciens, interim aspere minas et terroribus prouocans, persuadere non cessat regi quod optabat.¹⁰ Suggerebat eciam

---

¹ Illustration: The disabled Prince Offa I is seated at the feet of the elderly enthroned King Wermund, who laments that he is without decent heir, and to the right is nagged by the rebellious Rigan (Frontispiece and Fig. 14).

² *C* precedes this heading with: 'Gesta Offe Regis Merciorum.' *V* has no heading but a marginal note adds: 'Vita Warmundi Regis'.

³ *V* Warwich.

⁴ *V* potuit.

⁵ Presumably puzzlement caused by the apparently feminine ending of the king's name in a Latin context, pp. 5-6; this affirms that the first Offa, although not the second, had borne this name since childhood.

⁶ *V C* omit second 'sibi'.

⁷ *V* summatibus.

⁸ *V* reputabat.

⁹ *V* Idcirco.

¹⁰ *C* optat.

The Lives of Two Offas

Here begins the story of the first Offa, who by his efforts subjugated the greatest part of England to himself.[11] The second Offa was very like him.

Among the most illustrious kings of the West English,[12] King Wermund is celebrated with particular acclaim for excellence among those who used to save stories of the English people not just by word of mouth but also by putting them in books. He was the founder of a certain town named after himself,[13] which in the English language is Warwick, that is 'Wermund's court'. Right into his old age he remained without children except for a single son, whom he thought he could not set up as heir and successor to his kingdom due to the ill effect of disability since boyhood. For although this same – his only son, Offa or Offanus by name – was tall in stature, healthy in body and developing into a young man of most handsome appearance, he nevertheless remained bereft of sight from birth until his seventh year. He was dumb as well, not offering up a human word until his thirtieth year of age. The ill effect of this disability troubled not only the king, but also the leading men of the kingdom more than I can say.[14]

For when old age impinged on the father and, not knowing the day of his death, he did not know who else to appoint as his heir and successor to the kingdom. But a certain man called Rigan, a prominent man in the kingdom, with a certain henchman of his called Mittun, one ambitious man together with another, a deceiver with a traitor, seeing the elderly king wasting away in grief with no hope of begetting a son, took it upon himself to begin to aspire to the pinnacle of royal rank, contemptuous of the other noblemen, thinking only of himself, before all the rest, for this rank. Every day he nagged the king about this – accosted him impudently – that he be adopted in position of his heir. Sometimes enticing the king's heart with flattery, sometimes goading it fiercely with anxieties and alarms, he never stopped working on the king for what he wanted. In his avarice and malice he even used to suggest to the king through

---

[11] An overall location transferred from Offa II, see Introduction, p. xii.

[12] I.e. Mercians, considered separate from the East English (Northfolc and Southfolc), see Introduction, pp. xliii-xlv, Fig. 5.

[13] For Wermund's position in the Offa dynasty, see Fig. 6, Appendix A, pp. 133-4; and for the romance notion that he founded Warwick see Introduction, p. l.

[14] For conditions beyond mere teenage taciturnity see Introduction, pp. lii-liv.

regi per uiros potentes, complices cupiditatis et malicie sue,[15] se regni sui summum apicem, uiolentia et terroribus,[16] et ui extorquere, nisi arbitrio uoluntatis sue rex ipse pareret, faciendo uirtutem de necessitate. Super hoc itaque et aliis regni negociis, euocato semel concilio, proteruus ille a rege reprobatus discessit a curie presentia, iracundie calore fremens in semetipso, pro repulsa quam sustinuit.

Nec mora, accitis multis qui contra regis imperium partem suam confouebant, infra paucos dies, copiosum immo infinitum excercitum congregauit,[17] et sub spe uictorie uiriliter optinende, regem et suos ad hostile prelium prouocauit. Rex autem confectus senio, timens rebellare, declinauit aliquociens impetus aduersariorum.[18] Tandem uero, conuocatis in unum principibus et magnatibus suis, deliberare cepit quo facto opus haberet. Dum igitur tractarent in commune per aliquot dies,[19] secum deliberantes instantissime necescitatis articulum, affuit inter sermoci [2ᵛ] [20] nantes natus et unigenitus regis, eo usque elinguis et absque sermone, set aure purgata, singulorum uerba discernens. Cum autem patris senium, et se ipsum ad regni negocia quasi inutilem et minus efficacem despici et reprobari ab omnibus, perpenderet, contritus est et humiliatus in semetipso, usque in lacrimarum aduberem profusionem,[21] et exitus aquarum deduxerunt oculi eius. Et estuabat dolore cordis intrinsecus amarissimo. Et quam uerbis non [22] poterat, deo affectu intrinseco precordialiter suggerebat, [23] ingemiscens, reponensque lacrimabilem querelam coram ipso, orabat ut a spiritu sancto reciperet consolacionem, a patre luminum fortitudinem, et a filio patris unigenito sapiencie salutaris donatiuum. In breui igitur, contriti cordis uota prospiciens, is, cui nuda et aperta sunt omnia, resoluit os adolescentis in uerba discreta [24] et manifeste articulata. Sicque de regni principatu tumide et minaciter contra se et patrem suum perstrepentes, subito et ex insperato alloquitur: Quid adhuc me et patre meo superstite contra leges et iura uobis uendicatis regni iudicium enormiter contrectare, et me excluso, herede geneali, alium degenerem facinorosum eciam in minas et iniquitatis et prodicionis [25] arguere ualeamus. Quid, inquam, diffiduciacionem superbe nimis prorumpentem, subrogare ut uos non [26] immerito exteri, quid extranei [27] contra nos agere debeant, cum nos affines et domestici nostri a patria quam hactenus generis nostri successio iure possedit hereditario,[28] uelitis expellare.'

---

[15] *V* cupiditatuis et malicie sue complices.

[16] *V* terroribus uel dicare...

[17] *V* congregauit excercitum sepe numero regem et suos ad prelium prouocans.

[18] *V* hostiles.

[19] *V* Dum tractarent quodam die in.

[20] Illustration: Prince Offa I, praying for deliverance from from his disability, is relieved by the hand of God and presents himself to the enthroned King Wermund. Rigan and the rebels depart (Fig. 15).

[21] *V* usque effusionem lacrimarum aucarissima. Et quam uelis.

[22] *V* necdum.

[23] *V* suggerebat interius debilitatis per propter querelam, sic igitur breui contriti.

[24] *V* diserta.

[25] *V* 'possumus': we are able; repetitive if we accept 'ualeamus'.

[26] *V* non uos: not you.

[27] *V* Quid inquam quid exteri uel extranei.

[28] *V* hereditario possedit.

powerful men, henchmen, that he would extort[29] from him the highest position in his kingdom by violence, menaces and alarms, unless the king did what he wanted, himself of his own free will, making a virtue of necessity. A special council was called about this and other business of the kingdom. That impertinent man was reproved by the king and left the meeting of the court, muttering to himself in hot anger on account of the rebuttal he had suffered.

Straightway, many who had supported his cause against the rule of the king followed him, and within a few days he assembled an enormous – in fact infinite – army[30] and, in the hope of victory to be won by force, challenged the king and his side to a bloody battle. But the king, worn out with the frailty of old age and afraid of fighting, ignored the enemies' harassment over and over again. However, eventually he called together his chief men and magnates, and began to discuss what needed to be done. Well, whilst they turned it over together for several days,[31] discussing the hour of need with each other, among the speakers there was the king's son, his only son, who until then had been dumb and unable to talk; but now that his ears had been opened he could make out the words of people talking separately. But when he realised that he himself was as if worthless and of no use to the business of his father and the elders and the kingdom, he felt that he was to be despised and reproached by all; and he was contrite and humiliated in his very being, to the extent of a profuse flood of tears;[32] and his eyes shed streams of water. And the depths of his heart burned with the bitterest sorrow. And the fact that he was unable to speak was deeply impressed upon his heart in his emotions by God.[33] And, sighing and suppressing his tearful grief within, he prayed that he might receive consolation from the Holy Spirit, and the gift of saving wisdom from the Only Son of the Father.[34] Therefore, approving the prayers of a repentant heart, He to whom everything was plain and obvious, instantly opened his mouth with the voice of a youth, distinct[35] and clearly articulate. And so he suddenly and unexpectedly spoke out about the proud chief men of the kingdom and the men threatening himself and his father, and said: 'Why, against the laws and customs, are you claiming a right to lay your hands, in an improper manner, on the throne of the kingdom, whilst I and my father are still living, and exclude me, the heir by birth, and to put in our place another man, ignoble and most criminal, who is breaking out into such threats and outrageous treachery that we are able, not unjustly, to accuse you of disloyalty and treason. What foreigners, what aliens I ask, might act against us, whilst you are trying to expel us and our friends and servants from the country which up to now generations of our family have possessed by right of inheritance?'

[29] *V* by threats or imprisonment.
[30] *V* he collected an army of enormous number against the king.
[31] *V* on a certain day.
[32] *V* to the point of a very great outburst of tears.
[33] *V* he produced from deep within himself a complaint about his weakness, so thus in a short time of repentance.
[34] I.e. Jesus, cf. John III.16-18. Historically the English were not converted to Christianity until the seventh century.
[35] *V* fluent.

Et dum hec Offanus uel Offa, hoc enim nomen adolescentulo erat, qui iam nunc primo eterno nomine cum benedicionis memoria meruit intitulari, ore facundo, sermone rethorico, uultu sereno prosequeretur, omnium audientium plus quam dici potest attonitorum oculos, facies et corda in se conuertit. Et prosequens inceptum sermonem, continuando rationem, ait, intuens ad superna; 'Deum testor, omnesque celestis curie primates, quod tanti sceleris et discidii incentores,[36] nisi qui ceperint titubare, uiriliter erigantur in uirtutem pristinam roborati, indempnes, pro ut desides et formidolosi promeruerunt, ac[37] impunitos, non paciar. Fideles autem ac strenuos, omni honore prosequar confouebo.[38]

Audito igitur adolescentis sermone, quem mutum estimabant uanum et inutilem, consternati admodum et conterriti, ab eius presencia discesserunt, qui contra patrem suum et ipsum, mota sedicione, ausu temerario conspirauerant. Riganus tamen, contumax et superbus, comitante Mittunno cum aliis complicibus suis, qui iam iram in odium conuerterant, minas minis recessit cumulando, regemque delirum cum filio suo inutili ac uano murione, frontose diffiduciauit.

Econtra,[39] naturales ac fideles regis, ipsius minas paruipendentes, immo [3r][40] uilipendentes, inestimabili gaudio perfusi, regis et filii sui pedibus incuruati, sua suorumque corpora ad uindicandam regis iniuriam exponunt gratanter uniuersi. Nec mora, rex in sua et filii sui presentia generali edicto eos qui parti sue fauebant iubet assistere, uolens communi eorum consilio edoceri, qualiter in agendis suis procedere et negocia sua exequi habeat conuenienter.[41] Qui super hiis diebus aliquot deliberantes, inprimis consulunt regi ut filium suum moribus et etate ad hoc maturum, militari cingulo faciat insigniri. Vt ad bellum procedens, hostibus suis horrori fieret et [42] formidini. Rex autem sano et salubri consilio suorum obtemperans, celibri ad hoc condicto die, cum sollempni et regia pompa, gladio filium suum accinxit, adiunctis tirocinio suo strenuis adolescentibus generosis, quos rex ad decus et gloriam filii sui militaribus indui fecit, et honorari.

Cum autem post hec, aliquandiu cum sociis suis decertans, instrumenta[43] tiro Offanus experiretur, omnes eum strenuissimum et singulos superantem ueheementer admirabantur.

---

[36] *V* Deum testor quod incentores tanti discidii indempnes.

[37] *V* et.

[38] *C* prosequar et confouebo.

[39] *V* Econtra fideles et amici primus sui inestimabili leticia.

[40] Illustration: Prince Offa I is knighted (belted and spurred) by his father King Wermund, then vested with mailcoat. A man-at-arms stands by with shield and banner, its heraldry (gold saltire) anticipating that of Offa II (p. 41) and perhaps consequent upon that king's close patronage of St Andrew's cathedral at Rochester. This heraldic theme which has been attributed to the kingdom of Mercia at least since the thirteenth century (College of Arms MS. L.14), is still in use by the Borough of St Albans.

[41] *V* exequi conueniat.

[42] *V* atque.

[43] *V* instrumenta militaria conffissus.

And all the time this Offa, or 'Lump', for that was the name given to the youth[44] who now already deserved to be called by that first eternal name which recalls his blessedness[45] continued with eloquent speech, persuasive argument and smiling face, and attracted to himself the gaze and hearts of all his audience, with eyes more astonished than I can say. And following up the speech he had started, continuing with his argument, he said, looking up to heaven: 'God, and all the nobility in the court of Heaven, is my witness that the instigators of such great crime and discord, except for those who hesitated, must be firmly corrected, restored to their former virtue and pardoned; but I will not allow backsliders and cowards escape the punishment they have deserved. However, I will protect and honourably uphold all those who were loyal and active.'

When, therefore, they had heard the speech of the youth whom they had thought dumb, empty and useless, those who had stirred up rebellion and conspired with vile daring against him and his father were all scared and afraid. But Rigan, defiant and proud, with Mittun his companion and other henchmen, who had now turned anger into hatred, went away heaping threats upon threats in vain invective – shamelessly broke faith with a crazy king and his useless son.

On the other hand, those close to the king and faithful to him,[46] thinking little of these threats – in fact scorning them – were filled with enormous delight and bowed at the feet of the king, his son and their followers, and all gladly pledged their bodies to avenge the wrongs done to the king. Without delay the king, with those present with himself and his son, ordered by a general edict those who supported his cause to help him, wishing to learn from their mutual advice how he should proceed in his affairs and suitably carry out business. Conferring together for several days about this, they advised the king first of all to strap the belt of knight-hood on his son,[47] who was now mature enough in behaviour and age. So that, going into battle, he would instil fear and terror into his enemies. And complying with their wise and sensible advice, on an agreed date with formal and regal pomp the king girded his son with the sword for his novitiate; the king brought together for his military induction some active well-bred youths whom he had clad in armour and distinguished with knighthood for the honour and glory of his son.

And when, after these events, one day the novice Offa was trying out his tools, practising combat with his fellows, everyone marvelled at the great vigour and force with which he overcame each one.

---

[44] For the likely etymology 'lump', see Introduction, pp. lii-liii.

[45] The later Offa is repeatedly blessed in the St Albans liturgy, see Introduction, p. xxvii.

[46] *V* On the other hand his faithful followers and friends found inestimable happiness for the first time.

[47] From earliest times among north European peoples the presentation of arms by leader or respected kinsman had been equivalent to the Roman toga, signifying the coming-of-age of a young man (O.E. *cniht*) as member of state, Tacitus, *Germania*, 13, ed. M. Winterbottom and R.M. Ogilvie, *Opera Minora*, Oxford, 1975, p. 44, transl. J.B. Rives, Oxford, 1999, p. 82; thus William the Conqueror 'dubbed' his son Henry in 1085, *The Anglo-Saxon Chronicles*, s.a. 1085, ed. J. Earle and C. Plummer, Oxford, 1892-99, pp. 216-17; transl. M. Swanton, London, 1996, pp. 216-17, p. 220, fn. 1. For a thirteenth-century form of ceremony, see *Le Pontifical de Guillaume Durand*, I, 28, ed. M. Andrieu, *Studi e Testi*, 88, 3, (1940), pp. 447-50.

Rex igitur inde maiorem assumens audaciam, et in spem erectus alacriorem, communicato cum suis consilio, contra hostes regni sui insidiatores,[48] immo iam manifeste contra regnum suum insurgentes, et inito certamine aduersantes, resumpto spiritu bellum instaurari precepit. Potentissimus autem ille, qui regnum sibi usurpare moliebatur, cum fillis suis iuuenibus[49] duobus, uidelicet tironibus strenuissimis Otta et Milione nominatis, ascita quoque non minima multitudine, nichilominas audacter ad rebellandum, se suosque premunire cepit,[50] alacer et imperterritus. Et preliandi diem et locum,[51] hinc inde rex et eius emulus determinarunt.

Congregato itaque utrobique copiosissimo et formidabili nimis excercitu,[52] parati ad congressum, fixerunt tentoria e regione, nichilque interat nisi fluuius torrens in medio, qui utrumque excercitum sequestrabat. Et aliquandiu hinc inde meticulosi et consternati rapidi fluminis[53] alueum interpositum, qui uix erat homini uel equo transmeabilis transire distulerunt. Tela tamen sola, cum crebris comminacionibus et conuiciis, transuolarunt. Tandem indignatus Offa et egre ferens probrose more dispendia, electis de excercitu suo robustioribus et bello magis strenuis,[54] quos eciam credebat fideliores, subitus et improuisus flumen raptim pertransiens, facto impetu ueheementi, et repentino, hostes ei obuiam occurrentes, preocupatos tamen circa ripam fluminis, plurimos de aduersariorum[55] excercitu contriuit,[56] et in ore gladii trucidauit. Primosque omnes tribunos et primicerios potenter dissipauit, cum tamen sui commilitones, forte uolentes prescire in Offa preuio Martis fortunam, segniter amnem transmearent, qui latus suum tenebantur suffulcire, et[57] pocius [3ᵛ][58] circumuallando roborare. Et rusumpto spiritu uiuidiore, reliquos omnes, hinc inde ad modum nauis uelificantis et equora uelociter sulcantis, impetuosissime diuisit, ense terribiliter fulminante, et hostium cruore sepius inebriato,[59] donec sue omnes acies ad ipsum illese et indempnes transmearent.

Quo cum peruenirent sui commilitones, congregati circa ipsum dominum suum, excercitum magnum et fortem conflauerunt. Duces autem contrarii excercitus,[60]

---

[48] *V* alacriorem, cum suis communicato consilio, contra hostes et insidiatores regni sui bellum instaurari precepit.

[49] *V* iuuenibus bello strenuis ascita non minima multitudine.

[50] *V* ceperunt.

[51] *V* 'locum icc... condixerunt.' They agreed on that place.

[52] *V* utrobique non minimo excercitu fuerunt tentoria.

[53] *V* fluminis distulerunt.

[54] *V* strenuis, subitus et inprouisus pertranssiens.

[55] *V* hostili.

[56] *V* contriuit occidit et aggressus reliquos ab aluco distantes fortissim cum illis dum cauait donec omnis acies lite adcetuisse sunt. Duces...

[57] *C* eciam.

[58] Double-page illustration: The Battle of Mount Slaughter where Prince Offa I slays Brut, the first-born son of the rebel Rigan, cleaving his helmet by sword. A variety of heraldry displayed.

[59] The same image is used a few lines later and also p. 16. The concept is a familiar one, cf. the 'arrows drunk with blood' of Biblical Deuteronomy XXXII.42.

[60] *V* excercitus aue-ordinata precedunt equo et strage suorum exasperati fortissime, instant et non nullos sibi resistentes uel deiccinum seu nifugam constituit. Dum autem in accute magna eggresi, Offa cum hostibus dectaret aliis imperum non sustinentes, longius ab eo pedem retulerunt, et respirans paululum a labore altat diuitit cecidos uides cuneos suorum cessisse et hostilibus dedisse uehementer indoluit et cumgenti clamore suos conuertens

And so in consequence the king becoming bolder, his spirit restored, and buoyed up by a greater hope, having consulted with his council, ordered war to be declared against the hostile plotters of his kingdom, and especially those already openly rebelling against his throne and who, having initiated the fighting, were enemies. But most powerful was he who tried to usurp the throne for himself, with his two young sons, that is to say the most active novices called Otta and Mittun,[61] also a not insubstantial foreign force bold enough to rise against him; and he began to arm himself and his men, rapidly and without fear. And after that the king and his rival settled on the day and place of battle.

And so, when a very large and formidable army[62] had gathered on either side ready for the confrontation, they pitched their tents exactly opposite each other; and there was nothing between them except the river[63] rushing in the middle, which cut off one army from the other. Every so often from then on the timid and fearful disturbed the intervening channel of the rapid river (which was scarcely passable to man or horse) to cross over. But all that flew over it were javelins together with repeated threats and insults. Eventually Offa was exasperated, considering the price of delay to be dishonour and, having chosen from his army those strongest and most active in battle, who he also believed loyal, crossing the rapid river suddenly and surprisingly unexpectedly made a furious attack. The enemy ran towards them; however he destroyed and butchered with the edge of his sword many of the opposing army[64] taken unawares near the riverbank.[65] He forcibly scattered all the officers and leaders. And then his comrades-in-arms, very much needing to know in advance of the military success of Offa – gone ahead – slowly crossed the stream in order to support his flank, and even strengthen it, in a surrounding ward. And, when all the remainder had recovered their spirits, from here on in the manner of a ship under sail and swiftly charging horses, he ploughed around the great current, blade flashing terrifyingly and often soaked with enemy gore, until his whole vanguard passed over safe and unharmed to him.

When his comrades-in-arms reached him, they gathered round their lord, and produced a great and mighty army. But the leaders of the other army[66] violently

insequentibus se uiriliter apposuit. Hic sibimet procedunt obuiam plerumque primates uterusque excercitus hic ab uterusqe multo tempore decertatem est et uicissim hinc inde prouolentibus ferme usque uisi diei suspensa est uictoria.

[61] Differently named pp. 9-10.

[62] *V* no small foreign army.

[63] Historically the Continental Eider *alias* Fifeldor, see Introduction, Fig. 4, p. lxii, *et passim*.

[64] *V* of the enemy army.

[65] V he wore down, killed and attacked others far from the water-course, on guard until the lines of battle over their dispute were decided. The leaders...

[66] *V* the armies, out of formation, went before the cavalry, and were very angered by the slaughter of their men; they pressed on, and Offa stopped many of those who resisted... But as they passed out, not withstanding the attack, they withdrew further off from him, and he took a respite from his labours. The others, seeing that his troops had ceased from hostilities and had given up, and that he was in very great pain... turning his side back with a shout he threw himself against his opponents with manly determination. Here several noblemen set out to block the way of

sese densis agminibus et consertis aciebus, uiolenter opponunt aduentantibus. Et congressu inito cruentissimo, acclamatum est utrobique et exhortatum, ut res agatur pro capite, et certamen pro sua et uxorum suarum, et liberorum suorum, et possessionum liberacione, ineant iustissimum, auxilio diuino protegente. Perstrepunt igitur tube cum lituis, clamor exhortantium, equorum hinnitus, morientium et uulneratorum gemitus, fragor lancearum, gladiorum tinnitus. Ictuum tumultus, aera perturbare uidebantur. Aduersarii tandem Offe legiones deiciunt, et in fugam dissipates conuertunt.

Quod cum uideret Offa strenuissimus, et ex hostium cede cruentus, hausto spiritu alacriori, in hostes, more leonis et leene sublatis catulis, irruit truculenter, gladium suum cruore hostili inebriando. Quod cum uiderent trucidandi, fugitiui et meticulosi, pudore confusi, reuersi sunt super hostes, et ut famam redimerent, ferociores in obstantes fulminant et debacantur. Multoque tempore truculenter nimis decertatum est, et utrobique suspensa est uictoria.

Tandem post multorum ruinam, hostes fatigati pedem retulerunt, ut respirarent et pausarent post conflictum. Similiter eciam et excercitus Offani. Quod tamen moleste nimis tulit Offanus, cuius sanguis in ulcionem estuabat, et indefessus propugnator cessare erubescebat. Hic casu Offe obuiant duo filii diuitis illius,[67] qui regnum patris eius sibi attemptauit[68] usurpare. Nomen primogenito Brutus.[69] Et iuniori Sueno. Hii probra et[70] uerba turpia in Offam irreuerenter ingesserunt, et iuueni pudorato in conspectu excercituum,[71] non minus sermonibus quam armis, molesti extiterunt.[72] Offa igitur, magis lacessitus, et calore audacie scintillans, et iracundia usque ad fremitum succensus, in impetu spiritus sui in eosdem audacter irruit. Et eorum alterum, uidelicet Brutum, unico gladii ictu percussit, amputatoque galee cono, craneum usque ad cerebri medullam perforauit, et in morte singultantem sub equinis pedibus potenter precipitauit. Alterum uero, qui hoc uiso fugam iniit, repentinus insequens, uulnere letali sauciatum, contempsit et prostratum. Post hec deseuiens[73] in ceteros contrarii excercitus duces, gladius Offe quicquid obuiam habuit prosternendo[74] deuorauit, excercitu ipsius tali exemplo recencius in hostes insurgente, et iam gloriosius triumphante.

[Offa] himself, and both armies fought this way and that for a long time, and on both sides hither and thither the victory was undecided almost until daybreak for the rushing-around men.

[67] *V* illius diuitis.

[68] *V* temptauit.

[69] *N* 'siue Hildebrandus' marginal rubric.

[70] *V* uel uerba turpia meum iactantes iuueni pudorato.

[71] *V* excercitus.

[72] *V* extiterunt, uerbis eorum tamen magis exasperatus iracundie calore succensus in impetu spiritus sui in eosdem audacter irruit et eorum alterum unico gladii ictu debilitatum non solum gale e coronam set eciam cerebri intortora perforauit, alterum post hoc fugientem consecutus ictu letali campo prostratum contempsit.

[73] *C* Post deseuiens.

[74] *V* prostrauit.

obstructed advances with close-formed columns and serried ranks. After an initial most gory encounter, cries of encouragement went up on both sides, and exhortations to fight for their lives, and carry on this most righteous struggle for their liberty, and that of their wives and children, and their possessions, with divine help protecting them.[75] And so the trumpets and horns, the shouts of encouragement, the whinnying of the horses, the groans of the dying and wounded, the breaking of spears and clash of swords all made a great din. The rain of blows seemed to make the air tremble. Eventually the enemy beat Offa's troops back and forced them to scatter in flight.

When Offa, most active and covered in gore from the slaughter of the enemy, saw this, with spirit immediately revived, he rushed violently on the enemy like a lion or lioness when their cubs have been stolen, soaking his sword in enemy gore. When those being butchered, those who had fled, the cowardly and the timid, saw this, they turned on the enemy and, so as to regain their reputation, those more fierce stormed against their opponents and went on the rampage. For a long time very fierce fighting took place, but victory was denied either side.

Eventually, after many were lost, the exhausted enemy drew back their infantry to draw breath and rest after the fighting. And the same also in Offa's army. However, that annoyed Offa very much; his blood burned from a wound, and the unwearied champion was ashamed to stop. Then by chance the two sons of that elusive man who had attempted to usurp his father's kingdom approached Offa. The name of the first-born was Brut, and the younger Sweyn.[76] They rudely flung insults and foul words at Offa and, in full view of the armies,[77] continued to harass the modest young man no less with words than with weapons. So Offa,[78] seriously wounded and smarting from the sharp pain inflamed to screaming-point, on a sudden impulse of his spirit rushed boldly in between them. And he struck one of them, that is to say Brut, with a single blow of his sword and, having cut off the top of his helmet, he pierced his skull through to the marrow of his brain and flung him, gasping his life out, under the horses' feet. The other one, having seen this, began to flee but being suddenly turned upon was thrust down, sprawling, injured with a mortal wound. After this, storming against the other leaders of the opposing army, Offa's sword devoured whatever came in its way by throwing it down. And with such an example his army rose against the enemy anew and triumphed even more gloriously.

[75] Cf. Introduction, p. lxxxii.

[76] Different individuals or differently named pp. 7-8. Here the marginal note 'or Hildebrand' acknowledges an uncertainty.

[77] *V* of the army.

[78] *V* However, he was most upset by their words and, inflamed by the heat of anger, and with a sudden impulse of his spirit he rushed boldly in between them and knocked one of them senseless with a single blow of the sword not only the crown from the helmet but also piercing that twisted within the skull. After this, he thrust down the other, consequently in flight, sprawling on the ground with a mortal blow.

Pater, uero, predictorum iuuenum, perterritus et dolore intrinseco sauciatus, subterfugiens amnem oppositum, nitebatur [4ʳ] [79] pertransire, set interfectorum sanguine torrens fluuius, eum loricatum et armorum pondere grauatum et multipliciter fatigatum, cum multis[80] de suo excercitu simili incomodo prepeditis, ad ima submersit, et sine uulneribus; miseras animas exalarunt proditores, toti posteritati sue proba relinquentes. Amnis autem a Rigano ibi submerso sorciebatur uocabulum, et Riganburne, ut facti uiuat perpetuo memoria, nuncupatur.[81] Reliqui autem omnes de excercitu Rigani[82] qui sub ducatu Mitunni regebantur, in abissum despercionis demersi, et timore effeminati, cum eorum duce in quo magis Riganus confidebat, in noctis crepusculo trucidati, cum uictoria gloriosa, campum Offe strenuissimo in nulla parte corporis sui deformiter mutilato, nec eciam uel letaliter uel periculose uulnerato, licet ea die multis se letiferis opposuisset periculis reliquerunt.[83]

Sicque Offe circa iuuentutis sue primicias, a Domino data est uictoria in bello nimis ancipiti ac cruentissimo. Et inter alienigenas uirtutis et industrie sue nomen celebre[84] ipsius uentilatum, et odor longe lateque bonitatis ac ciuilitatis, nec non et strenuitatis eius circumfusus, nomen eius ad sidera subleuauit.

Porro in crastinum post uictoriam, hostium, spolia interfectorum et fugitiuorum magnifice contempnens,[85] nec sibi uolens aliquatenus usurpare, ne quomodolibet auaricie turpiter redargueretur, militibus suis stipendiariis, et naturalibus suis hominibus precipue[86] hiis quos nouerat indigere liberaliter dereliquit. Solos tamen magnates, quos ipsemet in prelio ceperat, sibi retinuit incarcerandos, redimendos, uel iudicialiter puniendos. Iussitque ut interfectorum duces et principes, quorum fama titulos magnificauit, et precipue eorum qui in prelio magnifice ac fideliter se habuerant, licet ei[87] aduersarentur, scorsum honorifice intumularentur,[88] factis eis obsequiis, cum lamentacionibus. Excercitus autem popularis cadauera, in arduo et eminenti loco, ad posteritatis memoriam, tradi iussit sepulture ignobiliori. Vnde locus ille hoc nomine Anglico Qualmhul,[89] a strage uidelicet et sepultura interfectorum merito meruit

---

[79] Double-page battle illustration contd: Offa I lances another of Rigan's sons who is pulled away by the retreating rebel army.

[80] *V* cum multis subterfugiens amnem oppositum nitebatur protelessire interfectorum sanguine torrens fluuius eum cum multis ad yma demeritus una nomine suo amnis denominatus est reliqui omnis excercitus circa noctis crepusculum attemptati sunt.

[81] *N* 'Hiic alio nomine Auene dicitur,' mariginal rubric.

[82] *N* 'qui et Aliel dicebatur,' marginal rubric.

[83] *C* dereliquerent.

[84] *V* Incesti pro uictoriam hostium spolia magnifice contempnens militibus et sequentibus ea exposit... atque interfectorum duces in arduo memoriam sepultura imperauat.

[85] *V* contempnes.

[86] *C* 'precipue' omitted.

[87] *C* licet aduersarentur.

[88] 'Covered by a mound'; what is presumably in mind is the kind of mound found at Sutton Hoo, M. Carver, *Sutton Hoo*, London, 2005, or Prittlewell or Taplow, see Introduction, p. xi, n. 10. The same word is used of St Æthelberht's burial later, pp. 99-100.

[89] *N* 'Qualmhul uel Qualmweld,' marginal rubric. Cf. A.H. Smith, *English Place-Name Elements*, English Place-Name Society, 25-26, Cambridge, 1956, I, pp. 121, 274-75, II, pp. 239-42.

Now the father of the aforesaid young men, terrified, and suffering from an internal injury, tried to cross the water opposite, escaping secretly, but the torrent, flowing with the blood of the slain, drowned him in the depths, loaded down by the weight of his hauberk and armour, and exhausted from several causes – he with many of his army similarly hampered in the same way,[90] and without wounds. The traitors breathed forth their miserable souls, leaving disgrace on all their posterity. However, the river changed its name because Rigan was drowned there and it is called Riganburn[91] so that the memory of what happened may live evermore. However, all the rest of Rigan's army,[92] who were under the leadership of Mittun, were plunged into an abyss of despair and emasculated by fear, and with their leader, in whom Rigan had placed great trust, were butchered in the dusk of the evening, in a glorious victory Offa most active in the field, maimed in no part of his body so as to disfigure it, or even wounded either fatally or dangerously, although he had exposed himself to many deadly dangers that day.[93]

And so a God-given victory in the dangerous and most gory war was granted to Offa around the beginning of his early manhood.[94] And the famous name[95] of this man for virtue and activity was aired among foreigners, and the redolence of his virtue and courtesy, not to mention his valour, spread far and wide; his name reached the stars.

Moreover, on the day after his victory, magnanimously rejecting booty from the enemy dead and flown, not wishing to take anything at all for himself, lest in any way he should be accused shamefully of greed, he liberally left it all to his stipendiary soldiers and men in his household, particularly those whom he knew were needy. Moreover he detained only those noblemen whom he himself had captured in battle, so as to imprison, ransom or legally punish them. And he ordered that the leaders and chief men among the dead, whose reputations had been increased by the reports told about them and those who had acted heroically and loyally in battle even though it had been against himself, should be separately honourably entombed, given funerals with mourning rituals.[96] However, the corpses of the common forces he ordered to be handed over for more ordinary burial in a steep and prominent place, as a reminder to posterity. From whence that place rightly deserved to be called by the English name of

---

[90] *V* fleeing with many in secret, he was prevented from getting across the river lying opposite, which was flowing with the blood of the slain, but deservedly pulled down into the depths with many others; this water was named after his name; but all the remnants of the army were attacked around dusk.

[91] *N* margin: 'This is called by another name, Auene.' No known by-name of the Eider; the name Avon, British **abon*, 'water', is applied to several rivers in different parts of southern and western England; of particular Mercian relevance is that which flows for ninety miles through the counties of Northampton, Leicester, Warwick, Gloucester and Worcestershire, to join the Severn at Tewkesbury, cf. E. Ekwall, *English River-Names*, Oxford, 1928, pp. 17, 20-23.

[92] *N* margin: who was also called Aliel.

[93] *C* they escaped.

[94] For appreciation of the stages of youth, see Introduction, p. lv.

[95] *V* famous... after victory, magnanimously refusing loot from the enemy, he offered these things to his soldiers and followers, and he commanded tombs on a steep... in memory of the leaders of the dead.

[96] So also Offa II, pp. 73-4. Cf the honour Allied forces accorded the corpse of First World War German fighter ace Baron von Richthofen in 1918, P. Kilduff, *The Red Baron*, London, 1994, pp. 204-05, plate between pp. 160-61.

intitulari. Multorum eciam et magnorum lapidum super eos, struem excercitus Offe, uoce preconia iussus, congessit eminentem. Totaque circumiacens planies[97] ab ipso cruentissimo certamine et notabili sepultura nomen et titulum indelebilem est sortita. Et Blodiweld[98] a sanguine interfectorum denominabatur.[99]

Deletis igitur et confusis hostibus,[100] Offa cum ingenti triumpho ac tripudio et gloria reuertitur ad propria.

Pater uero[101] Warmundus, qui sese receperat in locis tucioribus, rei euentum expectans, set iam fausto nuncio certificatus, comperiensque et securus[102] de carissimi filii uictoria,[103] cum ingenti leticia ei procedit obuius. Et in amplexus eius diutissime commoratus, conceptum [4^v][104] interius de filii sui palma gaudium tegere non uolens[105] set nec ualens, huius cum lacrimis exultacionis prorupit in uocem: 'Euge fili[106] dulcissime, quo affectu, quaue mentis leticia, laudes tuas prout dignum est prosequar. Tu enim es spes mea et subditorum[107] iubilus ex insperato, et exultacio. In te spes inopinata meis reuixit temporibus. In sinu tuo, leticia mea, immo spes pocius tocius regni est reposita. Tu populi tocius firmamentum. Tu pacis et libertatis mee basis et stabile, deo aspirante, fundamentum. Tibi debetur ruina poterui proditoris illius, quondam publici hostis nostri, qui regni fastigium quod mihi et de genere meo propagatis[108] iure debetur hereditario, tam impudenter quam imprudenter, contra leges et ius gentium usurpare moliebatur. Set uultus domini super eum et complices suos facientes mala, ut perderet de terra memoriam eorum, Deus ulcionum Dominus dissipauit consilium ipsius. Ipsum quoque Riganum in superbia rigentem, et immitem Mitunnum commilitonem ipsius, cum excercitu eorum proiecit in flumen rapacissimum. Descendunt quasi plumbum in aquis uehementibus. Deuorauit gladius tuus hostes nostros fulminans et cruentatus, hostili sanguine magnifice inebriatus.

---

[97] C 'planicies,' corrected from 'planies.' V congessit. Ita ut circumcacentis campi planicie locus sepulture eorum non opus nature, set magis opus hominis possit discerni. Deletis...

[98] C blodifeld. Similarly vernacular forms, cf. Smith, *English Place-Name Elements*, I, pp. 39, 166-68, II, pp. 239-42.

[99] V congessit etc.

[100] V hostibus suis, Offa.

[101] V Pater uero Offe in locis tucioribus.

[102] V comperiens tam securus et de filii uictoria cuius.

[103] N 'Gloria triumphi,' marginal rubric.

[104] Illustration: Entombment of the war-dead from the battle of Mount Slaughter whom Offa I mourned; the bodies shrouded, whilst a cleric standing by holds a separated head (believed to contain the spirit, see p. 96, n. 476). Nearby, a woman weeps and an attendant tears his hair (Fig. 16).

[105] V cogere non ualens.

[106] V filii.

[107] V subditorum meorum, tu salus regni, tu fortitudo mea et populi mei, tibi debetur ruina proterui illius quondam hostis nostri qui regni fastigium quo michi et de genere meo propagans ('-gatis' interlined) hereditario uire debetur inpudenter et inuercundie contra leges et ius gentium usurpare moliebatur. Set uisitauit dominus super se. Idcirco uicto eius indicio dexterea rita triumphante sepultis in inferno recipit igitur. Luctum.

[108] V propagatis hereditario iure debetur inpudenter et inuercundie contra leges.

Mount Slaughter,[109] that is to say, because of the massacre and burial of the dead. And on the eminence Offa's army, directed by loudly shouted orders, heaped a pile of many huge stones over them. The whole surrounding plain got its name and indelible title from this most gory battle and remarkable burial. And it was known as Bloody Wold from the blood of those who had died there.

So, the enemy[110] being wiped out and thrown into confusion, Offa returned home in great triumph and rejoicing and glory.

Indeed his father Wermund, who had hidden in safer places[111] awaiting the outcome of the affair, but now informed of the good news and learning about and reassured of the victory of his most dear son,[112] went to meet him with great satisfaction.[113] And he lingered for a long time in his embrace,[114] neither willing nor able[115] to conceal the delight he felt in his heart about the honour of his son; with tears of joy on his behalf, he burst out: 'Well done, my sweetest son! With what love, or contentment of mind, can I continue to praise you worthily enough? For surprisingly and delightfully you are my hope, and the joy of my subjects. In you, unexpected hope has revived in my times. In your breast rests my contentment – but more, in fact the hope of the whole kingdom. You, the people's whole bulwark. You, please God, the base and firm foundation of my peace and liberty. To you is owed the ruin of that bold traitor, our former public enemy,[116] who tried to usurp, against the laws and the custom of the people – as much impudently as imprudently[117] – the peak of the kingdom, which is owed to me and my family's offspring by hereditary right. But, the face of the Lord being against him and his henchmen engaged in evil, God the Lord of vengeance destroyed his schemes so that He might obliterate their memory from the earth. He threw that same Rigan, rigid with pride, and rough Mittun, his comrade-in-arms, with their armies into the most rapacious flood. They went down like lead into the turbulent waters. Your flashing

---

[109] Old English *cwealm-hylle*, must have been a common enough place-name, given that a local high point will frequently have been the place where retreat and final stand is made when the going is bad – and where the bodies will remain. *N*'s marginal variant Qualm-weld ('-upland') is presumably interpretative. Cf. Qualmestowe as 'place of execution'; perhaps supposed to have been Swamstey Common, high ground a dozen miles NE of St Albans, across which a major Roman road ran (J.E.B. Gover *et al.*, *The Place-Names of Hertfordshire*, English Place-Name Society, 15, Cambridge, 1938, p. 156). For royal jurisdiction over all such places: *omnes herestrete, omnia qualstowa* and *occidendorum loca*, see *Ancient Laws and Institutes of England*, ed. B. Thorpe, Rolls Series, 28, London, 1840, I, pp. 518-19.

[110] *V* his enemies.

[111] *V* Indeed, Offa's father in safer places.

[112] *V* so, reassured also about the victory of his son.

[113] *N* 'the glory of triumph' marginal rubric.

[114] *V* and in the embraces of his son.

[115] *V* unable to force.

[116] *V* of my subjects, you are the saviour of the kingdom, you are the strength of myself and of my people, to you is owed the fall of that ambitious man, our one-time enemy, who strove to usurp the pinnacle of the kingdom, which to me and to offspring of my stock is owed by hereditary right, strove impertinently and angrily to usurp against the laws and customs of the people. But the Lord visited him. On this matter his proof having been overcome, his right hand successfully triumphing, he received them into tombs in hell. Grief.

[117] *V* he impudently and ambitiously.

Non degener es fili mi genealis, set patrissans, patrum tuorum uestigia sequeris magnificorum. Sepultus in inferno noster hostis et aduersarius, fructus uiarum suarum condignos iam colligit, quos uiuus promerebatur. Luctum et miseriam quam senectuti mee malignus ille inferre disposuerat, uersa [118] uice, clementia diuina conuertit in tripuduum.[119] Quamobrem in presenti accipe, quod[120] tuis meritis exigentibus debetur, eciam si filius meus non esses, et si michi iure hereditario non succederes. Ecce iam cedo, et regnum Anglorum[121] uoluntatis tue arbitrio deinceps committo. Etas enim mea fragilis et iam decrepita, regni ceptrum ulterius sustinere non sufficit. Iccirco te fili desideratissime, [122] uicem meam supplere te conuenit, et corpus meum senio [123] confectum, donec morientis oculos clauseris, quietitradere liberiori. Vt a curis et secularibus sollicitudinibus, quibus discerpor liberatus, precibus uacem et contemplacioni. Armis hucusque materialibus dimicaui, restat ut de cetero uita mea que superest, militia sit super terram contra hostes spirituales. Ego uero pro incolumitate tua et regni statu, quod strenuitati ue, O anime mee dimidium, iam commisi, preces quales mea scis simiplicitas et potest imbecillitas, Deo fundam indefessas. Set quia[124] tempus perbreue amodo michi restat, et corpori meo solum superest sepulchrum, aurem benignam meis accomoda salutaribus consiliis, et cor credulum meis monitis inclina magnificis. tibi commendo,[125] diligendos, honorandos, promouendos. Verum ipsos qui nobiscum contra hostes publicos, Riganum uidelicet et Mitunnum [5ʳ][126] et eorum complices emulos nostros, fideliter steterunt, et periculoso discrimini pro nobis se opposuerunt, paterno amore. Eos autem qui decrepite senecutis mee menbra debilia contemptui habere ausi sunt,[127] asserentes uerba mea et regalia precepta esse senilia deliramenta, presumentes temere, apice regali me priuato te exheredare, suspectos habe et contemptibiles, si qui sint elapsi ab hoc bello, et a tuo gladio deuorante, eciam cum eorum posteritate, ne cum in ramusculos uirus pullulet, a radice, aliquid consimile tibi generetur in posterum. Non enim recolo me talem eorum promeruisse, qui me et te filium meum gratis oderunt, persecucionem.

---

[118] *V* gaudium.
[119] *V* conuersa.
[120] *V* quod tibi tuis.
[121] *V* Angligeruarum.
[122] *V* dilectissime.
[123] *V* senio fessum conquesticium.
[124] *V* qui ipse.
[125] *V* sepulchrum eos qui ceci que hostes et emulum tuit discemini se obiicentes te cum in bello stare ausi proximi amoris affectu tibi commendo.
[126] Illustration, unfinished without framework: King Wermund embraces his returning triumphant son Offa I, whose succession is indicated by Wermund pointing to his own crown. Homage is done to the young man; his heraldic shield is displayed on the wall behind (Fig. 17).
[127] *V* sunt omni tempori uite tue suspectos habeat, ne qui simile in ipsis inuentas silque et eos qui intera et inhonesta regni finibus etti sum inopere reuocare studeat, et in obsequio tuo ut familiares et amicos excipias laus industrie.

sword, blood-stained, magnificently soaked with enemy gore, devoured our enemies.[128] Son of my family, you are not degenerate but, taking after your ancestors, follow in the footsteps of your magnificent fathers.[129] Buried in hell, our enemy and adversary has now collected the fruit, deserved by his ways, which he earned when alive. The grief and misery which that pest had intended to bring me in old age is, on the contrary,[130] turned into rejoicing[131] by divine mercy. Wherefore, accept today what is yours,[132] because your merits would deserve it even if you were not my son, and were not to succeed me by right of inheritance. Behold, I now abdicate, and commit the kingdom of the English henceforth to the judgement of your will; for my fragile old age – and I am now decrepit – is no longer adequate to bear the sceptre of the kingdom. And so, most needed son,[133] it is proper that you should replace me, and that I should consign my body, worn out with old age,[134] to a freer life of quiet until you close my eyes in death. Thus I may have leisure for prayer and contemplation, free from the worldly cares and concerns by which I am torn to pieces. Up to now I have fought with material weapons; let it be that, for the remnant of my life that remains, my warfare on earth may be against spiritual enemies. Oh, one half of my soul I will pour out to God in unwearied prayers – such as you know my simplicity and weakness to be capable – for your safety and for the state of the kingdom which I have already entrusted to your valour. But because[135] henceforth only a very short time remains to me, and only the grave is left for my body, lend a kindly ear to my wholesome counsels and incline a believing heart to my great advice. Indeed, I recommend to you with fatherly love, esteem, honour and advancement for those who have loyally stood firm with us against our public enemies (that is to say our rivals Rigan and Mittun and their henchmen) who risked themselves on our behalf in a dangerous crisis.[136] However, you should hold as suspects and contemptibles those who dared to hold in contempt the weak limbs of my worn-out old age,[137] asserting my words and royal commands to be senile craziness, rashly taking it on themselves having stripped me of my royal rank to disinherit you. If there are any who have escaped from this war and your devouring sword – or among their posterity – do not let the virus spring up again like sprouts from the root, or something similar may happen to you in the future. I do not remember deserving such persecution from them, who have for no reason hated me and you my son.

---

[128] The notion of a devouring sword, drunk with the blood of enemies is familiar from many cultures including the Bible. Cf. Jeremiah II.30, XII.12, XLVI.10.

[129] For genealogy see Fig. 6, Appendix A, pp. 133-4.

[130] *V* quite the opposite.

[131] *V* delight.

[132] *V* what to you and yours.

[133] *V* most beloved son.

[134] *V* tired and overcome with old age.

[135] *V* who himself.

[136] *V* a tomb I recommend to you with the affection of love... those who fell, even although enemies,... who dared to stand in battle...

[137] *V* let them all be held suspect for all your life-time lest there be found those like them... and let there be trouble taken to recall those who... wrongful deeds... from the ends of the kingdom... you must receive into your allegiance those close to you and your friends with praiseworthy action.

Fig. 14) The disabled Prince Offa I is seated at the feet of the elderly enthroned King Wermund, who laments that he is without decent heir, and to the right is nagged by the rebellious Rigan.

MS Cotton Nero D I, f. 2ʳ © The British Library Board. All Rights Reserved.

Fig. 15) Prince Offa I, praying for deliverance from from his disability, is relieved by the hand of God and presents himself to the enthroned King Wermund. Rigan and the rebels depart.

MS Cotton Nero D i, f. 2ᵛ © The British Library Board. All Rights Reserved.

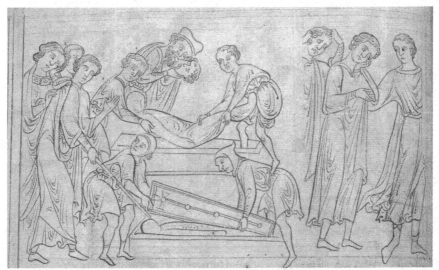

Fig. 16) Entombment of the war-dead from the battle of Mount Slaughter whom Offa I mourned; the bodies shrouded, whilst a cleric standing by holds a separated head. Nearby, a woman weeps and an attendant tears his hair. MS Cotton Nero D i, f. 4ᵛ © The British Library Board. All Rights Reserved.

Fig. 17) King Wermund embraces his returning triumphant son Offa I, whose succession is indicated by Wermund pointing to his own crown. Homage is done to the young man; his heraldic shield is displayed on the wall behind. MS Cotton Nero D i, f. 5ʳ © The British Library Board. All Rights Reserved.

Similiter eos, quos dicti proditores pro eo quod nobis fideliter adheserant, exulare coegerunt, uel qui impotentes rabiem eorum fugiendo resistere, ad horam declinauerunt, cum omni mansuetudine studeas reuocare, et honores eorum cum possessionibus ex innata tibi regali munificentia, gracius ampliare. Laus industrie tue et fame preconia, [138] et strenuitatis tue titulus, que adolescenciam tuam diuinitus illustrarunt, in posterum de te maiora promittunt. Desideranti [139] animo sicienter affecto, ipsumque Deum, qui te tibi, sua mera gracia reddidit et restaurauit, deprecor affectuose, ut has iuuentutis tue primicias, hoc inopinato triumpho subaratas, melior semper ac splendidior operum gloria subsequatur.[140] Et procul dubio post mortem meam, que non longe abest, iubente Domino, fame tue magnitudo, per orbem uniuersum dilatabitur, et felix suscipiet incrementum. Et que Deo placita sunt, opere felici consumabis, que diuinitus prosperabuntur.'

Hec autem filius deuotus et mansuetus, licet magnificus triumphator exaudisset et intenta aure intellexisset, flexis genibus et iunctis manibus, et exundantibus oculis, patri suo grates[141] rettulit accumulatas.

Rex itaque per fines Anglie[142] missis nunciis expeditissimis, qui mandata regia detulerunt, tocius dicionis sue conuocat nobilitatem. Que conuocata ex regis precepto, et persuasione, Offano filio suo unigenito ligiam fecerunt fidelitatem et homagium in patris presencia. Quod et omnes, animo uolenti, immo gaudenti, communiter perfecerunt.

Rex igitur quem pocius prona uoluntas, quam uigor prouexit corporalis, per climata regni sui proficiscitur securus et letabundus, nullo contradicente uel impediente, ut regni municiones et uarias possessiones, diu per inimicos suos alienatas et iniuste ac uiolenter possessas, ad sue dicionis reacciperet iure potestatem. Que omnia sibi sunt sine difficultate uel more dispendio restituta. Statimque pater filium, eorum possessionibus corporaliter inuestiuit, et paterno contulit affectu ac gratuito, proceribus congauden [5ᵛ][143] tibus super hoc uniuersis.

Post hec autem, Rex filio suo Offano erarium suum adaperiens, aurum suum et argentum, uasa concupiscibilia, gemmas, oloserica omnia, sue subdidit potestati. Sicque subactis et subtractis hostibus cunctis, aliquandiu per uniuersum regnum uiguit pax et securitas diu desiderabilis.[144]

---

[138] *V* preconia, qui in etate puerili tibi contigerunt, in posterum.

[139] *V* Idcirco magno opere desidero ut has iuuentutis.

[140] *V* prosequatur.

[141] *C* gracias.

[142] *V* Anglie cum filio suo secure, et nullo modo qui dicente perficisitur ut regni municiones qua dominio et potate sua pius recesserant iterum reciperent, et sine mora sibi restita sunt. Sique.

[143] Illustration: The seated King Wermund, dying, transfers his treasury to Prince Offa I, and is buried. Seated and smiling, King Offa I is crowned and annointed by flanking bishops.

[144] *V* securitas magna. Set et rex conuictui filii sui et presentia delectatus abosquto tempore uite sue inetas distulit per inestimabili gaudio et leticie magnitudine. Tandem defficiente natura fortis humane decessit, et discedens filio suo apicem pacatum et qui etuius reliquit, Offa uero prout patuit fuius obsequiat apparatu regio magnifice completas in loco regni sui celeberimo et nominacissimo honore regibus condigno in eminenciori ecclesia penes.

Similarly take care to call back with all benevolence those whom, because of their adherence to our cause, the aforesaid traitors forced into exile, or those who were unable to resist the temptation to flee and on the spur of the moment turned away. And with the natural, regal benevolence that is yours, graciously increase their standing with properties. The praise of your actions, the proclamation of your honour and the fame of your valour, divine embellishments of your youth,[145] promise greater things of you in the future. With a soul full of need[146] and longing emotion from the depths of my heart, I pray, I beseech God himself who returned and restored you to yourself by His grace alone, that better and more splendid, glorious feats may always follow these first-fruits of your early manhood that were harvested in[147] this unexpected victory. And without doubt after my death, which is not far off, the greatness of your fame will be spread throughout the whole world, the Lord willing, and receive happy increase. And you will happily achieve works pleasing to God, which will succeed with divine help.'

However, despite being a great champion, when the devoted and good-natured son had listened to these things closely and understood, he knelt and joined his hands and, eyes streaming, gave enormous thanks to his father.

And so the king[148] sent very swift messengers who carried the royal instruction to all the borders of the English land – summoned the nobility of his entire domain. These, summoned together at the king's command and direction, made liege fealty and homage to Offa, his only son, in his father's presence.[149] And they all did so together with willing spirit – in fact delightedly.

Therefore the king, borne less by strength of body than by a ready will, travelled safely and happily through the different regions of his domain, challenged or impeded by no one, to reclaim his rightful rule over the kingdom's fortifications and various properties that had long been taken over by his enemies unjustly and with force. All of which were restored to him without difficulty or waste. Immediately the father invested the son bodily with their possession, giving them freely with fatherly emotion, and all the leading men rejoiced with them about this.

And after this, opening his coffers, the king made over to his son Offa his gold and silver, valuable accoutrements, jewels and all silk robes.[150] And so with enemies altogether subjected or removed, the peace and security so long needed flourished throughout the whole kingdom briefly.[151]

---

[145] *V* fame, which you possessed as a child, in future.

[146] *V* on this matter I greatly wish that these things of your youth.

[147] Literally 'ploughed close to'.

[148] *V* Safely with his son, and without gainsaying of any kind, he set out piously for England so that the fortifications which had been lost to the kingdom and to the dominion and had receded from its power, they now took back again, and without delay they were restored to himself.

[149] Compare the act of Offa II with his son Ecgfrith at the Council of Chelsea in 787, pp. 101-2, Introduction, p. xcii.

[150] Silk items, imported from the Far East via Araby, were sufficiently valuable to be considered a fine gift from Charlemagne (pp. 77-8), or simply signalled out for comment (pp. 91-2). The fullest examination of such vesture remains *The Relics of St Cuthbert*, ed. C.F. Battiscombe, Durham, 1956, pp. 9-14, 375-539, plates xxiv-lv.

[151] *V* great security. But the king had his son for companionship and presents the delight... and in... time the measures of his life extended through unspeakable joy and great happiness. Eventually nature having failed this

Rex igitur filii sui prosperitate gauisus, qui eciam diatim de bono in melius gradatim ascendit, aliquo tempore uite sue metas distulit naturales. Iubilus quoque in corde senis conceptus, languores seniles plurimum mitigauit. Tandem Rex plenus dierum, cum benediccione omnium, qui ipsum eciam a romotis partibus per famam congnouerunt, nature debita persoluens, decessit. Et decedens, filio suo apicem regni sui pacatum et quietum reliquit, Offanus autem oculos patris sui pie claudens, lamentaciones mensurnas cum magnis eiulatibus, lacrimis et specialibus planctibus, prout moris tunc erat principibus magnificis, lugubriter pro tanto funere continuauit. Obsequiisque cum exequiis, magnifice tam in ecclesia quam in locis forinsecis conpletis, apparatu regio et loco celeberrimo et nominatissimo, regibus condigno, uidelicet in eminenciori ecclesia penes Glouerniam urbem[152] egregiam, eidem exhiberi iubet sepulturam.[153]

Offanus autem cum moribus omnibus foret redimitus, elegans corpora, armis strenuus, munificus et benignus, post obitum patris sui magnifici Warmandi, cuius mores tractatus exigit speciales, plenarie omium principum Regni dominium suscipit, et debitum cum omni deuocione, et mera uoluntate, famulatum. Cum igitur cuiusdam solempnitatis arrideret serenitas, Offanus cum sollempni tripudio, omnibus applaudentibus, et faustum omen acclamantibus, Anglie diademate feliciter est insignitus. Adquiescens igitur seniorum consiliis et sapientum persuasionibus, cepit tocius regni habenas[154] irreprehensibiliter, immo laudabiliter, habenas modernanter et sapienter gubernare.

Sic igitur subactis hostibus regni uniuersis, uiguit pax secura et firmata in finibus Anglorum, per tempora longa, precipue tamen per spacium temporis quinquennale. Erat autem iam triginta quatuor annos etatis attingens, annis prospere pubescentibus. Et cum Rex, more iuuenili, uenatus gracia per nemora frequenter, cum suis ad hoc conuocatis uenatoribus et canibus sagacibus, expeditus peragrasset, contigit die quadam quod aere turbato, longe a suorum caterua semotus, solus per nemoris opaca penitus ipsorum locorum, necnon et fortune ignarus, casu deambulabat. Dum autem sic per ignota diuerticula incaucius oberraret, et per inuia,[155] uocem lacrimabilem et miserabiliter querulam haut longe a se audiuit. Cuius sonitum secutus, inter densos

---

strong mortal, he died, and dying he handed on the crown in a peaceful and quiet state; and Offa prepared for his father funeral rights magnificently completed with royal pomp in the most famous and noted place of his kingdom, worthy of kings, in the centre of the most important church.

[152] *V* Gloucestriani.

[153] *V* penes Gl. egregiam eidem exhiberi iubet sepulturam prout obitum patris cuius subdius suis sibi fidelite obligans et afirmato inmanu impius regno securitatem undique ab hostibus suis nactus dictus est Offa uenatoria delectari. Quem ille iuuenilli more exitens, die quodam longe remotus a suorum catemia solus pre nemoris opata loci penitus ignarus fortune deambulabat. Dum autem sic aberaret preuicia contigit ut uxorem lacrimabilem...

[154] *C* 'habenus' deleted.

[155] *V* inuia contigit ut uocem.

And so the king rejoiced in his son's success; day by day he went from good to better, and for some time protracted the natural limits of his life. A joyful thought in the heart of an old man greatly soothes the weariness of old age. Eventually the king reached the end of his days, with the blessing of all – even those in remote parts who knew him only by repute. Paying the debt to nature, he passed away. And, passing away, he left his son the crown of his kingdom in peace and quietness. But Offa, devoutly closing his father's eyes, continued deep mourning in honour of so great a death with great lamentation, weeping and special obsequies for a month, as was then the custom for great leaders. When the funeral rites and procedures had been completed, as magnificently in church as in places outside, he ordered that the burial be displayed, with royal trappings,[156] in a very famous and well-known place, worthy of kings, that is to say in the main church in the centre of Gloucester, a major city.[157]

Now, after the death of his great father Wermund, Offa was winning favour in every way, becoming handsome of body, active in arms,[158] generous and kind. Management of the chief men of the kingdom demanded special skills; he took full responsibility for them, taking on this duty with all devotion, and this service with a pure will. And so, in the peace of a formal holiday, with formal ceremonies and general plaudits, everybody crying out that it promised well for the future, Offa was happily ordained with the diadem of England. And so, acting on the counsel of elders and advice of the wise, he began to take in hand the whole kingdom irreproachably in an up-to-date and wise way, in fact to govern excellently.

And so all the enemies of the kingdom had been vanquished, and secure and stable peace flourished within the borders of the English for a long time, but notably for a period of five years. However, he was now approaching thirty-four years of age, the peak of his marriageable years. And when the king, in the manner of young men, often summoned his huntsmen and hounds and rode freely through the glades to hunt, it happened one day that there was a storm, and by chance he was roaming completely by himself deep in the shady glades of the woods of that place, entirely unaware of what would happen. But whilst he was walking like this through unfamiliar places, off his guard, he found that he had wandered away from the path, and on the way he heard a voice not far away from him sobbing and wretchedly lamenting. Having followed this sound, he unexpectedly found among dense fruit trees[159] a maiden of

---

[156] Apparently imagining the kind of three-dimensional recumbent stone effigy provided for secular rulers from the twelfth century onwards and found in the majority of significant church buildings.

[157] With respect to the death of his father to whom he was obedient he was faithfully obliging to his men and to himself; and the kingdom having been affirmed in his hand and having achieved although inexperienced security on all sides from his enemies, Offa was said to delight in hunting. Which, going out to do in the manner of a young man, one day he was far removed from his band and was walking alone in the groves deep in the shady glades of the place, ignorant of his fortune. However whilst thus he wandered about, in his path it happened that a damsel in distress...

[158] As reflected in the skeletal remains, those of the strongest physique belonged to the wealthier, better-fed members of the community, naturally taller, capable of the powerful over-shoulder slashing stroke – the poets' *sweord-geswing* or *sweord-slege* – for which the Anglo-Saxon sword was intended.

[159] *V* among thorn bushes and dense low fruit trees.

frutices [160] [6^r] [161] uirginem singularis forme et regii apparatus, set decore uenustissimam,[162] ex insperato repperit. Rex uero, rei euentum[163] admirans, que ibi ageret, et querele causas blande alloquens, cepit sciscitari.[164] Que ex imo pectoris flebilia[165] trahens suspiria, regi respondit. Nequaquam in auctorem set in seipsam reatum retorquens 'Peccatis meis' inquit[166] 'exigentibus infortunii huius calamitas michi accidit.' Erat autem reguli cuiusdam filia qui Eboracensibus preerat. Huius incomparabilis pulchritudinis singularem eminentiam[167] pater admirans, amatorio demone seductus, cepit[168] eam incestu libidinoso concupiscere, et ad amorem illicitum sepe sollicitare ipsam puellam, minis, pollicitis, blanditiis, atque muneribus adolescentule temptans emollire constantiam. Illa autem operi nephario nullatenus adquiescens,[169] cum pater tamen[170] minas minis exaggeraret, et promissa promissis accumularet, munera muneribus adaugeret, iuxta illud poeticum:

imperium, promissa, preces, confudit in unum,[171]

elegit magis incidere in manus hominum,[172] et eciam ferarum qualiumcunque, uel gladii subire sententiam, quam Dei offensam [173] incurrere, pro tam graui culpa manifestam. Pater itaque ipsam [174] sibi parere constanter renuentem, euocatis quibusdam maligne mentis hominibus quos ad hoc elegerat, precepit eam in desertum, solitudinis remote duci, uel pocius trahi, et crudelissima morte condempnatam, bestiis ibidem derelinqui. Qui[175] cum in locum[176] horroris et uaste solitudinis peruenissent, trahentes eam seductores illi, Deo ut creditur inspirante, miserti pulchritudini[177] illius, eam ibidem sine[178] trucidacione et membrorum mutilacione, uiuam, set tamen sine aliquorum uictualium alimento, exceptis talibus qui de radicibus et frondibus uel herbis colligi, urgente ultima fame, possunt, dimiserunt.

---

[160] *V* inter uepres et frutices densos simos.

[161] Illustration, the folio repaired prior to drawing: A mounted King Offa I encounters in the forest a damsel in distress (Thryth, daughter of the king of Northumbria) her dress washed light red, and subsequently, standing, he places her in the care of his court (Fig. 18).

[162] *V* uestitam.

[163] *V* aduentum.

[164] *V* blande cepit eam alloquens.

[165] *V* alta.

[166] *V* inquit meis.

[167] *V* pulchritudinis decorem pater amatorio.

[168] *V* cepit qui naturam concupiscere.

[169] *V* probens assensum.

[170] *V* tamen acupilcencia sua excercatus minas et perorutera intenderet, elegit magis.

[171] Ovid, *Metamorphoses*, IV, 472, ed. F.J. Miller, London, 1916, II, pp. 210-11.

[172] *N* 'hominum' inserted from margin.

[173] *V* indicium.

[174] *V* eam.

[175] *V* Que.

[176] *V* locum remotissime uastitatis educeretur seductores illi.

[177] *C* pulcritudinis.

[178] *V* sine periculo mortis ac membrorum determento uiuo dimiserunt.

matchless looks and regal bearing, and extremely beautifully adorned.[179] Well, the king, wondering how this had happened,[180] began to speak, gently enquiring what she was doing there, and the reasons for her grief. Heaving a doleful[181] sigh from the breast, she replied to the king. Putting the blame not on the perpetrator but on herself, she said 'My sins have brought the calamity of this misfortune upon me.' She was the daughter of a certain prince who ruled over the people of York. Her father, admiring the outstanding quality of her unique beauty[182] and deceived by the demon of love, began to lust after her with incestuous lechery,[183] and frequently to persuade the girl to unlawful lovemaking with threats, assurances, sweet words and gifts, trying to wear down her virtue like an importunate youth. But she would no way acquiesce[184] to this heinous deed and, when her father piled threat upon threat, supplemented promise with promise, added gifts upon gifts, just as in the poem:

> poured out power, promises, entreaties as one,[185]

she chose to fall into the hands of men, or even beasts of any kind, or to suffer the sentence of sword rather than commit an offence[186] to God which was so obviously a grave sin.[187] And so, as she constantly refused to obey him, her father summoned certain men of malignant mind whom he had chosen for this, and commanded her to be taken, or rather to be dragged, to a remote, isolated wilderness and condemned to a most cruel death, left there to the wild beasts. Those deceivers dragged her along, and when they had reached a horrifying and completely deserted spot,[188] taking pity on her beauty, apparently inspired by God, they left her there alive, without butchery or mutilation of her limbs, but nevertheless without the sustenance of any kind of food against final starvation, except such as could be collected from roots, leaves and plants.

[179] *V* beautifully clothed.

[180] *V* come about.

[181] *V* deep.

[182] *V* loveliness.

[183] *V* began to desire she who was related. A familiar 'romance' situation, cf. Introduction, pp. lxxvi-lxxviii.

[184] *V* show assent.

[185] A line quoted commonly by Matthew Paris among others, cf. *Chronica Majora*, ed. H.R. Luard, Rolls Series, 57, London, 1872-83, IV, pp. 61, 122, V, p. 55.

[186] *V* 'indicium' cause for confession.

[187] Marriage or any sexual act with a near relative was strictly forbidden in the Bible. Leviticus XVIII.6-18, XX.10-21.

[188] *V* to be led to a place of very remote vastness, those seducers.

Cum hac rex aliquandiu habens sermonem,[189] comitem itineris sui illam habuit, donec solitarii cuiusdam habitacionem reperissent. Vbi nocte superueniente quiescentes pernoctauerunt. In crastinum autem solitarius ille[190] uiarium et semitarum peritus, regem cum comite sua, usque ad fines domesticos, et loca regi non ingnota[191] conduxit. Ad suos itaque rex rediens, desolate illius quam nuper inuenerat curam gerens familiaribus et domesticis generis sui sub diligenti custodia commisit.[192]

Post hec aliquot annis elapsis, cum rex celibem agens uitam, mente castus et corpore perseueraret,[193] proceres dicionis sue, non solum de tunc presenti, set de futuro sibi[194] periculo precauentes, et nimirum multum solliciti, dominum suum de uxore ducenda unanimiter conuenerunt, ne sibi et regno successorem et heredem non habens, post obitum ipsius iminens periculum generaret.[195]

Etatis enim iuuenilis pubertas, morum maturitas, et urgens regni necessitas, necnon et honoris dignitas, itidem postularunt. [6ᵛ][196] Et cum super hoc negocio, sepius regem sollicitarentur, et[197] alloquerentur, ipse multociens ioculando, et talia uerba asserendo interludia fuisse uanitatis, procerum suorum constantiam [198] dissimulando differendoque delusit. Quod quidam aduertentes, communicato cum aliis consilio, regem ad nubendum incuntabiliter urgere ceperunt.

Rex uero more optimi principis, cuius primordia iam bene subarrauerat, nolens uoluntati magnatum suorum resistere, diu secum de thori socia, libra profunde rationis, studiose cepit deliberare.[199] Cumque hoc in mente sua solliciensis[200] tractaret, uenit forte in mentem suam illius iuuencule memoria, quam dudum inter uenandum inuenit, uagabundam solam, feris et predonibus miserabiliter expositam, quam ad tuciora ducens, familiaribus generis sui commiserat alendam, ac carius custodiendam. Que, ut rex audiuit, moribus laudabiliter redimita, decoris existens expectabilis, omnibus sibi cognitis amabilem exhibuit et laudabilem.

Hec igitur sola, relictis multis,[201] eciam regalis stematis sibi oblatis, complacuit, illamque solam in matrimonium sibi adoptauit. Cum autem eam duxisset in uxorem, non interueniente multa mora, elegantissime forme utriusque sexus liberos ex eadem procreauit. Itaque cum prius esset rex propria seueritate subditis suis formidabilis,

[189] *V* sermonens.
[190] *V* ille ne moris et uixarum.
[191] *C* ignota. *V* incognita.
[192] *V* custodia eam commisit.
[193] *V* persouaret.
[194] *V* non solum inpresenti set de infuturo sibi pariter et regno solliciti.
[195] *V* immineret.
[196] Illustration, the folio repaired prior to drawing: A standing Offa I is betrothed to Thryth, placing a ring on her finger. Seated, he receives a request from the King of Northumbria.
[197] *V* et illi serio alloquerentur, ipse tamen multociens occulare uanitatis uerbis.
[198] *V* instantiam.
[199] *V* Quorum uoluntati resistere nolens diu secum de thori sui socia deliberarit.
[200] *V* ducius. *V* summarises the remainder of this paragraph, the opening sentence of the next and concludes at that point.
[201] *V* multis, regi placuit. Hanc solam.

Having talked to her for some time, the king took her as his travelling companion until they found the dwelling of a certain hermit. There, with night arriving, they rested and spent the night. The next day however, the solitary, who knew all the roads and paths well,[202] conducted the king and his companion right up to his own boundary, and places not unknown to the king. And so, returning home, the king handed her over to members of his household and his family servants, desolately assigning to their diligent attention the care of her whom he had recently found.

Some time later, when a few years had passed, the king was leading a celibate life, persevering chaste in mind and body, the leading men of his domain realised not only the present risk, but the danger to themselves in the future.[203] And in fact with many concerns, they all had a meeting together with their lord to discuss his marriage, inasmuch as his lack of successor and heir to himself and the kingdom after his death presented a threatening danger.[204]

Indeed, everything argued the same way: it was a young man of marriageable age, mature in behaviour, and the needs of the kingdom requiring it – and it was an honourable estate as well. They would frequently solicit and[205] exhort the king about this matter – he often declaring in an amused manner that such words were pleasantries. And he foiled the persistence[206] of his leading men by pretence and evasion. Noticing this, some of them having conferred with others, began to urge the king to marriage without delay.

In fact the king, in the manner of a very good leader who had practised self-discipline in his early years, not wishing to resist the will of his chief men, eventually began to discuss a bed partner carefully with them, in an open and serious way. And as he earnestly[207] turned this over in his mind, there came strongly into his mind that childhood memory of the damsel whom he had found long ago whilst hunting – a lonely waif, wretched prey to wild animals and brigands – and rescued and consigned to his own household to be fed and carefully looked after. Who, so the king heard, had proved her worth by her excellent conduct. Promising great beauty, she behaved in a lovable and excellent manner to all who knew her.

Well, she alone[208] pleased him more than all the others, even those of royal line offered him, and he chose just her in marriage. And when he had taken her as wife, without much delay he had lovely children of both sexes by her. And, although when initially king he inspired fear in his subjects by his severity, his chief men and indeed all his people were encouraged by the appearance of heirs and successors, which promised both confidence and contentment for the kingdom. And the king enjoyed

---

[202] *V* he least of the custom and hardly then.
[203] *V* concerned not only in the present but for their own future.
[204] *V* it would threaten.
[205] *V* and those men spoke to him in turn; however to hide the vanity in the words he often.
[206] *V* vehemence.
[207] *V* lengthily. *V* summarises the remainder of this paragraph, the opening of the next and ends at that point.
[208] *V* many, pleased the king. Her alone.

magnates eius, necnon et populus eius uniuersus, heredum et successorum apparentia animati, regni robur et leticiam geminarunt. Rex quoque ab uniuersis suis, et non solum prope positis, immo alienigenis et remotis, extitit honori, ueneracioni, ac dileccioni. Et cum inter se in Britannia, que tunc temporis in plurima regna multiphariam diuisa fuisset, reguli sibi finitimi hostiliter se impeterent, solus Rex Offa pace regni sui potitus feliciter, se sibique subditos in pace regebat, et libertate. Vnde et adiacencium prouinciarum reges, eius mendicabant auxilium, et in neccessitatis articulo, consilium. Rex itaque Northamhimbrorum, a barbara Scotorum gente, et eciam aliquibus suorum, grauiter et usque ferme ad internecionem percussus, et proprie defensionis auxilio destitutus, ad Offam regem potentem legatos destinat, et pacificum, supplicans, ut presidii eius solacio contra hostes suos roboretur, tali mediante condicione, ut Offe filiam sibi matrimonio copularet, et non se proprii regni, set Offam, primarium ac principem preferret, et se cum suis omnibus ipsi subiugaret. Nichil itaque dotis cum Offe filia rogitauit, hoc sane contentus premio, ut a regni sui finibus, barbaros illos potenter et frequenter experta fugaret strenuitate. Cum autem legatorum uerba rex Offa succepisset, consilio suorum fretus sup [7r][209] plicantis uoluntati ac precibus adquieuit, si tamen rex ille pactum huiusmodi, tactis sacrosanctis ewangeliis,[210] et obsidum tradicione, fideliter tenendum confirmaret.

Sic igitur Rex Offa, super hiis condicionibus sub certa forma confirmatus, et ad plenum certificatus, in partes illas cum equitum numerosa multitudine proficiscitur. Cum autem illuc peruenisset, timore eius consternata pars aduersa, cessit, fuge presidio se saluando. Quam tamen rex Offa audacter prosecutus, non prius destitit fugare fugientem donec eam ex integro contriuisset. Set nec eo contentus, ulterius progreditur, barbaros expugnaturus. Interea ad patriam suam nuncium imperitum destinauit, ad primates et precipuos regni sui, quibus tocius dicionis sue regimen commendauerat. Et literas regii sigilli sui munimine consingnatas, eidem nuncio commisit deferendas.

Qui autem destinatus fuit, iter arripiens uersus Offe regnum, ut casu accidit, inter eundum, hospitandi gracia aulam regiam introiuit illius regis, cuius filiam Offa sibi matrimonio copulauerat. Rex autem ille, cum de statu et causa itineris sui subdole requirendo cognouisset, uultus sui serenitate, animi uersuciam mentitus, specie tenus illum amantissime suscepit. Et uelamen sceleris sui querens, a conspectu publico, sub quodam dileccionis pretextu, ad regii thalami secreta penetralia ipsum nuncium nichil sinistri suspicantem introduxit, magnoque studio elaborauit, ut ipsum, uino estuanti madentem, redderet temulentum. Et ipso nuncio uel dormiente uel aliquo alio modo ignorante mandata domini sui regis Offe, tacitus ac subdolus apertis et explicatis literis perscrutabatur. Cepitque perniciose immutare et peruertere sub Offe nomine sigillum

---

[209] Illustration: Offa I in the front line of battle against the Northumbrian king's enemies lances their leading cavalryman, who is pulled away by a man-at-arms.
[210] C ewangelii.

honour, reverence and affection from all his people and not only those near to him, in fact, but in foreign and far off places. Although the princes on his borders kept attacking each other in a hostile manner in many places in Britain, which at that time had been divided into several kingdoms,[211] King Offa alone successfully achieved peace in his kingdom and reigned in peace and liberty over those subject to him. And so princes in adjacent provinces used to beg for his aid and his advice in an hour of need. Therefore the king of the Northumbrians, who was under serious attack by the barbarous Scottish people and also some of his own, to the point of being nearly wiped out and, totally lacking support from his own defendants, sent ambassadors to the powerful King Offa, beseeching him, the peacemaker, to relieve them with reinforcements against their enemies, with the following match to unite them that he might join with Offa's daughter in marriage and he would put no other kingdoms before, but hold Offa as his chief and prince and subject himself with all his people to him. And so he sought no dowry with Offa's daughter but was extremely satisfied with the prize that those barbarians be efficiently and frequently repelled from the borders of his kingdom, with proven strength. And, when King Offa received what the ambassadors said, he trusted in their advice and the wish of the supplicant and agreed to what they asked, on condition that the king, with his hand on the Holy Gospels, swear to faithfully keep such a pact and to hand over hostages.

And so, ready to keep these conditions according to the terms, and fully confident, King Offa set out for those regions with a very large mounted force. Then on his arrival, those coming to meet him were alarmed in fright of him, shied and gave way, whilst their escort fled. However, King Offa boldly pursued them, nor did he stop following as they fled until he had harried them anew. Nor was he satisfied with that, but went on further with the intention of attacking the barbarians. Meanwhile, he had sent an inexperienced messenger to his own country, to the men of first rank and noblemen of his kingdom to whom he had given charge of his whole domain. And he entrusted to the same messenger letters to be delivered, which he had signed and closed with his royal seal.

It happened by chance that the man who had been sent, broke his journey on the way to Offa's kingdom to ask for shelter, entering the royal court of that king whose daughter Offa had taken in marriage. So when that king had discovered the nature and cause of his journey, asking craftily – his face smiling but counterfeit in mind, he received him most warmly to all outward appearances. And, seeking to cloak his crime from open view, on some pretence of friendship, he took that messenger, who suspected nothing wrong, into the innermost part of the royal apartment and with great care ensured that he would be rendered drunk and sodden with intoxicating wine. And, with this messenger either sleeping or in some other way disregarding the instructions of his lord King Offa, he quietly and craftily opened and unfolded the letters and read them. And he took them and began to perniciously change and alter

---

[211] For the heptarchic situation at the time of the second Offa, here anticipated, see pp. 51-2, and Introduction, pp. xliii-xlv, Fig. 5.

adulterans, fallacesque et perniciosas literas loco inuentarum occultauit. Forma autem adulterinarum[212] hec est, que subscribitur[213]:

> Rex Offa,[214] maioribus et precipuis regni sui, salutis et prosperitatis augmentum. Vniuersitati uestre notum facio, in itinere quod arripui infortunia et aduersa plurima tam michi quam subditis meis accidisse, et maiores excercitus mei, non ignauia propria, uel hostium oppugnantium uirtute, set pocius peccatis nostris iusto Dei iudicio interisse. Ego autem instantis periculi causam pertractans. Et consciencie mee intima perscrutatus, in memetipso, nichil aliud conicio altissimo displicere, nisi quod perditam et maleficam illam absque meorum consensu uxorem imperito et infelici duxi matrimonio.
>
> Vt ergo de malefica memorata, uoluntati uestre ad plenum quam temere offendi satisfiat, asportetur cum liberis ex ea genitis ad loca deserta, hominibus incongnita, [7ᵛ][215] feris et auibus aut siluestribus predonibus frequentata. Vbi cum pueris suis puerpera, truncata manus et pedes, exemplo pereat inaudito.

Nuncius autem mane facto, uino quo maduerat digesto, compos iam sui effectus, discessit. Et post aliquot dies perueniens ad propria, magnatibus qui regno regis Offe preerant, literas domini sui sigillo signatas exposuit.

In quarum auditu perlecta mandati serie, in stuporem et uehementissimam admiracionem uniuersi, plus quam dici possit, rapiuntur. Et super hiis, aliquot diebus communicato cum magnatibas consilio deliberantes, periculosum ducebant[216] mandatis ac iussionibus, regiis non obtemperare. Misera igitur seducta, deducta est in remotissimum et inhabitabilem locum horroris et uaste solitudinis, cum qua eciam liberi eius miseri et miserabiles querali et uagientes, absque misericordia, ut cum ea traherentur occidendi, iudicium acceperunt. Nec mora, memorati apparitores matrem cum pignoribus suis in desertum uastissimum trahebant. Matri uero propter eius formam admirabilem parcentes, liberos eius, nec forme, nec sexui, etati uel condicioni parcentes, detruncarunt menbratim; immo pocius frustratim, crudeliter in bestialem feritatem seuientes. Completaque tam crudeli sentencia, cruenti apparitores ocius reuertuntur.

Nec mora, solitarius quidam uitam in omni sanctitate, uigiliis assiduis, ieiuniis crebris, et continuis orationibus, ducens heremiticam, circa noctis crepusculum eo pertransiens, mulieris cuiusdam luctus lacrimabiles et querelas usque ad intima cordis

---

[212] *C* adulterinarum literarum.
[213] *C* scribitur.
[214] *N* 'Epistola,' marginal rubric in a separate hand.
[215] Illustration: A standing Offa I despatches a courier, kneeling, to the Mercian court. Intercepted and now falsified, Offa I's letter is returned to the courier, who presents it to a shocked home court.
[216] *C* dicebant.

them, forging the seal in Offa's name, and secreted false and pernicious letters in place of those found.[217] But here written below is the form of the forgery:

'King Offa sends greetings and regards to the elders and princes of his kingdom. I wish to inform you all that, on the journey I made, many misfortunes and setbacks happened to me and my subordinates, and beset the leaders of my army, not because of their own cowardice or the strength of the opposing enemy, but rather by the righteous judgement of God because of our sins. However, I bear the blame for our immediate danger. And having thoroughly examined the depth of my conscience, I have realised that nothing else has displeased the Most High other than that, inexperienced and childless, I married that lost and evil woman without the agreement of my people.

So in order fully to make amends for the offence – however you like, but dishonourably – let the notorious evildoer with her offspring be taken to a wild place, unknown to men, the haunt of beasts, birds and outlaws. There let her perish together with the children she has mothered, with hands and feet cut off, an unheard of example.'

So the messenger, it being morning, now fully in control of himself, sober after the wine he had drunk, left. And after a few days arriving home, he showed the letters signed with his lord's seal to the noblemen who were in charge of Offa's kingdom.

They heard the series of instructions contained therein all rapt in astonishment and the most extreme amazement beyond description. And after that, discussing the message together for several days, the noblemen decided[218] it would be dangerous not to comply with the royal instructions and commands. Therefore the wretched woman was led away, taken to a most remote and uninhabitable place of horrors and enormous solitude; and her miserable wretches with her also, whining and crying, condemned to be handed over without mercy to be murdered with her. No delay but the notorious officers dragged the mother with her progeny into this most enormous wilderness. Sparing the mother because of her wonderful looks, but not sparing her children, on account of either looks or sex, state or condition, they tore them limb from limb; in fact, savaging cruelly with the ferocity of beasts, it was rather deceptive. And having carried out so cruel a sentence, the blood-stained officers rapidly returned.

Just then a certain solitary, who was leading a hermit's life in all sanctity – assiduous vigils, frequent fasts and continual prayers – walking through that place around the dusk of evening, heard the woman's tearful grief and – what went right to his heart and

---

[217] It was easy to scrape clean and write over the surface of the velum (dried animal skin) of manuscript documents, or to transfer wax seals; witness, for example, the comments in P.H. Sawyer, *Anglo-Saxon Charters: an Annotated List,* London, 1968, *passim.*

[218] *C* they said.

et ossuum[219] medullas penetratiuas, quas Dominus ex mortuorum corporibus licet laceratis elicuit, audiuit. Infantulorumque uagitus lugubres nimis, cum doloris ululatibus quasi in materno sinu audiendo similiter annotauit. Misericordia autem sanctus Dei motus, usque ad lacrimarum aduberem effusionem, quo ipsa uox ipsum uocabat, Domino ducente peruenit. Et cum illuc peruenisset, nec aliud quam corpora humana in frusta detruncata reperisset, congnouit in spiritu ipsa alicuius innocentis corpus, uel aliquorum innocentium corpuscula extitisse, que tam inhumanam sentenciam subierunt. Nec sine martirii palma, ipsos quorum hec fuerunt exuuie, ab hoc seculo[220] transmigrasse suspicabatur. Auxilium tamen pro Dei amore et caritatis intuitu postulatum non denegans, se pro illorum reparacione prostrauit in deuotissimam cum lacrimis oracionem, maxime propter uocem celitus emissam, quam profecto congnouit per Deum linguas cadauerum protulisse. Piis igitur sanctu commotus uisceribus, igneque succensus caritatis ex congnicione eius, quam, ut iam dictum, dudum uiderat, habuit, factus hilarior, pro ipsis [8r][221] flexis genibus, inundantibus oculis, iunctisque palmis orauit, dicens: 'Domine Jesu Christe, qui Lazarum quatriduanum ac fetidum resuscitasti. Immo qui omnium nostrorum corpora in extremo examine suscitabis, uestram oro misericordiam, ut non habens ad me peccatorem, set ad horum innocentum pressuras respectum piissimum, corpuscula hec iubeas resuscitari, ad laudem et gloriam tuam in sempiternum, ut omnes qui mortis horum causam et formam audierint, te glorificent Deum et Dominum mundi Saluatorem.'

Sic igitur sanctus iste, Domine,[222] de fidei sui[223] uirtute in Domino presumens et confidens, inter orandum, membra precisa recolligens, et sibi particulas adaptans et coniungens, et in quantum potuit redintegrans, in parcium quam plurimum, set in integritatem pocius delectatus, Domino rei consummacionem qui mortificat et uiuificat commendauit.

Coniuncta igitur corpora, signo crucis triumphali consignauit. Mira fidei uirtus et efficacia. Signo crucis uiuifice et orationis ac fidei serui Dei uirtute, non solum matris orbate animus reparatur, set et filiorum corpuscula, in pristinum et integrum nature sunt reformata decorem, necnon et anime mortuorum ad sua pristina domicilia sunt reuerse. Ad mansiuncule igitur sue septa, a qua elongatus fuerat, gracia lignorum ad pulmentaria dequoquenda colligendorum, ipse senex, qui prius detruncati fuerant, Domino iubente integri uiui et alacres sunt reuersi, ducem sanctum suum sequentes pedetentim. Vbi more patris, ipsam desolatam cum liberis sibi ipsis restitutis, alimentis

---

[219] C ossium.
[220] C ab seculo.
[221] Illustration: Queen Thryth is abandoned in the forest with bodies of her murdered children whilst a hermit kneels nearby and prays; the hand of God descending. Offa I and company return to his home court.
[222] If this apparently superfluous vocative does not maintain the previous 'dramatic' air, hereabouts perhaps it reflects circumstances of dictation in the scriptorium.
[223] C sue.

the marrow of his bones – lamentations which the Lord drew from the bodies of the dead even though torn apart. And he noticed the doleful whining of little children especially, whilst at the same time hearing sorrowful wailing as though from the mother's breast. But holy God was moved with pity, for he arrived, the Lord leading him, at the most copious outpouring of tears, in which the voice itself called him. And when he reached that place he found nothing but human bodies mindlessly dismembered and realised that these remains were the body of an innocent, or the little bodies of some innocents, who had suffered such an inhuman punishment. It could well be that those, of whom these were the remains, had not left this world without the palm of martyrdom.[224] So, for the love of God and out of charity, not refusing the help that was asked of him, in tears he prostrated himself in the most devout prayer for their recovery – above all because of the voice coming from heaven, which he truly knew had given the corpses tongue through God. Therefore the holy man, inwardly moved, and kindled with the fire of charity from his earlier-perceived insight as said already – felt happier, went down on his knees, eyes brimming, and clasping his hands together prayed, saying: 'Lord Jesus Christ, who brought Lazarus back to life after four days – and putrefaction,[225] in fact who will raise all our bodies at the Last Judgement,[226] I beseech your mercy that, regardless of me a sinner, should turn your loving gaze instead on the tortures done to these innocents; order these little bodies to live again, to your eternal praise and glory, so that all who shall hear the cause and manner of their death may glorify you, God and Lord, Saviour of the world.'

And so that holy man, Lord, relying on and trusting in the Lord, strong in his faith, between prayers, collected together the severed limbs and took pleasure in fitting the pieces together and joining them, and so far as he could restoring them, some partly[227] but more of them wholly; he commended the completion of the affair to the Lord who gives death and life.

And so, having put together the bodies, he made the sign of the triumphant cross over them. The strength of faith is wonderful and effective. At the sign of the life-giving cross and because of the virtue of the prayer and faith of the servant of God, not only did the soul of the bereft mother recover, but also the little bodies of her sons returned to the former and complete beauty of their state, not to mention the fact that the souls of the dead returned to their former lodging. So now the old man and those who had earlier been mutilated but at the Lord's will were whole and alive and in good spirits, following their holy leader on foot, returned to his little enclosed dwelling, which he had left in order to collect kindling for cooking. There like a father with goodness and mercy he tended that desolate one, with her own children restored to her,

---

[224] The palm tree an ancient symbol of the spirit's victory over the flesh, especially applicable to Christian martyrdom.

[225] John XI.1-44.

[226] An apocalyptic concept, Revelation XX.12-15.

[227] Presumably inferred from the nature of remnants. An inventory of holy relics remaining at St Albans in the early fifteenth century is printed as an appendix to the *Gesta Abbatum Monasterii Sancti Albani*, ed. H.T. Riley, Rolls Series, 28, London, 1867-69, III, pp. 539-45.

quibus potuit, et que ad manum habuit, pie ac misericorditer confouebat.

Nesciens ergo quo migraret regina, cum suis infantulis intra uastissimam heremum cum memorato solitario, diu moram ibidem, orationibus, uigiliis, ac aliis sanctis operibus eius intenta et iam iam conuenienter informata, et edulio siluestri sustentata, continuabat.

Post duorum uero mensium curricula, Rex Offa uictoriosissimus domum letus remeauit, spolia deuictorum suis magnatibus regali munificentia gloriose distribuendo. Verumtamen, ne lacrime gaudia regis, et eorum qui cum eo[228] aduenerant, miserabiliter interrumperent, consiliarii regi que de regina et liberis eius acciderant, diu sub silencio caute dissimulando, et causas absencie eius fictas annectendo, concelabant.

Tandem cum rex uehementer admiraretur ubinam regina delituisset, que ipsi regi ab ancipiti bello reuertenti occurrisse gaudenter teneretur, et in osculis et amplexibus ceteris gaudentius triumphatorem aduentantem suscepisse; sciscitabatur instantius, et toruius et proteruius, quid de ipsa fieret uel euenisset.

Suspicabatur enim eam morbo detentam, ipsamque cum liberis [8ᵛ][229] suis, regis et aliorum hominum, ut quieti uacaret, frequentiam declinasse. Tandem cum iratus nullatenus se uelle amplius ignorare, cum iuramento, quid de uxore sua et liberis euenisset, uultu toruo asseruisset, unus ex edituis omnia que acciderant, de tirannico eius mandato, et mandati plenaria execucione, seriatim enarrauit.

Hiis auditis, risus in luctum, gaudium in lamenta, iubilus in singultus flebiter conuertuntur. Totaque regia ululatibus personuit et meroribus. Lugensque rex diu tam immane infortunium, induit se sacca cilicino, aspersum cinere, ac multipliciter deformatum. Tandem monitu suorum, qui dicebant non uirorum magnificorum set pocius effeminatorum, dolorem interiecto solacio nolle temperare,[230] esse proprium et consuetudinem, rex cepit respirare, et dolori modum imponere.

Consilio igitur peritorum, qui nouerant regem libenter in tempore prospero in studio uenatico plurimum delectari, conuocantur uenatores, ut rex spaciaturus uenando, dolorem suum diminueret et luctum solacio demulceret. Qui inter uenandum dum per siluarum abdita, Deo misericordiarum et tocius consolacionis ducente, feliciter solus per inuia oberrauit, et tandem heremitorium memorati heremite directe peruenit. Eiusque exiguum domicilium subintrans, humanisse et cum summo gaudio receptus est. Et cum humili residens sedili, menbra fatigata quieti daret ad horam; recolens qualiter uxorem suam ibidem quondam diuinitus reperisset, et feliciter educasset, et educatam duxisset in uxorem, et quam elegantem ex ea prolem protulisset, eruperunt lacrime cum gemitibus, et in querelas lugubres ora resoluens, hospiti suo sinistrum de

---

[228] *N* 'eo' inserted from margin.
[229] Illustration: Counsellors persuade the grieving King Offa I to engage in the pastime of hunting as a distraction whereat he encounters the hermit, seated beneath a Romanesque arch.
[230] *C* obtemperare.

with such food that he had and what was to hand.

So, like that for a long time not knowing where to go, the queen remained with her little children in the vast wasteland with the aforesaid solitary, intent on prayer, vigils and her other holy acts, and teaching was conveniently continuous; and she lived on fodder from the woods.

After a period of two months had passed, King Offa returned home happy and most victorious, jubilantly distributing the spoils of the vanquished to his chief men with royal generosity. Nevertheless, lest tears should dolefully interrupt the pleasure of the king and those who had arrived with him, the king's counsellors for a long time concealed what had happened to the queen and her children by carefully dissembling quietly, and supplying invented reasons for her absence.

Eventually however, the king was extremely perplexed as to the whereabouts of the queen who was expected to have run up delightedly to the king himself coming back from the dangers of war, and to have received the returning champion with kisses and other fond embraces. He kept asking more and more persistently, more fiercely and more passionately, what had become of her or happened to her.

He supposed that she was kept away by sickness, and that she with her children had asked to be left in peace, avoiding the company of the king and other men. Eventually, when with an oath he insisted angrily with a wrathful expression that he really refused to be kept in ignorance about what had happened to his wife and children, one of the palace wardens told him everything that had happened, from his despotic command to the complete execution of that instruction.

When he heard these things, laughter turned to grief, delight to laments, joyfulness to doleful sobs. The whole kingdom resounded with wailing and grief. And mourning such a dreadful tragedy for a long time, the king put on sackcloth, sprinkled himself with ashes and disfigured himself in many other ways. When eventually his advisers said that to be unwilling to temper mourning with consolation was not the mark and habit of great men but rather of effeminate ones, the king began to draw breath and mourned in moderation.

So, on the recommendation of the experienced, who knew that in prosperous times the king really loved to go hunting, they sent for the huntsmen, so that, at leisure by hunting, the king might lessen his sorrow, and soften his grief with solace. During a break in the hunting, he was in the hidden places of the woods; the God of mercies and all consolations leading him, he fortunately wandered away from the path alone, and eventually came right to the hermitage of the aforesaid hermit. And entering his tiny dwelling, he was received with great courtesy and extreme pleasure. And sitting on a humble little seat, he rested his exhausted limbs for an hour. Recalling how once by divine inspiration he had found his wife in this very place, and brought her up happily, and when brought up had married her, and what handsome offspring she had borne him, he burst into tears with groans; and this sad grief loosening his tongue, he told his

uxore sua qui infausto sidere nuper euenerat, quam et ipse quondam uiderat, enarrauit.

At senex sereno uultu, factus ex intrinsecus concepto gaudio alacrior, consolatus est regem. Et in uocem exultacionis eminus prorumpens: 'Eia domine mi rex, eia,' ait, 'uere Deus misericordiarum, Dominus, famulos suos quasi pater filios in omni tribulacione post pressuras consolatur, percutit et medetur, deicit ut gloriosius eleuet pregrauatum. Viuit uxor tua, cum liberis tuis in omni sospitate restauratis. Non meis meritis, set pocius tuis, integritati sanitati et leticie plenius qui trucidabantur restituuntur.

Recongnosce quanta fecit tibi Dominus, et in laudes et graciarum acciones totus exurge.' Tunc prosiliens sanctus pre gaudio, euocauit reginam, que in interiori diuerticulo, pueros suos balneo micius materno studio confouebat. Que cum ad regem intoisset, uix se [9^r]^{231} gaudio capiens, pedibus mariti sui prouoluta, in lacrimis exultacionis inundauit. In cuius amplexus desideratissimos ruens rex, ipsam in maius quam dici possit gaudium suscepit. Interim senex, pueros elegantissimos et ex ablucione elegantiores, uestit, comit et paterno more et affectu componit, et ad presentiam patris et matris introducit. Quos pater intra brachia suscipiens, et ad pectus arctioribus amplexibus applicans, roseis uultibus infantum oscula imprimit multiplicata. Quos tamen rore lacrimarum, pre nimia mentis exultacione, madefecit. Et cum diucius eorum colloquiis pasceretur, conuersus rex ad senem, ait: 'O pater sancte, pater dulcissime,^{232} mentis mee reparator, et gaudii cordis mei restaurator, qua, merita uestra, caritatis officia, pietatisque beneficia, prosequar remuneracione. Accipe ergo, licet multo maiora exigant merita tua, quicquid erarium meum ualet effundere, me, meos, et mea, tue expono uoluntati.' At sanctus, 'Domine mi rex, non decet me peccatorem conuersum ad Dominum, ad insanias quas reliqui falsas respicere. Tu uero pocius pro animabus patris tui et matris tue, quibus quandoque carus fueram ac familiaris, et tua, et uxoris tue, et liberorum tuorum corporali sanitate, et salute spirituali, regni tui soliditate, et successorum tuorum prosperitate, Deo gratus, qui tot in te congessit beneficia, cenobium quoddam fundare, uel aliquod dirutum studeas restaurare. In quo digne et laudabiliter Deo in perpetuum seruiatur, et tui memoria cum precibus ad Dominum fusis, cum benediccionibus semper recenter recolatur.' Et conuersus ad reginam, ait: 'Et tu, filia, quamuis mulier, non tamen muliebriter, ad hoc regem accendas et admoneas diligenter, filiosque tuos instrui facias, ut^{233} et Dominum Deum, qui eos uite reparauit, studeant gratanter honorare, et eidem fideliter famulando fundandi cenobii possessiones ampliare, et tueri libertates.'

---

^{231} Illustration: Offa I is reunited with Queen Thryth and his now healthy children by the hermit. Subsequently the hermit, shrouded but bearing the heavenly crown of eternal life, is entombed by monks.
^{232} *C* sancte et dulcissime.
^{233} *N & C* 'ut' interlined.

host the treachery concerning his wife – whom he himself had seen – that had recently occurred under an unlucky star.[234]

But the old man, with a smiling face brought about by the deep delight he felt within, consoled the king. And exclaiming in a voice of great joy: 'Ah my lord king, Ah!' he said, 'truly the Lord God of mercies consoles his servants in all their tribulations after troubles as a father does his sons; he strikes and then heals, throws down so that he may lift up the burdened more gloriously. Your wife is alive, with your children restored in complete safety. Not because of my merits, but rather yours, those who were butchered are restored to greater health, soundness of mind and contentment.

Recognise how much the Lord has done for you, and go and give wholehearted praise and thanksgiving.' Then, leaping up full of delight, the holy man called the queen who with motherly care was tenderly seeing to her boys in a bath in an inner room. When she came to the king, almost beside herself with delight, she flew to the feet of her husband and bathed them in tears of joy. Rushing into the embrace he so much desired, the king received her with indescribable delight. Meanwhile the old man dressed the boys – very pretty, and all the prettier after washing – groomed and arranged them with both the manner and affection of a father, and brought them into the presence of father and mother. Their father took them into his arms and, hugging them tightly to his breast, planted many kisses on the rosy faces of the little children. And he was so overjoyed he drenched them with a dew of tears. And at last when he had taken in all they had to say, the king turned to the old man and said, 'Oh holy father, most sweet father, you have restored my mind, and retrieved my heart's delight. How can I appropriately reward your deserts, works of charity and good deeds of devotion? For although your deserts demand much more, accept whatever my coffers can pour out; I put myself, mine and my goods at your disposal.' However the holy man [replied], 'My lord king, it is not proper that I, a sinner, should against the will of the Lord have regard for the false insanities relinquished. But rather, for the souls of your father and your mother, to whom I was once dear and a friend, and in your interests, and your wife's, and for the bodily health and spiritual well-being of your children and the security of your kingdom, and the prosperity of your successors – thanks be to God, who has granted you so many blessings – turn your mind to founding a monastery, or to restoring business to a wrecked one. In that God would be served for evermore, worthily and excellently, and memory of you with all your recent blessings always be recalled, joined with prayers to the Lord.' And turning to the queen, he said: 'And you, daughter, although female you're not effeminate; prompt and remind this king diligently, and have your children so taught that they both strive to honour the Lord God who restored them to life, and by faithful service to the monastic foundation, increase its possessions and safeguard its franchises.'

---

[234] In *The Anglo-Saxon Chronicles* a flying star is reported presaging such events as the death of prominent men, famine or terrifying weather (*s.a.a.* 678, 729, 975, 995 *et al*). But sufficiently heretical a concept to attract persistent clerical denunciation, by e.g. the eleventh-century Ælfric, *Catholic Homilies*, ed. P. Clemoes, Early English Text Society, Suppl. Series 17 (1997), pp. 229-30. Generally T.O. Wedel, *The Mediæval Attitude towards Astrology, particularly in England*, Oxford, 1920, pp. 44-48.

Fig. 18) *A mounted King Offa I encounters in the forest a damsel in distress (Thryth, daughter of the king of Northumbria) her dress washed light red, and subsequently, standing, he places her in the care of his court. MS Cotton Nero D i, f. 6ʳ* © The British Library Board. All Rights Reserved.

Fig. 19) *The disabled boy Wynfrith [future Offa II], duly considered by his parents, is offered to God, the lad kneeling on the altar steps of a Romanesque chapel.*

MS Cotton Nero D i, f. 9ᵛ © The British Library Board. All Rights Reserved.

Fig. 20) Wynfrith [the future Offa II] now lightly bearded, is knighted, (belted and spurred), in the same manner as Offa I, a man-at-arms with similar heraldry present [see Fig .17]. The allegiance of magnates recognises the seated man as future king.

MS Cotton Nero D i, f. 10ʳ © The British Library Board. All Rights Reserved.

Fig 21) The enthroned Offa II, sword in one hand sceptre the other, is crowned by flanking men, one the abdicating king; the whole beneath a complex foliate canopy. The damsel Thryth II arrives in a dragon-prowed boat that could devour the branches of a shoreline tree.

MS Cotton Nero D i, f. 11ʳ © The British Library Board. All Rights Reserved.

Descensus ad secundum Offam.

Sanctus autem ad cellam reuersus, post paucum temporis ab incolatu huius mundi migrauit ad Dominum, mercedem eternam pro labore temporali recepturus. Rex autem, cito monita ipsius salubria dans obliuioni et incurie, ex tunc ocio ac paci uacauit, prolemque copiosam utriusque sexus expectabilis pulchritudinis procreauit. Vnde semen regium a latere et descensu felix suscepit incrementum. Qui completo uite sue tempore, post etatem bonam quieuit in pace. Et regaliter sepultus, appositus est ad patres suos. In eo multum redarguendus, quod scenobium [235] uotiuo affectu repromissum, thesauris parcendo non contruxit. Post uictorias enim a Domino[236] sibi collatas, amplexibus et ignauie necnon auaricie plus equo indulsit. Prosperitas enim secularis, animos, licet uiri [9ᵛ][237] les, solet frequenter effeminare. Verumtamen hoc onus humeris filii sui moriturus apposuit, qui cum deuota assercione, illud sibi suscepit. Set nec ipse Deo auerso pollicita, prout patri suo promiserat, compleuit. Set filio suo huius uoti obligacionem in fine uite sue dereliquit. Et sic memorati uoti uinculum, sine efficacia complementi de patre in filium descendens, usque ad tempora Pineredi[238] filii Tuinfreth suspendebatur. Quibus pro pena negligentie, tale euenit infortunium, ut omnes principes quos Offa magnificus edomuerat, a subieccione ipsius Offe, et posteritatis sue procaciter recesserunt, et ipsum morientem despexerunt. Quia ut predictum est, ad mortem uergens, deliciis et senii ualitudine marcuit eneruatus.

De ortu secundi Offe.

Natus est igitur memorato Tuinfred, et[239] qui de stemate regum fuit, filius, uidelicet Pineredus, usque ad annos adolescentie inutilis, poplitibus contractis, qui nec oculorum uel aurium plene officio naturali fungeretur. Vnde patri suo Tuinfredo et matri sue Marcelline, oneri fuit non honori, confusioni et non exultacioni. Et licet unicus eis fuisset, mallent prole caruisse, quam talem habuisse. Verumtamen memorie reducentes euentum Offe magni, qui in tenera etate penitus erat inutilis, et postea, Deo propicio, penitus sibi restitutus, mirabili strenuitate omnes suos edomuit aduersarios, et bello prepotens, gloriose multociens de magnis hostibus triumphauit, spem conceperunt, quod eodem medico medente, Christo uidelicet, qui eciam mortuos suscitat, propiciatus, posset similiter uisitari et sibi restitui. Pater igitur eius et mater ipsam puerum inito salubri consilio, in templo presentarunt Domino, uotiua deuocione

---

[235] Spelling with initial 's' found in *N* only on ff. 9-10; *C* initial 's' erased and spelled cenobium thereafter.

[236] *C* Deo.

[237] Illustration: The disabled boy Wynfrith [future Offa II], duly considered by his parents, is offered to God, the lad kneeling on the altar steps of a Romanesque chapel (Fig. 19).

[238] For the common manuscript error of the vernacular graph *Wyn* for Latin *P*, see Introduction, p. xxxii.

[239] *C* Tuinfreth qui de stemate.

The Descent to Offa II.

The holy man went back to his cell, a short time after which he journeyed from the habitation of this world to the Lord, received an eternal reward for his temporal labour. But his sound advice soon abandoned by forgetfulness and neglect, the king then led an empty life of ease and leisure, and had numerous offspring of both sexes, all remarkably good looking. And so the royal seed was blessed with increase, laterally and directly. When he came to the end of his days, at a good age, he fell asleep in peace. And regally buried, he was laid with his fathers. He is greatly to be criticised inasmuch as, in order to spare the treasury, he did not build the monastery that he had promised with a loving vow. Indeed, after the victories conferred on him by the Lord, he gave way to the temptations of excessive idleness and greed. For worldly success will often emasculate souls, even virile ones. However, upon dying, he placed this burden on the shoulders of his son, who took it on himself with positive devotion. But, God being against the assurance, he did not carry out what he promised his father. But at the end of his life he left the obligation of this vow to his son. And thus the link of the aforesaid vow, descending from father to son without ever being carried out, remained unfulfilled right up to the time of Wynfrith son of Thingfrith. [240] As punishment of their negligence, a most unfortunate thing occurred in that all the leaders whom the great Offa had subdued disdained him when dying, for they had impertinently withdrawn from subjection to that Offa and his posterity because, as said, when approaching death he was very weak and yielded to luxuries in old age.

On the rise of Offa II.

And so to the aforesaid Thingfrith was born a son, and this son, that is to say Wynfrith, who was of the royal line, was useless right up to the years of his youth, [241] with crippled knees and neither eyes nor ears that fully performed their natural function. [242] So his father Thingfrith and his mother Marcellina found it a source of anxiety not respect, of bewilderment and not joy. And although he was their only one, they would have preferred to be without children than to have one like this. Nevertheless, casting the mind back to what had happened to the great Offa, who had been very sickly and almost entirely useless, and later by the grace of God entirely restored to himself, how he had with miraculous strength subdued all his opponents, was valiant in war, and many times triumphed gloriously over powerful enemies, they took hope, because with the same doctor treating him, that is to say Christ who can even raise the dead, he might mercifully at the same time be visited and restored to himself. So his father and mother, with sound initial advice, presented the boy in the temple to the Lord, [243] firmly

---

[240] See Appendix A, pp. 133-4.
[241] For appreciation of the stages of youth, see Introduction, p. lv.
[242] For comments on the nature of such disability see Introduction, pp. lii-liv.
[243] Compare the presentation of the infant Jesus, following Jewish tradition, Luke II.22-52.

firmiter promittentes: 'Ut si ipsum Deus restauraret, quod parentes eius negligenter omiserunt, ipse puer cum se facultas offerret fideliter adimpleret.' Videlicet de scenobio, cuius mencio prelibata est, honorifice construendo, uel de diruto restaurando. Et cum hec tam puer quam pater et mater deuotissime postularent, exaudia est oratio eorum a Deo, qui se nunquam difficilem exhibet precibus iustis supplicantium, hoc modo.

Quomodo prosperabatur.

Erat in eadem regione, Merciorum uidelicet, quidam tirannus, pocius destruens et dissipans regni nobilitatem, quam regens, nomine Beormredus.[244] Hic generosos, quos regius sanguis preclaros,[245] usque ad internecionem subdole persequebatur, relegauit, et occulta nece perdidit iugulandos. Sciebat enim, quod uniuersis de regno, merito extitit, odiosus. Et ne aliquis loco ipsius subrogaretur, et presertim de sanguine regio propagatus, uehementer formidabat. Tetendit insuper laqueos Tuinfredo et uxori eius, ut ipsos de terra expelleret, uel pocius perderet trucidatos. [10ʳ][246] Puerum autem Penefredum[247] spreuit, nec ipsum querere ad perdendum dignabatur, reputans eum inutilem et ualitudinarium.

Fugientes igitur memoratus Tuinfredus et uxor eius et familia a facie persequentis, sese in locis tucioribus receperunt, ne generali calumpnie inuoluerentur. Quod comperiens Pinefredus adolescens, quasi a graui sompno expergefactus, erexit se. Et compagibus neruorum laxatis, et miraculose protensis, sese de longa desidia redarguens, fecit alices, brachia, crura, pedes, extendendo. Et aliquociens oscitans, cum loqui conaretur, solutum est uinculum lingue eius, et loquebatur recte, uerbe proferens ore facundo prompcier articulata. Quid plura, de contracto, muto, et ceco, fit elegans corpore, eloquens sermone,[248] acie perspicax oculorum. Qui tempore modico in tantam floruit ac uiguit strenuitatem, ut nullus in regno Merciorum, ipsi in moribus et probitate multiplici ualuit comparari. Vnde ipsi Mercii, secundum Offam, et non Pinefredum, iam nominantes, quia a Deo respectus et electus fuisset, eodem modo quo et rex Offa filius regis Warmundi, ceperunt ipsi quasi Domino uniuersaliter adherere. Ipsumque iam factum militem, contra regem Beormredum et eius insidias, potenter ac prudenter protegere, dantes ei dextras, et fedus eum ipso, prestitis iuramentis, ineuntes.

Quod audiens Beormredus doluit, et dolens timuit sibi uehementer. Penituitque eum amarissime, ipsum Pinefredum, qui iam Offa nominabatur, cum ceteris fraudulenter non interemisse.

---

[244] *N C* rubric: 'De tirannide Beormredi regis Mercie.'
[245] *C* 'fecerat' inserted from margin in a later hand.
[246] Illustration: Wynfrith [the future Offa II] now lightly bearded, is knighted, (belted and spurred), in the same manner as Offa I, the man-at-arms with similar heraldry present (f. 3ʳ). The allegiance of magnates recognises the seated man as future king (Fig. 20).
[247] *N* has 'i' above the first 'e' *of* 'Penefredum'; *C* 'Pinefredum' and thus hereafter.
[248] *C* 'eloquens sermone' inserted from margin in separate hand.

promising with a vow of devotion, that if the Lord restored, the boy himself would faithfully fulfil when he was given the ability – that is to say the worthy construction of a monastery or restoration of a wrecked one, which has been mentioned before.[249] And when these things were devoutly asked for the boy by his father and mother alike, their prayer was heard by God – who never shows himself obdurate to the righteous prayers of supplicants – in this way.

How he acceded.

There was in the same province, that is to say Mercia, a certain despot called Beornred,[250] destroying and scattering the nobility of the kingdom rather than ruling. He persecuted those well-bred[251] who were distinguished by royal blood, even to the point of crafty murder; put them away and did them down by secret, clandestine throat-cuttings. But he knew that he was hated – and deservedly so – by the entire kingdom. And he was very much afraid of anyone usurping his place, in particular anyone of royal blood. Above all he was out to ensnare Thingfrith and his wife in order to expel them from the land, or preferably destroy them by butchery. But he spared the boy Wynfrith, considering him not worth destroying, thinking him useless and a weakling.

So the aforesaid Thingfrith and his wife and household fleeing from the face of their persecutor hid in a place of safety so that they would not be involved in the general calumny. Learning this, the youth Wynfrith raised himself up as though waking from a heavy sleep.[252] The joints of his sinews were both loosened and miraculously stretched out, and, belying his long inactivity, he threw himself about – arms, legs, feet extended. And every so often gulping when he tried to talk, the fetter of his tongue was loosened, and he spoke properly, forming words in his mouth by making clearer utterances. What else, but that the crippled, dumb and blind man became handsome in body, eloquent in speech and most keen of eye! In a short time he flourished and grew to such strength that no one in the kingdom of the Mercians could be compared to him in character and every kind of uprightness. The Mercians themselves now called him a second Offa, and not Wynfrith, because he had been looked upon and chosen by God in the same way as had King Offa the son of King Wermund. Universally they began to adhere to him as if their lord. He had now been made a knight and, giving him their right hands and entering a pact with him after taking oaths, they began powerfully and prudently to protect him against King Beornred and his plotters.

Hearing about this, Beornred worried, and, worrying, he greatly feared for himself. And he regretted very bitterly that he had not treacherously suppressed this Wynfrith – who was now called Offa – with the rest.

---

[249] See above, pp. 35-6.

[250] *C* Rubric: Concerning the tyrant Beornred king of Mercia. For Beornred see generally Introduction, p. lii.

[251] *C* he had done inserted from margin.

[252] For escape from trauma, see Introduction, pp. liv-lv.

De bello inito inter Beormredum et Offam.

Congregato igitur utrobique excercitu copiosissimo, pugnam cruentissimam inierunt, hinc rex Beormredus cum suis complicibus, inde Offa adolescens strenuissimis[253] cum suis Merciis sibi indissolubiliter adherentibus. Decertantibusque utrimque uiriliter partibus ex aduerso, ceciderunt quamplures exanimati. Multi quoque letaliter uulnerati elapsisunt, qui cito postea miserabiliter expirarunt. Tandem suspensa diu uictoria, cum iam nox diremptura certamen immineret, adolescens Offa, cuius adhuc sicut mane spiritus recenter feruebat, suos exhortabatur dicens, uoce alacriter exaltata: 'O nobiles commilitones non alienigene set indigene, non amore pecunie set libertatis, uobis debite michi coniuncti, qui me super uos elegistis, et non ego ad hunc apicem me ingessi, expergiscimini. Res uestra agitur. Quid pigritantes fatigamini? Sequimini me preuium. Ecce prelii negotium finem expectat adoptatum. Sol iam uergit in occasum. Nunquid in tenebris [254] quas desiderant, manus nostras euadent hostes nostri. Hucusque prosperatum[255] opus Martium feliciter ex parte nostra. Incepta, uiriliter prosequimini.'

Ad hunc clamorem, clamor subiectorum resonat, et ipso [10v][256] preuio, et densam aciem hostium ad instar [257] tellurem sulcantis, hinc inde dissipat, aduersarios et obstantes prosternendo. Quem merciorum prestanciores a tergo et e uestigio subsequentes, uiam aperiunt laciorem. Sese igitur ad inuicem clamor exhortantium, ascendit ad sidera, puluis aera perturbat, fragor hastarum, tinnitus gladiorum, gemitus uulneratorum; tubarum et lituorum clangor.[258] Ictuum strepitus repetitorum, corda potuit exterruisse magnanimorum. Sic sique funestissimo bello cum rediuiuo certamine renouato, multi corruunt[259] utrobique, animas cum sanguine sub equinis pedibus miserabiliter eructantes.

De gloriosa uictoria Offe adolescentis contra Beormredum tyrannum dimicantis.

Tandem cum iam adueniente crepusculo nox atra immineret, uersum est pondus prelii super Beormredum. Qui letaliter uulneratus, in tenebris a manibus animam suam querentium, ereptus est et elapsus. Igitur antequam nox opaca certamen diremisset, contritus est et dissipatus Beormredi tiranni totus exercitus, et cruentissima hostium quos fuga non eripuit, et tenebre non occultauerunt, strages irrestaurabilis consummata. Conuocatis igitur militaribus per notos lituos et clamores agminibus, Offa gloriose triumphans, sese in municionem propinquam recipiens, cum leticia sopori dedit, ac secure quieti menbra nimis fatigata. Que Deo in causa sua iustissima protegente penitus illesa conseruauit. Ibique aliquot diebus, fatigati quiete recreantur, uulnerati

---

[253] C strenuosissimus.
[254] C in intenebris.
[255] C prosperatum est.
[256] Illustration: The battle against the rebel Beornred. Offa II, in crested helmet, takes the front line, lancing the leading enemy cavalryman whilst others turn to flee.
[257] C 'instaris' with final '–is' erased ; N –'ri' erased.
[258] Cf the description of battle p. 9.
[259] C corruerunt.

On the war that began between Beornred and Offa.

So when a very numerous army had gathered on either side, they joined in a very gory battle – here King Beornred with his henchmen, over there the most vigorous youth Offa with his staunch Mercian adherents. And, sections having fought hard on both sides in hostile opposition, very many dropped lifeless. Also numbers fell fatally wounded, who very soon afterwards wretchedly expired. Eventually, with victory in the balance for a long time, and now with night already about to fall and interrupt the struggle, the youth Offa, who had until then continually burned with day-break spirit, roused his men, saying fervently in a raised voice: 'Oh noble comrades-in-arms, let us bestir ourselves! You have not joined with me for foreign but for native land, not for love of money but of liberty – your right. It is you who elected me to lead you, and not I who put myself in such an exalted position. It is your affair. Why slacken off, exhausted ones? Follow with me in front. Behold, the battle we are engaged in awaits a winning end. The sun is already beginning to set. Are our enemies going to slip out of our hands in the darkness, as they want? The work of Mars[260] has brought success, happily on our part so far. Vigorously carry on what is begun.'[261]

At this cry, a cry of the defeated went up, and he himself was seen in front of the line, scattering the dense line of the enemy hither and thither, by thrusting to the ground those who opposed or obstructed him, just like ploughing the earth. The flower of the Mercians following on from behind and in his footsteps opened up a wider path. From then on cries encouraging one another ascended to the stars; tumult[262] shook the air: there was the breaking of spears, the clash of swords, the groans of the wounded, the blast of trumpets and horns. The racket of repeated blows might have terrified the hearts of the courageous. In mortal combat on all sides, in fresh outbursts of conflict many rushed in all directions, wretchedly belching forth souls with blood, beneath the horses' feet.

On the glorious victory of the youth Offa over forces of the despot Beornred.

Eventually, as dusk really drew nigh and night threatened, the weight of the battle went against Beornred. He was fatally wounded, and was snatched from the hands of those seeking his soul and escaped in the darkness. And so before shady night put an end to the struggle, the whole of the despot Beornred's army was crushed and scattered; and those enemy not snatched by most bloody flight, and not hidden by darkness, were swallowed up in irretrievable massacre. So Offa, gloriously triumphant, having summoned his troops by the familiar trumpets and calls in the ranks, retiring to a nearby stronghold, gave himself up to the satisfaction of sleep, the rest of peace to his over-exhausted limbs, which God, safeguarding in his most righteous cause, kept entirely unharmed. And there for a few days the exhausted were refreshed in peace,

---

[260] Roman god of war. Also pp. 55-6, 65-6, 71-2.
[261] As frequently, *C*'s run-over can be confused. *C our initiatives courageously.*
[262] Here *pulsus* replacing MSS *puluis*, 'dust'.

medicaminibus mitigantur, membris contriti balneis et unguentibus confouentur. Sicque factum[263] ut in triduo, nec Beormredus, nec aliquis de ipsius complicibus in regno Merciorum inueniretur.

Pater Offe et mater et totum semen Regium respirarunt.

Hec autem eum audisset Tuinfredus comes, pater uidelicet Offe, et comitissa Marcella mater, ac eorum familia, qui sub protectione cuiusdam potentis contermini latuerant, quasi ab exilio ad propria gaudenter remearunt. Patri igitur aduentanti occurrit Offa triumphator magnificus, [264] et in mutuos ruentes, sese piis lacrimis et letis fletibus irrorarunt. Et singultibus sermonem prorumpentibus ait pater filio: 'O fili, unice fili genealis, fili Offa karissime, quem michi senescenti dedit Deus solatium, et ad gaudium et gloriam restaurauit, non tantum sanum, set eciam uictoriosum faciendo, accipe hereditatem tuam comitatum meum. Quia et si filius meus non esses, hec et plura pro meritorum retribucione promeruisti. Inimicum enim generis nostri prostrauisti, et regnum Merciorum pristine libertati potente restituisti. Ego iam delibor, etenim senui, et caligauerunt oculi mei. Precibus et contemplacioni cum uxore mea de cetero quiescius incumbam, pro alacritate tua et generis nostri Deo preces, de cetero porrigam indefessas, in scenobio quod uita comite fundaturus es, [11ʳ][265] habitum religionis assumpturus.' Hec cum audisset Offa, commota sunt uiscera sua. Et cum gemitu ait: 'Absit hoc pater mi uenerande, ut dum uitales auras hauseris, status uestre dignitatis in aliquo me uiuente mutiletur, immo potius, felix suscipiet incrementum. Ecclesiam autem quam Deo multociens promissi me edificaturum, profecto me polleceor, nam Deo nunc magis obligor, non ignobiliter perfecturum.

Qualiter Offa in regem Merciorum sublimatur.

Cum autem hoc pium certamen potentes Merciorum audissent, ipsum Offam quasi animam suam diligere ceperunt.[266] Et irruentes, ipsum iuuenum a patris amplexibus certatim rapientes, unanimi consensu uociferabantur. 'Nequaquam comes, set rex noster eris magnificus. Hoc enim sanguis regius expostulat, et merita tua hoc multipliciter precesserunt. Te enim auctore, te duce, persecutorem nostrum contriuimus. Et ad hoc Deus te [267] tibi mirabiliter, misericorditer, ac miraculose restaurauit. Tu omnes regno Merciorum rebelles, potenter edomabis. Et quod Deo

---

[263] C 'est' added in margin in later hand.
[264] C 'amplexus' added in margin.
[265] Illustration: The enthroned Offa II, sword in one hand sceptre the other, is crowned by flanking men, one the abdicating king; the whole beneath a complex foliate canopy. The damsel Thryth II arrives in a dragon-prowed boat that could devour the branches of a shoreline tree (Fig. 21).
[266] C run on.
[267] C 'te' omitted.

wounds soothed with medicines, crushed limbs tended with baths and ointments. And so it came about that within three days neither Beornred nor any of his henchmen was found in the kingdom of the Mercians.

The father and mother of Offa and all the royal seed draw breath.

When Earl[268] Thingfrith, that is to say Offa's father, Lady Marcellina his mother and their household, who had been in sanctuary under the protection of a certain neighbouring power, heard this they returned delightedly home as though from exile. Then Offa, the great champion, ran to meet his father as he was approaching; and rushing into each other's arms,[269] they sprinkled each other with tears of affection and joyful weeping. And the father said to his son, interspersing his words with sobs: 'Oh son, only son of my family, dearest son Offa, whom God has given me as a consolation in my old age, and restored for delight and glory, not only in health but even made victorious, receive your inheritance – my office. Because, even if you were not my son, you have deserved this and more in reward of virtue. Because you have thrown down our family's enemy, and powerfully restored the kingdom of the Mercians to its former liberty. I am already worn out, in fact elderly, and my eyes have clouded over. For the remainder of my life I am going to devote myself more quietly to prayer and contemplation with my wife, having taken the religious habit in the monastery which you are going to found for the common life; I will offer continual prayers to God for the success of you and our family.' When Offa heard this, he was inwardly moved. And with a sigh he said: 'Forbid it! my reverend father, for as long as you draw breath of life, your high rank will never be degraded as long as I live; on the contrary may it preferably grow greater. Moreover, now I am more indebted to God, the church I have many times promised God that I would build, I swear that I will complete in no mean fashion.'

How Offa was raised to be king of the Mercians.

But when the magnates of the Mercians heard this loving dispute, they began to value Offa on account of his spirit. And rushing in, eagerly dragging this young man from the embrace of his father, they cried with one voice: 'Although only an earl, you will be our great king.[270] Because by this royal blood is obvious, and your deserts many times preceded it. For with you as ruler, you as leader, we have crushed our persecutor. And to this end God restored you to yourself wonderfully, mercifully and miraculously. You have powerfully subdued all rebels in the kingdom of the Mercians. And what

---

[268] *Comes* and *Comitissa* ('Count' and 'Countess') are found in a footnote to f. 9ᵛ, but were not terms used in Anglo-Saxon England. The title *cuntesse* was introduced early into post-Conquest English, cf. *Anglo-Saxon Chronicle, s.a.* 1140, providing a feminine partner of English 'earl'. *Count* is never used other than as applied to a Continental social equivalent of earl. See generally A.T. Thacker, 'Some terms for noblemen in Anglo-Saxon England, *c.* 650-900', *Anglo-Saxon Studies in Archaeology and History*, 2 (1981), 201-36 (pp. 207-9).

[269] C 'embraces' provided in margin.

[270] C 'great for this'.

uotiuo affectu promisisti, ex hoc nobilius consumabis. Congregati igitur uniuersi Merciorum potentes, Offam supra se constituunt sollempniter coronatum. Dixeruntque ei: 'Ex hoc nunc et deinceps, non tantum similis, set Offe magno censeberis simillimus. Sequere igitur ipsius pedetentim uestigia, et eos quos et ipse regno huic potenter subiugauit, et postea insolentes de sub iugo eius colla nequitur excusserunt, tu potentius ad corone tue reuoca soliditatem. Nos autem uno animo et alacri uoluntate, tibi per omnia consilium efficax, et auxilium, usque ad mortem propensius impendemus.

Coronato igitur Offa, in soliique[271] culmine constituto, refloruit pax Merciorum, et prosperitas, populus respirauit. Seminis regii propago restauratur. Leges pacifice suscitantur, et nobiles quos Beormredus tirannus expulerat a regno reuocantur.

Qualiter Offa rex uxorem duxerit.

Diebus itaque sub eisdem, regnante in Francia Karolo rege magno ac uictoriosissimo, quedam puella, facie uenusta, set mente nimis inhonesta, ipsi regi consanguinea, pro quodam quod patrauerat crimine flagiciosissimo, addicta est iudicialiter morti ignominiose.

Verum, ob regie dignitatis reuerentiam, igni uel ferro tradenda non iudicatur, set in nauicula armamentis carente, apposito uictu tenui, uentis et mari, eorumque ambiguis casibus exponitur condempnata. Que diu uariis uariis[272] procellis exagitata, tandem fortuna trahente, litori Britonum est appulsa. Et cum in terra subiecta potestati regis Offe memorata cimba applicuisset, conspectui regis protinus presentatur. Interogata autem quenam esset, respondens, patria lingua affirmauit, se Karolo regi Francorum fuisse consanguinitate propinquam, Dridamque nominatam. Set per tirannidem [11^v][273] quorundam ignobilium, quorum nuptias ne degeneraret spreuit, tali fuisse discrimini adiudicatam. Abortisque lacrimis addidit dicens: 'Deus autem qui innocentes a laqueis insidiantium liberat, me captiuam ad alas tue protecionis, regum serenissime, feliciter transmisit, ut meum infortunium, in auspicium fortunatum transmutetur, et beatior in exilio quam in natali patria, ab omni predicer posteritate.' Rex autem uerborum suorum ornatum et eloquentiam, et corporis puellaris cultum et elegantiam,[274] motus

---

[271] C Offa eciam in solii culmine.
[272] C 'uariis' duplicated and the second deleted.
[273] Illustration: Counsellors with raised hands express disapproval as King Offa II, one forefinger pointing, the other raised in authority, determines to marry Thryth. The king is betrothed to Thryth by two men in secular dress, one pointing at her.
[274] C 'considerans' added in margin in correcting hand.

you have promised to God in a loving vow, you will complete famously hereafter.' So, having gathered together, all the magnates of the Mercians decided to formally crown Offa to rule them. And they said to him: 'From now and henceforth, you will be considered not just like, but exceptionally like Offa the Great. So follow in his footsteps with care, and very powerfully call back into unity under your crown those insolent rebels whom he once powerfully subjugated to this kingdom – and who later shook their necks from under his yoke. And we, with one mind and ready willingness, will providently supply you with effective counsel and support throughout everything, until death.'

So, with Offa crowned on high on a secure throne, peace and prosperity flourished once more for the Mercians, the people drew breath. Propagation of the royal seed would be renewed, the laws upheld in peace,[275] and the noblemen whom Beornred the despot had banished from the kingdom recalled.

How King Offa married a wife.

Now in the days that followed, whilst there reigned in France Charles – a great and most victorious king[276] – a certain girl, a blood relative of the king himself, beautiful of face but too dishonest of mind, was legally condemned to an ignominious death for a certain deed that she had disgracefully committed by acting very criminally.

In fact, out of respect for her royal status, her sentence would not be committal to fire or iron, but condemnation to a small unrigged boat, a little food put in, and exposure to the winds and waves and their uncertain outcomes. Eventually, tossed by various storms for a long time, fortune delivering her, she was driven onto the coast of Britain. And when the said tub was moored on land in the power of King Offa, she was immediately brought into the presence of the king. However, asked who she was, replying in her native tongue[277] she declared that she was a blood relative of Charles king of the Franks, and was called Thryth.[278] But she had been condemned to this through the tyranny of certain common men, with whom she had refused marriage because of losing status. And having shed tears she continued, saying: 'But God who frees the innocent from the snares of plotters, has happily sent me captive to your protecting wings, Oh most serene king, so that my misfortune might be changed into good fortune; and I may be said by all posterity to be happier in exile than in the land of my birth.' So the king, moved to pity by the beauty and eloquence of her words and the appearance and grace of the girl's body, commanded that she should be taken to

---

[275] No laws of Offa II himself survive, see Introduction, p. xcii.

[276] This reference is to the Frankish Charlemagne, 768-814, but there is subsequent confusion with his older brother Carloman, see pp. 51-6, and Introduction, pp. xc-xci.

[277] Records of the Germanic Frankish language are minimal. Charlemagne is said to have ordered their heroic poetry to be written down and for a vernacular grammar to be begun (Einhard, *Vita Karoli Magni*, ed. O. Holder-Egger, *Monumenta Germaniae Historica, Scriptores rerum Germanicarum*, Hanover, 1911, p. 33; transl. L. Thorpe, *Two Lives of Charlemagne*, Harmondsworth, 1969, p. 82) but nothing of this survives. The western Franks were in more or less constant contact with the Roman world from the fourth century onwards and by the ninth century Romance Old French, developed from Vulgar Latin, was becoming standard.

[278] See Introduction, pp. lxxvii, lxxxiv-lxxxv.

pietate, precepit ut ad comitissam Marcelline matrem suam tucius duceretur alenda, ac mitius sub tam honeste matrone custodia, donec regium mandatum audiret, confouenda.

Puelle igitur infra paucos dies, macie et pallore per alimenta depulsis, rediit decor pristinus, ita ut mulierum pulcherima censeretur. Set cito in uerba iactantie et elacionis, secundum patrie sue consuetudinem, prorumpens, domine sue comitisse, que materno affectu eam dulciter educauerat, molesta nimis fuit, ipsam procaciter contempnendo. Set comitissa, pro amore filii sui regis, omnia pacienter tolerauit, licet et ipsa dicta puella inter comitem et comitissam uerba discordie seminasset.

Vna igitur dierum, cum rex ipsam causa uisitacionis adiens, uerbis consolatoriis alloqueretur, incidit in retia amoris illius. Erat enim iam species illius concupiscibilis.

Clandestino igitur ac repentino matrimonio ipsam sibi, inconsultis patre et matre, necnon et magnatibus suis uniuersis, copulauit. Vnde uterque parentum, dolore ac tedio in etate senili contabescens, dies uite abreuiando, sue mortis horam lugubriter anticiparunt. Sciebant enim ipsam mulierculam fuisse, et regalibus amplexibus prorsus indignam. Perpendebantque iam iam ueraciss [279] ueracissime, non sine causa exilio lacrimabili, ipsam, ut predictum est, fuisse condepmnatam. Cum autem annos longeue senectutis[280] comes Tuinfredus, et pre senectute caligassent oculi eius, data filio suo regi benedicione, nature debita persoluit. Cuius corpus magnifice, prout decuit, tradidit sepulture. Anno quoque sub eodem uxor eius comitissa Marcellina, mater uidelicet regis, ualedicens filio, ab huius incolatu seculi feliciter transmigrauit.

Qualiter patre et matre iam defunctis, Rex Offa in cunctis prospere se habuit.

Rex itaque Offa uel Offanus utroque parentum iam orbatus, consolaconem a Domino Iesu Christo, cui se palam et frequenter confitebatur obligatum, postulauit et accepit. Ex regina igitur uxore sua, que se Petronillam nominauit, prolem suscepit sexus imfra[281] biennium utriusque, filiumque suum primogenitum Ecgfridum iussit nominari.

Interea utpote sagax fortunatus et bellicosus, hostes conterminos audacter impetendo, fines [12ʳ][282] regni Merciorum sub temporis breuitate, inopinabiliter dilatauit. Vnde tum pro sobole sibi a Deo concessa, tum pro corporis strenuitate, tum pro cordis sagacitate, factus est hostibus non mediocriter formidabilis.

Hostes Offe Karolo Regi Francorum confederantur.

Rex igitur Offa secundus, primo similimus, in omnibus agendis primo studuit conformari. Dilatata est igitur fama magnifencie[283] sue, et ceperunt uniuersi reges quos Offa primus sibi subiugarat magis ac magis potentiam suam formidare. Inito igitur

---

[279] C ueracium.

[280] C 'uixisset' inserted from margin.

[281] C infra.

[282] Illustration: The three kings of the anti-Mercian alliance, standing, despatch a courier to the Frankish king Carloman (see p. 51-2), seated, who then replies.

[283] C magnificencie.

his mother, the Lady Marcellina, for protection, to be fed and looked after more tenderly in the care of so honourable a matron, until she heard the king's instructions.

So within a few days the girl's emaciation and pallor were dispelled by food, and her former beauty returned so that she was considered a very lovely woman. But soon breaking out into boastful and passionate words, as was customary in her native country, she behaved very badly by being impertinently contemptuous of the Lady who had gently nurtured her with maternal affection. But the Lady bore everything patiently for love of her son the king, although this said girl had sown words of discord between the Earl and Lady.

Then one day, when the king was going to pay her a visit, so as to address her with consoling words, he fell into the net of her love, for she was now an attractive sight.

And so he took her to himself in a secret, hasty marriage, without consulting his father and mother, or any of the chief men at all. In consequence, both his parents worrying with grief and anxiety, which shortened the days of their life, anticipated the hour of their death sorrowfully. For they knew that she had been a little hussy and utterly unworthy of the king's embrace. And now they were truly convinced that it was not without cause she had been condemned to this lamentable exile, as said above. But when Earl Thingfrith had lived[284] to a great old age, and his eyes had clouded over with age, having blessed his son the king, he paid the debt to nature. His body was committed to burial in a splendid manner. And the year after that his wife also, that is to say the king's mother the Lady Marcellina, bidding farewell to her son, happily left the habitation of this world.

How, with father and mother now dead, King Offa succeeded in every way.

And so King Offa (or Offanus), now bereft of both parents, asked and received consolation from the Lord Jesus Christ, to whom he openly and often confessed himself bound, obliged and indebted. And then he had offspring by the queen, his wife (who called herself Petronilla[285]), of both sexes in under two years, and he ordered his first-born son to be called Ecgfrith.

Meanwhile, very wise, fortunate and warlike, he boldly invaded neighbouring enemies, unexpectedly extending the borders of the kingdom of the Mercians in a short time. Hence he became no small threat to his enemies, partly because of the offspring granted him by God, then because of strength of body, then because of wisdom of heart.

Offa's enemies form an alliance with Charles, king of the Franks.

So the second King Offa, who resembled the first, strove to imitate the first in every way. So the fame of his greatness spread, and all the kings whom the first Offa himself had subjugated[286] began to fear his power more and more. So there began a general

[284] C synonym 'he had lived' inserted from margin.
[285] The name of an early virgin martyr whose cult Charlemagne's court strongly subscribed. For this and similar by-names, see Introduction, p. lxxxv.
[286] Cf. pp. 27-8.

communi consilio. Rex Cantuariensium et Kenttensium, Rex Occidentalium Saxonum, Rex Northambrorum, Rex Australium Saxonum, Rex Orientalium Anglorum, consultius arbitrabantur Karolo Magno Francorum regi, solempnibus nunciis ad hoc destinatis amicicias postulando confederari. Cartam igitur huius exempli eidem transmiserunt:

> Karolo Regi Francorum magno, triumphatori inuincibili. Quinque Britannie Reges potentissimi,[287] uidelicet Cantii Occidentalium Saxonum, Northambrorum, Australium Saxonum, Orientalium Anglorum, salutem et fedus amicicie. Cum Offanus Rex Merciorum in tantam proruperit proteruiam ut maiestatis nostre hostiliter inuaserit potenciam, et temere presumat conterere; ad sinum uestre protectionis confugimus; ut et nos, qui quamuis uulpinas eius insidias non timeamus, tua nos prudencia moderetur, confortet consilium; et si emerserit necessitas, contra ipsum cuius maior est [288] superbia quam fortitudo, iuuet et corroboret patrocinium. Nos quoque simili federe relatiuo uobis si res expostulet generaliter in adiutorium uestrum contra uobis rebelles insurgemus. Tuam igitur petimus serenitatem quatinus furorem suum terribilis, epistola uestra compescat, ne sponte perire compellatur. Tue uero donacioni mille aureos pro munere mittimus primitiuo, hoc donatiuo futuram amiciciam subarrantes.

Karolus incipit protegere hostes Regis Offe.

Hec cum audisset Karolus eorum mandata et munera gratanter acceptauit. Transmisit igitur epistolam comminatoriam et preces imperiosas continentem Regi Offe consulens et imperans ut desisteret Britanniam inquietare, aut reges conterminos sibi, qui eidem fuerantnouo federe sociati, aliquo modo subiugare. Quod si attemptaret, sibi Karolum omni mortali formidabilem sentiret inimicum.

Offa contempto mandato Karoli, expugnat sibi rebelles.

Ad hec magnanimus Rex Merciorum Offa respondit: 'Quid michi et Karolo transmarino. Et ipsum si michi iniuriaretur hostiliter impeterem et conarer michi et regno meo ipsum cogere famulari.'

In spiritum igitur iracundie omnes sibi militare seruicium debentes uoce preconia congregauit, et ait: 'Amici et commilitones mei qui me ad libertatis uestre unanimiter

---

[287] N 'potentissimi' inserted from margin.
[288] C run on; 'subi' deleted.

discussion. Upon consideration, the king of the Eastern and Western Kentish men,[289] the king of the West Saxons, the king of the Northumbrians, the king of the South Saxons, the king of the East English, decided on negotiation with Charles the Great,[290] king of the Franks, by means of official messengers designated expressly to ask for his friendship in an alliance. So they sent him a document of this kind:[291]

> 'To Charles the Great, King of the Franks, invincible champion, five most powerful kings of Britain, that is to say: of the people of Kent, of the West Saxons, Northumbrians, South Saxons, East English, send greetings and a pact of friendship. Because Offa, king of the Mercians, has risen up with such impudence that he has invaded our realms and rashly dares harry us, we flee to the bosom of your protection, so that, although his wolfish plots do not frighten us, we may be both restrained by your prudence and comforted by your advice; and if need arises your military support might help and strengthen us against a man whose pride exceeds his power. We too, by a similar pact regarding you, will arm ourselves to help suppress those rebelling against you if the general occasion demands it. So we seek your favour in order that a letter from you will restrain his terrible rage, not wanting annihilation. We are sending you a thousand gold pieces as merely a preliminary gift, looking for future friendship with this donation.'

Charles begins to protect King Offa's enemies.

When Charles heard these things, he willingly accepted their commissions and gifts. So he sent a warning letter to King Offa that contained imperial requests advising and ordering that he desist from disruption in Britain or in any other way oppressing his neighbouring kings who had united in a new pact against him. If he tried that, wholly mortal, he would feel mighty Charles's enmity.

At Charles's contemptible instruction Offa attacks his rebels.

To these things the mighty Offa, King of the Mercians, replied: 'And what is Charles overseas to me? If he wrongfully assaulted me I would send forces to attack him, and force him to serve me and my kingdom.'

So in a wrathful spirit he had the voice of a herald gather all those owing him military service, and said: 'My friends and comrades-in-arms who have unanimously

---

[289] A racial distinction since the time of the Settlements, reflected to the present day in the separation of the respective dioceses of eastern Canterbury and western Rochester (Fig. 13), although not recognised in the Alliance's letter to Charles (pp. 51-2). See generally B.A.E. Yorke, 'Joint kingship in Kent *c.* 560 to 785', *Archaeologia Cantiana*, 99 (1983), 1-19.

[290] For textual confusion between Carloman and Charlemagne, see pp. 49-58, and Introduction, pp. xc-xci.

[291] No separate copy of this letter survives in Carolingian archives.

non meis meritis set sola liberalitate uestra conuocastis tuicionem; [12ᵛ]²⁹² ecce hostes mei, immo uestri, Karolo Regi Francorum superbo, in perniciem uestram confederati ruinam Merciorum fraudulenter machinantur. Set ut audiui immo constanter certificor, ipse in Ytalicis et aliis transmarinis et transalpinis partibus negociis bellicis occupatus inimicis circundatur et²⁹³ impugnatur. Interim et nos inimicos nostros uigilanter impetamus. Vt sic antequam idem Karolus sibi uacet ut nostris hostibus suffragentur, ipsos irrestaurabiliter prosternamus.' Interea memoratus rex Karolus a Saxonum gente prouocatus, illuc lora dirigit et uexilla, et ipsos multis preliis, que speciales tractatus exigeret, suo dominio²⁹⁴ multis utrobique principibus interfectis tandem triumphaliter mancipauit.

Rex Estanglorum ab Offa Rege Merciorum expugnatur.

Magnates autem Merciorum cum super libertate regni sic per regem sollicitarentur, constanter et unanimiter quasi uno spiritu responderunt, se ipsum regem usque ad exposicionem capitum fideliter secuturos. Rex igitur Offa dum Karolus Rex in Saxonie partibus, uariis preliorum casibus detineretur, non dormiens neque dormitans, regem Estanglorum, collectis uiribus, studuit potenter impetere. Sed cum hic ipsius hostilem aduentum cognosceret, ipsum Offam alacriter in ore gladii suscepit. Vnde in loco qui Feldhard ab incolis nuncupatur, commissum est prelium cruentissimum. Et post certamen a summo mane usque ad meridiem hostiliter continuatum, cessit Offe uictoria.²⁹⁵ Vnde triumphali titulo gloriose insignitus, Offa letus et illesus ad propria remeauit.

Moritur Karolus Rex francorum Substituitur Karolus frater eius priore potencior.

Cum autem post tropheum exultans rex preciperet munifice spolia uictorum et captiuos suis distribui commilitonibus et ut²⁹⁶ qui pondus et estus prelii, uulnera uel amicorum iacturas sustinuerunt premia reportarent pro suis meritis uberiora; redierunt²⁹⁷ quos clanculo miserat de transmarinis partibus sui exploratores, qui affirmarunt²⁹⁸ Karolum Francorum regem in medio suorum procerum morte repentina

---

²⁹² Illustration: At the battle of Feldhard against the East Anglians, Offa II in the front line, without heraldry but wearing a distinctively crested helmet, lances the leader of the enemy cavalry, who then turn to flee.

²⁹³ *C* 'et' erased.

²⁹⁴ *C* domino.

²⁹⁵ *N* 'cessit Offe uictoria' underlined in later hand presumably in reference to the illustration at the top of the page.

²⁹⁶ *C* 'ut' interlined.

²⁹⁷ *C* 'redieruit' and insertion mark but nothing supplied. The Rev. W. Watts's transcript, never wholly accurate, here inserts 'etiam', *Uitæ duorum Offarum… Et uiginti trium abbatum Sancti Albani*, London, 1639, p. 14.

²⁹⁸ *C* affirmauerunt.

called me your liberator – of your own free will, not out of duty to me but out of your generosity alone – behold, my enemies – in fact yours – have to your harm allied themselves to proud Charles king of the Franks; treacherously planned the ruin of the Mercians. But as I hear – in fact get constant confirmation of – he is personally occupied somewhere in Italy and other overseas parts beyond the Alps in military campaigns, and under attack surrounded by foes.[299] Taking note, we also meanwhile will attack our foes. So that before Charles so extricates himself as to lend aid to our enemies, we will irretrievably cut them down.' In the meantime the renowned King Charles, being harassed by the people of Saxony,[300] sent there cavalry and infantry and these [fought] many battles which demanded special manoeuvres; and eventually, after widespread killing of their chief men, he triumphantly subjected them to his domination.

Offa, king of the Mercians, attacks the king of the East English.

But when the magnates of the Mercians were freely approached in this way by the king, they replied loyally and unanimously as if with one heart that they would follow their king even at cost of their lives. So whilst King Charles, neither sleeping nor slumbering, was delayed in various different battles somewhere in Saxony, King Offa – after summoning his men – engaged in a concerted attack on the king of the East English.[301] But when this man learned about the invasion he swiftly offered battle to Offa. Then a most gory battle began with the local people in a place called Feldhard.[302] Once the struggle started, there was continuous fighting from mid-morning until midday, ending with victory to Offa. Gloriously distinguished by the title of champion, Offa returned home, happy and unharmed.

Charles, king of the Franks, dies and his brother Charles takes over, more powerful than the former.

But then the king, celebrating after his triumph, generously ordered the spoils of victims and captives to be distributed among his comrades-in-arms, so that those who had endured the burden and heat of battle, injuries or loss of friends, obtained richer booty according to their deserts. The scouts whom he had secretly sent returned from overseas, and confirmed that Charles the king of the Franks had suddenly collapsed

---

[299] For Charlemagne's Langobard campaign see below, pp. 75-6, 79-80.

[300] Charlemagne had long regarded the pagan Saxons as a threat to his domain. He first invaded their territory in 772 and in 782 organised Saxony as a Frankish province, deporting many of its original inhabitants. Rebellions broke out regularly thereafter. Einhard, *Vita Karoli Magni*, Holder-Egger, pp. 9-11; Thorpe, pp. 6, 61-4.

[301] Hun, Beonna and Alberht had divided the kingdom between them in 749. Æthelberht acceded at some stage, dying at Offa II's palace in 794 (pp. 89-96), cf. Introduction, pp. lxxxvi-lxxxvii.

[302] Location unknown. The name is composed of Old English *feld*, commonly used at that time for a tract of open country; and *heard* with a semantic spread over 'difficult to till' and, relevant here, 'cheerless', cf. Smith, *English Place-Name Elements*, I, pp. 166-8, 239.

corruisse ueneno uel apoplexiea subito suffocatus. Quod cum audisset Offa, non iam semipleno sed exuberanti gaudio recreatus, ait: 'Eia milites laboris et gaudii mei participes, fauente nobis ad uotum, Marte, immo pocius ipso Christo Domino excercituum; ceciderunt hic et in partibus transmarinis nostri eminus inimici. Karolus namque dum de Saxonia superbus remearet pro triumpho, in medio agminum suorum offenso Deo cruentus, interitu periit repentino. Qui hostibus nostris contra nos dimicaturis auxilium et consilium prestiturum se promisit. Manifestum est igitur Deum nobis fauorem et patrocinium celitus contulisse.' Ad hoc omnes cum gaudio uociferati dixerunt: 'Et si uiueret Karolus, nec ipsum [13r][303] nec alium sub te duce fortunato timeremus.'

Hostes Offe iterum Karolo secundo potentissimo confederantur.

Defuncto igitur ut dictum est Karolo qui cum fratre suo Karolo, patris sui monarchiam participando dimidiabat, substitutus est ille dictus Karolus natu minor monarchie memorate. Vnde reges Britannie predicti qui Offe hostiliter aduersabantur, nouis et preciosioribus muneribus cum legatis preclaris et solempnibus ad ipsum festinanter transmiserunt ut cum ipso confederati in Offam insurgerent tuciores, immo pocius forciores. Qui ad ipsum peruenientes dixerunt: 'O regum excellentissime, audiuit ut creditur imperialis maiestas uestra qualiter frater tuus Karolus regibus qui in Britannia iniuriosos impetus Offe Regis Merciorum sustinent, consilium salutiferum et efficax libenter conferret patrocinium. Quo uniuerse carnis uiam ingresso et te loco ipsius feliciter subrogato, tuam propensius condecet dominacionem, magnificentius suplere quod spopondit, cum maiori potestate sublimeris.' Acceptans igitur hoc mandatum Karolus cum muneribus concupiscibilibus, sereno uultu respondit: 'Amici mei, Dominus uestris munificis ac magnificis regibus Britannie qui fratri beniuoli et benefici, et me[304] renouatis respexerunt donatiuis, grata respondebo uicissitudine, in plenitudine, tamen potestatis michi debite stabilitus. Expectent igitur paciencer, donec fidelium meorum receperim iuramenta plenius et obligaciones. Ego autem interim temeritates Offe freno terribilis comminacionis cohibebo.'

Comminacio secundi Karoli, S. Maximi, ne inquietet reges sibi rebelles.

Scripsit igitur Karolus maximus Offe Regi hunc modum:

---

[303] Illustration: King Offa II, enthroned and ensceptred beneath a tripartite Romanesque arch with foliated capitals receives Charlemagne's warning with a gesture of rejection; and then standing sends his reply.
[304] C 'me' interlined.

and died in the midst of his noblemen, suddenly suffocated by poison or apoplexy.[305] When Offa heard this, now buoyed up with delight, not moderate but overwhelming, he said: 'Hooray! You soldiers who have willingly shared my toil and and delights, Mars, in fact one greater – Christ the Lord of Hosts – has granted our prayer![306] Our powerful enemies here and in overseas parts, have fallen. For whilst the proud Charles was returning in triumph from Saxony, still on the march, he suddenly died in the midst of his troops, blood-stained from their offence to God – he who earlier promised aid and advice to our enemies in a struggle against us. Thus it is clear that God has granted us progress and patronage from heaven.' At this everyone exclaiming with delight, said: 'Under your happy leadership even if Charles were alive, we would fear neither him nor anyone else.'

Offa's enemies again form an alliance with a second very powerful Charles.

Therefore, as said, with the death of Charles who divided with his brother Charles their father's kingdom by sharing it,[307] this said younger Charles took over from him in the aforementioned kingdom. So the aforesaid kings of Britain, who hostilely opposed Offa, quickly despatched formal, distinguished ambassadors with yet more valuable gifts, so that with his support they might revive the alliance against Offa – in fact in greater security and strength. Who, coming to him, said: 'Oh most excellent of kings, we believe that your imperial majesty has heard how your brother Charles readily conferred sound advice and effective patronage on the kings in Britain who are suffering wrongful attacks by Offa, king of the Mercians. He having gone the way of all flesh and you raised to greater power, we feel it would be proper and advantageous to your rule to generously fulfil what he pledged.' So Charles, accepting this mandate, together with the attractive gifts, replied with a smiling face: 'My friends, your lord will respond with glad exchanges to your generosity and to the great kings of Britain who wished well and acted well towards my brother, and who have shown regard for me with new gifts – though not until my power is secure. So let them wait patiently until I have received more fully the oaths and allegiance of my subjects. But in the meantime I will restrain Offa's temerity by the control of terrible warnings.'

A warning from the second Charles, the Holy and Great, that he should not disrupt the kings rebellious to him.

So Charles the Great wrote to King Offa in this way:

---

[305] Einhard, their contemporary, says merely that Carloman died due to 'illness' (*morbo decessit*), *Vita Karoli Magni*, Holder-Egger, p. 6, Thorpe, p. 58. And there is no evidence for Carloman rather than Charlemagne conducting anti-Saxon campaigns.

[306] The term is frequently used of God by Old Testament prophets Isaiah, Jeremiah, Malachi and Zechariah and thus readily transferred to post-resurrection Jesus, cf Augustine, *Enarrationes in Psalmos*, ed. J.P. Migne, *Patrologia Latina*, 37, *passim*.

[307] See Introduction, pp. xc-xci.

Karolus Regum potentissimus et imperiali diademate decorandus illustri regi Merciorum Offe, salutem. Cum regum nobilium tibi finitimorum impaciens in tantam proruperis proteruiam, ut omnes tibi temere coneris inclinare, reprimat te epistola nostra imperialis, ne prout presumptuo se nimis incepisti, ipsos amplius audeas amplius[308] hostiliter impetere, aut modis aliquibus ulterius inquietare. Non enim deesse poterit nostrum eis in necessitatis articulo patrocinium. Consule igitur tue gratissime iuuentuti, me te cogar conterere, regno tuo miserabiliter irrestaurabiliter spoliatum.

Offa paratur uiriliter et reges sibi rebelles conterere.

Hec igitur cum audisset Offa magnanimus conuocatis suis commilitonibus, ait: 'Ecce mandatum[309] Karoli secundi rediuiuum. Segnes nos existimat et desidiosos, necnon et formidolosos credit et effeminatos, cum solis minis suis uincere nos speret et turpiter incuruare. Sed O generosi sortis mee participes, non tam mea sed res uestra, non specialis, sed publica causa uentilatur. Negocium hoc arduum nimis nullam capit dilacionem. Dum enim Karolus ad instar [13ᵛ][310] plantule que non dum radices in altum transmisit, robur non accipit, inimicos nostros sceleriter[311] conteramus.

Animatur populus Merciorum ad conterendum reges sibi aduersantes.

Cum autem taliter Offa perorasset, responderunt ei nobiles Merciorum: 'Utquid nos existimat Karolus ignauos et degeneres? Vires suas minime formidamus. Qui et si Karolo iam defuncto maior est, et tu Rex noster Offa maior es Offano magno tuo predecessore. Et si ille maximus inter suos, tu maximus inter tuos choruscabis.[312] Dimicet maximus eum maximo, ut maximi uirtus manifestius comprobetur. Et si nobis quos hactenus Deus protexit aduersetur, eodem uindice quo et frater eius corruit, corruet et ille a Deo reprobatus! Ex tunc autem omnes ad certamen martium quodcunque Offa dispositurus et agressurus erat generaliter animantur.

---

[308] *C* second 'amplius' of the two omitted.
[309] *C* mandati.
[310] Illustration. At the battle of Otford, Kent (AD. 776), Offa II in the front line of Mercian cavalry lances the king of Kent.
[311] *C* celeriter.
[312] *N* 'h' interlined.

'Charles, most powerful of kings, and adorned with the imperial diadem,[313] greets Offa, illustrious king of the Mercians. Because you have been so intolerant of the noble kings on your borders, as to presumptuously intend to shamefully subject every one to yourself, may this our imperial letter curb you; do not be so very audacious as you have been up to now – boldly perpetrating more and more hostilities toward them – or disrupt them any more in other ways. For I cannot withhold my support from them in their hour of need. So consider carefully what is in your best interests, young man,[314] lest I be forced to crush you, miserably, irretrievably despoil your kingdom.'

Offa prepares boldly to crush the kings rebelling against him.

When the great-hearted Offa heard this, therefore, he summoned his comrades-in-arms and said: 'Look! a fresh instruction from a second Charles. He reckons us lazy and idle, and also believes us cowardly and effeminate, if he hopes to overcome us merely by his threats and to shamefully turn us from our purpose. But, Oh well-bred sharers in my fate, let us not consider my affairs but yours, not one man's interest but that of all. This really tough business brooks no delay. So let us quickly[315] crush our enemies whilst Charles is still like a young plant that hasn't yet put down deep roots, and hasn't grown strong.'

The Mercian people are encouraged to crush the kings opposing them.

Well, when Offa had addressed them in this way, the Mercian nobles replied: 'Why does Charles reckon us stupid and corrupt? We aren't afraid of his forces. And even if he is now greater than the dead Charles, you too, our King Offa, are greater than the great Offa your predecessor. And if he is the best among his people, you will be celebrated as the best among yours. Let best be compared with best, so that the strength of the best may be clearly shown. And if it goes against us, who up to now God has protected, he will die of the same penalty by which his brother died, reproved by God.' So from then on everyone was generally encouraged to fight and do whatever Offa suggested or proposed.

---

[313] Not in fact crowned emperor until Christmas Day, AD. 800. See Introduction, p. xxxiii.

[314] Offa II might perhaps refer to himself as 'a child by nature' but actually the Mercian ruler was Charlemagne's senior by two or three decades (see Introduction, p. lviii). The expression 'young man' is still to be heard as a patronizing form of address in English at the present time.

[315] Here C 's *celeriter*, 'quickly', is preferred to N's *sceleriter*, 'criminally', although cf. D.J. Tyler, 'Orchestrated violence and the "supremacy of the Mercian kings"', in *Æthelbald and Offa*, pp. 27-33.

Rex Cantuariensium uel Kentensium a Rege Offa conteritur.

Conuocatis igitur uniuersis officium militare sibi debentibus, Regem Cantuariensem uel Kentensem hostiliter aggreditur. Cui accurrunt alii reges memorati Regi Offe rebelles, in eorum adiutorium. Offa uero dispositis milicie sue legionibus, oppositum excercitum potenter et audacter ad similitudinem fulguris choruscantis inuadit. Et dissipates obstantibus uniuersis, bellum inchoat cruentissimum. Vnde equorum et armorum et armatorum, tubarum et lituorum strepitus horribilis, aciesque sese glomeratim comprimentium, ad nubes ascendere uidebatur. Et timor qui super constantissimos cadere poterat, corda concutit intuencium. Quid plura, congressum utrobique grauiter, et suspensa est uictoria equipollentibus uiribus tempore diuturno. Et dum hec agerentur inuictissimus Rex Offa tedio affectus uocem eleuans cum clamore ualido, ait: 'O consortes, amici et commilitones mei, confusionis uel glorie mee consortes, quid hucusque pueriliter hostibus publicis allusistis? Numquid hic simultas latitat? Vbi nam Merciorum probitas frequenter experta? Sequimini me preuium. Et Kentensem proditorem in spiritu furoris nostri et impetu repentino adeamus uniuersi. Et eius miseram animam nichil aliud pro meritis expectantem in Tartara detrudamus.'

Hec uerba compleuerat, equinum calcaribus latus utrumque cruentans, in ipsum tyrannum Kentensem quasi turbine raptus inuehitur truculenter, nec eum acies interposite quin turmas densissimas dissiparet; et uias latas aperiret, retardare potuerunt. Vibrata igitur hasta cruentata totis uiribus in Kentensem, corpus eius hastili mucrone transuerberauit, quod nec obice clipei uel lorice poterat premuniri. Et cum miseram animam eructans corruisset, exclamauit moribundus: 'Heu, heu, miser, peccata mea inueterata recens michi dedecus [14ʳ] [316] reseruarunt. Verumptamen inuictissimi commilitones mei hoc meum et uestrum dapnum et dedecus uiriliter uindicate.' Et sic moriens extremum spiritum sub equinis pedibus exalauit. Hec cruenta cedes apud Otteford perhibetur fuisse consummata.

Fugerunt a facie Offe reges[317] uicti qui in adiutorium eorum uenerant qui eidem Offe aduersabantur.

Rex Offa interim Norhthamhinbrorum, [318] Australium et Occidentalium turmis in ipsum truculenter irruentibus, undique circumuallatur et impetitur uiolenter, adeo ut

---

[316] Illustration: A confrontation between Mercians and others at the Battle of Benson, Oxfordshire (AD. 777). The leading mounted figure on either side fights with a long-sword.
[317] C 'es' of 'reges' erased, and last four words of heading omitted.
[318] C 'Northamhinbrorum' and similarly hereafter.

The king of the Men of Kent, or Kentish men,[319] is crushed by King Offa.

So having called up all those owing him military service, an attack was made on the king of the Men of Kent or Kentish men. Other afore-mentioned kings who were rebels against King Offa, came to their aid.[320] However, Offa, having positioned the troops of his fighting force, attacked the opposing army powerfully and boldly, like a flash of lightning. And all those standing in his way being scattered, he began a very bloody battle. From then on, with the vanguard amassed, the horrendous racket of horses and arms and of armed men, of trumpets and horns, seemed to rise up to the clouds. And the fear that could fall on the most resolute struck the hearts of onlookers. What else! Serious combat on all sides, and victory delayed for a long time between forces of equal strength. Whilst these things were happening, the most invincible King Offa, distressed, raised his voice and shouted out loudly: 'Oh my partners, friends and comrades-in-arms! Partners in my defeat or glory, why have you been playing children's games with the public enemy until now? What hides the fierceness here? Where the often-proved Mercian vigour? Follow my lead! And with our fighting rage let us make a concerted and sudden attack on the Kentish traitor. And let us oust his miserable soul which deserves nothing but Hell.'

These words finished, bloodying both flanks of the horse with spurs,[321] he rode violently towards the Kentish despot[322] as if seized by a whirlwind; nor was the front-line lying between able to prevent him from scattering very dense cavalry indeed, and opening wide paths. So having brandished a blood-stained spear against the Kentish man with full might, he ran his body through with the head of a spear which neither shield nor breastplate was able to deflect. And after he had fallen, belching forth his miserable soul, he exclaimed when dying: 'Alas, alas for me, my besetting sins have stored up this new humiliation for me. Nevertheless, my invincible comrades-in-arms, rigorously avenge this my – and your – condemnation and humiliation.' And dying thus, he breathed forth his soul beneath the horses' feet. This bloody slaughter is said to have taken place at Otford.[323]

The defeated kings who had supported them against Offa now flee upon Offa's appearance.

Meanwhile, cavalry of Northumbrians, Southerners and Westerners[324] violently rushed in on King Offa, surrounded him on all sides and attacked so fiercely that the points of

---

[319] Cf. p. 52, n. 289.

[320] *The Anglo-Saxon Chronicles* mention only Kentish being at the Battle of Otford, 776, (eds cit., pp. 50-51).

[321] See generally, R.H.C. Davis, 'Did the Anglo-Saxons have warhorses?', in S.C. Hawkes, ed., *Weapons and Warfare in Anglo-Saxon England*, Oxford, 1989, pp. 141-44.

[322] The Kentish leader is given no name, but the rulership of Kent was commonly divided at this period, see above p. 52, n. 289.

[323] A.D. 776, *Anglo-Saxon Chronicles*, eds cit., pp. 50-51. At a strategic crossing of the River Darent.

[324] As shown a few lines later, this is not a confused echo of the old Deira, Bernicia divide of Northumbria, but rather an allusion to the cavalry of South and West Saxons.

lancearum cuspidibus in pectore, dorso et utroque latere applicatis et impulsis, diuersis hinc inde pellentibus immotus permansit et ab inuitis ne prosterneretur, est adiutus. Et circumtinnientes[325] gladii hostiles caput suum undique mallearent, ita ut iam discrimini letali pateret Rex Offanus.

Ecce acies Merciorum inuictissima, ad instar torrentis saxa rotantis, irruit in obstantes. Et in Northhamhinbros, Occidentales et Australes Saxones qui iam pene Regem Offam contriuerant, tanto impetu et mentis acerbissimo furore, ut omnes eis resistentes perturbarunt, et dissipatos ante solis occasum fugam inire compulerunt. In quo grauissimo conflictu multi de nobilioribus qui memoratis regibus adheserunt contra Offam, ceciderunt. De manu uero mediocri, innumerabiles. Hoc autem bellum horribile nimis apud Bensintonam est commissum, in obsidione eiusdem castri.

Elapso autem Kenulpho rege Occidentalium Saxonum in noctis caligine, aduersi martis minoratus est casu infortunato, totus exercitus qui Offe aduersabantur. Offa uero triumphator magnificus ipsum castrum quod ibidem obsederat, cum illis quos in eo inuenerat in sua suscepit. Fugerunt ergo residui, et insequebatur eos Offa et multos ex eis fugientes a dorso lancea perforauit. Sui autem commilitones, quos apprehendebant uel eos qui se quasi uictos eis manciparunt, uiuos et illesos reseruabant, in seruitutem redigendos uel grauiter redimendos. Omnes autem ad uotum comprehendent[326] uel peremissent nisi in cuiusdam municipii refugio ad quod conuolabant sese Northambrorum et Australium Saxonum reges celeriter recepissent.

Quos Rex Offa qui sicut erat in pace mansuetissimus ita et in bello fuit hominum ferocissimus, iussit in girum obsidione[327] castrum donec omnes inclusi uel fame contabescerent, uel uiolenter capti, iudicialiter punirentur.

Nocte uero tertia sequente dum excubitores fatigati quiescerent, ipsi reges memorati omni carentes alimento dum caligo nimis opace noctis oculos omnium detineret, clanculo cum suis omnibus aufugerunt, nec lora retinuerunt donec ad Wallie confinia peruenissent. Vbi cum regem Wallie Marmodium inuenissent, eius humiliter protectionem et receptacionem [14^v][328] contra Offanum eorum animas querentem, et postea regnum uiolenter occupare proponentem, postularunt. Ac ipse nimis credulus dictis eorum, timens ne iuxta eorum afferconem regnum Wallie expugnaret, recepit eos

---

[325] C 'Et cum circumtinnientes' the anticipated syllable 'cum' requiring no grammatical accommodation.
[326] C 'comprehendissent'. Corrected thus in margin of N by a later hand. 'they would have understood' ('pluperfect' subjunctive used conditionally)
[327] C 'uallari' inserted from the margin.
[328] Illustration: Offa II sends a letter to the Welsh king Meredith; subsequently massed ranks of Mercian and Welsh cavalry encounter each other (although without indication as to which is which), and the right-hand-most turn to flee.

lances touched and entered the chest, back and both sides; here he remained unable to move because of various blows and was helped lest he was thrown down by adversaries. And clashing enemy swords hammered around his head, in such a way that now King Offa was exposed to mortal danger.

And behold, against Northumbrians, Western and Southern Saxons, who just now had almost destroyed King Offa, the most invincible vanguard of Mercians — just like a torrent rushing around rocks — streamed against obstructions, with such force and so intense rage that everyone resisting them were in havoc, and those scattered were compelled to flee before sunset. In this most important conflict died many of the nobles who adhered to the aforesaid kings against Offa. And countless ordinary troops in fact. But the greater part of this terrible war took place at Benson,[329] in the siege of that fort.[330]

For after Cynewulf king of the West Saxons escaped into the darkness of the night,[331] the whole army which had opposed Offa was now reduced by the misfortune of adverse war. Indeed, Offa the great champion himself seized that very fort which he had besieged in that same place, along with those he found in it. And so the rest fled, and Offa pursued them, and killed many of those fleeing with a lance piercing the back. But those whom his own comrades-in-arms took prisoner or those who, almost overcome, surrendered themselves, they kept alive and unharmed, to be reduced into slavery or heavily ransomed. But they would have seized or destroyed them all at will if the kings of the Northumbrians and the South Saxons had not swiftly escaped to the refuge of a certain stronghold to which they fled.

King Offa, who was a man just as ferocious in war as he was good-natured in peace, ordered the fort to be besieged around,[332] until all those inside either died of hunger or, taken by force, were punished by law.

On the third night following, whilst the exhausted watchmen were resting, these aforesaid kings, having nothing to eat, whilst no one could see them in the gloom of the dark night, secretly escaped with all their followers, not to draw rein until they had reached the Welsh border. There, when they had found King Meredith of Wales,[333] they asked for his protection and defence against Offa who was seeking their souls, and afterwards proposing to violently occupy the kingdom. And he believed their words entirely, and was afraid that, in accord with their report, the kingdom of Wales might be invaded. He received them, through whom he hoped to have the advantage of a

---

[329] *Benesingtun, Anglo-Saxon Chronicles*, AD, 779; cf. M. Gelling, *The Place-Names of Oxfordshire*, English Place-Name Society, 23-24, Cambridge, 1953-54, p. 116. A major crossing of the Thames, near Wallingford (Berks.); remembered as being captured by the West Saxons in AD. 571, *Anglo-Saxon Chronicles*, eds cit., p. 19.

[330] Presumably Frithela's Fort on Wytham Hill, later said to have been built at that time, *Chronicon de Abingdon*, ed. R.S. Stevenson, Rolls Series, 2, London, 1858, I, p. 8; II, pp. 269-70.

[331] This is the Cynewulf whose dramatic death in 786 in confrontation with his rival Cyneheard is related at length in *The Anglo-Saxon Chronicles s.a.* 755, (eds cit. pp. 46-49).

[332] C 's marginal 'to be walled round' possibly referring to a besiegers' counter-fort.

[333] Maredudd, a king of Dyfed, *ob.* 796, about whom very little is known: J.E. Lloyd, *A History of Wales*, 3rd edn, London, 1939, I, p. 262. But generally Lloyd, 'The personal name-system in Old Welsh', *Y Cymrodor*, 9 (1888), 39-55 (pp. 50-51).

benigne, per quos sperabat magna roborari defensione. Vnde non tantum in terra sua refugium et latibulum sed defensionem spopondit et iuuamen.

Offa Northamhinbrorum et Australium Saxonum Reges fugientes in Waliam insequitur.

Cum hec autem[334] regi Offe plenius innotuissent, excubitorum desidiam quamplurimum redarguens, reges memoratos usque ad Wallie contermina hostiliter insequitur non percunctans. Destinatisque solempnibus nunciis significauit Regi Marmodio sub hac forma:

> 'Nobile Walensium Regi Marmodio, Offa Merciorum Basileus salutem et honorem. Nouit fama referente prudentia tua ut creditur qualiter Northamhinbrorum et Australium reges potentiem Regni Merciorum a longo tempore subiugati, meam procaciter spreuerunt dominacionem, et ad alas protectionis Karoli Francorum Regis ut me contererent fraudulenter conuolarunt. Vnde supplico moneo et consulo, quatinus talibus fauorem nullatenus prebeas aut iuuamen, quod si temere acceptaueris, noueris me tibi inimicum grauiter suscitatum, et te cum illis similibus calamitatibus inuoluendum. Vale.'

Hiis auditis, Rex Wallie Marmodius conuocatis regibus supradictis, epistolam sibi ex parte Offe Regis transmissam exposuit per ordinem. At ipsi affirmarunt ipsum Offanum prophanum semper minis habundasse et sub ouina pelle uulpinas insidias et lupinas semper palliasse rapinas. Nec ipsum Marmodium Regem potentem, Offam regulum desipientem et arreptium[335] minime debere formidare. Quibus fallacibus sermocinacionibus animatus Rex Marmodius per ipsos Offe legatos eidem Offe renunciauit: 'Inhonestum fore ac formidolosum ipsos deserere desolatos quos susceperat misericorditer protegendos.' Quos si[336] impetere prosumpsisset,[337] uires totius Wallie effunderet in eorum defunsionem.

Dum autem legati istis occuparentur,[338] Rex Offa presagus futurorum terras et municiones regum fugitiuorum sibi prudenter ac potenter occupauit; et suis obsequiis acceptis obsidibus et iuramentis indissolubiliter mancipauit. Et in eorum ciuitatibus et castris suos fideles ad custodiam ordinauit, ut ex tunc fugitiui penitus excluderentur.

---

[334] C autem hec.
[335] C arepticium.
[336] N inserted from margin in later hand.
[337] C presumpsisset.
[338] N marginal rubric: 'Cautela Offe.'

great means of defence, favourably. Wherefore he promised not only a refuge and hideout in his land but also defence and support.

Offa pursues the kings of Northumbrians and South Saxons as they flee to Wales.

But after they had told these things to Offa in great detail, he was very angry with the careless watchmen, and straightway hotly pursued the said kings as far as neighbouring Wales. And he sent word to King Meredith through official messengers in this way:

> 'Oh noble Meredith king of the Welsh people, Offa emperor of the Mercians[339] sends greetings and respects. You must realise, for the report is widespread so it is understood, that the kings of the Northumbrians and the Southerners, having been subject[340] to the power of the kingdom of the Mercians for a long time, impertinently scorned my domination and fled to the protecting wings of Charles king of the Franks so that they might treacherously attack me. So I beseech, recommend and advise that you give no favour or help at all to such men. If you do foolishly comply with them, realise that I would be an enemy seriously raised against you, and that you would share in that same disaster. Farewell.'

When he heard these things, Meredith king of Wales summoned the aforesaid kings, and one after another showed them the letter sent to him by Offa. But they declared that this profane Offa had always abounded in threats, and always foxy plots and wolfish plundering under his sheep's clothing. Nor ought he — powerful King Meredith — to be in the least afraid of Offa, a mad and crazy prince. Emboldened by which mistaken talk, King Meredith sent a rebuttal to Offa himself, through Offa's own ambassadors: 'It would be shameful and cowardly to desert those whom he had mercifully admitted in order to protect, whom he would have poured out the forces of all Wales to defend, should he have given orders to attack.'

But whilst the ambassadors were busied with this,[341] King Offa was looking ahead, and prudently and powerfully occupied the lands and the strongholds of the fugitive kings for himself, and, having accepted their surrender, hostages and oaths, he subjected them irrecoverably. And he posted his followers to guard their towns and forts, so that from then on the fugitives would be entirely excluded.

---

[339] A title also used a little later (pp. 69-70), but fitting ill with what we are told elsewhere of Offa II's modesty in such respects pp. 71-2, 121-2.

[340] In fact Northumbria was harried rather than subjugated by Mercia, unlike the southern Anglo-Saxon kingdoms.

[341] *N* marginal rubric: Offa's precaution.

De pugna inter Offam et reges Walensium, Northamhinbrorum et Australium Saxonum.

Rex igitur Offanus super premissis per legatos suos plenius certificatus, tam regem Walensium quam Northamhinbrorum et Australium Saxonum diffiduciauit. Statutis igitur die et loco prelium imanissimum contra ipsos commisit. Et ceciderunt utrobique quamplurimi trucidati et uulnerabantur multi letaliter. Et dum usque solis occasum hinc inde uiriliter est decertatum, superuiens nox certamen [15ʳ]³⁴² letale diremit in crastinum tamen continuatum. Sub noctis igitur silencio Rex Wallensium Marmodius licet illud tempus sacrum id non admittebat, dolum machinari studuit hoc modo.

De dolo Marmodio Regis Wallie.

Nox atra nimis mundum obsuscauit. Eratque tempus quo Aduentus Domini, iminente eiusdem Natiuitate celebratur. Conuocatis igitur suis sub caliginose noctis silencio magnatibus, ait: 'Cernitis O mei commilitones, quod Rex Offa inuincibilis apparet, nec audet aliquis ipsius impetum expectare, non enim ualet quis ictus suos sustinere. Victoriosus est insuper et triumphator magnificus. Cor eciam habet feruens et erectum in spem meliorem eo quod Marte sibi fauente de multis suis eciam regibus ad uotum triumphauit. Ipsum igitur qui uiribus inuincibilis est, prudentia nostra prudenter conteret, que multociens efficacius operatur. Quod summopere elaborandum ³⁴³ impercunctanter, ut ad finem optatum perducatur. Significabimus igitur ipsi Offe uerbis amicabilibus caute, ut utrobique pax acclametur suspensiua que Treuga uulgariter nuncupatur, diebus aliquot, ut respirent fatigati, foueantur contriti, et sanentur uulnerati, donec dies natalicii Domini celebrentur, et uerna temperies dies protelauerit sereniores. Et si interim pax poterit amicabiliter perpetuari, firmetur feliciter. Si non redeamus in id³⁴⁴ ipsum. Si igitur fauorem exhibuerit, excercitus eius inermis, ociis indulgebit et conuiuiis. Nos igitur una noctium que nunc temporis protenduntur, impetum repentinum facientes, omnes ante expectatum occupabimus, et dicabimur multipliciter. Quicquid enim ipse Offa uiolenter ac morose sibi adquisiuit; nos una nocte uel die nobis prudenter ac potenter adquiremus.

Consensus et prosecutio prodicionis.

Hic igitur sermo prodicionis cum tam regibus fugitiuis quam magnatibus Wallie complacuisset, confirmatum est inter eos hoc sacramentum secretissimum, nulli

---

³⁴² Illustration: Welsh king Meredith with fugitive kings of Sussex and Northumbria, standing, direct two couriers to the Frankish king Charlemagne, seated, who duly receives their missive.

³⁴³ C 'est' inserted from margin.

³⁴⁴ C 'id' interlined.

On the battle between Offa and the kings of the Welsh, Northumbrians and South Saxons.[345]

So King Offa, fully informed about all these previous things by his ambassadors, distrusted the kings of the Welsh equally with those of the Northumbrians and the South Saxons. So, having set the day and the place, he staged the most enormous battle against them. And on both sides a great number were butchered and many fatally wounded. And, although there was fierce fighting on all sides until sunset, when night fell the deadly battle continued uninterrupted into the following day. So in the silence of the night King Meredith of the Welsh put his mind to contriving a trick in this fashion, although it did not respect that holy season.

On the trickery of King Meredith of Wales.

Black night hid the world completely. It was the season in which the Advent of the Lord was celebrated,[346] and his Nativity imminent. So, having sent for his chief men in the darkness of the silent night, he said: 'You have seen, Oh my comrades-in-arms, how King Offa seems invincible; no-one dares await his attack, nor is even able to withstand his blows. He is always victorious and a great champion. Also he has a brave heart and is always confident so that, Mars favouring him, he has easily conquered even many of his own kings.[347] So let our caution, which has proved effective many times, cautiously wear down one who is invincible by force. Measures ought to be taken on this matter immediately, so that a good outcome results. So we will carefully communicate with Offa in friendly terms so that on both sides a break for peace, commonly known as a 'truce', is announced for a few days so that the exhausted can draw breath, the worn out be tended, and the wounded treated, until the days of the Lord's Birth are celebrated, and spring weather ushers in milder days.[348] And if, in the meantime, peace can be protracted in a friendly way, let it be confirmed happily. If not, let us return to the present situation. So if it seems worthwhile, he will permit revels and feasts with his army disarmed. And then on one of those now late nights, we making a sudden attack will seize them all before they are expecting it, and we shall be ready for all sorts of things. For, whatever Offa has himself acquired violently and by cunning, we ourselves will prudently and powerfully acquire, one night or day.'

Agreement to carry out the treason.

Because this treacherous talk pleased the Welsh chief men as much as the fugitive kings, it was affirmed among them that this vow was very secret, revealed to absolutely

---

[345] This goes without mention by the English chroniclers in general.

[346] The four weeks from late November to Christmas Day, 25th December – which is traditionally a time of festivity and relaxation from work.

[347] Presumably sub-reguli of whom there were numbers.

[348] We might compare the unofficial, lower-ranks truce between German and British armies during the First World War, from 24th December (Christmas Eve) 1914 – 1st January 1915: M. Brown and S. Seaton, *Christmas Truce*, London, 1984; M. Jürgs, *Der kleine Frieden im Grossen Krieg*, Munich, 2003.

prorsus reuelandum. Missa igitur legatione cum donatiuis impreciabilibus Regi Offe complacuit ei mandatum pacificum excercitque eius, tum ut excercitus quiete recrearetur, famelici cibarentur, equi restaurarentur et sanarentur sauciati, tum ut dies sollepnis[349] qui instabat uidelicet Natiuitatis Dominice, in ebdomada proximo sequente, serenius, letius et quiescius choruscaret. Fauorem igitur promptius prebuit postulatis, nesciens doli uenenum mollitis et mellitis sublituisse.

Veruntamen cum nollent uel exercitus Regis Offe uel Walensium inde procul recedere, Rex Offa ad cautelam inter ipsos duos excercitus communi assensu unum fossatum longum nimis et profundum effodi, aggere terrestri uersus Wallenses eminenter eleuato, ne fallatium hostium irruptionibus repentinis preocuparetur. Et ut tucius ac quiecius diuinis obsequiis in tanta solempnitate uacaret, unam ibidem construxit ecclesiolam. [15ᵛ][350] Que omnia prout temporis breuitas exigebat, ante natale Domini uidelicet duodecim diebus licet breuissimis sunt completa. Cuius rei ut memoria perpetuetur, fossa illa Offe dicitur et ecclesia Offekirk[351] usque in hodiernum diem appellatur.

Reges reuocant sous sibi quondam subiectos in internecionem[352] *Offe.*

Interim reges supradicti amicos suos et consanguineos et alios quondam sibi subiectos, de quorum fidelitate plenius confidebant, in regnis eorum existentesil secretius in eorum adiutorium uocauerunt; ut infra Natalis Domini diem, Walensium exercitui prudenter et clanculo sese associarent,[353] de uictoria que profecto preparabatur non formidantes. Qui rupto federe quo Regi Offe uinciebantur, pristinis Dominis suis, relictis uxoribus suis et liberis nec non et mansionibus, credentes se cum omni alacritate multiplicatis diuiciis redituros, paruerunt. Rex insuper Walensium Marmodius omnem quamcunque potuit ad illum quem prefixit diem multitudinem adunauit.

Offa delusus fugit et ab inimicis suis fugatur.

Cumque tempus leticie ac requiei die Natalis Domini totum excercitum Offanis immo totum mundum exhilarauit, nocte sequenti, uidelicet nocte beati Stephani, cum

---

[349] C sollempnis.

[350] Another double-page battle illustration, cf. ff. 3ᵛ-4ʳ, much erased and repaired; the heraldry corrected. The Mercian army depicted across the centrefold is attacked from both left and right; thus Offa II's heraldic shield is visible. Spearmen carry small round targes. Offa II in the van of densely massed cavalry confronts the opposing king, whilst to the rear the Mercian army turns to retreat across the fold to where, now moving from left to right, Offa II lances one of the retreating Welsh cavalry (Figs. 22 and 24).

[351] This apparently Scandinavian form with –*kirk* is found once again *s.a.* 1196 in *The Chancellor's Roll*, ed. D.M. Stenton, The Pipe Roll Society, 45 (1930), p. 57.

[352] C internencione.

[353] C associanerunt. De uictoria.

no one. So when an ambassador had been sent to King Offa with supplicatory gifts, the call for peace pleased him – that the army could refresh itself in quiet, the hungry fed, the horses rested and the injured treated; then that the ceremonial day which approached in the next week following, that is to say the Nativity of the Lord, could be sung more gladly, joyfully and calmly. So he consented to the request very readily, unaware that the poison of treason had been secretly softened and honeyed.

Well, because it was unclear as to whether it was the army of King Offa or of the Welsh which was to withdraw to a distance, King Offa as a precaution, by common consent between the two armies, dug one very long and deep dyke,[354] a land rampart raised up high against the Welsh, to prevent an attack by the sudden invasion of a deceptive enemy. And so that he might be free to solemnise the divine rites at such a formal festival in greater safety and peace he built a little church in the same place.[355] All of which was done in the very short time there was before the Lord's Birthday, that is to say in twelve, albeit very short, days.[356] It is still remembered right up to this day that the dyke is called Offa's and the church is called Offchurch.[357]

The kings recall to them their one-time subjects, to kill Offa.

Meanwhile the aforesaid kings secretly called to their aid their friends, blood relatives and others once their subjects, in whose loyalty they felt fully confident, living in their kingdoms; so that at the Lord's Birthday they might associate themselves cautiously and stealthily with the army of the Welsh, unconcerned about the victory that was certainly in preparation. Who, having broken the pact by which they were bound to King Offa, showed allegiance to their former lords, left their wives and children and even houses, believing that they would return with all speed having increased their wealth. In all, King Meredith of the Welsh brought together all the forces he could on that prearranged day.[358]

Offa, tricked, retreats and is pursued by his foes.

And when the period of comfort and leisure on the Lord's Birthday was encouraging the whole of Offa's army – in fact the whole world – on the following night, that is to

---

[354] For the character and surviving remains of 'Offa's Dyke', see Introduction, pp. lxix-lxxv, Fig. 9. Replication of a short stretch suggests that the whole could have taken well over a thousand men two years to construct.

[355] If the place in question is Offchurch at the crossing of the Roman Fosse Way with a major Welsh drove-road, it is some seventy miles east of Offa's Dyke. Nothing remains of the eighth-century church, but William Camden supposed that Offchurch Bury here was the location of the king's palace where a certain Offa's son Fremund was murdered and buried, *Britannia*, London, 1586, p. 317. Cf. below, pp. 127-8. Graves found here appear to have been pagan in date, J.T. Burgess, 'Saxon remains at Offchurch', *Journal of the British Archaeological Association*, 32 (1876), 464-67.

[356] The 'twelve days of Christmas' was a period of traditional merrymaking, not prior but subsequent to Christmas Day on the 25th December, ending with 'Twelfth Night' on 5th January. See also Introduction, p. lxxii.

[357] Cf. J.E.B. Gover *et al.*, *The Place-Names of Warwickshire*, English Place-Name Society, 13, Cambridge, 1936, pp. 177-78.

[358] A plan to be regarded as particularly noxious because of its arrangement for a day recognised as of religious sanctity, and especially of peace, for the Church.

se cuncti Merciorum principes immo eciam excubitores nichil sinistri pertimescentes se securo sopori dederunt, ipsi reges Walensium, Northamhimbrorum, Australium Saxonum, cum suis complicibus, tota ipsa opaca nocte, silenter ac furtim magnam partem predicte fosse, officio rusticorum propere repleuerunt. Et illam in iter planum quantum arcus iacere posset[359] breui tempore repleuerunt.

Summo igitur mane Rex Walensium Marmodius cum suis consentaneis facto impetu repentino prout prelocutum fuit, Regem Offam immunitum et inermem, ad instar tempestatis borealis truculenter inuadunt.

Vnde excercitus Offe subito consternatus in magna parte passus est[360] diminucionem et irrestaurabile detrimentum. Interim armantur festinanter Rex Offa et sui et qui sibi proximi,[361] electi commilitones et primicerii. Et irruit rex frendens ut aper in incendio ire sue in hostium turmas, pre immanitate iracundie, periculum mortis contempnendo; et inuocato de summis auxilio, sui prodigus se in medium[362] inimicorum suorum inuexit. Et hinc inde resistentes prosternendo, uiam ferro suis potenter aperuit; sed militares acies que uel inermes uel incomposite pre nimia festinacione armabantur, sequi pertimescentes, uix ipsum Regem Offam a discrimine mortis eripuerunt. Et sic inuiti retrocedentes, cum iacturam irrecuperabilem tolerassent, fugam usque ad sua tentoria et castra miserabiliter inierunt. Nix autem hiemalis et tempestas horrida ac nimis tenebrosa locique palustres, certamen bellicum, usque ad consummacionem continuare, Deo sic uolente, non sinebat. Et sic Rex Offa donec fortior resurgeret ad propria remeauit. [16^r][363] Interea cum redisset Offanus dolens et inglorius obsides eorum qui ad reges suos rupto federe redierunt, iussit arctioribus uinculis mancipari, uxores et familiam ultime seruituti ascribi uel uenundari. Possessiones autem eorum uel suis distribuit hereditarie possidendas, uel edicto regio iussit redigi in fauillas; et sic omnia in pace suscipiens regni negocia feliciter disposuit, cogitans tamen sibi illatas iniurias in tempore retribucionis potenter ac grauiter uindicare, si pacis formam sibi non inueniret acceptabilem.

Rex Walensium Marmodius cum suis consentaneis uincitur, Offa triumphante.

Offa autem Merciorum Basileus bellipotens moras multas prioribus casibus non annetens temporis nacta oportunitate, ualidissimam in confinia uallie contra hostes suos nimis debacantes et superbientes expedicionem[364] armis et uictualibus sufficienter

---

[359] *N* 'posset' inserted from margin in later hand. *C* 'iacere posset breui' over erasure.
[360] *C* 'est' interlined.
[361] *C* 'fuerant' inserted from margin in later hand.
[362] *N* An anticipatory 'in medium' with 'medium' deleted. *C* prodigus in medium se.
[363] The double-page battle illustration begun on f. 15^v contd: The Mercian forces now advancing from left to right, Offa II lances one of the retreating Welsh cavalry (Fig. 24).
[364] *C* 'debacantes et superbientes expedicionem construtiunt' over erasure.

say the night of the blessed Stephen,[365] when all the Mercian chief men, in fact even the watchmen, fearing nothing wrong, were safely asleep, the kings of the Welsh, Northumbrians and South Saxons with their henchmen, in that totally dark night, silently and stealthily quickly filled in a great part of the aforesaid dyke, in the manner of peasants. And in a short time they filled it up into a level path, for as far as a bow can shoot.[366]

Then early in the morning, because he was stationed in front, King Meredith of the Welsh and his supporters made a sudden attack and rushed fiercely, just like a tempest from the north, upon King Offa who was defenceless and unarmed.

And as a result a large section of Offa's army promptly panicked, suffered depletion and irreparable damage. Meanwhile King Offa and his men and those around him,[367] chosen comrades-in-arms and chief men, hastily armed themselves. And the king rushed in gnashing his teeth like a wild boar, hot with wrath, into the enemy cavalry, savage in wrathfulness, scorning the danger of death. And having called for help from on high, he carried himself into the midst of his enemies, reckless of himself. And, everywhere throwing to the ground those resisting him, with iron he powerfully opened up a path for his men; but the military vanguard, who were either unarmed or disordered and very slow to arm, being afraid to follow, barely snatched King Offa himself from danger of death. And so, unwillingly drawing back because they had suffered irrecoverable loss, they began to retreat miserably to their camps and fortifications. But, it being the will of God to continue right up to the end, there was no lessening in the struggle of warfare in winter and the wild and extremely dark tempests in the swamps of the place.[368] And so King Offa went back home until he could re-emerge more strongly. In the meantime, after Offa had returned lamenting and in shame, he ordered the hostages from those who returned to their kings having broken the pact to be subjected to tighter bonds, wives and households to be assigned to the lowest servitude or for sale. But their possessions he either distributed to his followers as heritable properties, or ordered them by royal edict reduced to ashes. And so, resuming everything in peace, he happily dealt with the affairs of the kingdom – thinking, however, to impose a serious and forceful period of retribution for the injuries done to him, should he not find the form of peace acceptable to him.

King Meredith of the Welsh with his supporters is beaten, and Offa is triumphant.

But Offa, Emperor of the Mercians, taking no longer time than he had previously done, militarily powerful, sufficiently, in fact abundantly, furnished with weapons and provisions, seized the moment and made a very strong expedition into the Welsh

---

[365] A martyr of the early Church in Jerusalem. Acts VI-VII.

[366] Typically perhaps two or three hundred yards (about 230m.) and regularly understood as a unit of measure in medieval usage, especially in respect of combatants on the battle-field, cf. *Middle English Dictionary*, ed. H. Kurath, S.M. Kuhn *et al.*, Ann Arbor, Michigan, 1952-2001, sv. *arwe-shot*, *boue-draught*, pp. A, 409, B, 1080-81, and references there cited. Also see *Laws of Early Iceland*, ed. A. Dennis, P. Foote and R. Perkins, Winnipeg, 2000, p. 30 *et passim*.

[367] Inserted from margin.

[368] The River Leam meanders through extensive floodplains at this point before joining the River Avon at Stratford.

immo habundanter communitam. Que omnes ibidem existentes Regi Offe contradicentes pluribus annis irremediabiler dapnificando[369] fatigarunt, adeo quod in arcto constituti non minimum doluerunt se Regem Offan offendisse.

Dum igitur eis Mars eminus aduersaretur, Offa Rex collectis sue dicionis uiribus, iter illuc[370] dirigit et uexilla. Et cum eidem aduentanti obstare presumpsissent, in loco quo prius transeuntes fossatum triumpharunt, credentes locum sibi fortunatum, prelium maximum conseruerunt; et multociens ad latibula consueta redeuntes et in tempore in exercitum regis argumentose prosilientes, frequenter ipsum repulerunt.

Vna igitur dierum Rex Offa tedio affectus et indignacione intumescens eo quod tale uulgus tam diu resistere ualuit et uoluit, suis ait commilitonibus: 'O formidolosi et desides, quam diu hos pecuales tolerabimus; aut hodie me interempto confundemini, aut eorum insolentiam penitus hodie suprimetis.'

Hiis dictis, signo crucis se premuniens, facie sue clipeum opponens, in hostes se totum ingessit confidenter, uiam patulam preuius suis adaperiens. Quem nobiles in ira indignacionis sue e uestigio sequentes, et in modum piramidis cornu militare componentes, omnem Walensium turmam potenter dissiparunt; et inimicos a facie eorum fugam inire compulerunt. Quos insequens Rex Offa tantam sanguinis fudit habundantiam, ut planicies illa cruore cesorum tincta uideretur. Iussitque Rex Offa omnes uallie mares, uix reseruatis mulieribus cum infantulis trucidari. Et quia hoc in furore ire[371] sue hic rex preceperat, paucis admodum lictores pepercerunt. Sed ne preceptum regium uacuum uideretur, stragem ex ipsis exercuerunt inauditam.

De humilitate Regis Offe in prosperis.

Tot igitur insignitus Rex Offa, et tot prosperis fortunatus, arrogantia nunquam intumuit nun [16ᵛ][372] quam in iactantiam tumide resolutus se supra se pomposius exaltando. Sed omnia Deo non sue strenuitati ascribens, more Christianissimi principis, gratas et solempnes ipsi soli Christo[373] qui uincit, regnat et imperat sapienter cum omni humilitate impendebat. Omnibusque diebus uite sue se solum regem Merciorum in titulis scriptorum in salutacionibus in relacionibus, quamuis pluribus prefuerit regnis, se precepit et constituit nominari, unde quod a laude eius non uacat, multorum sepius adulatorum huius precepti redarguit acriter transgressionem. Indignum quippe

---

[369] C irremedialiter dampnificando.
[370] C illuc iter.
[371] C 'ire' omitted.
[372] Illustration: Offa II ensures the shrouded war-dead honourable entombment then, returning from battle, is shriven by monks sprinkling water.
[373] C 'grãs' inserted from margin in later hand.

borders against enemies debauching too much and exhilarating excessively. All alike, they supposed that in opposing King Offa they had injured him for many years by wholly irredeemable crushing — to such a degree that they when hard-pressed were not a little sorry that they had offended King Offa.

So, whilst Mars on high[374] was against them, King Offa, having mustered his men, directed his way there with standards. And when they had presumed to withstand his advance, at the place where they had been triumphant when first crossing the dyke, believing it to be a lucky place for them, they kept the upper hand. Many times retiring to their customary hideouts and sometimes springing out to harry the king's army, they frequently drove it back.

So one day King Offa felt weary and, swelling with exasperation to the point where he thought and decided that it was ignoble to be at a standstill so long, he said to his comrades-in-arms: 'Oh you cowardly and lazy men, how long are we going to tolerate these herdsmen? Either all be slain with me today – or today entirely suppress their insolence.'

Having said this, protecting himself with the sign of the cross, lifting his shield in front of him, he confidently bore himself fully into the enemy, opening up a broad path before his men. His nobles, wrathful with exasperation, followed his tracks, and in wedge formation they made up a wing and powerfully scattered all the Welsh cavalry, forcing their enemies to flee in front of them. Following them, King Offa spilled such a quantity of blood that the plain seemed dyed with the gore of the slain. And King Offa ordered all Welsh mothers to be butchered, scarcely excepting women with little children. And because the king was in a furious wrath[375] when he had commanded this, the officers spared only a few. They wrought an unheard-of massacre among them, lest they should appear not to have heard the royal command.

On the humility of King Offa in success.

Although so distinguished and fortunate with such success, King Offa never became inflated with arrogance — never became ostentatious by proudly vaunting himself in a pompous fashion. But, in the manner of a most Christian prince, he ascribed everything to the working of God, not himself. In wisdom and all humility he offered thanks and sacrifice to Christ himself, who alone conquers, rules and controls. All the days of his life he commanded and ordered that, although he ruled over several kingdoms, he should be called only 'King of the Mercians' in document headings, in addresses and titles, as a result of which, that did not detract from the praise, the many frequent flatteries, keenly criticised as a transgression of these commands.[376] Certainly he

---

[374] Names and properties of the Classical gods had been transferred to the planets in Ancient times: F. Cumont, 'Les noms des planètes', *L'Antiquité Classique*, 3 (1935), 5-43. For the generally maleficent and specifically martial influence of Mars on human affairs see Ptolemy, *Tetrabiblos*, ed. and transl. F.E. Robbins, Cambridge, Mass., 1940, pp. 182-5.

[375] C was in a fury.

[376] Our text elsewhere calls him 'Emperor (*basileus*) of the Mercians' in speaking of his relations with the Welsh, pp. 63-4, 69-70. For use of this term in documents of the weakling Eadred (946-55) or incompetent Eadwig (955-59), see

reputabat se regem uel dominum acclamari regnorum quorum erat possessor uiolentus, licet haberet in hostes suos expugnandos actionem iustissimam.

De humanitate et pietate Regis Offe, in mortuis honeste sepeliendis.

Die igitur crastina proximo uidelicet sequente illum diem uictoriosum et exultacionis plenum, iussit Rex Offanus piissimus gloriose triumphans corpora occisorum humanitus et honeste sepeliri que nobilitate uel generositate aliquatenus fuerant [377] insignita. Ignobilium uero et popularium corpora et membra detruncta que fuerat[378] suis intermixta, quorum non erat cognito[379] propter sanguinis inundantiam que quidem totam illam tinxerat planiciem, colligi diligenter precepit.

Et in ipsa sepedicta fossa quam et ipsi eruderauerant, ne a bestiis dilaniata deuorarentur uel aera tabe corrumperent, iussit sepeliri. Et ipsum terestrem aggerem uidelicet limbum fosse super ipsa dispargi et accumulari. Necnon diuina pro animabus eorum quibus et ipse interfuit tam missis quam aliis exequiis celebrari.

De eiusdem regis munificencia post uictoriam.

Occupatis igitur omnibus. Et spoliis cum terris et possessionibus, suis ciuiliter commilitonibus distributes, regressus est Rex Offa cum summa exultacione triumphali. Et cum ad fines Mercie peruenisset, occurrerunt aduentanti incole non mediocriter exultantes, uidelicet prelati ecclesiarum solempniter adornati cantantes et applaudentes cum uexillis et cereis. Nobiles quoque qui custodes regni remanserant; ciues quoque et utriusque multitudo cum facibus accensis et uariis musicis instrumentis, obuiam[380] ei per multam uiarum distanciam gaudenter perrexerunt. Quibus et multa contulit donaria et nouas concessit libertates. Collata est igitur celitus hec gloriosa Offe uictoria anno gratie secentesimo [381] septuagesimo quinto. Ex quibus annos circiter decem expendit rex in expedicionibus precedentibus in quibus omnes suos contriuit inimicos.

Quomodo hec uictoria Regis Offe clausula fuit laborum et sollicitudinum.

Et cum hec uictoria suorum laborum clausula fuisset et sollicitudinum, pacis perpetue confirmatiua, nec insurgentium aliquorum in circuitu regni sui impetum uel mali cuiuslibet machinationes formidaret, cogitauit Rex prouidus quod et eciam Karolo

---

Cartularium Saxonicum, ed. W.G. Birch, London, 1885-99, III, pp. 72, 143 *et passim*. Generally M.J. Swanton, *Crisis and Development in Germanic Society*, Göppingen, 1982.

[377] N 'fuerant' inserted from margin in later hand.

[378] C detruncata que fuerant.

[379] C 'drā non erat propter' over erasure.

[380] C 'ea' added but deleted.

[381] C sexcentesimo

considered it improper for him to be acknowledged as king or lord of kingdoms of which he was the possessor by violence, although he had acted entirely righteously in attacking his enemies.

On the compassion and faith of King Offa in honourably burying the dead.

So on the next morning, that is to say the day following the day of victory, so full of joy in his triumphant glory, the most devout King Offa ordered that bodies of the slain which had any marks of nobility or good birth should be given decent and dignified burial.[382] He commanded the bodies of the common or ordinary people, and the dismembered limbs that had been mixed up with them that were unidentifiable because of the inundation of blood that had indeed dyed the whole plain, to be carefully collected. And he ordered them to be buried in that renowned dyke which they themselves had fashioned, lest, torn apart, they should be devoured by wild beasts, or putrefied by corruption in the air; and the earth rampart itself, that is to say the side of the dyke, to be spread and heaped up over them,[383] and also divine services, masses and other ceremonies, which he himself attended, to be celebrated for their souls.

On the generosity of this same king after victory.

So everything was taken over. And with spoils, land and properties courteously distributed to his comrades-in-arms, King Offa returned with the greatest triumphant exultation. And, when he came to the borders of Mercia, on his arrival the inhabitants ran up to him exulting in no small way: that is to say, the clergy of the churches formally vested, singing and applauding, with banners and wax tapers; also the nobles who had remained behind as guardians of the kingdom, and also townspeople and a host of others with lighted torches and various musical instruments delightedly made journeys of a great distance to meet him.[384] Upon these he conferred many gifts and allowed new rights. Heaven bestowed this glorious victory on Offa in the year of grace seven hundred and seventy five.[385] From which date the king spent about a decade in remaining expeditions in which he crushed all his enemies.

How this victory brought to an end King Offa's toil and cares.

And now that this victory – an affirmation of perpetual peace – brought an end to his toil and cares, fearing neither the attack of any insurgents within the confines of his kingdom nor the machinations of any evildoer, the prudent king thought that it would be a very good thing to be reconciled both to Charles, the great king of the Franks

---

[382] Compare his predecessor Offa I, pp. 11-12, n. 96.

[383] Archaeological evidence is as yet lacking.

[384] C 'with this' added but deleted.

[385] MSS six hundred and seventy five. Various chronicles offer no help.

Regi Francorum maximo, quem uehementer offenderat eoque regibus [17ʳ] [386] supradictis pro quibus tam pater dicti Karoli quam et ipse tunc presens scripserat, spreto ipsius mandato cum grauibus comminacionibus, non pepercit, multum expediret reconciliari. Non enim mediocriter offensus idem Karolus eciam mercatorum et peregrinorum quos ad Offam nouerat pertinere commeantium, pacem et transitum perturbabat. [387] Et nisi bellicis in Ytalia arduis negociis detineretur, ipsum Offam hostiliter impugnasset.

Sano igitur ac modesto Rex Offa fretus consilio, ipsi Karolo iam Ytaliam et Ytalicos nec non et Saxoniam et Saxones pertrectanti, Ticina nobilissima Longobardorum ciuitate occupata, rege eius desiderio capto et incarcerato, legatos sollempnes destinauit; et per eosdem munera concupiscibilia et prioribus preciosiora frequenter transmisit; supplicans attentius ut conceptam iram et indignacionem freno racionis et regie modestie choiberet.[388] Scripsitque ei huius tenoris epistolam.

Epistola Regis Offe ad Karolam Magnum Francorum Regem.[389]

Regi Francorum Maximo inuictissimo triumphatori Karolo, Rex Merciorum Offanus salutem et honorem. Cum omnium regum terrenorum potentissimus et iustissimus fama testificante prediceris, indignum est et prorsus execrabile aliquibus proditoribus uel profugis a debito seruicio colla executere uolentibus, sinum aperire proteccionis. Tu uero hostium meorum sermocinacionibus nimis credulus, et super hoc ignarus ueritatis pro ipsis michi scripsit tua serenitas, ut eisdem parcerem, michi superbe et insolenter resistentibus. Cum igitur iniustum sit ut alicui sua fraus suffragetur, noueris eorum falsis persuasionibus tuam mansuetudinem circumueniri et decipi fraudulenter. Oro igitur et sicienter desidero, sinceritatem amicicie et federis soliditatem inter nos reformari.

Vt communis utilitas et respublica felix suscipiat incrementum. Ipsos enim reges cum suis fere omnibus complicibus potenter contriui michi rebellantes, eos iterum respirare non permissurus. Hec omnia Domino nostro Iesu Christo[390] sic uolente et disponente, qui uincit, regnat et imperat, regna et imperia commutat et cui uult tribuit, sapienter, cui eciam contraire te uelle nullatenus arbitramur. Vale.

---

[386] Illustration: King Offa II, seated and sceptred despatches letter by kneeling courier, subsequently received by enthroned discountenanced Charlemagne.

[387] C run on.

[388] C cohiberet.

[389] See Introduction, pp. xix, xc-xcii.

[390] C 'Christo' omitted.

whom he had mightily offended, and to the aforesaid kings on whose behalf the father[391] of the said Charles, and he himself then present, had written; spurning his instruction accompanied by grave warnings, he showed no forbearance. Now not a little offended, the same Charles even interfered with the peace and passage of merchants and pilgrims whom he knew would have contact with Offa.[392] And had he not been detained in Italy on pressing matters of war, he would have ferociously attacked Offa himself.

So King Offa, trusting in sound and sensible advice, despatched formal ambassadors to Charles himself as he dealt with Italy and the Italians, and also Saxony and the Saxons, Pavia, the noblest city of the Langobards being occupied, their king Daufer captured and imprisoned.[393] And through them he often sent attractive gifts and exceptional valuables, beseeching most earnestly that the rein of reason and royal moderation temper the wrath and exasperation aroused. And he wrote a letter along these lines:

Letter of King Offa to Charles the Great, King of the Franks.

'Offa King of the Mercians sends greeting and respect to Charles, most invincible champion, great king of the Franks. As your fame declares you the most powerful and righteous of all earthly kings, it is unworthy and utterly execrable to harbour and protect any traitors, fugitives or people absconding from due service. Too ready to believe the talk of my enemies, and on top of this, ignorant of the truth, your Serenity has written to me on their behalf – that I should spare them who proudly and insolently resist me. Because it is wrong that anyone's deceit should be aided by another, be aware that their false arguments have tricked and treacherously deceived your benevolence. So I ask and beseech you fervently that sincere friendship and a firm pact be renewed between us.

I powerfully destroyed those same kings who rebelled against me, with nearly all their henchmen, not allowing them to draw breath again, so that the general good and prosperity of the state should increase. May Our Lord Jesus Christ who conquers, reigns and rules, bestows kingdoms and empires, and who wisely gives to whom he wishes – whose will we think you do not wish to contravene – want and carry out all these things. Farewell.'

---

[391] In fact his brother Charles (Carloman). For the author's general confusion as to this relationship see Introduction, pp. xxx, xc.

[392] Below, pp. 77-8; and referred to by Alcuin, *Epistolae Karolini Aevi*, II, Dümmler, pp. 32-33, transl. S. Allott, *Alcuin of York*, York, 1974, p. 43.

[393] With the excuse of their anti-papal activity, Charlemagne had invaded Langobard north Italy, taken Pavia in 774 and confined the last of the Langobard kings Daufer (756-86) to a monastery, assuming for himself the additional title *Rex Langobardorum*: Einhard, *Vita Karoli Magni*, Holder-Egger, pp. 8-9, Thorpe, pp. 60-61.

Rescriptum Offe Regis Karolo.[394]

Hec autem cum plenius Regi Karolo innotuissent, ut pote regum mansuetissimus et Christianissimus uidens quod non aliter facere necesse fuit inito prouidorum consilio, Regi Offe scripsit amicabiliter in hunc modum:

Karolus gratia Dei Rex Francorum et Longobardorum et patricius Romanorum uiro uenerando et fratri karissimo, Offe Regi Merciorum salutem. Primo gratias agimus omnipotente Deo de catholice fidei sinceritate, quam in uestris laudabiliter paginis reperimus exaratam. De peregrinis uero qui pro amore Dei et salute animarum suarum, beatorum apostolorum limina desiderant adire, cum pace sine omni perturbatione uadant. Sed si aliqui non religiosi seruientes, sed lucra sectanctes inueniantur inter eos locis oportunis statuta soluant thelonia.

[17ᵛ] [395] Negociatores quoque uolumus ut ex mandato nostro patrocinium habeant in regno nostro legitime. Et si in aliquo loco iniusta affligantur oppressione, reclament se ad nos et [396] nostros iudices et plenam iubebimus inde iustitiam fieri.

Cognoscat quoque dilectio uestra quod aliquam benignitatem de dalmaticis nostris uel palliis ad singulas sedes episcopales regni uestri uel Etheldredi direximus in elemosinam domini apostolici Adriani, deprecantes ut pro eo intercedi iubeatis, nullam habentes dubitacionem beatam illius animam in requie esse. Sed ut fidem et dilectionem in amicum nobis karissimum. Sed et de thesauro humanarum rerum quam Dominus Iesus gratuita pietate[397] concessit, aliquid per metropolitanas ciuitates direximus. Vestre quoque dilectioni unum balteum et unum gladium Huniscum[398] et duo pallia serica duximus destinanda.

Item aliud manifestum argumentum dileccionis et amicicie inter Karolum et Regem Offam.

Et post hos non multos dies postquam talem eidem Regi Offano Rex Karolus misit epistolam, hoc eidem[399] significauit eulogium: [400]

---

[394] C 'Rescriptum' the remainder of the chapter heading erased.
[395] Illustration: Clerics present synodal decrees to King Offa II, enthroned and sceptred. Mounted missioners travel to Rome.
[396] Matthew and William (see p. 78, n. 401) both read 'uel' ('or').
[397] C 'pietate' repeated; the second deleted.
[398] '-isc' a Germanic (and thus Anglo-Saxon and Frankish) adjectival element.
[399] C idem.
[400] N 'epistola' marginal rubric.

The reply from Charles to King Offa.[401]

But when King Charles had taken full account of these things, seeing that he only need carry out what the wise had already counselled, like the most good-natured and most Christian of kings, he wrote amicably to King Offa in this way:

'Charles by the grace of God King of the Franks and Langobards and Patrician of the Romans, greets the honourable Offa, King of the Mercians and dearest brother. Firstly we give thanks to Almighty God for the sincere catholic faith that we find excellently revealed in your pages. As for those pilgrims who truly wish for the love of God and the well-being of their souls to reach the thresholds of the blessed Apostles, they may travel in peace without any hindrance. But if others serving not religion but chasing profit are found among them they must pay the statutory tolls at the proper places.

Also at our instruction we intend merchants to have lawful protection in our kingdom. And if in any place they are treated with unjust repression, let them appeal to us and our judges and then we will order full justice to be done.

My beloved you should also know that we have sent to each episcopal see in your kingdom, or Æthelred's,[402] a present from our dalmatics or stoles[403] as alms for the apostolic lord Adrian, praying that you order intercessions for him – not that we have any doubt that his blessed soul is at rest [404] but in faith and love of our dearest friend. But we have sent something for the archiepiscopal cities from the treasury of human things that the Lord Jesus has bestowed out of pure mercy. Also for your friendship we have thought fit to send a sword-belt and a Hunnish sword[405] and two silk robes.'[406]

Also another clear proof of the love and friendship between Charles and King Offa.

And later, not many days after this, King Charles sent a letter to the same King Offa, expressing praise of the same:

[401] A significantly condensed and summarised version of that we may believe to derive from the Frankish archive: *Monumenta Germaniae Historica, Epistolae Karolini Aevi,* ed. E. Dümmler, Berlin, 1895, II, pp. 145-46; transl. *English Historical Documents,* I, ed. D. Whitelock, London, 2nd edition, 1979, pp. 848-49. Except in details, it corresponds with the version to be used by Matthew Paris, *Chronica Majora,* I, pp. 348-9, and William of Malmesbury, *Gesta Regum Anglorum,* ed. and transl. R.A.B. Mynors, *et al.,* Oxford, 1998-99, I, pp. 136-37.

[402] Æthelred, ruling Northumbria 774-96, a land clearly considered separable. See Introduction, pp. xliii-xliv.

[403] Vestments (*hreave*) at Hereford were worth stealing when the cathedral was looted in AD 1055, cf. *Anglo-Saxon Chronicle* version C, eds cit., p. 186.

[404] Pope Adrian I had died recently, on Christmas Day 795.

[405] Hun was the name used for a confederation of nomadic mounted warrior people moving westwards from the southern Russian steppes. The present of a sword, perhaps a Sarmatian horseman's broadsword, probably had significance over and above that of merely interesting gift, see Introduction, pp. xlvii, lv-lvii.

[406] Cf. p. 20, n. 150.

Karolus et cetera ut supra, Offano Merciorum Regi salutem honorem et amorem. Cum deceat et expediat reges potentes et famosos amicicie federe conuinciri, et mutuis gaudiis ad inuincem gratulari, ut in uinculo caritatis Christus in omnibus et ab omnibus glorificetur; uestre serenitati hoc eulogium duximus destinandum. Cum nobilissimam Longobardorum ciuitatem cum suis ciuibus omnibus nostro Dominatui potenter subiugauerimus, et Ytaliam totam nostro imperio feliciter subiugauerimus, [407] Christi adiutorio cui famulari desideramus, Rex Desiderius Langobardorum Ducesque Saxonie quos nostris nutibus inclinauimus, Withmundus et Albion, cum fere omnibus incolis Saxonie baptismi susceperunt sacramentum, Domino Iesu Christo de cetero famulaturi. Hoc igitur salubri mandato ego Karolus Regum Christianorum orientalium potentissimus, uos, O Offane Regum Occidentalium Christianorum potentissime, cupio letificare, et te in dilectione speciali amplecti sincerius.

Mittit Karolus Rex quedam sinodalia et epistolas ad confirmandam fidem catholicam, et amiciciam, Offe. [408]

Ex quo autem hec Offano plenius nunciabantur, creuit diatim inter ipsos Reges magnificos, amicicia, federa firmabantur, munera preciosa, mutuo deferebantur, regna utrobique non modicum roborantur, et prosperitas utriusque suscipit incrementum.

Inter cetera uero dilectionis insignia misit[409] memoratus rex Karolus, qui sicut erat regum potentissimus, ita et erat regum mansuetissimus, Offano Regum occidentalium maximo et piissimo, quasdam trasmissit epistolas cum quibus statutis synodalibus quasi quedam fidei catholice fidei[410] rudumenta,[411] ad informandum corda aliquorum suorum prelatorum, quos rudes credidit et imcompositos.[412] Et ad amiciciam inter ipsos incho [18ʳ][413] atam feliciter perpetuandam. Quam et idem Offa quasi hostiam sibi celitus transmissam gratanter et gaudenter suscepit.

Archiepiscopatus Cantuariensis transfertur apud Lichefeldam.

Roboratus igitur suo[414] Rex Offanus, nullas formidans hostium insidias uel rebelliones, formam induit prelati religiosi et pastoris ecclesiastici, curam et sollicitudinem gerentis de grege dominico. Quarundam igitur ecclesiarum cathedralium sedes in melius studet

---

[407] C subiugauerimis potenter.
[408] C Rege Offe.
[409] N 'misit' lightly deleted.
[410] N first 'fidei' deleted by later hand.
[411] C rudimenta.
[412] C 'imcompositos' corrected to 'incompositos'.
[413] Illustration, the folio repaired prior to drawing: An enthroned pope blesses kneeling missioners and grants the king's request. An Archbishop of Lichfield is enthroned by two fellow bishops.
[414] N 'suo' marked with a cross, but no correction; C 'suis'.

'Charles etc. as above,[415] to Offa King of the Mercians greetings, honour and love. Because it is right and fitting for powerful and well-known kings to be bound together in a pact of friendship and to greet each other with mutual delight, so that Christ be glorified in bonds of love in all and by all, we have thought fit to send this letter of praise to your Serenity. When we powerfully subjugated the most noble city of the Langobards with all its citizens to our domination,[416] and happily subjugated the whole of Italy to our rule, with the help of Christ whom we long to serve, King Daufer of the Langobards, and the leaders of Saxons whom we have brought under our authority, Withmund and Albion,[417] received the sacrament of baptism with almost all the inhabitants of Saxony, to serve the Lord Jesus Christ in future. Therefore with this salutary instruction, I Charles, most powerful of the Christian kings of the east, wish to please you, O Offa most powerful of the Christian kings of the west, and embrace you most sincerely with special affection.'

King Charles sends certain synodal decrees and letters to affirm the catholic faith, and friendship, to Offa.

From the time that these words fully reached Offa the friendship and pact between those great kings increased daily, and was confirmed; precious gifts were exchanged, the kingdoms on either side strengthened in no small way, and the prosperity of both met with increase.

Among other symbols of affection the aforesaid King Charles — who, just as he was the most powerful of kings was also the most good-natured of kings — sent to Offa, the greatest and most devout of kings of the west, certain letters and with them synodal decrees in the form of certain rudiments of the catholic faith, to instruct the hearts of some of his prelates, whom he considered irregular and ill-organised. And this was to continue the happily begun friendship between them. Which likewise Offa received gratefully and delightedly as if a consecrated host sent to him from heaven.

The Archbishopric of Canterbury is transferred to Lichfield.

So King Offa, resolved in himself, fearing no enemy plots or rebellions, assumed the role of a religious prelate and ecclesiastical pastor, showing anxiety and concern for the flock of the Lord. So he took pains to better arrange and assemble some of the

---

[415] I.e. pp. 77-8. A decidedly secretarial mode.

[416] I.e. Pavia, pp. 75-6.

[417] And visiting Charlemagne. In other sources the name used is not Withmund but Wittikind. See generally H.H. Howorth, 'The Ethnology of Germany, IV. The Saxons of Nether Saxony', *Journal of the Anthropological Institute*, 9 (1880), 406-36 (p. 427).

ordinare et salubriter ut consciuit transmutare. Accusatus est autem Lambertus[418] archiepiscous Cantuariensis coram Rege Offa accusacionibus perualidis. Quarum una fuit quod Cantuaria nimis uicina fuit Regnis Karoli transmarinis. Cui eciam ante contracta federa promiserat idem lambertus Karolo, quod si hostiliter ingressurus Britanniam adueniret, liberum in archiepiscopatum suum, introitum inueniret, fauorem et adiutorium. Preterea persuasum erat Regi Offe, ut ubi gloriose de inimicis suis triumpharat, ibidem uel prope, locum cathedralem archiepiscopatu et primatu reuerenter merito foret sublimandum. Misit igitur ad Papam Adrianum tunc presidentem, cui Rex Offa fuerat propter suam supereminentem sancitatem amicissimus, nuncios discretos et facundos, honore atque fauore condignos, insuper donatiuis conferendis premunitos. Nouerat enim rex desideria Romanorum. Postulauit igitur rex instanter et non nullis datis muneribus impetrauit, ut contra ueterem consuetudinem approbatam Ealdulphum archiepiscopum constitueret Lichefeldensem. Vt uidelicet omnes prouincie Merciorum, quarum prouinciarum, et episcoporum earum[419] et hec sunt nomina, antistiti subicerentur memorato.

Nomina prouinciarum et episcoporum.[420]

Denebertus, Wigorniensis episcopus; Werebertus Legrecestrensis; Eadulphus [421] Sinacestrensis; Wluardus[422] Herefordensis. Episcopi Orientalium Anglorum: Haraldus Helmamensis. Et Tedfordensis.[423] Et sic per negligentiam diuisa immo pocius dissipata est primacia, ipso Cantuariensi tepide resistente regis impetui ut decuit et expediuit.

Remanserunt autem antistiti Lamberto episcopi Londonensis, Wintoniensis, Rofensis, Sireburnensis. Stetit autem hec regis uiolentia totis[424] Lamberti presulatus tempore quamuis idem archiepiscopus nichil uel sumptibus uel laboribus parceret ut pristina gauderet ecclesia sua dignitate. Procurante igitur Rege Offa efficaciter Ealdulphus Licheldensis[425] archiepiscopus pallium suscepit. Ipso autem tempore Werebertus[426] Legrecestrensis episcopus quartus diem cum clausisset extremum, substitus[427] est Vnwona regis cancellarius et consiliarius familiarissimus. Et cito post Ealdulpho Lichefeldensi archiepiscopo defuncto, subrogatus est Humbertus quem quidam

---

[418] The text's by-name for Jænberht, archbishop of Canterbury, 765-92, cf. W.G. Searle, *Onomasticon Anglo-Saxonicum*, Cambridge, 1897, pp. 313, 323; the form possibly influenced by that of the eminent Benedictine chronicler Lambert of St Bertin (France), *c.* 1060-1125.

[419] C quorum.

[420] See Introduction, pp. xxxii, xciv-xcvi.

[421] C Ealdulphus.

[422] C Wolwardus.

[423] A later hand has interlined 'Ep' before 'Tedfordensis'. Matthew Paris reads 'Tidfert Domucensis', *Chronica Majora*, I, p. 345.

[424] C 'toto' for all.

[425] C Lichfeldensis.

[426] N abbreviated 'W[...]'; C spelled fully.

[427] C 'substitutus' placed next (for 'suscepit', he supported).

ecclesiastical cathedral sees so as to reform beneficially.[428] Well, Jænberht, archbishop of Canterbury, was accused at the court of King Offa with accusations, one of which was that Canterbury was too close to the overseas kingdom of Charles.[429] Before the pact came about, this same Jænberht had even promised Charles that if he came to Britain aggressively as for an invasion, he would find free passage and support and aid in his archbishopric. Besides, King Offa was convinced that at the place where he triumphed gloriously over his enemies, there or nearby, an archiepiscopal and episcopal cathedral might with justification be honourably raised. So he sent to Pope Adrian, then supreme, to whom King Offa had been very friendly on account of his exceptional sanctity, messengers who were discreet and articulate, worthy both of esteem and applause – and additionally reinforced with gifts to offer because the king knew the wishes of Romans. So the king asked that, against ancient sanctioned custom, having been given quite a few gifts, he would immediately appoint Aldwulf as archbishop of Lichfield; that is to say of all the dioceses of the Mercians, of which dioceses and their bishops here are the names to be committed to memory.

Names of the dioceses and bishops.

Deneberht, bishop of Worcester; Wernberht of Leicester, Ealdwulf of Lindsey,[430] Wulheard of Hereford, the bishops of the East English: Alhheard of Elmham and of Thetford.[431] And thus through indifference the primacy was divided, in fact scattered, with even Canterbury resisting in lukewarm fashion, because the king decided on impulse that this was right and carried it through.

But there remained as prelates under Jænberht, the bishops of: London, Winchester, Rochester, Sherborne.[432] But the king ceased his interference during the whole of Jænberht's period of office, even though this archbishop spared no expense or labour to restore the church to its original status. So under King Offa's administration, Aldwulf archbishop of Lichfield effectively received the pallium.[433] But when Wernberht, fourth bishop of Leicester, came to the end of his days, Unwona the king's chancellor and very close advisor, replaced him.[434] And soon after Aldwulf archbishop of Lichfield had died,

---

[428] See generally Introduction, pp. xciv-xcvi.

[429] Geographically close (cf. Introduction, Fig. 13) as well as politically.

[430] Northern Lincolnshire, the bishop's seat as yet unidentified. *Sina-cestrensis*, literally 'without a city', is possibly an error for Sidnacester, but see E.M. Sympson, 'Where was Sidnacester?', *Reports and Papers of the Associated Architectural and Archaeological Societies*, 28 (1905), 87-94. The appointment was variously interrupted, and post-Conquest was abandoned in favour of Lincoln. Also see Introduction, p. xxxii.

[431] Of Dunwich. The author knows there is more than one bishop but, unlike Matthew, makes no reference to Dunwich, which ceased to exist *c.* 880. However, a see was set up at Thetford, separating from Elmham, in 1072, and it may be that the form of the bishop's name has resulted in confusion. Unusually, at this point the ink runs dry for a line or two.

[432] There is no reference to Selsey, transferred to nearby Chichester in 1075.

[433] Hygeberht who was elevated to archiepiscopal status in 787, had retired by 801, with Lichfield reverting to its former status when he died in 803. Aldwulf's incumbency (*c.* 799-*c.* 814) which spanned the reversion seems to have begun after Offa II's death.

[434] Wernberht, *c.* 801- *c.* 814, seems in fact to have been the seventh bishop of Leicester, succeeding not preceding Unwona, *c.* 781- *c.* 801.

Bertum appellarant sillaba[435] subtracta. Iste Humbertus magne sanctitatis uir fuit, literature et prudentie secularis, Regis capellanus conscius eiusdem secretorum, et confessor, atque morum informator.

Hic cum Vnwona episcopo supradicto inuencioni beati Albani Anglorum protho-martiris interfu[436] [18ᵛ][437] sicut superius suo loco dicetur plenius ad audientium informacionem et martiris gloriam et honorem.

De prima Danorum irrupcione in Britanniam repressa per Regem Offanum.

Regente igitur tam prudenter quam potenter regna Merciorum Rege Offano, gens Danorum piratica rapina uiuere assueta tribus magnis aduecta nauibus, in terminis regionis dicioni Regis Offe subiecte, uiolenter et hostiliter applicans, irrupciones dapnosas et repentinas excercebant, flammis et cedibus intendentes. Et nescientes bellipotentis Regis Offe miliciam ac strenuitatem, interiora terre iam temere penetrando cum tirannide magna ceperunt inuadere. Opidanum quoque cum quodam uillico qui ad resictendum[438] eis cum plebe compatriotarum collecta parabantur, peremerunt; et uulgo perturbato et fugam inire compulso, predis et spoliis ausu temerario procedentes procaciter intendebant. Et hii fuerunt primi qui per Danicam tirannidem in Britannia ceciderunt. Heu heu Deo nimis irato quot milia immo milium milia postea eorum insania uidelicet Danorum in Britannia miserabiliter perierunt.

Quorum aduentus primus et tam temarius postquam Offano Regi innotuit, missa expedicione, non enim pro tanto populo dignabatur excercitum publicum conuocare, eorum potenter repressit arrogantiam, et dissipatos et magna parte diminutos, ad naues suas turpiter recurrere coegit, predis suis sequentibus omnibus derelictis. Cum autem regales primicerii aliquos eorum captiuos detinuissent, confessi sunt idem captiui ut ubertatem terre diligenter explorarent, a primatibus Dacie premissos fuisse. Addideruntque quod sequentibus temporibus infinita Danorum multitudo Britones et

---

[435] *C* silbā.

[436] Probably the copyist's page-break error; *C* 'interfuit' was among.

[437] Illustration, the folio repaired prior to drawing: Heavily armed Viking invaders, on foot with axes and long-swords, land from a dragon-prowed ship, slay unarmed inhabitants and are repelled by King Offa II counter-attacking at the head of his cavalry (Fig. 23).

[438] *N C* interlined in later hand; *C* 'resistendum'.

Hunberht – who some call 'Bert,[439] with a syllable subtracted[440] – was put in his place.[441] This Hunberht was a man of great sanctity, well-read and worldly wise, the king's chaplain, confidant, his confessor and spiritual instructor.

He, with Unwona the aforesaid bishop, was present at the discovery of blessed Alban the first martyr of the English, as is described more fully above[442] in a passage dedicated to him, for readers' fuller information, and for the honour and glory of the martyr.

On the first invasion of Danes into Britain, put down by King Offa.

So, with King Offa reigning both wisely and powerfully thus in the kingdom of the Mercians, the piratical race of Danes,[443] who used to live through plunder, sailed in three great ships,[444] mooring at the border of the region subject to the rule of King Offa, violently and hostilely carrying out destructive and sudden raids, spreading fire and slaughter. And not knowing the forces and strength of the militarily powerful King Offa, they now began to invade the interior of the land – vile intrusion with great tyranny. Also, when a certain bailiff appeared together with a crowd of compatriots collected to resist them, they devastated the town;[445] and with the mass confused and forced to flee, they presumptuously pressed on, looting and plundering with vile boldness. And these were the first who fell to the tyrannical Danes in Britain. Alas, alas, because of God's great wrath how many thousands, in fact thousands of thousands, perished wretchedly in the wake of their, that is to say the Danes', mania in Britain.

When their first, so vile, invasion came to the attention of King Offa, he sent an expeditionary force, because it was not worth recruiting a public army, forcefully repressed their arrogance, and compelled those dispersed, and in large part depleted, to return shamefully to their ships, their plunder abandoned to all those following. But, when regal noblemen had seized some of them as captives, these captives confessed that they had been sent ahead by the leaders of Denmark to diligently explore the prosperity of the land. And they added that some time later an infinite number of

---

[439] For such monothematic forms see Searle, *Onomasticon Anglo-Saxonicum*, p. 87 *et passim*.

[440] Roger of Wendover (I, p. 239) and thus Matthew Paris (I, p. 346) curiously account for the popular name by transposition (*transposita*) of syllables.

[441] Apparently an error for Hygeberht. Bishop Hunberht acceded a dozen or so years afterwards in 830, in fact, with two intervening occupants (Herewine and Æthelwald).

[442] In fact below, pp. 107-8.

[443] *The Anglo-Saxon Chronicles*, *s.a.* 787, which use the terms Danes and Northmen synonymously, specify that they came from Hordaland (the district around Hardanger Fjord in West Norway), Appendix A, pp. 137-8, eds cit., pp. 54-55.

[444] The largest military ships at this time, 30m in length with a draught of little more than one metre allowing easy estuary access, were each capable of carrying more than eighty men: O. Crumlin-Pedersen, 'Ship types and sizes AD 800-1400', in *Aspects of Maritime Scandinavia AD 200-1200*, Roskilde, 1991, pp. 69-82, and later discoveries.

[445] The *Annals of St Neots* (ed. D.N. Dumville and M. Lapidge, Cambridge, 1984, p. 39) tell us that they landed on Portland off the coast of Dorset, and *The Chronicle of Æthelweard* (ed. A. Campbell, London, 1962, p. 27) that the bailiff was Beaduheard from the nearest royal town, Dorchester.

omnes Anglie indigenas expugnatura[446] in exterminio furibundi. Quo audito, Offa magnanimus iussit talia prenunciantes ad propria remitti illesos et indempnes ut nunciarent Danis, quod Rege Offano uiuente, qualia primi, talia forent sequentes premia consecuturi. Vnde ipsis Danis stupefactis, in pace remansit Anglia omnibus diebus Offani Regis, nullius contermini irrupcionibus uiolentis inquietata.

Quomodo pacificatis sibi regibus quos uicerat tradidit Rex Offa filia suas nuptui, duas.[447]

Rex autem Offa triumphator ubique magnificus, humilitatis et sapientie spiritu ductus, omnes reges quos antea suo dominatui inclinauerat, piissimum reputauit, ut uel ipsos si uiui possent inueniri, uel eorum saguine propinquos reuocare, et in regnis suis misericorditer stabilire. Vt eidem regi suo Offe et suis successoribus, auitis regnis gratia regia substituti fidelius et sinc eriori corde famularentur. Et sic tucior in temporalibus quiescens senesceret et in spiritualibus. Quo facto, tantam omnium gratiam adeptus Rex Offa ut pro eo gratanter omni se [19r][448] exponerent discrimini et obicerent periculo.

Qualiter in hoc facto omnium gratiam adeptus est.

Confluebant igitur ad eum, quasi ad patulum sinum patris ac domini omnes finitimi, eidem Regi Offe desiderantes affinitate specialius federari. Inter quos rex Occidentalium Saxonum Brithricus, ut ampliorem gratiam apud Regem Offam et sibi propinquos inueniret, et hostibus timori et amicis foret honori et dilectioni filiam eiusdem Regis Offe, ut ei matrimonio copularetur postulauit et obtinuit. Adolescens enim erat indolis florentis et strenuitate laudabilis.

Eodemque anno Ætheldredus Northamhimbrorum rex corpore elegans, corde maganimus, qui eciam Offanum Regem sincero corde diligebat, aliam filiam Offe natu minorem puellam electissime speciei, eisdem quibus et Brithricus causis ductus et racionibus, sibi peciit dari in uxorem.

---

[446] C 'foret' inserted from margin.

[447] C filias suas nuptui.

[448] Illustration: King Offa II gives his three daughters as 'peace-weaving' brides to the now subordinate kings of Wessex and Northumbria, and offers the youngest to the king of East Anglia. Three couples stand in order across the page. The girls adopt a similar bodily posture, but are depicted in relative degrees of relationship to the kings. The first couple, Eadburh and King Brihtric of Wessex, stand hand in hand. In the second, King Æthelred I of Northumbria has his arm around the shoulder of Ælflæd who, grimacing, stands with raised hands, palms stretched outwards. The third, Æthelburh with palms out-turned, stands away from the young, unbearded King Æthelberht of East Anglia. (Fig. 25).

Danes was going to make a frenzied assault on the Britons and all the inhabitants of England,[449] to extermination. Having heard which, the great-hearted Offa ordered that those revealing all this should be sent home uninjured and unharmed so that they might report to the Danes that, with King Offa living, those following would procure the same spoils as the first. As a result, the Danes stunned at this, England remained in peace all the days of King Offa, untroubled by the violent disruptions of any neighbour.

How King Offa gave the kings he had vanquished two of his daughters in marriage as peace-weavers for him.[450]

But King Offa, great conqueror everywhere, led by a spirit of humility and wisdom, considered it the kindest thing to recall all the kings whom he had bent to his domination — either them, if they had survived, or their blood relations, and sympathetically establish them in their kingdoms. So that, restored by royal favour to their ancestral kingdoms, they might serve this their own king, Offa and his successors, more faithfully and with a more sincere heart. And in this way, secure in temporal affairs and in spiritual matters, he might grow old peacefully. Having done this, King Offa earned such gratitude from everyone that they would all have willingly exposed themselves to risk and thrown themselves into danger on his behalf.

How by this action he gained the favour of all.

So all those on his frontiers flocked to him as though to the open bosom of a father and lord, wanting to be allied to King Offa by a special pact. Among these, Beorhtric king of the West Saxons,[451] asked if he might join with the daughter of King Offa in marriage, so as to find greater favour with King Offa and his relatives, and be an object of fear to enemies and of honour and affection to friends. And he acquired her,[452] for the lad blossomed with natural talents and ready excellence.

And the same year Æthelred, king of Northumbrians,[453] handsome in body, with a generous heart, who also revered King Offa with a sincere heart, led by the same motives and reasons as Beorhtric, was delighted that another daughter of Offa, a younger girl of most attractive appearance, was given to himself as wife.[454]

---

[449] C 'hereabouts' inserted from margin.

[450] For the 'peace-weaver' principle of intermarriage see Introduction, pp. lxxix-lxxxi.

[451] 786-802.

[452] Eadburh, who married in 789, was said to be responsible for poisoning a favourite of her husband, perhaps inheriting the manner of her mother (although Asser says her father). Upon her husband's death she fled to Charlemagne's court but was despatched to a nunnery from which she was expelled in due course to die in poverty. We know of her from Asser's *Life of King Alfred*, ed. W.H. Stevenson, revd. D. Whitelock, Oxford, 1959, pp. 12-14, 205-08; transl. S. Keynes and M. Lapidge, *Alfred the Great*, Harmondsworth, 1983, pp. 71-72, 235-36.

[453] 774-96; exiled 779-90.

[454] Ælflæd, whom he married (his second wife) on 29 September 792, *Anglo-Saxon Chronicle*, eds cit., p. 55; at Catterick, Yorkshire, says Simeon of Durham, *Historia Regum*, ed. T. Arnold, Rolls Series, 75, London, 1882-85, II, p. 54.

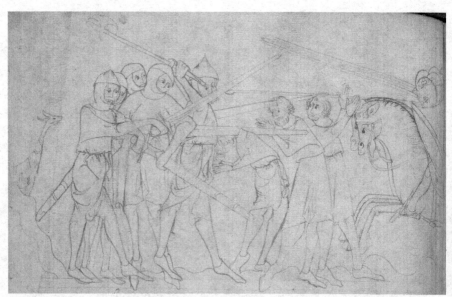

Fig. 23) Heavily armed Viking invaders, on foot with axes and long-swords, land from a dragon-prowed ship, slay unarmed inhabitants and are repelled by King Offa II counter-attacking at the head of his cavalry.

Figs. 22 & 24 Top left and Above) The Mercian army depicted across the centrefold is attacked from both left and right; thus Offa II's heraldic shield is visible. Spearmen carry small round targes. Offa II in the van of densely massed cavalry confronts the opposing king, whilst to the rear the Mercian army turns to retreat across the fold to where, now moving from left to right, Offa II lances one of the retreating Welsh cavalry.

MS Cotton Nero D i, ff. 15^v & 16^r © The British Library Board. All Rights Reserved.

De sancto Ælberto cui tercia filia regis Offe tradenda fuit nuptui.

Erat quoque quidam iuuenis, cui rex Offa regnum Orientalium Anglorum, quod eum iure sanguinis contingebat, concesserat, nomine Ælbertus. De cuius uirtutibus [455] quidam uersificator, solitus regum laudes et gesta describere, eleganter ait:

> Ælbertus iuuenis fuerat rex, fortis ad arma,
> Pace pius, pulcher corpore, mente sagax.

Cumque Humbertus Archiepiscopus Lichefeldensis, et Vnwona Episcopus Legrecestrensis, uiri sancti et discreti, et de nobili stirpe Merciorum oriundi, speciales essent regis consiliarii, et semper que honesta erant et iusta atque utilia, regi Offe suggessissent, inuidebat eis regina uxor Offe, que prius Drida, postea uero Quendrida, id est regina Drida, quia regi ex insperato nupsit, est appellata, sicut in precedentibus plenius enarratur. Mulier auara et subdola, superbiens, eo quod ex stirpe Karoli originem. Et inexorabili odio uiros memoratos persequebatur, tendens eis muscipulas muliebres.

Porro cum ipsi reges supradictos regi Offe in spiritu consilii salubriter reconciliassent, et ut eidem regi federe matrimoniali specialius coniungerentur, diligenter et efficaciter procurassent, ipsa mulier facta eorum nitebatur in irritum reuocare, nec poterat, quibus acriter inuidebat. Ipsas enim puellas filias suas, ultramarinis, alienigenis, in regis supplantacionem et regni Merciorum perniciem, credidit tradidisse maritandas. Cuius rei prescii dicti episcopi, muliebre consilium prudencie repagulis impediebant.

Verum et adhuc tercia filia Regis Offe in thalamo regine remansit maritanda, Ælfleda nomine. Procurantibus igitur supradictis episcopis, inclinatum est cor regis ad consensum, licet contradiceret regina, ut et [456] hec regi Ælberto nuptui traderetur, ut et sic specialius Regi Offe, teneretur in fidelitate dilecionis obligatus. Vocatus igitur rex Ælbertus, a rege Offa, ut filiam suam desponsaret, affuit festinus [19v] [457] et gaudens, ob honorem sibi a tanto rege oblatum. Cui amicabiliter rex occurrens aduentanti, recepit ipsum in osculo et paterno amplexu, dicens: 'Prospere ueneris fili, et gener. Ex hoc, iuuenis amantissime, te in filium adopto specialem.' Sed hec postquam efferate regine plenius innotuerunt, plus accensa est liuore ac furore, dolens eum pietatis in [458] manu

---

[455] N 'uirtutibus' added in margin in later hand; C 'uirtutibus quidam uersificator' over erasure.

[456] C 'et' omitted.

[457] Illustration: King Offa II, enthroned and sceptred, a hand raised in rejection, turns his head away as Queen Thryth makes an abhorrent suggestion. Subsequently the queen herself superintends the murder of King Æthelberht, now lightly bearded; one man beheads him, half down the pit, whilst another carries in a pillow for his suffocation (Fig. 26).

[458] C in pietatis.

On Saint Æthelberht to whom King Offa's third daughter was to have been handed over in marriage.[459]

There was also a certain young man to whom King Offa had conceded the kingdom of the East English because he was close to him by blood relationship, by the name of Æthelberht, about whose virtues a certain lyrist, accustomed to singing the praises and deeds of kings,[460] eloquently said:

> The young man Æthelberht was a king, militarily powerful,
> Devoted to peace, lovely in body, wise in mind.

Now although Hunberht, archbishop of Lichfield, and Unwona, bishop of Leicester,[461] holy and prudent men, and sprung from the noble race of Mercians, were special advisers of the king and had always suggested what was honest and righteous and also practical to King Offa, they were resented by the queen, Offa's wife – who was originally Thryth but later Cwenthryth, that is Queen Thryth, because she had suddenly married the king, as related more fully in earlier pages.[462] She was a greedy and crafty woman, swelling with pride because she came from the race of Charles. And she persecuted the previously mentioned men with inexorable hatred, setting a woman's mousetraps for them.

Moreover, when in their capacity as advisers they had worthily reconciled the aforesaid kings to King Offa, and carefully and effectively arranged that they should be united to that king more specially by a marriage alliance, that woman, bitterly jealous of them, strove to reverse their deeds, but was unable. For she believed that these girls, her daughters, should have been handed over to be married off to men overseas, foreigners, in usurpation of the king and to the detriment of the kingdom of the Mercians. Aware of this fact, the said bishops put a bar on the womanly-wise advice.

In fact King Offa's third daughter, Ælflæd by name, still remained in the queen's apartment, awaiting marriage. So the aforesaid bishops prevailed on the king to agree, albeit against the will of the queen, that she be handed over in marriage to King Æthelberht; and thus he would be bound to remain especially loyal to King Offa through affection. So King Æthelberht, summoned by King Offa so that he could wed him to his daughter, came quickly and delighting, on account of the honour offered him by such a king – who, running up to him when he arrived, greeted him with a kiss and fatherly embrace saying: 'You are successful in love, son and son-in-law. Henceforth, most beloved young man, I adopt you as my special son.' But after they made this fully known to the savage queen she was more inflamed with rancour and

---

[459] See generally M.R. James, 'Two Lives of St. Ethelbert, king and martyr', *English Historical Review*, 32 (1917), 214-44, and C.E. Wright, *The Cultivation of Saga in Anglo-Saxon England*, Edinburgh, 1939, pp. 95-106.

[460] The early Hereford *Life* of Æthelberht ed. James mentions songs sung about the saint's ancestors (*op. cit.*, p. 219). The fourteenth-century *Life* of him by Richard of Cirencester uses Virgil's Aeneid, *Speculum Historiale*, ed. J.E.B. Mayor, Rolls Series, 30, London, 1863-69, I, pp. 262-94.

[461] For chronological disparity as to these names see notes above.

[462] Above, pp. 47-50.

regis et suorum fidelium prosperari. Vidensque sue nequicie argumenta minime preualere, nec hanc saltem terciam filia suam, ad uoluntatem suam alicui transmarino amico suo, in regni subuersionem, quod certissime sperauerat, dare nuptui, cum non preualuisset in dictos episcopos huius rei auctores eminus malignari, in Ælbertum regem uiris sue malicie truculenter euomuit, hoc modo.

Fraus muliebris crudelissima.[463]

Rex huius rei ignarus tantam latitasse fraudem non credebat, immo pocius credebat hec ipsi omia placitura. Cum igitur rex piissimus ipsam super premissimis secrecius conueniret, consilium querens qualiter et quando forent complenda, hec respondit: 'Ecce tradidit Deus hodie inimicum tuum, tibi caute, si sapis, trucidandum, qui sub specie superficiali, uenenum prodicionis in te et regnum tuum exercende, nequiter, ut fertur, occultauit. Et te cupit iam senescentem, cum sit iuuenis et elegans, de regno supplantando precipitare, et posterum suorum, immo et multorum, ut iactitat, quos regnis et possessionibus uiolenter et iniuste spoliasti, iniurias uindicare. In cuius rei fidem, michi a meis amicis significatum est, quod regis Karoli multis muneribus et nunciis ocultis intermeantibus, implorat ad hoc patrocinium, se spondens ei fore tributarium. Illo igitur, dum se tibi fortuna prebet fauorabilem, extincto latenter, regnum eius in ius tuumet successorum tuorum transeat in eternum.'

Cui rex mente nimium perturbatus, et de uerbis quibus credidit inesse ueraciter falsitatem et fraudem, cum indignacione ipsam increpando, respondit: 'Quasi una de stultis mulieribus locuta es. Absit a me, absit, tam detestabile factum. Quo perpetrato, michi meisque successoribus foret obprobrium sempiternum. Et peccatum in genus meum cum graui uindicta diucius propagabile.'

Et hiis dictis, rex iratus, ab ea recessit, detestans tantos ac tales occultos laqueos, in muliere latitasse.

Interea mentis perturbacione paulatim deposita, et hiis ciuiliter dissimulatis, reges consederunt ad mensam pransuri, ubi regalibus esculentis et poculentis, in timpanis, citharis et choris, diem totum in ingenti gaudio expleuerunt. Sed regina malefica, interim a ferali proposito non recedens, iussit in dolo thalamum more regio pallis sericis et auleis sollempniter adornari, in quo rex Ælbertus nocturnum caperet sompnum. Iuxta stratum quoque regium sedile preparari fecit, cultu nobilissimo extructum, et cortinis undique redimitum. Sub quo eciam fossam preparari fecit profundam, [20r][464] ut nephandum propositum perduceret ad effectum.

---

[463] Irregularly laid out chapter heading.

[464] Illustration: A blind man stumbles upon the decapitated head of King Æthelberht whose body is carried away. The right-hand space is occupied by the remainder of this chapter otherwise omitted by the copyist, although the folio's footnote indicates that it had been intended to depict Offa II in mourning and Queen Thryth dying in a cesspit (*in puteo*) (Fig. 27). See Introduction, pp. xxiv-xxv.

rage, bemoaning that he was successful in the hands of the king and his followers. And, seeing that her worthless arguments did not prevail, that not even this the third of her daughters was given in marriage according to her wishes, to some overseas friend of hers, to the ruin of the kingdom, which she had most certainly hoped, when she had not prevailed over the said bishops, authors of this business, from a distance, she violently spewed forth the poison of her malice against King Æthelberht in this way.

The woman's most cruel deceit.

The king, unaware of these things, did not believe that such deceit had lain hidden, in fact believed rather that everything would please her. Then when the most devout king had a private discussion with her in advance, looking for advice as to how and when to carry it out, she replied: 'Look, today God has handed over your enemy to you for careful butchery, if you are wise – he who, it is said, has, hidden under a beautiful exterior, the poison of treason to be wickedly used against you and your kingdom. And he wants to usurp you, now an old man, whilst he is a young and handsome one, from the kingdom, to avenge the wrongs done to his followers, and in fact the many that you have violently and unjustly despoiled of their kingdoms and properties. I have been told by my friends who believe that many gifts and secret intermediaries have passed between him and King Charles, that he asked for this protection, offering himself as a tributary to him. So do away with him under cover, whilst Fortune shows herself favourable to you, and let his kingdom lawfully pass to you and your successor's rule for ever.'

At this the king did not change his mind at all, but believed there to be actually falsehood and deceit in her words. In exasperation he replied to her in remonstration: 'You have spoken like a crazy woman. Forbid it! Forbid that I commit such a detestable deed. If I did, it would be an eternal disgrace on me and my successors and a sin to pass down in my race, having serious consequences.'

And having said this, the angry king left her, abhorring the fact that such great, secret snares had lain hidden in the woman.

In the meantime – perturbation gradually put aside, and such things courteously concealed – the kings sat down together at table to eat, where they spent the whole day in huge delight, in royal feasting and drinking, with tambourines, harps and songs. But meanwhile, the evil queen, not relinquishing her beastly plan, treacherously ordered an apartment in royal fashion, formally hung with silken drapes and covers, in which King Æthelberht would spend the night asleep. And next to the royal couch she also had a seat prepared, fashioned in the most elegant style and surrounded with curtains on every side. Under which a deep trench was prepared for the heinous plan to be carried through.[465]

---

[465] We might perhaps assume this to be closet and cess-pit in view of her own eventual fate (pp. 97-100). Cf Introduction, pp. lxxxvi-lxxxvii.

Fig. 25) King Offa II gives his three daughters as 'peace-weaving' brides to the now subordinate kings of Wessex and Northumbria, and offers the youngest to the king of East Anglia. Three couples stand in order across the page. The girls adopt a similar bodily posture, but are depicted in relative degrees of relationship to the kings. The first couple, Eadburh and King Brihtric of Wessex, stand hand in hand. In the second, King Æthelred I of Northumbria has his arm around the shoulder of Ælflæd who, grimacing, stands with raised hands, palms stretched outwards. The third, Æthelburh with palms out-turned, stands away from the young, unbearded King Æthelberht of East Anglia. MS Cotton Nero D i, f. 19ʳ © The British Library Board. All Rights Reserved.

Fig. 26) King Offa II, enthroned and sceptred, a hand raised in rejection, turns his head away as Queen Thryth makes an abhorrent suggestion. Subsequently the queen herself superintends the murder of King Æthelberht, now lightly bearded; one man beheads him, half down the pit, whilst another carries in a pillow for his suffocation. MS Cotton Nero D i, f. 19ᵛ © The British Library Board. All Rights Reserved.

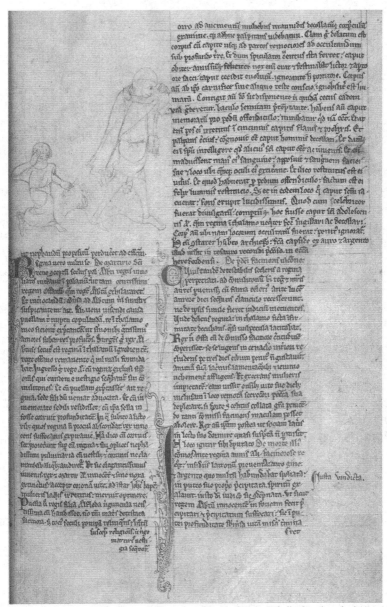

De martirio Sancti Ælberti regis innocentissimi.

Regina uero uultu sereno conceptum scelus pallians, intrauit in palatium, ut tam regem Offanum quam regem Ælbertum exhilararet. Et interuocandum Quendrida ad Ælbertum nichil sinistri suspicantem, ait:[466] 'Fili, ueni uisendi causa puellam tibi nuptu copulandam, te in thalamo meo sicienter expectantem, ut sermonibus gratissimis amores subarres profuturos.' Surgens igitur rex Ælbertus, secutus est reginam in thalamum ingredientem. Rege Offano remanente, qui nil mali formidabat. Ingresso igitur rege Ælberto cum regina, exclusi sunt omnes qui eundem e uestigio sequebantur sui commilitones, et cum puellam expectasset, ait regina: 'Sede fili dum ueniat aduocata.' Et cum in memorato sedili residisset, eum ipsa sella in fosse corruit profunditatem. In qua, subito a lictoribus quos regina non procul absconderat, rex innocens suffocatus expirauit. Nam ilicocum corruisset, proiecerunt super eum regina et sui complices nephandissimi puluinaria cum uestibus et cortinis, ne clamans ab aliquibus audiretur. Et sic elegantissimus iuuenis, rex et martir Ælbertus, innocenter et sine noxa extinctus, accepit coronam uite quam[467] ad instar Iohannis baptiste mulieris laqueis irretitus, meruit optinere.

Puella uero regis filia Ælfleda[468] uirguncula uenustissima, cum hec audisset, non tantum matris detestata facinora, sed tocius seculi pompam relinquens, habitum[469] suscepit religionis, ut uirgo martiris uestigia sequeretur.[470]

Porro ad aucmentum muliebris tirannidis,[471] decollatum est corpusculum exanime, quia adhuc palpitans uidebatur. Clam igitur delatum est corpus cum capite, usque ad partes remociores ad occultandum sub profundo terre. Et dum spiculator cruentus ista ferret, caput obiter amissum est feliciter,[472] nox enim erat, et festinabat lictor, et aperto ore sacci, caput cecidit euolutum, ignorante hoc portitore.

Corpus autem ab ipso carnifice sine aliquo teste conscio ignobiliter, est humatum. Contigit autem, Deo sic disponente, ut quidam cecus eadem uia graderetur, baculo semitam pretemptante. Habens autem caput memoratum pro pedum offendiculo, mirabatur quidnam esset. Erat enim pes eius irretitus in cincinnis capitis flauis et prolixis. Et palpans cercius, congnouit esse caput hominis decollati. Et datum est sue et loco ubi quandoque oculi eius extiterant. Et ilico restitutus est ei uisus. Et quod habuerat pro pedum offendiculo, factum est ei felix ei in spiritu intelligere, quod alicuius sancti caput esset, ac iuuenis. Et cum maduissent manus eius sanguine,

---

[466] C nichil sinistrum ait.

[467] N 'quam' added in margin in later hand.

[468] Presumably Offa's daughter Æthelburh, alias Eugenia abbess of Fladbury, Worcestershire, the form of the name confused with that of her who married Æthelred of Northumbria, p. 86, n. 454. See generally J. Story, *Carolingian Connections: Anglo Saxon England and Carolingian Francia*, Aldershot, 2003, pp. 183-84.

[469] The remainder of this chapter, omitted by the copyist, is inserted in the top right-hand space intended for illustration (Fig. 27). For the layout of this folio see Introduction, pp. xxiv-xxv.

[470] N Last seven words omitted and added in lower margin.

[471] C facinoris.

[472] N 'feliciter' over erasure.

On the martyrdom of Saint Æthelberht, most innocent of kings.

Now, with a smiling face cloaking the crime thought up, the queen went into the palace, where King Offa was delighted with King Æthelberht. And speaking to Æthelberht who suspected nothing wrong, Cwenthryth said: 'Son, come and see the girl to be joined with you in marriage, thirstily awaiting you in my apartment, so that you may make future love certain with pleasing conversation.' So, getting up, King Æthelberht followed the queen entering the apartment – King Offa, who supposed nothing wrong, staying behind. So, King Æthelberht having entered with the queen, all his comrades-in-arms who had followed in his footsteps were excluded. And when he expected to see the girl, the queen said: 'Sit down son, until she comes – she's been sent for.' And when he settled on the aforesaid seat, he collapsed together with the chair into the bottom of the trench. In that the innocent king expired, immediately suffocated by officers whom the queen had concealed not far away. For, immediately he had collapsed, the queen and her most heinous henchman[473] threw cushions with clothes and curtains over him so that no cries were heard by anyone. And so the most handsome young man Æthelberht, king and martyr, done away with, innocent and without fault, received the crown of life that he deserved to gain when entangled in a woman's snares like John the Baptist.[474]

Now when the maiden Æthelflæd, the king's daughter, a very beautiful young girl, heard of these things she took the habit of a nun,[475] distancing herself from not only the mother's detestable crimes but the whole vanity of the world, so that, a virgin, she might follow in the footsteps of a martyr.

Moreover, to add to the woman's despotic deeds,[476] the lifeless young body was beheaded,[477] because it seemed to be still throbbing. Then the body and the head were covertly borne to a remote area to be hidden deep under the earth. And as the blood-stained assassin carried them, on the way the head was happily lost; because it was night-time and the officer was in a hurry and, the mouth of the sack open, the rolling head fell out without the carrier knowing.

However, the body was buried by that murderer in a secret place without any witness. But it happened, God willing it, that a certain blind man was going along that road, feeling the footpath with a stick. Finding the aforesaid head a stumbling block to the feet however, he wondered what it was, because his foot was tangled up in the head's long golden curls. And touching it more carefully, he realised that it was the head of a decapitated man. And intuitively he realised that this was the head of

---

[473] Named as Winberht in the *Life* by Giraldus Cambrensis, ed. James, *op. cit.*, p. 228; cf. Introduction, p. lxxxvii.

[474] Matthew XIV.4-11; Mark VI.18-28.

[475] At Croyland, south Lincolnshire, an abbey founded by St Guthlac. Encouraged by Alcuin to enter Christ's apartment: *in coenobio militet Christo, quae thalamo priuata est uiri*, J.P. Migne, *Patrologia Latini*, 100, Paris, 1863, col. 228.

[476] C crime. The act of beheading would be regarded as particularly despicable inasmuch as that which was thought to identify and thus embody the spirit of the individual was separated from the remainder.

[477] With his own sword, naively entrusted to Winberht, above, n. 473.

apposuit et sanguinem faciei luminis restitucio. Sed et in eodem loco quo caput sanctum iacuerat, fons erupit lucidissimus. Quod cum celebriter[478] fuerat diuulgatum, compertum est hoc fuisse caput sancti adolescentis Ælberti, quem regina in thalamo nequiter fecit sugillari ac decollari. Corpus autem ubinam locorum occultatum fuerat, penitus ignoratur.

Hoc cum constaret Humberto Archiepiscopo, facta capside ex auro et argento, illud iussit in tesauro recondi precioso, in ecclesia Herefordensi.

De predicti facinoris ulcione.

Cuius tandem detestabilis sceleris a regina perpetrati[479] ad commilitonum beati regis et martiris aures peruenisset cum[480] fama celerius ante lucem aurore diei sequentis clanculo recesserunt, ne de ipsis simile fieret iudicium metuentes. Vnde dolens regina, in thalamo ficta infirmitate decubans, quasi uulpecula latitabat.

Rex uero Offa cum de commisso facinore certitudinem comperisset, sese lugens, in cenaculo interiori recludens, pe[481] tres dies cibum penitus non gustauit, animate suam lacrimis, lamentacionibus, et ieiunio uehementer affligens. Et execrans mulieris impietatem, eam iussit omnibus uite sue diebus inclusam in loco remotam secreciori peccata sua deplorare, si forte sibi celitus collata gracia, penitendo tanti commissi facinoris maculam posset abolere. Rex autem ipsam postea ut sociam lateris in lecto suo[482] dormire quasi suspectam non permisit.

De morte illius facinorose regine.

In loco igitur sibi deputato, commorante regina annis aliquot, insidiis latronum preuenta, auro et argento quo multum habundabat spoliata,[483] in puteo suo proprio precipitata, spiritum exalauit, iusto dei iudicio sic condempnata. Vt sicut regem Ælbertum innocentem in foueam fecit precipitari, et precipitatum suffocari, sic in putei

---

[478] N 'scelebriter' perhaps assuming 'scelerate', 'criminally', but 's' erased; C 'celeriter', 'quickly'.
[479] C 'cum' added in margin in later hand.
[480] C corrected to 'cum peruenisset' in later hand over erasure.
[481] C per.
[482] C 'in lecto suo' omitted; 'nullatenus' added in margin.
[483] N C 'Iusta Vindicata' in margin.

someone holy, and a young man.[484] And when his hands had been steeped in blood, and sometimes in the place where his eyes had been, he put the blood on his face. And immediately his sight was restored. And what had been a stumbling block for his feet became for him a blessed restorative of light. And in the very place where the holy head had fallen the clearest spring arose.[485] When news of this spread, it was discovered that this had been the head of the holy youth Æthelberht, whom the queen in her apartment had wickedly had beaten senseless and beheaded. But the place where the body had been hidden is entirely unknown.

When this was agreed with Archbishop Hunberht, he had a box made from gold and silver that he ordered to be kept in the treasury of valuables in the church of Hereford.

On the punishment of the aforesaid wrong.

When the detestable crime committed by the queen eventually reached the ears of the comrades-in-arms of the blessed king and martyr, very quickly, before light of dawn the following day, they secretly withdrew, fearing that a similar sentence might be meted out to themselves. Whereupon the queen, upset, lurked like a little vixen, lying in the apartment feigning illness.

In fact when King Offa learned the facts about the crime committed, he did not touch food for three entire days, weeping in private, shutting himself in an inner chamber, severely afflicting his soul with tears, lamentations and fasting. And, cursing the woman's wickedness, he ordered her to deplore her sins all the days of her life, confined, removed to a very distant place. Perhaps, if grace were bestowed on her from heaven, she would be able with penance to wipe out the stain of having committed such a great crime. But, because untrustworthy, as it were,[486] after that, the king did not allow her to sleep as a partner by his side in bed.[487]

On the death of that criminal queen.

So the queen, staying for some years in the place assigned to her, lost out to the plots of thieves, was robbed of the gold and silver of which she had plenty.[488] Thrown into her own cesspit[489] she breathed forth her soul, thus condemned by the righteous judgement of God. So, just as she caused the innocent King Æthelberht to be thrown into a hole

---

[484] For the blind man, let alone one in an era that could consider itself still heroic, a death by execution would be preferrable to one through suffocation in sewage by an indignant prospective mother-in-law.

[485] A phenomenon characteristically associated with the decapitation of early Anglo-Saxon female virgin saints, e.g. Osyth of Essex, Winifred of Holywell, Urith of Chittlehampton, Juthware at Sherborne, in the tradition of pagan well guardians. Generally M. J. Swanton, *St. Sidwell: an Exeter Legend*, Exeter, 1986, pp. 12-16, and references there cited. But the head of a saint would often be separately enshrined whether or not decapitated at a martyrdom.

[486] Cf. M. Swanton, 'Die altenglische Judith: Weiblicher Held oder frauliche Heldin', in *Heldensage und Heldendichtung im Germanischen*, ed. H. Beck, Berlin, 1988, pp. 289-304.

[487] C 'not at all' added in margin.

[488] N 'Justly Punished' in margin.

[489] Cf pp. 92-3; Introduction, pp. lxxxvi-lxxxvii, n. 363.

profunditate submersa, uitam miseram terminaret. [20ᵛ][490]

De intumulacione sancti corporis eiusdem regis Alberti et martiris.

Humbertus uero Lichefeldensis Archiepiscopus corpus regis et martiris Alberti, sibi dari a rege Offano humiliter ac pie postulauit. Sciebat enim ut pote confessor[491] sanctissimus, ipsum regem Albertum purum et innocentem, sine aliqua culpa et offensa occubuisse. Et illud ad ecclesian Lechefeldensem, solempniter cum canticis et obsequiis deferri fecit obsequialibus, et conuocatis suis omnibus diaconibus et clericis sepeliri. Vbi minus honeste quam decebat tumulatus, omnibus latebat diu incognitus, donec corpus eius celesti lumine declaratum, a fidelibus est[492] inuentum, et apud Herefordensem delatum ciuitatem, nunc sedem episcopalem, miraculis exornat et uirtutibus illustrat.[493]

Regnum Orientalium Anglorum sine difficultate cedit in potestatem Offe Regis Merciorum.

Rex autem Offa magnificus, postquam consolacionem ex mellifluo affatu sanctorum episcoporum supradictorum acceperat, qui penitus a morte regis fuerat immunis, missa expedicione perualida,[494] regnum Orientalium Anglorum suo regno prudenter copulando solidauit. Non enim prenominatus Rex Albertus liberos habuit aut legitimum successorem. Et sic dominacio sua, licenter non mediocriter est adaucta.[495]

Adrianus[496] legatos mittit in Britanniam.

Eisdem annis, Adrianus Papa[497] legatos misit in Britanniam, ad fidem quam Augustinus episcopus predicauerat, renouandam et confirmandam. Qui et uerbis et operibus sancte doctrine et uirtutem, populos adhuc rudes salubriter imformarent. Ipsi igitur a rege et clero honorifice ac reuenter suscepti, super stabile fidei catholice fundamentum sane ac prudenter, Christi cooperante gratia edificauerunt. Vt hec autem

---

[490] Illustration: the body of St Æthelberht, decapitated and enshrouded, is entombed in a church at Lichfield by Archbishop Humbert. King Offa II knights his bearded son Prince Ecgfrith, belted and spurred. The scene as previously (f. 10ʳ), a man-at-arms standing to the right with banner and shield, but without heraldry depicted.

[491] C 'alussimus' [perhaps intended for albusissimus - very white] added and deleted.

[492] N 'est' interlined in later hand.

[493] The sentence is largely similar to that found in Matthew Paris, *Chronica Majora*, I, p. 355.

[494] C ne ualida.

[495] N 'adaucta' 'a' of second syllable interlined. C second two syllables written over erasure.

[496] N 'lig' added but deleted.

[497] N 'Papa' erased; C 'Adranus Papa'.

and, thrown in, suffocated, so she ended her miserable life drowned in the depth of a cesspit.

On the entombment of the holy body of this same Æthelberht, king and martyr.

In fact Hunberht, archbishop of Lichfield, asked humbly and devoutly that the body of Æthelberht king and martyr be given him by King Offa. For the most holy confessor knew moreover that this King Æthelberht had passed away pure and innocent, without any fault or offence. And, after he had summoned all his deacons and priests, he had it taken formally with chanting and funeral rituals to a Lichfield church, and buried. Where, entombed less honourably than fitting, it lay hidden to all for a long time, unknown until, indicated by a light from heaven, his body was discovered by the faithful and borne to the city of Hereford[498] (now the seat of a bishop[499]), enhanced by miracles and made glorious with marvels.[500]

The kingdom of the East English cedes without difficulty to the power of Offa, king of the Mercians.

However, the great King Offa afterwards received consolation in the sweet talk of the aforesaid holy bishops. He who was entirely innocent of the king's death, having sent a very strong expedition, prudently secured the kingdom of the East English by union with his own kingdom. For the aforenamed King Æthelberht had no children or legitimate successor. And thus legally, his realm was considerably extended.[501]

Adrian sends legates[502] to Britain.

At that time, Pope Adrian sent legates to Britain to renew and confirm the faith that Bishop Augustine [503] had preached. They were to wholesomely instruct a still uncultivated people in words and deeds about holy doctrine and virtues. [504] So, received by the king and clergy with honour and reverence, these men, with the aid of the grace of Christ, built soundly and prudently on a firm foundation of orthodox

---

[498] Richard of Cirencester, who provides a full narrative account of the episode, tells us that it was a miraculous light that enabled the body, *inhoneste tumulatus omnibus latebat incognitos*, to be identified and transferred to Hereford, although the head would be enshrined at Westminster, where Richard himself was a monk, *Speculum Historiale*, ed. Mayor, I, pp. 289-93.

[499] An episcopal see since the seventh century, but the exact dates of most pre-Conquest occupancies are uncertain. During the twelfth century the seat was frequently unoccupied for more than a year. William of Malmesbury remarks the overall confusion of bishoprics during Jænberht's time, *Gesta Pontificum Anglorum*, ed. and transl. M. Winterbottom, Oxford, 2007, I, pp. 122-23.

[500] Cf. Giraldus Cambrensis, *Opera*, ed. Brewer, III, pp. 425-30.

[501] There is no hard evidence for a separate kingdom of East Anglia for about thirty years.

[502] Neighbouring Italian bishops: George of Ostia and Theophylact of Todi.

[503] Leader of the sixth-century Roman mission, cf. Bede, *Ecclesiastical History of the English People*, I, 23-26, ed. and transl. B. Colgrave and R.A.B. Mynors, Oxford, 1969, pp. 68-79.

[504] Sent to confront a latter-day rise of Pelagianism, see below, pp. 105-6.

sapientius, rite prosequerentur, tenuerunt concilium apud Chalcuthe, ubi eciam Lambertus Archiepiscopus Cantuariensis, partem sui episcopatus, Archiepiscopo Lichefeldensi, sponte quam postulauerat, resignauit.

Ecgfridus Regis Offe primogenitus, in regem Merciorum patre uiuente sollempniter coronatur.

In illo quoque concilio, Offa Merciorum potentissimus, in regem fecit sollempniter coronari filium suum primogenitum Ecgfridum, iuuenem strenuum et elegantem, moribusque decenter redimitum. Qui deinceps cum patre, eidem militans et in omnibus obsecundans, usque ad[505] finem uite eius conregnauit.

Rex Offa orat sibi gratiam dari in uoto suo complendo.

Rex autem Offa magnificus ac piissimus, post mortem uxoris sue regine, uidelicet Quendride, uitam celibem ducens, salubribus monitis et doctrinis sanctorum Humberti Archiepiscopi et Vnwone Episcopi, et aliorum, quos iustos nouerat et prudentes, diligenter intendebat, et eorum consilio cum filio suo Ecgfrido regebatur. Pacis enim undique tranquillitate congaudebant. Vna autem dierum suscitato sermone de uoto supra dicto quo Rex Offa a multis[506] retroactis temporibus Deo tenebatur astrictus, cuius execucionem Regina [21ʳ][507] Quendrida iam defuncta, nequiter retardando impediuerat,[508] trahens ab alto Rex suspiria, uiris memoratis et aliis magnatibus sibi specialibus, ait, Deo tamen fundens orationem. 'O Deus, qui me ab onnium hostium insidiis et impugnacionibus, nec non et a coniugis mee laqueis, misericorditer ac potenter liberasti, da michi condigne tibi famulando, gratam rependere uicissitudinem. Oro Domine Iesu Christe[509] congnitor secretorum, et presage futurorum, ut michi famulo tuo manifeste concedas certificari, de cenobio tibi te propicio, constituendo, de quo fundando uotiuo affectum me nosti[510] strictius obligatum. De loco insuper, et cuinam sancto tuo sit intitulandum, per angelum ueritatis flagito cercius edoceri.' Et conuersus rex ad circumsedentes abortis lachrimis et coniunctis manibus, ait: 'Hoc quoque patres ac fratres karissimi, qui Deo sic uolente nunc presentes estis, oro deuocius quatinus sincera mente, totaque deuocione, Deum omnipotentem deprecemini, ut ad beneplacitum suum honorem et gloriam, ad effectum meum perducat desiderium.' Et cum omnes gaudentes hoc concessissent, intrauit Archiepiscopus Humbertus cum Vnwona Episcopo et aliis quos aduocauerant[511] clericis, in oratorium quod prope erat, super hoc propensius oraturus. Et premisso

---

[505] C in.
[506] C 'annis' added and deleted.
[507] Illustration: An angel from heaven informs the sleeping King Offa II as to where St Alban's remains may be found. A light descends between holly and oak trees.
[508] C impedierat.
[509] C 'Christe' omitted.
[510] C 'nosti'; N 'nostis' final 's' erased.
[511] C aduocauerat.

faith.[512] However, so that these things should be properly followed up, they wisely held a Council at Chelsea[513] – also where Jænberht, archbishop of Canterbury, voluntarily resigned part of his province to the archbishop of Lichfield, as he had asked.

Ecgfrith the first-born of King Offa, is formally crowned as king of the Mercians with his father still living.

From then on, fighting for him and obeying him in everything, [Ecgfrith] jointly reigned with his father right to the end of his life.[514] Also at that council Offa, mightiest of the Mercians, had his first first-born son Ecgfrith – an active and handsome young man, and endowed with decent moral principals – formally crowned king.

King Offa prays that grace be given him to carry out his vow.

But the great and most devout King Offa, leading a celibate life after the death of his wife the queen, that is to say Cwenthryth, listened carefully to the sound advice and teachings of the holy Archbishop Hunberht and Bishop Unwona and others whom he knew to be righteous and prudent, and by their counsel governed together with his son Ecgfrith. Indeed, they rejoiced together everywhere in the tranquillity of peace. One day however talk turned to the aforesaid vow[515] by which King Offa was held bound to God from a long time ago, the fulfilment of which Queen Cwenthryth, now dead, had wickedly delayed by impediments. Heaving deep sighs the king spoke to the aforesaid men and other of his close noblemen, although pouring out a prayer to God:

'Oh God, who has mercifully and powerfully freed me from all the plots and attacks of the enemy, let alone the snares of my spouse, grant grace to repay the other side of the bargain so that I may worthily serve you. I pray Lord Jesus Christ, who knows the unknown and foresees the future, that you who are merciful will agree to make manifest to me your servant about the establishment of a monastery in your honour, the votive foundation of which I know myself responsible under a heavy obligation. Moreover I beg you that I be distinctly told by an angel of truth about the location, and to which saint it should be dedicated.' With tears ended and hands clasped, the king turned to those sitting round him and said: 'Dearest fathers and brothers who are now present by the will of God, I also devoutly pray this, that with sincere mind and complete devotion you beseech Almighty God that, to please his honour and glory, he may lead me to put my wish into effect.' And when all, in delight, had agreed to this, Archbishop Hunberht with Bishop Unwona and the other clerics they had sent for,

---

[512] Their report exists: *Epistolae Karolini Aevi*, II, ed. Dümmler, pp. 20-29, transl. Whitelock, *English Historical Documents*, I, 2nd edn, pp. 836-40.

[513] A convenient location on the Thames in Middlesex, in 787 (*Anglo-Saxon Chronicles*, eds cit., pp. 52-4); the venue of a dozen councils, one of a limited number of sites to which assemblies repeatedly returned through the late eighth or early ninth century.

[514] I.e. Offa II's life, see Introduction, p. xcii.

[515] His ancestor's vow to found or restore á monastery, pp. 35-6.

ymno[516] Veni Creator Spiritus, orauerunt deuotissime, ut Dominus iustum Regis desiderium ad effectum duceret gloriosum. Et cum prolixius orassent, ecce lux emissa celitus totam cellulam illam in qua erant, a summo tecti fastigio usque ad pauimentum perlustrauit. In qua fauor Dei manifeste significabatur. Vnde rex illud regale manerium in quo hec euenerunt, uidelicet Wineslaue cum pertinenciis illi cenobio quod adhuc fundaturus erat rex, regali contulit munificentia, tali munere locum subarrando, quem adhuc penitus ignorauit.

De reuelacione Angelica facta Regi Merciorum Offe de Inuencione Sancti Albani Anglorum Prothomartiris.[517]

Post hos uero dies non multos, Rex Merciorum Offa potentissimus, cum in urbe Bathonia residens, post diei laborem, noctis quietem in stratu regio caperet, angelo nuntiante diuino est amonitus oraculo, ut sanctum Anglorum siue Britonum prothomartirem Albanum de terra leuaret, et reliquias eius in scrinio dignius collocaret.

Rex uero diuinis ilico studens obtemperare preceptis, accito Humberto Merciorum Archiepiscopo, cuius sedes apud Lichefeld ut predictum est nuper ab eodem rege fuerat constituta, diuinam ei uoluntatem indicat de premissis. Tunc archiepiscopus sepedictus assumptis continuo secum Ceoluulfo Lindesiensi et Vnwona Legrecestri Episcopis suis suffraganeis, cum innumera utriusque sexus et diuerse etatis multitudine, regi die sibi statuta, apud Verolamium occurrerunt. Rex uero dum illuc iter expediret, lucis radium in modum ingentis facule celitus emissum super locum sepulchri quasi fulminare conspexit.

Hoc quoque diuino miraculo manifeste[518] ab omnibus aspecto gaudentes, tali indicio extiterunt de uisionis ueritate effecti [21ᵛ][519] cerciores. Tunc populo in ieiuniis et orationibus sanctificato, antistites sacri sacerdotalibus infulis adornati, affore sibi beati martiris auxilium flagitabant. Fuerat nanque[520] locus, et memoria martiris post aduentum Sancti Germani Autissiodorensis Episcopi, qui cum beato Lupo Trecasine

---

[516] C ympno.

[517] The wording of this section bears an overall resemblance to that used by Matthew Paris, *Chronica Majora*, I, p. 356.

[518] C 'manifeste' omitted.

[519] Illustration: At King Offa II's direction, accompanied by two bishops one presenting 'the host', trees are felled and soil excavated seeking the remains of Saint Alban. Labourers are depicted with axe and mattock, bucket and spade. Bones are to be seen in the trench. A monk in attendance chants the 'Te deum' (Fig. 28).

[520] C Fuerant namque.

entered the oratory which was nearby, to pray about this very willingly. And having started with the hymn 'Come Creator Spirit' they prayed most devoutly that the Lord would lead the king's righteous wish into glorious effect. And when they had prayed lengthily, behold, a light from heaven – in which God's favour was clearly shown – lit up the whole of that chapel where they were, from the top of the roof gable down to the paving-stones. Wherefore the king gave the royal manor in which these things happened – that is to say Winslow, with its appurtenances[521] – to that monastery which the king yet had to found,[522] endowing the place with generosity such as was entirely unknown before.

On the angelic revelation made to Offa, king of the Mercians, about the discovery of Saint Alban, First Martyr of the English.

Not many days after that, when Offa, most powerful king of the Mercians, staying in the city of Bath,[523] took his nightly rest on the royal couch after the day's labours, he was advised by an angel speaking with a divine message that he should exhume holy Alban, first martyr of the English or Britons,[524] and place his relics in a worthier casket.

So the king, immediately wondering how to comply with the divine commands, having sent for Hunberht, archbishop of the Mercians, whose seat at Lichfield had been recently established by the same king, as said above,[525] pointed out to him the divine will from what had happened. Then, on a day decided by the king himself, they met at Verulamium,[526] the renowned archbishop having taken with him his suffragans, Ceolwulf of Lindsey and Unwona, bishop of Leicester,[527] with a countless number of either sex and various ages. Now whilst the king made his way there, he spied a beam of light, resembling a huge torch sent down from heaven, like lightning onto the place of the grave.

Delighting in this divine miracle, clearly seen by all, they remained impressed by a sign of this kind, more certain of the truth of the vision. Then, with the people sanctified by fasting and prayer, the holy prelates adorned with priestly vestments begged that the blessed martyr would help them. For indeed, the place and memory of the martyr had been entirely wiped out after the arrival of Saint Germanus, bishop of

---

[521] Including 'demon's mound', two dozen miles to the north-east of St Albans. See generally A.H.J. Baines, 'The Winslow charter of 792 and the boundaries of Granborough', *Records of Buckinghamshire*, 22 (1980), 1-18.

[522] *Charters of St Albans*, ed. J. Crick, Oxford, 2007, pp. 119-31.

[523] In Somerset. Aquae Sulis, a former Roman spa city with extensive naturally hot therapeutic baths. Lying on the Mercian border with Wessex, the place was of strategic importance to Offa II, who spent much time acquiring land thereabouts.

[524] The regular formula used, as in this chapter heading, is 'first martyr of the English'; but at this point is correctly hesitant, inasmuch as at the time of Alban's martyrdom (283 or 286 A.D. according to the *Anglo-Saxon Chronicles*, eds cit. pp. 10-11) the English immigration, let alone their conversion to Christianity, had yet to take place. Cf. pp. 105-6 and Introduction pp. xl-xlvi.

[525] Above, pp. 79-82.

[526] A small British town, developed in Roman times and fortified under the Emperor Hadrian; but already in decline by the third century and later ruined: R. Niblett, *Verulamium, the Roman City of St Albans*, Stroud, 2001.

[527] Ceolwulf, 767-96; Unwona, *c.* 781- *c.* 801.

urbis Episcopo, ad extirpandam heresim Pelagianam in Britanniam uenerant, annis circiter trecentis et xliiii, omnino deleta; sed tantum in codicibus historiarum, et relatu senum, cum paucis uestigiis representata. Siquidem gens pagana, Saxonum, Iutorum, et Anglorum, Britonibus expulsis, sibi[528] subiugauerant. Qui agros cum horreis feraliter depopulantes, ignem in ciuitates, opida et pagos succenderunt, ecclesias solo tenus complanantes, prelatos quoque membratim detruncantes, omnem pene Britannicam insulam a mari usque ad mare hostili exterminio, uelut in desertum redegerunt.

Hac itaque tempestate ecclesia beati Anglorum prothomartiris Albani, quam Beda in Anglorum Historia miro tabulatu lapideo scripsit fuisse constructam, inter ceteras regionis ecclesias, funditus est subuersa. Vnde et sepulchrum eius quod in aduentu Sancti Germani et ante a passione martiris, usque ad illius patrie desolacionem, ab omnibus notu propter antique fame celebritatem, et miraculorum frequentiam, ab omnibus fuerat adoratum compatriotis et honoratum uniuersis, tempore quo Offe Regi inuictissimo angelico fuerat ministerio reuelatum. Locus autem sepulchri et loci distincti cognicio penitus delebatur.

Manifestius inuencionis indicium.[529]

Facta igitur ut diximus oratione a clero et populo cum elemosina et ieiunio, terram percuciunt, et passim martiris sepulturam offendunt. Nec fuit necesse locum diu querere, quem diuina clementia dignata est celesti lumine reuelare. Martiris igitur corpus astante Offa Rege Christianissimo in theca lignea in qua prius a Christi fidelibus propter barbarorum seuitiam fuerat tempore discriminis occultatum reperiunt, cum ipsis sacris omnium Apostolorum diuersorumque martirum reliquiis, quas ibi dudum sanctus deposuerat Germanus, intercessione beati martiris de Pelegianis triumphans.

Mouit[530] hec inuencio tam clerum quam populum uniuersum ad lacrimas, et ob hoc maxime quod fidem fecit Dominus de sanctorum patrum reliquiis ibidem cum corpore

---

[528] *C* 'insulam' inserted from margin.

[529] The wording used by Matthew Paris bears a close resemblance to the greater part of the first two paragraphs, *Chronica Majora*, I, p. 357.

[530] *N* marginal rubric: 'Testimonia fidei quibus contradici non potest'; *C* rubric within column.

Auxerre, who together with blessed Lupus, bishop of the town of Troyes, came to Britain to root out the Pelagian heresy[531] in the years around three hundred and forty four.[532] They were such as described in history books[533] and old men's tales, and traced with a few lines.[534] In fact a pagan race of Saxons, Jutes and English, having banished the Britons, subjugated the place.[535] Like wild animals they depopulated the fields along with their barns, set fire to cities, towns and villages, razed churches to the ground – dismembered the prelates as well – reduced the whole island of Britain to a wilderness with violent destruction from sea to sea.

The church of blessed Alban, first martyr of the English – of which Bede wrote in his *History of the English* that it had been constructed on wonderful stone flooring[536] – was ruined to its foundations by this tempest, among other churches in the region. And henceforth his grave which at the arrival of Saint Germanus and before that from the death of the martyr until the devestation of his country, was known by all because of the fame of its ancient proclamation and frequency of its miracles, and had been revered by all his fellow-citizens and universally honoured at the time it had been revealed by a ministering angel to the most invincible King Offa. But the situation of the grave and clear knowledge of the location was totally wiped out.

A clearer sign of the discovery.

So after the clergy and people had, as we said, offered prayers with almsgiving and fasting, they excavated the earth and came upon the martyr's grave there. Nor was there need to search the place long for him whom divine clemency honoured to reveal by a heavenly light. For with the most Christian King Offa standing by, they found the martyr's body in the wooden case in which it had been hidden earlier by Christ's faithful, on account of the ferocity of the barbarians at the time of danger; together with the sacred relics of all the apostles and various martyrs which holy Germanus had placed there long ago when triumphing over the Pelagians through the intercession of the blessed martyr.[537]

This discovery moved all the clergy and people equally to tears,[538] and above all because, as we read, the Lord had relics of the holy fathers deposited in the same place

---

[531] Pelagius was a British monk arguing against the orthodox notion of original sin. Bede, *Ecclesiastical History*, I, 17, 21, Colgrave and Mynors, pp. 54-67. Generally E.A. Thompson, *Saint Germanus of Auxerre and the end of Roman Britain*, Woodbridge, 1984.

[532] An error for 429 AD. A second visit took place some time after 437 AD.

[533] A summary of Bede, *loc. cit.*, and fifth-century Constantius, *Vita Germani*, ed. B. Krusch and W. Levison, *Passiones Vitaeque Sanctorum Aevi Merovingici*, Hanover, 1919, pp. 225-83 (pp. 259-65), transl. F.R. Hoare, *The Western Fathers*, London, 1954, pp. 281-320 (pp. 295-302).

[534] Presumably sketches rather than surviving plans.

[535] C marginal modification reads: 'the island'.

[536] Perhaps from the adjacent ruined Roman town of Verulamium. See Fig. 1, Introduction, p. xcviii.

[537] No explicit intercession by St Alban is described either by Bede or in Constantius' *Vita Germani*, although the martyr's help was said by both to have ensured Germanus a safe voyage home: Bede, I, 20, Colgrave and Mynors, pp. 64-5; Constantius, 18, Krusch and Levison, p. 265, Hoare, p. 302.

[538] N C rubric: 'Faithful witnesses whom it is not possible to contradict'.

martiris prout legimus depositis; quas ut pium est credere uoluit Dominus quasi ad solatium eiusdem martiris corpori diu soli fuisse associatas.

Roborauit insuper fidem regis et eius fidelium diuinum testimonium, cum apud Wineslaue lux cum miri odoris fragrantia, cellam presulum orantium illuminauit; et regis propositum cercius solidauit. Plus tamen ceteris omnium corda erexit, radius igneus ab ethere missu super locum eciam in die descendens et solare sicut et lunare lumen adaugens, regem cum suis sodalibus, quasi stella Magorum dux donec staret supra Domum ubi erat puer Christus, ad locum perduxit, memoratis reliquiis insignitum; ut uere dici possit, testimonia tua Christe credibilia facta sunt ni [22^r][539] mis. Et iccirco domum tuam Domine, tali loco fundandam, decet sanctitudo in longitudine dierum hoc est in sempiternum.

De testimonies miraculorum in conspectu populi ibidem celebratum.

Quem utique thesaurum super aurum et topazion preciosum, sub cespite diu absconditum, et iam diuinitus inuentum, Archiepiscopus Humbertus cum suis coepiscopis et clericis, astante rege reuerenter leuantes de sepulchro, precedente sollempni processione in hymnis et laudum preconiis transtulerunt in quandam ecclesiolam, ibidem extra urbem Verolamium, a neophitis in honorem beati martiris constructam; ubi martir percussus sanguinem suum fudit pro Christo, quam persecutores quia paruulam eiecto locello corpus suum continente diruere dedignabantur.

Ibidem igitur in eodem locello reliquiis ordinate dipositis[540] et pallis inuolutis et crane[541] aureo circulo a rege circundato, in[542] quo scriptum fuit: 'Hoc est caput Sancti Albani Anglorum prothomartiris', missa sollempniter celebratur. Et interim miracula eterna recordacione ibidem celebrantur,[543] in conspectu regis,[544] et antistitum et omnium illic existentium. Nam mortui ad uitam reuocantur semineces ad sospitatem[545] restaurantur, leprosi mundantur. Paralitici solidantur, febricitantes curantur, contracti eriguntur, muti, surdi, ceci et arrepticii, immo omnes languidi et se male[546] habentes malorum remedia recipiunt.

---

[539] Illustration, the outer edge of the folio repaired before drawing: In the presence of Offa II, St Alban's reliquary is carried by a group of monks in formal procession headed by some bearing cross, torches and sprinkler, and followed by one holding up an open book from which another chants. They pass disabled people awaiting cure.
[540] C disponitis.
[541] C craneo.
[542] C 'a rege circundato' over erasure; 'in' omitted. N In.
[543] C celebratur.
[544] C 's' corrected over erasure.
[545] C 'respitatem' added but deleted.
[546] C male se.

with the body of the martyr;[547] which it is a piety to believe the Lord wished to be associated with the body of the martyr as a consolation for being so long in the earth, as it were.

Divine evidence affirmed the faith of the king and his faithful, when at Winslow a light accompanied by an odour of wonderful fragrance lit up the chamber of praying bishops; and the king's intention was certainly confirmed.[548] But the beam, fiery even in daylight, descending on the place from its airy source, lifted the hearts of everyone even more, increasing both sunlight and moonlight alike, led the king with his companions to the place distinguished by the aforesaid relics, like the star that was the guide of the Magi until it stopped above the house where the Christ child was,[549] so that it can be truly said, your witnesses, Christ, were made completely believable. And for that reason, Oh Lord, it is appropriate for your house to be founded here on such a spot, in sanctity for length of days and eternity.

On witnesses to the miracles executed there in sight of the people.

This treasure, certainly more precious than gold and topaz,[550] hidden for so long under the turf and now divinely revealed was lifted from the grave by Archbishop Hunberht with his fellow-bishops and clergy, the king reverently standing by. Moving in formal procession with prayers and hymns of praise, it was transferred to a certain small church built by converts in honour of the blessed martyr in the same place outside[551] the city of Verulamium where the martyr being struck shed his blood for Christ, which, after throwing out the coffin containing his body, ravagers did not bother to destroy because it was small.[552]

So after the relics had been arranged in order in the same coffin, and palls wrapped round, and the head crowned by the king with a golden circlet, on which was written: 'This is the head of Saint Alban, first martyr of the English', mass was formally celebrated. And meanwhile, in sight of the king and the prelates and all in attendance there, miracles were executed as an eternal record in that place. For the dead are recalled to life, the half-dead restored to health, lepers cleansed. The paralyzed are strengthened, the invalid cured, cripples made straight, the dumb, the deaf, the blind and the insane – in fact all those weak and infirm – receive remedies for their infirmities.[553]

---

[547] By Germanus, Bede, *loc. cit.*

[548] See above, pp. 101-2.

[549] Cf. Matthew II.9.

[550] A valuable gemstone then associated with royalty, *English Mediaeval Lapidaries*, ed. J. Evans and M.S. Sergeantson, London, 1933, pp. 19, 105-07.

[551] For issues as to location, see Introduction, pp. xcvi-xcviii.

[552] We have been told differently a little earlier, pp. 103-4.

[553] Cf. Matthew VIII.1-17, IX.2-8, 18-31, XI.5; Luke VII.21-22, VIII.41-55.

Que Dei beneficia usque in hodiernum diem fieri non desistunt, sine ea que pluris est, animarum salute que eodem loco deuotis largiter impertitur.

De multiplici honore quem Rex Offa contulit sancto corpori iam inuento.

Rex igitur Offa Christianissimus locellum memoratum laminis aureis et argentis gemmisque preciosis, de thesauro suo munifice sumptis decenter adornari. Et ecclesiam ipsius in qua ut iam dictum est corpus collocabatur, picturis, auleis, et aliis ornamentis, donec amplior multis ditanda possessionibus et honoribus edificaretur, iussit decorari. Acta autem sunt hec a passione sepedicti martiris, anno quingentesimo septimo, ab aduentu Anglorum in Britanniam, trecentesimo, quadragesimo quarto. Indictione prima, kalendis Augusti.

Ut Rex Offa Romam pergens pratum emerit peregrinis.[554]

Merito autem, ut pretactum est, uitam celibem agenti uictoriosissimo Regi Offe, angelo celitus destinato, et inuento Anglorum prothomartire Albano, celesti indicio, creuit sub dierum breuitate per totam regionem honor martiris et reuerentia.

Eodem quoque mense rex ibidem prouinciale concilium [555] cum Archiepiscopo Humberto suisque suffraganeis et primatibus suis uniuersis, cum tractet [556] diligenter et efficaciter de conuentu monachorum in loco illo congregando, atque cenobio constituendo et magnifice ac regaliter priuilegiando, ubi prothomartiris regni sui immo tocius Britannie uel Anglie reliquias inuenit, et quem locum suo sanguine consecrauit.

Placet omnibus pium regis propositum [22v][557] eique episcoporum consulit prudentia ut auctoritate Romani Pontificis et si alias hoc factum fuerit, quia non iterari inutiliter dicitur quod non scitur perpetratum, canonizetur simul et priuilegietur monasterium, in honorem eiusdem martiris nouiter construendum. Et hec omnia ut digniorem et firmiorem fortiantur essectum consilium uirorum sanctorum et discretorum suscipit et exaudit, ut per legatos sollempnes[558] a latere regis destinatos, aut pocius in propria persona rex ipse super hiis cum curia tractet Romana diligenter.

[554] Roger of Wendover's account of the penitent Offa II's journey to Rome is often verbally identical, even to the extent of using this chapter-heading in common: *Ut rex Offa Romam pergens pratum peregrinis emerit*, Coxe, I, p. 254. For Roger see generally Introduction, p. xxviii.

[555] C 'tenuit' inserted from margin.

[556] C 'cum' erased, and replaced by: 'Ut tractarent'.

[557] Illustration, the outer edge of the folio repaired before drawing: A ship leaves a tree-lined shore, the raised anchor looped over the stern. King Offa II, standing amidships accompanied by clerical dignitary, directs sailors; one steers another hauls on sheets.

[558] C 'nuncios' added and deleted.

These blessings of God do not cease to happen right up to present days,[559] not to mention what is more important, the well-being of souls, which is widely imparted in that place of religion.

On the manifold honour that King Offa paid to the holy body now discovered.

So the most Christian King Offa ordered that the aforesaid coffin should be appropriately embellished with gold and silver leaf and precious stones generously supplied from his treasury and that the church, in which as has already been said the body was placed, should be decorated with paintings, hangings and other ornaments, until a larger one, to be endowed with properties and honours, might be built. This was done in the 507th year after the death of the renowned martyr, 344 after the arrival of the English in Britain, on the first of August, 792.[560]

King Offa on his way to Rome buys a meadow from foreigners.

So, as already touched upon, after an angel had deservedly been sent from heaven to the most victorious King Offa who was leading a celibate life, and after the discovery of Alban, first martyr of the English, through a heavenly sign, honour and reverence of the martyr increased in a very short time throughout the whole region.

And in the same month the king held[561] a provincial council there, with Archbishop Hunberht and his suffragans and all his chief men, that they might deal[562] thoroughly and effectively about the community of monks to be gathered in that place, and the establishment of a monastery splendidly and regally privileged,[563] where he discovered the relics of the first martyr of his kingdom – in fact of the whole of Britain or England – and which place he consecrated with his blood.

The king's devout proposal pleased everyone, and the sagacity of the bishops commended him that because, as they say, you have to do something again if you know it was not done properly first time, a monastery should be newly built in honour of the same martyr, both canonised and endowed with privileges by the authority of the Roman pontiff in case things should be done differently. And so that all these things should support the nurturing advice of the holy and prudent men with added dignity and strength, the king undertook and granted that his personal formal ambassadors[564] – or even the king in his own person, because he was superior to these – should go and carefully negotiate with the papal court at Rome.

---

[559] Cf. Bede, *Ecclesiastical History*, I, 7, 20, Colgrave and Mynors, pp. 34-35, 64-65.

[560] Alban was killed in the late third century (see above, p. 104, n. 524), and according to the *Anglo Saxon Chronicles* the English arrived in 449 (eds. cit., pp. 12-13).

[561] C The verb 'held' supplied in the margin.

[562] C 'when' erased and replaced by: [in order] 'that they might treat'.

[563] Below, pp. 117-20.

[564] C 'messengers' added and deleted.

De prosecucione pii propositi Regis piissimi Offe.

Offa igitur rex piissimus suorum magnatum sano adquiescens consilio, diuino ductus spiritu, transalpinum ualde sibi laboriosum et sumptuosum iter arripit sine more dispendio. Nec eum cura rei familiaris uel regni custodiendi necessitas, uel comminantis senii[565] grauitas, nec laboris immanitas, uel pecunie inestimabilis effusio, ipsum poterant retardare. Stabilem retinens in proposito cordis intencionem, ut sicut beatus Albanus, prothomartir refulsit Angligenis, ita et monasterium eius omnibus regni cenobiis, possessionibus similiter[566] et libertatis nec non et priuilegiis prefulgeat et preponatur.

Transfretat Rex Romam profecturus.[567]

Preparatis igitur edicto regio nauibus cum nauium armamentis, rex puppes ascendit. Et sinuatis uelis prospero cursu in quodam portu maris in Flandria applicuit desiderato. Veniensque ad quoddam opidum ubi quoddam erat monasteriolum,[568] hospitandi gratia illuc diuertit. Vbi iumentis suis pabula non inueniens, miratur ualde quoniam locus ille pratorum copia conspicitur habundare. Querit ergo rex cuius sint prata illa. Responsum accipit quod dominos plures haberent. Qui iubentur omnes ante regem comparere; conuenit igitur eos de uendicione pratorum illorum.[569] At ipsi responderunt dicentes se nolle prata sua uendere, cum auro et argento satis habundassent, nec habebant propter egestatem necesse alicui precipue transeunti sua uel prata uel sura uendere. Quos cum audisset rex diuiciis omnimodis[570] habundare, ait rex magnificus et munificus: 'Credo quod non sic habundetis, quin non possitis amplius habundare. Nos prata uestra comparabimus non secundum eorum estimacionem, set iuxta uestram. Nec erit ulla difficultas de precio, licet nulla sit propriacio sit[571] in contrahendo.' Ipsi uero considerantes regis licet piissimi potentiam et quoque si uellet paruo nutu posset eos obruisse, responderunt, se uelle uoluntati sue obsecundare, si tot milia ipsis uellet numerare. Et nominauerunt tot milia quot credebant regem nullo modo licet prodigalissimus esset et inestimabiliter habundaret illis uelle numerari, quia prata sua uendere non curabant.

---

[565] *N* margin in light hand: 'Regnauerat enim iam xxx et sex annis'.
[566] *C* simul.
[567] Occasional sentences in this section and the next bear a resemblance to the text of Matthew Paris, *Chronica Majora*, I, pp. 358-9.
[568] The statement in one version of the *Chronica Majora* that this town was called Monasteriolum apparently results from grammatical confusion, I, p. 358. There is no good reason to associate this with European place-names such as Monistrol-sur-Loire or Monistrol de Montserrat, Barcelona.
[569] *C* 'illorum' omitted.
[570] *C* ommniodis.
[571] *C* 'sit' omitted.

On the implementation of the devout proposal of the most devout King Offa.

So, taking the good advice of his chief men, led by the divine spirit, the most devout King Offa undertook a journey across the Alps that was very difficult and costly to him, without sparing expense.[572] Nor could the king's domestic duties, or administrative needs of the kingdom, or risks in the frailties of old age, nor pressure of work, or the expenditure of enormous sums, delay him. Keeping this steadfast intention at heart, just as blessed Alban the first martyr illumined the inhabitants of England, so his abbey outshone all the monasteries of the kingdom, pre-eminent in properties and equally[573] in rights, not to mention privileges.[574]

Having set out for Rome, the king crosses the Channel.

So when the ships had been furnished with an armed crew by royal edict, the king boarded the poop.[575] And, furling sail after a successful crossing, he put into a certain seaport in Flanders. And reaching a certain town where there was a certain small monastery he stopped off there for lodgings. Finding no fodder there for his mules, he was very surprised, because it was clear the place had plenty of meadows. So the king asked whose the meadows were. The response received was that they had several owners. These were all ordered to show themselves before the king; so they gathered to talk about the sale of their meadows. But they replied saying that they did not want to sell their meadows, because they had quite enough gold and silver and did not need because of poverty to sell either their meadows or pig-pastures in a hurry to someone passing through. When the king heard that they were super-abounding in every kind of wealth, the great and generous king said: 'I don't believe you've got so much that you couldn't have even more. We'll assess your meadows not at what they're worth but what you think. Nor will there be any difficulty over the price, even if there be no proof of ownership in the contract.' They, considering the probity of the king and also that, although a most devout man, he could do away with them at a nod if he wished, replied that they would be willing to fall in with his wish if he were willing to pay their price. And because they did not want to sell their meadows, they named such a high price as they believed the king, although he was a great spender and had enormous wealth, would in no way be willing to pay.

---

[572] N marginal comment: 'For he had reigned now for 36 years.' i.e. 793.

[573] C at the same time.

[574] See below, pp. 113-24.

[575] For the little we know of English ship design in early times, see generally D. Ellmers, 'Die Shiffe der Angelsachsen', in *Sachsen und Angelsachsen*, ed. C. Ahrens, Hamburg, 1978, pp. 495-509, and references there cited. By the twelfth century the sides of the hull had grown upward and consequently braced with a new system of cross-beams that in turn permitted high-level decking – the poop deck a point of accommodation and authority.

Ut Rex Offa Romam perueniens cenobium beati[576] Albani priuilegiauerit.

Dinumerata denique[577] pro distraccione pratorum pecunia, a loco rex progreditur, et Romam tandem perueniens, optata apostolorum [23ʳ] [578] limina contingit, et diuersorum loca sanctorum percurrit. Demum Adriano summo pontifici sui causam aduentus explicans, et de loco simul et beato Albano canonizando et magnificando, cenobioque constituendo deuote preces porrigens, peticioni sue Romanam de facili curiam inclinauit; presertim cum martiris inuencio celitus mortalibus sit declarata. Adaugebat quoque omnium deuocionem, quod non cuilibet de populo, sed tanto talique regi, tam magni martiris sui pignera Dominus relielauit.[579]

De monasterio igitur conuentuali uidelicet cenobiali digne ac celebrari [580] constituendo et ab omni episcoporum subiectione emancipando, Papam et totam curiam consulit cum effectu.

Colloquium efficax Regis Offe cum Papa.[581]

Cumque inclitus Rex Offa eleganter perorasset, Romanus Pontifex humiliter ac fauorabiliter inclinato capite sic respondit: 'O regum Christianissime fili Offa, deuocionem tuam circa regni tui prothomartirem non mediocriter commendamus. Nec nos quamuis remotos latet uestra strenuitas uel sincera sanctitas.

Vere celibem uitam agentibus merito mittendus fuit angelus, cum castitati cognata sit puritas angelica. Et cum fauorabilis sit persona tua, fauorabilior est causa quam proponis in medio. Et labor tue peregrinacionis acceptus est altissimo.

De monasterio uero construendo et priuilegiando peticioni tue assensum prebemus gratissimum, iniungentes tibi in tuorum remissionem peccatorum ut prospere ac feliciter rediens cum Dei et mea benedicione in terram ac regnum tuum, consilio episcoporum et optimatum tuorum, quas uolueris possessiones siue libertates beati Albani Anglorum prothomartiris cenobio[582] conferas; et tuo priuilegio inde facto, nos originale tuum priuilegio nostro inuiolabili gratanter roborabimus et confirmabimus consequenter. Et monasterium illud in specialem Romane ecclesie filiam adoptabimus,

---

[576] C Sancti.

[577] The reading of Roger of Wendover, Coxe, I, p. 255, agrees with our text, whereas Matthew Paris, apparently not recognizing the sense of *dinumerata* here, prefers *Innumerata denique soluta*, *Chronica Majora*, I, p. 359.

[578] Illustration: King Offa II kneeling, crown in hand, is presented to Pope Adrian who, two fingers raised in blessing, grants the king's request in respect of his new foundation.

[579] C reuelauit.

[580] C 'celebriter' over erasure.

[581] N 'Papa' largely erased.

[582] N 'cenobio' with decayed illumination.

How King Offa on reaching Rome obtained privileges for the monastery of blessed Alban.

At last, the money for the acquisition of the meadows having been paid,[583] the king left the place and, eventually arriving in Rome,[584] he reached the longed-for thresholds of the Apostles, and went around the places of various saints. Finally, explaining to the high pontiff Adrian[585] the reason for his coming, and talking about the place and at the same time about having the blessed Alban canonised and exalted, asking devoutly for their requests as to establishing the monastery, he won over the Roman curia to his simple petition; especially when the heavenly disclosure of the martyr to humanity was reported. It also increased general devotion because it was not to just anyone among the people, but to such a very great king that the Lord revealed his pledge of so great a martyr.

And so he consulted the pope and the whole court with effect about the abbey, that is to say a communal monastery,[586] to be established with prestige and celebration[587] and to be exempt from all the authority of bishops.

The successful conversation of King Offa with the Pope.

And when the renowned King Offa had ended his eloquent request, the Roman pontiff humbly and approvingly nodding replied thus: 'Oh son Offa, most Christian king, we commend your devotion to the first martyr of your kingdom in no small way. Nor are your great deeds and sincere saintliness hidden from us although we live far away.

It is true that an angel should deservedly have been sent to those leading a celibate life, because the chaste are familiar with angelic purity. And because your person is exemplary, the matter that you bring forward in here is the more exemplary. And the effort of your pilgrimage has been accepted by the most high.

We grant most ready approval of your petition about building and granting privileges to the abbey, enjoining you for the remission of your sins that, returning successfully and happily with God's and my blessing to your country and kingdom, on the advice of your bishops and nobles you confer on the monastery of blessed Alban, first martyr of the English, what possessions or rights you wish; and then, your privilege given, we will in consequence gladly strengthen and confirm your initial one with our inviolable privilege. And we will adopt this abbey as a special daughter of the Roman Church and, making it subject to our apostolic authority alone, we will protect

---

[583] Matthew Paris adds that the property had been donated for the use of future pilgrims (I, p. 359) which suggests that the story was still being developed at this time, S. Matthews, 'Legends of Offa: the journey to Rome', in *Æthelbald and Offa*, 55-58 (p. 55).

[584] No formal record survives of the visit described, see Introduction, p. xcix, notes 422-3.

[585] Adrian I's pontificate AD 772-95.

[586] The term *monasticus* early denoted 'solitary'.

[587] C 'famously' over erasure.

et nostro tantum illud Apostolatui subicientes, ab omni nociuo cuiuslibet mortalium impetu specialiter Gregorio[588] mediante episcopo siue archiepiscopo protegemus.'

De Denario Sancti Petri.[589]

Hiis igitur auditis, rex quid digne tante benignitati compenset[590] secum studiose pertractat. Tandem diuina inspirante gratia, consilium inuenit salubre, et in die crastina, scholam Anglorum qui[591] tunc Rome floruit ingressus, dedit ibi ex regali munificentia ad sustentacionem gentis regni sui illuc uenientis singulos argenteos de familiis singulis omnibus in posterum diebus singulis annis; quibus uidelicet sors tantum contulit extra domos in pascuis, ut triginta argenteorum precium excederet. Hoc autem per totam suam dicionem teneri in perpetuum constituit, excepta tota[592] Sancti Albani suo monasterio conferenda, prout postea collata priuilegia protestantur.

Vt illo denario a generali contribucione sic excepto, et dicto monasterio, [23ᵛ][593] sic collato, memoria donatoris indelebiliter perpetuetur. Et hoc tali largitate optinuit et condicione, ut de regno Anglie nullus publice penitens pro execucione sibi iniuncte penitencie subiret exilium.

Redit Offa Rex et fundat cenobium.

Celebrata igitur donacione predicta et de peccatis omnibus precipue tamen de preliorum multorum commissione facta confessione, et pro predicta cenobii funda[594] accepta penitentia, cum benedicione deuota summi Pontificis, rex ad propria prospere remeauit.

Constituto cenobio ordinatur ibidem abbas cum conuentu.[595]

Tunc congregato apud Verolamium episcoporum et optimatum suorum consilio, rex unanimi omnium consensu et beniuola uoluntate beato Albano amplas contulit terras

---

[588] N 'Gregorio' with decayed illumination, and next two words inserted from margin in lighter hand. Pope Gregory I was the man believed to have sent the mission of the Roman Church to England, see Bede, *Ecclesiastical History*, II, 1, Colgrave and Mynors, pp. 132-35.

[589] The opening two sentences bear a broad similarity to Matthew Paris, *Chronica Majora*, I, p. 360.

[590] N 'compenset' in different hand over erasure.

[591] C que.

[592] C 'terra' added.

[593] Illustration: Offa II gives instructions to an architect bearing compass and square and the abbey begins to be built. Labourers winch up baskets of stone blocks to masons, one with plumb-line, on a rising wall (Fig. 29).

[594] C fundatione.

[595] C 'cum conuentu' omitted.

it from harmful attack by anyone mortal at all, especially an intervening bishop or archbishop.'[596]

On Saint Peter's Pence.[597]

So, having heard these things, the king thought carefully to himself as to what gesture could repay such kindness. Eventually, by the inspiration of divine grace, he found a sound idea; and the next day, going into the English School[598] which then flourished at Rome, he there granted out of royal generosity, for the support of the people of his kingdom coming there, one silver piece[599] from each household on one day[600] every year in future – that is to say a sum, collected in the pastures outside the fold, that in value might exceed the thirty pieces of silver.[601] And he laid down that this should be done in perpetuity throughout the whole of his realm, except for all that[602] to be conferred on his abbey of Saint Alban, just as the privileges bestowed would later declare.

And so the said abbey, being thus exempt from the general payment of the pence, thus bestowed, the memory of the benefactor could be indelibly perpetuated. And through such largesse and favour, he obtained that no public penitent from the kingdom of England need undergo exile to carry out penance enjoined on him.[603]

King Offa returns and founds the monastery.

So, the aforesaid donation celebrated, and confession made of all his sins, especially for engaging in many battles, and the foundation of the aforesaid monastery accepted in penance, the king successfully made his way back home with the devout blessing of the high pontiff.

With the monastery consecrated, so likewise is the abbot together with the community.

Then, with the council of his bishops and nobles gathered at Verulamium, the king, with the unanimous agreement and good will of all, donated to blessed Alban

---

[596] Cf. J.E. Sayers, 'Papal privileges for St. Albans abbey and its dependencies', in *The Study of Medieval Records*, ed. D.A. Bullough and R.L. Storey, Oxford, 1971, pp. 57-84.

[597] A tribute of one penny on every household, levied annually and paid to Rome until abolished by Henry VIII in 1534. Its association with the name of St Peter was presumably because it was he whom Christ charged with finding the tax levied on himself, Matthew XVII.24-7. See generally Introduction, p. c.

[598] A colony of Anglo-Saxon merchants and others, adjacent to St Peter's, see Introduction, pp. xcix-c.

[599] It was Offa II who replaced the ancient Anglo-Saxon coinage of irregular local design with the uniform silver *penig*; see Introduction, pp. xcii-xciii.

[600] Said later in our text to be the Feast of St Peter in Chains, pp. 121-2.

[601] Reference to Christ's role as the Good Shepherd, John X.11; and the sum for which Judas betrayed him, Matthew XXVI.15, XXVII.3-9.

[602] C adds: 'the land'.

[603] Roger of Wendover tells us that this was directly in recognition of Offa II's generosity to the English School, *Chronica*, ed. Coxe, I, p. 257, Giles, I, pp. 163-64.

et possessiones innumeras considerans quod ibidem elemosinaris uigeret[604] hospitalitas. Nam ibidem patet uia ab aquilone uenientibus et ab austro redeuntibus communis; et strata generaliter dicta Watlinges strate.[605] Et pium ei uidebatur ut omnes intermeantes ibidem pium ex suis elemosinis domicilium inuenirent. Locum igitur memoratum cenobio addictum libertatum multiplici insigniuit priuilegio. Monachorum quoque conuentum ex domibus ordinate religionis maxime[606] tamen ex domo Becci in Neustria, ad tumbam congregauit.[607] Et abbatem eis nomine Willegodum, quod interpretatur uolens bonum.[608] Vere enim uir bone fuit uoluntatis, et de stirpe regia oriundus, regique Offe consanguinitate propinquus. Qui cum inuencioni dicti martiris interfuisset, uiso celesti luminis radio qui eo inueniendo et leuando de terra, comparuit et ipso eodem martire inuento et leuato quasi suo perfuncto officio disparuit, statim se monachum habitum religionis assumpturum, Deoque et tam digno martiri omnibus uite sue ministraturum.[609]

Vnde licenter anticipate narracione, post inuencionem memoratam, statim rex ecclesiam cepit edificare, ponens primum lapidem in fundamento dicens: 'In honore Dei omnipotentis Patris et Filii et Spiritus Sancti, et martiris sui Albani tocius terre mea prothomartiris.' Et addens ait, iunctis manibus, flexis genibus, lacrimisque profusis.

Oracio Christianissimi Regis Offe super opus suum.

'Domine Iesu Christe tibi hanc tuam Domum et tibi martir Albane et tibi Willegode commendo fideliter custodiendam. Cuius omnes aduersarii uel perturbatores uel spiritualibus uel,[610] diminutores, maledicantur. Omnes quoque benefactores, premia recipiant sempiterna.'

Willegodo autem[611] iam monacho, regii thesauri contulit habundantiam, et prefecit fabrice ecclesiastice preceptorem. Et omnia ei iura regalia et libertates concessit. Et hoc fecit rex prouidus antequam iter arriperet transalpinum, ignorans quid Deus de uita sua ordinauerat. Set postquam rediit cum prosperitate, hec omnia sollempet[612] renouauit et confirmauit; et sepedictum Willegodum [24ʳ][613] presentibus filio suo Ecgfrido uniuersorum herede Humberto quoque Lichefeldensi archiepiscopo cum aliis

---

[604] C 'uiget' 'does flourish' - present tense for imperf. subj. of N.

[605] Vernacular form, taken from the name of an otherwise unknown group of early Anglo-Saxon settlers (*Wætlingas*) living at Verulamium. Cf. generally A. Mawer and F.M. Stenton, *The Place-Names of Bedfordshire and Huntingdonshire*, English Place-Name Society, 3, Cambridge, 1926, pp. 5-7.

[606] N 'maxime' deleted.

[607] C 'maxime... congregauit' omitted, with 'ad tumbam martiris congregauit' inserted from margin.

[608] C 'cuius iusset' over erasure.

[609] C sue diebus ministrauit deuotiti.

[610] C uel in spiritualibus et interpalibus diminutores.

[611] C 'autem' omitted.

[612] C sollempniter.

[613] Illustration: Offa II hands a beardless Willegode his abbot's crosier of office, and then both men together, one kneeling either side, place on the altar the abbey's charter of privileges. The whole beneath an Early Gothic arch.

considerable tracts of land and countless properties, reckoning that where there are almsgivers hospitality should flourish. For at that spot the road lies open, in common to those coming from the north and those returning from the south; and the street is generally called Watling Street.[614] And it seemed a devout notion that, as a result of his alms, all those travelling should find a devout dwelling-place there. So the aforesaid place was dedicated for a monastery, distinguished by manifold privilege of rights. Also a community of monks from the most regulated religious houses, although especially from the house of Bec in Normandy,[615] gathered at the tomb.[616] And their abbot's name was Willegod,[617] which translates as 'Goodwill'. He was certainly[618] a man of goodwill and, sprung from the royal race,[619] a close blood relative of King Offa. He had been present at the discovery of the said martyr. Having seen the heavenly beam of light, which discovered and raised him from the earth, as if compared with the discovery and exhumation of that same martyr, having discharged his office, he left and immediately became a monk, to assume the habit of religion and serve God and such a worthy martyr, for the whole of his life.[620]

Then, the scenario is easy to predict. After the aforesaid discovery, the king immediately began to build a church, laying the first stone on the foundation saying: 'In honour of God the Almighty Father and of the Son and of the Holy Spirit, and of their martyr Alban, the first martyr of all my land.' And going down on his knees, in floods of tears, joining his hands adding, he said:

The prayer of the most Christian King Offa over his work.

'Lord Jesus Christ, I faithfully commit this your house to your protection — and to you martyr Alban, and to you Willegode. May all those who oppose, or disrupt or diminish either its spiritual or intercessory[621] works be accursed. And also may all its benefactors receive eternal rewards.'

But Willegode, already a monk, and appointed a director for the church building contributed a great amount to the king's treasury. And [Offa] granted it all royal rights and franchises. And the provident king did this before he undertook his journey across the Alps, not knowing what God had ordained for his life. But when he came back with success he formally renewed and confirmed all these things. And in the presence of his son Ecgfrith, his heir in everything, also of Hunberht, archbishop of Lichfield, with the

---

[614] An important Roman road running north-west from London to Wroxeter and diverted from the ruined Roman town of Verulamium so as to pass by the monastery when established. See Fig. 1.

[615] A curious blunder: see Introduction, pp. xiv-xv. The Benedictine abbey at le Bec, Dept. Eure, renowned for exceptional austerity, would not be founded for another three centuries, Lanfranc, *Chronicon Beccensis abbatiae*, ed. J.P. Migne, *Patrologia Latina*, 150, cols. 639-90.

[616] C 'greatly... gathered' omitted and 'gathered at the tomb of the martyr' added in margin.

[617] An unknown period of rule, but dying only a few months after Offa.

[618] C 'for he governed truly.'

[619] Like his successor, Eadric: *Gesta Abbatum*, I, pp. 8-9.

[620] C 'devotedly served all his days.'

[621] C *interpalibus* perhaps for *interpollibus* 'intercessory' matters.

multis episcopis et terre optimatibus prefecit in abbatem, quem fidelissimum in conseruacione regni filio suo et ipsi commissi dum Romam pergeret certissime expertus fuerat. Et conuentum ex ordinatissimis domibus electum, ut pretactum est, ordinauit et instituit. Et[622] edificia omnia, preterquam pristinum quod inuenit, de ueteribus edificiis paganorum pridem factum, sumptibus propriis construxit. Et in eadem ecclesia Rex Christianissimus Offa uices agens yconomi et custodis specialis, uitam per aliquot annos continuauit; et una dierum iussit afferri cartas et omnia instrumenta data et adquisita super maius altare offerens reposuit.

De amplitudine dominacionis et regni Regis Offe.

Dominabatur Offa Rex magnus in uiginti tribus prouinciis,[623] quas Angli ssiras appellant; id est in Herefordensi, cuius episcopus sedem habet in eadem urbe. In prouinciis Wigorniensi et Glouernensi, quarum episcopus sedem habet in Wigornia, in Warewicensi, Cestrensi, Stafordensi, Scopesbiriensi et Derebiensi. Quarum episcopus habet sedem in Lichefeld. In Legrecestri, cuius episcopus in eadem urbe sedem habet.[624] In Lincolniensi, cuius episcopus sedem habet in Lindeseia, in Northamtonensi, Oxoniensi, Bukingehamensi, Bedefordensi, Huntendunensi, Cantebrigensi. Et dimidia Hertfordensi, quarum episcopus apud Dorkecestram sedem habet. In prouinciis Esexie et Middelsexie et dimidia Hertfordensi, quarum antistes sedem habet in urbe Londoniarum; in Northfolc et Suthfol, duo sunt episcopi, unus Helmhamensis et alter Domuensis.[625]

Dominabatur eciam Snotingensi prouincie, cuius Christianitas ad archiepiscopum spectat Eboracensem.

Ex hiis omnibus prouinciis dedit rex prefatus Offa denarium beati Petri. Eo tamen retento et collato post recepcionem beato Albano per totam eiusdem martiris terram, et iccirco beati Petri denarius appellatur quia sepedictus Rex Offa die Sancti Petri qui dicitur ad uincula ipsum martirem ipso die meruit celitus inuenire; et ipsum annuum redditum ipso die Romane ecclesie pro redepcione anime sue contulit ad sustentacionem uidelicet schole memorate propter Anglorum rudium et illuc peregrinantium erudicionem.

---

[622] *C* run on.

[623] For the list, cf. Matthew Paris, *Chronica Majora*, I, p. 360. See generally Introduction, p. xxxii.

[624] *C* habet sedem.

[625] *C* Domnicensis.

many other bishops and nobles of the land, he appointed as abbot the renowned Willegod, who had most certainly proved most faithful in safeguarding the kingdom committed to his son [Ecgfrith] and him whilst he went to Rome. And he organised and set up the community chosen from the most regulated houses, as already touched upon. And, except for the original one that he found,[626] he constructed all the buildings out of expensive materials from the old buildings of the pagans.[627] And the most Christian King Offa continued to live for a number of years, acting in the role of patron and special custodian of the church. And one day he ordered all the charters and bonds given and acquired, to be brought and placed them on the main altar as an offering.

On the extent of the domain and kingdom of King Offa.

King Offa the Great ruled over twenty-three counties, which the English call shires; that is: of Hereford, the bishop of which has his seat in the same city; the counties of Worcester and Gloucester, the bishop of which has his seat in Worcester; of Warwick, Chester, Stafford, Shrewsbury and Derby, the bishop of which has his seat in Lichfield; of Leicester, the bishop of which has his seat in the same city; of Lincoln, the bishop of which has his seat in Lindsey;[628] of Northampton, Oxford, Buckingham, Bedford, Huntingdon,[629] Cambridge and half of Hertford, the bishop of which has his seat at Dorchester; of the counties of Essex and Middlesex and half of Hertfordshire, the prelate of which has his seat in the city of London; of Norfolk and Suffolk there are two bishops, one of Elmham and the other of Dunwich.[630]

He even had dominion over the county of Nottingham, in which Christendom looks to the archbishop of York.[631]

From all these counties the aforesaid King Offa gave the blessed Peter's Pence. Throughout the whole of that martyr's land, however, after collection it was retained and bestowed upon the blessed Alban.[632] And the reason it was called the blessed Peter's Pence was because the very day that the renowned King Offa was honoured to discover the martyr himself by heavenly revelation was the Saint Peter's Day entitled 'in Chains'.[633] And he collected the annual returns on that very day of the Roman Church, for the redemption of his soul, that is to say in support of the aforesaid school for the uncultivated English and those making the educational pilgrimage.

---

[626] Bede had heard of the 'marvellous workmanship' of which the early chapel was made: *Ecclesiastical History*, I, 7, Colgrave and Mynors, pp. 34-35.

[627] Roman Verulamium, see Introduction, pp. xii-xiv, xcvi-xcviii.

[628] Confused; for which diocese see p. 82, n. 430.

[629] C of Lindsey, Buckingham, Huntingdon.

[630] C of Middlesex, Hertford, Norfolk, Suffolk, Elmham, Dunwich.

[631] At least from the mid-tenth century, J.C. Cox, 'Ecclesiastical History' in *The Victoria History of the County of Nottingham*, London, 1906-10, II, pp. 37-38.

[632] Cf. below, pp. 121-4.

[633] The Church festival that recalls the Apostle Peter's imprisonment by Herod Agrippa (Acts XII.3), was traditionally celebrated on 1st August.

Festiuitas tamen Inuencionis Sancti Albani in crastino festiuitatis inuencionis eiusdem celebratur, ne Sancti Petri celebritas detrimentum aut diminucionem paciatur.

De humilitate Regis Offe.

Nec censeo pretereundum quod tante fuerit Rex Offa humilitatis et modestie, quod nunquam quamuis in tantis et tot prouinciis regnaret et dominaretur et regnantibus et dominantibus prefuisset, uoluit appellariuel in epistolis uel cartis suis intitulari, nisi hoc solo dignitatis nomine, Rege Merciorum. Quia illud solum regnum illum[634] ratione sanguinis contingebat. Alia autem regna in ore gladii sibi uiolenter que tamen ad eum iure pertinebant adquisiuit.

Nota quod hic adinuenit et precepit primus quod tubicines[635] faciem regis preirent eciam tempore tubis canentes. [636]

Et sciendum quod quia tocius Britannie exceptis paucis particulis sibi potenter adquisiuit [24ᵛ][637] prenominatas prouincias, propter sui singularem dominacionem et prerogatiuam non tamen per superbiam, adinuenit et obseruari precepit, ut eciam in tempore pacis tubicines eum et successores eius cum per ciuitates transitum facientes, tubis canentes preirent. In signum quod rex omnibus uidentibus et audientibus, timori esse debet esse[638] et honori. Clangor enim tube quam uulgus trumpam uocat, timorem incutit audientibus.

De possessionibus ab Offa Rege monasterio Sancti Albani collatis.

Dedit preterea immortalis memorie Rex Offa potentissimus beato Anglorum prothomartiri Albano uillam suam dominicam que uiginti ferme miliariis a Verolamio distat et Wineslawuue nuncupatur, ut pretactum est, et tantundem per circuitum sicut usque hodie scripta regis protestantur ab eodem rege testantum et in ecclesia memorata reseruantur. Que tanta libertate priuilegiata refulget, ut ab Apostolica consuetudine et redditu qui Romscot dicitur Anglice, denarius Sancti Petri Latine, unde satis predictum est, cum neque rex, neque archiepiscopus, uel episcopus uel prior, aut

---

[634] C 'illum' inserted from margin.

[635] C tibitines.

[636] C last four words of heading omitted.

[637] Illustration: Offa II, shrouded but crowned, is entombed by unbearded men, a bearded bishop recites from a book held up and open by an attendant monk. There are present weeping men and Prince Ecgfrith, the crown hovering above his head.

[638] C 'esse' omitted.

But the Festival of the Discovery of Saint Alban is celebrated the day after the actual anniversary of the discovery,[639] lest celebration of Saint Peter suffer diminishment or detriment.

On the humility of King Offa.

Nor do I think it ought to be overlooked that, so great was King Offa's humility and modesty, although he reigned and had dominion over such great and numerous counties, and held sway over kings and princes, he wished to be called or named in his letters and charters, only by this one title of rank: 'King of The Mercians', because only that one kingdom was his by hereditary right. But other kingdoms he had acquired himself violently at the point of his sword nevertheless belonged to him legally.[640]

A note that here he was the first to devise and command that trumpeters[641] should proceed in front of the king, keeping pace, playing trumpets.

And it should be known that, because he powerfully acquired for himself the aforenamed counties of the whole of Britain except for a certain few ones, on account of his sole rule and prerogative but not through pride, he devised and commanded it to be observed that, even in time of peace, trumpeters playing trumpets should go in front of him and his successors when they progressed through the cities – as a sign that the king ought to be feared and honoured, by all who saw and heard. Certainly the blast of the horn that is commonly known as a trumpet struck fear into those who heard.

On the properties bestowed by King Offa on the Abbey of Saint Alban.

The most powerful King Offa of immortal memory also gave to blessed Alban, first martyr of the English, the manor from his demesne that lies almost twenty miles from Verulamium and is called Winslow, as already touched upon,[642] and as much around about as the writings of the king that are kept in the aforesaid church right up to this day declare. And it shines with such privileged rights that, when neither king, nor archbishop, or bishop or prior, nor anyone from the kingdom or in the kingdom can be immune from paying it, only the actual church called 'the Basilica of St Peter' is free from the Apostolic customary,[643] and the levy which is called 'Rome-Tax' in English, 'Saint Peter's Pence' in Latin, about which enough has already been said.[644] Moreover,

---

[639] The 'Invention' of St Alban, *i.e.* the discovery and the exhumation of the man's remains, traditionally celebrated on 2nd August. Celebration of Alban's martyrdom was placed on 22nd June, *Nova Legenda Anglie*, ed. C. Horstman, Oxford, 1891-1901, I, p. xix.

[640] See generally above, pp. 71-4.

[641] C 'pipers'; the second reference to trumpeters omitted.

[642] Where the king had been staying when inspired to take in hand his inherited pledge to found or restore a monastery (above, pp. 103-4).

[643] The hierarchical authority of the pre-Reformation western Church, deriving from the supposed origin of the Roman papacy in St Peter.

[644] Above, pp. 115-16, and see Introduction, pp. xcix-c.

quilibet de regno uel in regno ab illius solucione sit immunis, ipsa quidem ecclesia que Basilica Sancti Petri dicitur, sola quieta est. In presbiteros autem et laicos tocius possessionis sue abbas uel archidiaconus monachus sub ipso constitutus ius pontificale excercet, ita ut nulli archiepiscopo uel episcopo, uel legato, nisi summo tantum pontifici subiectionem impendant.

Hoc quoque sciendum est, quod Offa Rex magnificus tempore quo beati Petri uicario, Romane urbis pontifici redditum statutum id est Romscot de regno suo concessit, ipse a pontifice Romano impetrauit, ut ecclesia beati Albani Anglorum prothomartiris eundem redditum ab omni Hertfordensi prouincia in qua sita est ecclesia sepedicta fideliter colligeret, et collectum in usus proprios retineret. Vnde et ipsa ecclesia sicut a regia omnia iura regalia, ita habet abbas loci illius qui pro tempore fuerit pontificalia ornamenta, et in quantum licet alicui abbati habere pontificalem dignitatem, prout tam noua quam uetera instrumenta inde optenta manifeste protestantur. Que in hoc libro uidelicet in sequentibus annotantur. Gesta quoque abbatum omnium qui a tempore Regis Offani fundatoris ecclesie Sancti Albani in eadem ecclesia extiterunt, usque ad annum gratie millesimum, ducentesimum, quinquagesimum similiter in presenti uolumine denotantur.

De morte et sepultura Offe Regis Merciorum.

Cum autem immortalis [645] memorie Rex Offanus, fere omnia officin[a] [646] edificia laudabiliter in cenobio suo quod [25ʳ] [647] a fundamentis inchoauerat, edificauerat, infra quartum quintum uel annum postquam pium opus illud inchoauerat, ordinato conuentu circiter centum monachorum ordinatissimorum, in uilla que Offeleia nuncupatur, iuxta multorum oppinionem, diem clausit extremum. Cuius corpus apud uillam de Bedeford delatum in capella quadam, quia sic tunc exigebat temporis necessitas, extra urbem super ripam Vsce fluminis sitam, more regio dicitur fuisse sepultum.

Refert autem usque in hodiernum diem omnium fere conprouincialium assercio, quod capella prefata longo usu et uiolentia illius fluminis corrosa, cit submersa, atque eius rapacitate cum ipso regis sepulchro ad nichilum, redacta, uel saltem ut quamplurimi perhibent, in medio fluminis alueo quia firmissimo sarchofago continebatur corpus memoratum, sit ut ruinosa irrestaurabiliter precipitata. Vnde et usque in presens sepulchrum illud ab incolis loci tempore estiuo ibidem balneantibus

---

[645] C mortalis.

[646] N space left for case-ending probably due to uncertainty. In C the word is omitted.

[647] Illustration: A triptych, King Offa II enthroned, with on his lap an accurately arcaded model of St Albans Abbey at which he points, and holding an architecturally embellished sceptre presumably referring to his role as founder, his feet resting on a 'lion couchant, guardant. The whole is flanked by seated monks displaying large scrolls, uninscribed (Fig. 30).

the abbot, or monk appointed archdeacon beneath him, exercises pontifical jurisdiction over the priests and laity who are totally under his control, in such a way that none of them bend to archbishop or bishop or legate, except to the high pontiff alone.

It should also be known that, at the time the great King Offa granted the vicar of blessed Peter, pontiff of the city of Rome, the statuary return, that is Rome-tax, from his kingdom, he himself gained from the Roman pontiff that the church of blessed Alban the first martyr of the English should faithfully collect the returns coming from the whole of the county of Hertfordshire in which the renowned church is situated, and keep what they collect for their own use. And, just as that church has all regal rights from the king, so the abbot of the place shall have pontifical dress to wear for the time being; and any abbot is to have as much pontifical authority as allowed, just as extensively as recent documents or ancient, or any you choose, clearly declare, as are plainly noted subsequently in this book.[648] And similarly pointed out in the present volume are the Deeds of all the Abbots who have been in the same church from the time of King Offa, the founder[649] of the Church of Saint Alban, right up to the year of grace one thousand two hundred and fifty.[650]

On the death and burial of Offa King of the Mercians.

But when King Offa of immortal memory had splendidly built almost all the domestic buildings in his monastery that he had begun from the foundations – less than four or five years after having begun that holy work – after ordaining a community of about a hundred most disciplined monks, he ended his days, according to the opinion of many, in a manor called Offley.[651] Then, inasmuch as necessitated by the exigencies of time,[652] his body was borne to a certain chapel in a manor near Bedford,[653] outside the town situated on the River Ouse, where it is said that he was buried in a regal manner.[654]

But significant nowadays is the testimony of nearly all from that region that the said chapel, long worn and damaged by the force of that river,[655] should flood and be reduced to nothing by the surge, together with the actual sepulchre of the king. Or at least, as many maintain, because the famous body was contained in a very strong sarcophagus, it should be hurled, as if irrestorably in ruins, into the middle of the riverbed. From when on, and up to the present day according to local people bathing

---

[648] Ff. 149-61; cf Crick, *Charters of St Albans*, pp. 49-51.

[649] Probably not founder but renovator, see Introduction, p. xcviii.

[650] Ff. 30-69ʳ. The *Gesta Abbatum Monasterii Sancti Albani*, ed. H.T. Riley, Rolls Series, 28, London, 1867-69.

[651] Offley ('Offa's clearing or wood'), a dozen miles north of St Albans. Gover *et al.*, *Place-Names of Hertfordshire*, p. 19.

[652] Factors such as weather would have been significant in the decision. Sixteen miles north of Offley, Bedford was perhaps intended to be on his way back to Lichfield.

[653] Possibly Clapham, a valuable estate on the river a mile north of Bedford, and with evidence of a fine early church, E.A. Fisher, *The Greater Anglo-Saxon Churches*, London, 1962, pp. 153-55.

[654] So also, in words very similar to this, Roger, *Chronica*, Coxe, I, p. 262.

[655] The river-plain hereabouts commonly floods to the present day.

quandoque in aque profunditate uidetur esse consumptum; et quamuis licet diligentissime queratur ac si res fatalis esset, non inuenitur.

O[656] primitiuorum abbatum et monachorum huius ecclesie supine fatuitas. O ignauia inexcusabilis. O negligentia reprehensibilis. Et ut uerius concludam execrabilis ingratitudo, qui tanti benefactoris, talis regis, carnis, demonis, mundi ac mundanorum hostium magnifi triumphatoris, tam boni patroni ac fundatoris huius ecclesie, tam diligentis sui propositi executoris et consummatoris exuuias noluerunt cum potuerunt colligere, et in hac sua domo desideratissimum honorifice tradere sepulture. Set quia constat tanti benefactoris nomen in libro uite indelebiliter scribi, consolatur nos in hoc casu poeta qui talem iacturam subeuntes affatur dicens: 'Facilis iactura sepulchri est', et 'Celo tegitur, qui non habet urnam.' Quod enim debiti honoris de est corpori, anima que prestancior est in perpetua cum aucmento in eterna percipiat retribucione. Vt sicut in hoc mundo regnauit et multipliciter triumphauit corona transitoria, sic in celo perpetuo diademate regnet feliciter redimitus. Et corpore sibi restituto quo modo non gaudemus, stola duplici gaudeat restauratus, Amen.

Explicit Hystoria de Offa Rege Merciorum, fundatore Cenobii Sancti Albani Anglorum prothomartiris, et eiusdem martiris inuentore et de terra leuatore.

C omits this Explicit, and continues:

De pluribus regibus infra regnum Anglie Offe uocabulo uocatur.

Sed quia plures fuerunt qui Offe uocabulo insigniti, fueres et reges insuper extiteres ne error surrepat, et ignorantes historias deducat in deuium ut unum pro altero predicent, et extollant, nos de singulis huius uocabuli regibus perticulariter disseremus. Erat nempe apud Orientales Saxones Offa Rex dictus minor Offa, ad differenciam superioris Offe, qui fuit ilius [657] Sigeri Regis est Saxonum qui Romam cum Benredo [658]

---

[656] N 'Exclamacio' marginal rubric.
[657] 'Filius' inserted from margin.
[658] Presumably confused with the usurper Beornred who Offa II drove out in 757 (pp. 41-6) and who died in Rome in 769, see Introduction, p. lii.

there in summertime, the sepulchre seems to have been swallowed up when it got into the deep water, and in spite of the most thorough search, would not be found – as if a predestined matter.[659]

Oh the slothful lethargy of the early abbots and monks of the church here! Oh the inexcusable indolence![660] Oh the reprehensible negligence! And may I say finally, most truly, what execrable ingratitude of those who did not want, when they could, to collect the relics of so great a benefactor, such a king, magnificent champion over the flesh, the devil, the world and worldly enemies, of such a good patron and founder of this church, of someone who faithfully carried out and completed his intentions – and honourably bring them into this his most longed for house for burial. But because it is certain that the name of such a great benefactor is written indelibly in the book of life,[661] the poet consoles us, as we are suffering such a loss in this case, saying eloquently: 'A sepulchre is easily broken down',[662] and 'He who has no urn is covered by heaven'.[663] For our soul, which takes prime place in eternity and grows in stature, realises in eternal retribution how the body fails to give it due respect. So that, just as in this world a transient crown has ruled and triumphed in many ways, so in heaven crowning with an eternal diadem will reign blessedly. And when a man's body is renewed in him, in what way don't we rejoice; let one restored to the double cloak[664] rejoice. Amen.

Here ends the story of Offa King of the Mercians, founder of the monastery of Saint Alban, first martyr of the English, and of the discovery and exhumation of that martyr.

C omits this Explicit, and continues:

On more kings in English kingdoms called by the name Offa.

But in order that no error creep between those above and other additional kings, and divert ignorant accounts down a side-road so that one person is discussed and praised instead of another – because there have been many designated by the name of Offa[665] – we will make a review of the only kings of this name in particular. There was in fact another King Offa among the East Saxons[666] (called Offa 'the Less' to distinguish him from the greater Offa[667]) who was the son of King Sighere of the Saxons;[668] he went to

---

[659] Matthew Paris's account bears a broad resemblance to this, *Chronica Majora*, I, p. 363.

[660] The word 'Exclamation!' written in the margin in a later hand.

[661] Revelation XX.12, XXI.27.

[662] Virgil, *Aeneid*, II, 646, ed. and transl. H.R. Fairclough, London, 1934-35, I, pp. 336-37.

[663] Lucan, *The Civil War*, VII, 819, ed. and transl. J.D. Duff, London, 1928, pp. 428-29.

[664] I.e. in body and soul, cf Augustine, *Enarrationes in Psalmos*, ed. Migne, *Patrologia Latina*, 37, col. 1444.

[665] Searle lists many royal and other Offas, *Onomasticon Anglo-Saxonicum*, pp. 364, 569.

[666] A folk settled in present day Essex, cf. Introduction, pp. xli-xliv.

[667] It is possible that this refers to one 'Offa father of Æscwine', mentioned in British Library MS Additional 23211 – or another who wanted Penda's daughter Cyneswyth for a wife, *The Kalendre of the Newe Legende of Englande*, ed. M. Görlach, Heidelberg, 1994, pp. 130-31.

[668] Reigning jointly with Sebbi by c. 664-83, Bede, *Ecclesiastical History*, V, 24, ed. Colgrave and Mynors, pp. 516-17.

Rege Merciorum et Egwyno Wicciorum antistite spreto regno suo mit ubi tempore uale fecit. Erat et alter Offa uocatus rex Orientalium Anglorum qui genuit sanctem Fremundum, regem et martirem, de quo in Vita Sancti Fremundi multa narrantur que nusquam nitronicis poterunt reperiri. Fuit et alius rex Orientalium Anglorum nominatissiimus, sed paganus Uffa uocatus qui plerumque ab imperitis appellatur Offa, sed ignorantibus historias, uel historiarum non habentibus copias ignostond osti.

Rome with Coenred[669] king of the Mercians and Ecgwine prelate of the Hwicce,[670] spurning his kingdom when he bade farewell to the world.[671] And there was another Offa called king of the East English[672] who was the father of Saint Fremund, king and martyr,[673] about whom many things are told in the *Life of Saint Fremund*[674] that can be found nowhere in ballads.[675] And there was another most notable king of the East English, but he was a rustic called Wuffa[676] who was often named Offa by the ignorant, but they were people unfamiliar with history, or not having copies of the histories.

[669] Coenred succeeded in 704, abdicating to go to Rome in 709, Bede, *Ecclesiastical History*, V, 24, Colgrave and Mynors, pp. 566-67; *The Kalendre of the Newe Legende of Englande*, Görlach, pp. 101-02, 208.

[670] A folk occupying the south-west Midlands, their name surviving in the area called Wychwood Forest; see generally A.H. Smith, 'The Hwicce', in *Medieval and Linguistic Studies in Honor of Francis Peabody Magoun*, ed. J.B. Bessinger and R.P. Creed, London, 1965, pp. 56-65; D. Hooke, *Kingdom of the Hwicce*, Manchester, 1985. Ecgwine's seat was at Worcester, 693-717.

[671] 708/9 AD; cf Bede, *Ecclesiastical History*, V, 19, Colgrave and Mynors, pp. 516-17.

[672] Probably sub-regulus or merely a nobleman, having taken up the life of an anchorite but killed by an apostate relative in 866; buried at Offchurch (Offa kirk) see above p. 68, n. 355.

[673] A ninth-century name surrounded by legend, including the conversion to Christianity of his royal parents and the whole of the country, cf. *The Kalendre of the Newe Legende of Englande*, Görlach, pp. 101-02, 208.

[674] *Nova Legenda Anglie*, Horstman, II, pp. 689-98.

[675] Apparently *historiis* for *nitonicis*.

[676] An early figure in the genealogies, about whom nothing is otherwise known. Roger of Wendover assigned his accession to 571, *Chronica*, Coxe, I, p. 84; Giles, p. 49.

Fig. 28) At King Offa II's direction, accompanied by two bishops one presenting 'the host', trees are felled and soil excavated seeking the remains of Saint Alban. Labourers are depicted with axe and mattock, bucket and spade. Bones are to be seen in the trench.

Fig. 29) Offa II gives instructions to an architect bearing compass and square and the abbey begins to be built. Labourers winch up baskets of stone blocks to masons, one with plumb-line, on a rising wall.

Fig. 30) A triptych, King Offa II enthroned, with on his lap an accurately arcaded model of St Albans Abbey at which he points, and holding an architecturally embellished sceptre presumably referring to his role as founder, his feet resting on a lion 'couchant guardant'. The whole is flanked by seated monks displaying large scrolls, uninscribed.

MS Cotton Nero D i, f. 25ʳ © The British Library Board. All Rights Reserved.

Appendices

Selections from:

Appendix A:

The Anglo-Saxon Chronicle, AD 755-96

The Anglo-Saxon Chronicle had its origins in the ninth-century England of King Alfred. It consists of a sequence of anonymous vernacular annals, beginning with a retrospective view from the time of Julius Caesar onwards, and at one institution was maintained into the mid-twelfth century. Texts vary in detail depending on where they were copied out and maintained. Here is used a manuscript (Oxford, Bodleian Library MS Laud 636) from the scriptorium of Peterborough Abbey, apparently copying a book borrowed from a Kentish library *circa* 1120. Chronological discrepancies are adjusted within square brackets for the translation. Edited J. Earle and C. Plummer, *Two of the Saxon Chronicles Parallel,* Oxford, 1892; transl. M. Swanton, *The Anglo-Saxon Chronicles,* London, 2000.

> 755. ... Ond þy ilcan geare man ofsloh Æðelbald Myrcene cining...; ond he rixade xli wintra. Ond þa feng Beornred to rice, ond litle hwile heold ond ungefealice. Ond þa ilcan geare Offa geflymde Beornred ond feng to þam rice, ond heold xxxix wintra; ond his sunu Ecgferð heold xli daga ond c daga. Se Offa wæs Þingcferþing.

A Winchester manuscript (Cambridge, Corpus Christi College, MS 173A), attaches the following Mercian regal pedigree to this annal:

> Se Offa wæs Þincgferþing, Þincgferþ Eanwulfing, Eanwulf Osmoding, Osmod Eawing, Eawa Pybing, Pybba Creoding, Creoda Cynewalding; Cynewald Cnebbing, Cnebba Iceling, Icel Eomæring, Eomær Angelþowing, Angelþeow Offing, Offa Wærmunding, Wærmund Wyhtlæging, Wihtlæg Wodening.

[Cf. genealogical tree, Fig. 6.]

> 757. Her Eadberht Norðhymbra cining feng to scære, ond Osulf his sunu feng to þam rice, ond rixade i gear, ond hine of slogon his hiwan on ix kl Augusti.

The Anglo-Saxon Chronicle, AD 755-96

[757]. ... And the same year Æthelbald, king of Mercia, was killed...; and he ruled 41 years. And then Beornred succeeded to the kingdom, and held it a little while and unhappily; and that same year Offa put Beornred to flight and succeeded to the kingdom, and held it 39 years; and his son Ecgfrith held it 141 days. That Offa was Thingfrith's offspring.

A Winchester manuscript (Cambridge, Corpus Christi College, MS 173A), attaches the following Mercian regal pedigree to this annal:

That Offa was Thingfrith's offspring, Thingfrith Eanwulf's offspring, Eanwulf Osmod's offspring, Osmod Eawas's offspring, Eawa Pybba's offspring, Pybba Creoda's offspring, Creoda Cynewald's offspring, Cynewald Cnebba's offspring, Cnebba Icel's offspring, Icel Eomer's offspring, Eomer Angeltheow's offspring, Angeltheow Offa's offspring, Offa Wærmund's offspring, Wærmund Wihtlæg's offspring, Wihtlæg Woden's offspring.

[Cf. genealogical tree, Fig. 6.]

757. Here Eadberht, king of Northumbria, received the tonsure, and Oswulf, his son, succeeded to the kingdom and ruled 1 year; and his household killed him on 24 July.

758. ...

759. Her... Moll Æðelwold feng to rice on Norðhymbrum, ond rixade ui winter, ond hit þa forlet.

760. ...

761. Her wæs se myccla winter. Ond Moll Norþhymbra cining ofsloh Oswine æt Ædwines clife on octauo id Augusti.

762. Her Ianbeht wæs gehadod to ærceb on ðon xl dæg ofer midewinter...

769. *Initium regni Karoli regis.*

774. Her Norðhymbra fordrifon heora cining Alhred of Eoferwic on Eastertid ond genamon Æðelred Molles sunu heom to hlaforde. Ond se rixade iiii gear. Ond men gesegon read Cristes mel on heofenum æfter sunnan setlan gange. On þy geare gefuhton Myrce ond Cantwara æt Ottanforda. Ond wundorlice nædran wæron geseogene on Suðseaxna lande.

776. ...

777. Her Cynewulf ond Offa geflyton ymb Benesingtun, ond Offa genam þone tun...

778. Her Æðebald ond Hearberht ofslogon iii heah gerefan: Ealdulf Bosing æt Cininges clife, ond Cynewulf ond Ecgan æt Helaþyrnum on xi kl Apr. Ond þa feng Alfwold to rice ond Æðelred bedraf on lande. Ond he rixade x winter. *Karolus in Hispanias intrauit. Karolus Saxoniam uenit. Karolus Pampileniam urbem destruxit, atque Cesar Augustam, exercitum suum coniunxit, et acceptis obsidibus, subiugatis Sarracenis, per Narbonam Wasconiam Franciam rediit.*

779. Her Ealdseaxe ond Francon gefuhton. Ond Norðhymbra heah gerefan forbearndon Beorn ealdorman on Seletune on ix k Ianr.

780. ...

782. Her forðferde Wærburh Ceolredes cwen...

784. Her Cyneheard ofsloh Cynewulf cining; ond he wærð þær ofslagen ond lxxxiiii manna mid him. Ond þa onfeng Brihtric West Seaxna cining to rice; ond he rixade xui gear; ond his lic lið ær Wærham; ond his riht fædern cyn gæð to Certice.

785. ... Ond her wæs geflitfullic sinoð æt Cealchyðe. Ond Ianberht erceb forlet sumne dæl his biscopdomes. Ond fram Offan cininge Hygebriht wes gecoren. Ond Ecgferð to cining gehalgode. Ond in ðas tid wæren ærendracen gesend of Rome fram Adrianum papan to Ængla lande to niwianne þone geleafan ond þa sibbe ðe Scs Gregorius us sende þurh þone b Augustinum, ond hi man mid wurðscipe underfeng.

[760]. ...

759. Here Æthelwald Moll succeeded to the kingdom in Northumbria and ruled 6 years, and then abandoned it.

[762]. ...

[763-4]. Here was the big winter; and [761] Moll, the Northumbrian king, killed Oswine at Edwin's Cliff on 6 August.

[765] Here Jænberht was ordained as archbishop on the 40th day after mid-winter...

769. *The beginning of the rule of King Charles.*

774. Here the Northumbrians drove out their king Alhred from York at Eastertide, and took Æthelred, son of Moll, as their lord, and he ruled 4 years. And [776] men saw a red sign of Christ in the heavens after the sun's setting. In that year the Mercians and the inhabitants of Kent fought at Otford. And snakes were seen extraordinarily in the land of the South Saxons.

776. ...

[779]. Here Cynewulf and Offa contended around Benson, and Offa took the settlement...

778. Here on 22 March Æthelbald and Heardberht killed 3 high-reeves: Ealdwulf, Bosa's offspring, at Coniscliffe and Cynewulf and Ecga at Helathyrne. And then Ælfwald succeeded to the kingdom and drove Æthelred into the country; and he ruled for 10 years. *Charles entered Spain. Charles came to Saxony. Charles destroyed the cities of Pamplona and Saragossa, joined his army and, having received hostages and subjected the Saracens, returned to the Franks through Narbonne in Gascony.*

[782]. Here the Old Saxons and the Franks fought. And [780] on 24 December the Northumbrian high-reeves burned Ealdorman Beorn in Seletun...

780. ...

782. Here passed away Wærburh, Ceolred's queen...

[786]. Here Cyneheard killed King Cynewulf, and he [too] was killed and 84 men with him; and then Beorhtric, king of the West Saxons, succeeded to the kingdom, and he ruled 16 years; and his body lies at Wareham, and his direct paternal ancestry goes back to Cerdic.

[787] Here there was a contentious synod at Chelsea and Archbishop Jænberht relinquished some part of his bishopric, and Hygeberht was chosen by King Offa, and Ecgfrith consecrated as king. And at this time messengers were sent from Rome by Pope Adrian to England to renew the faith and the peace which St Gregory sent to us through Bishop Augustine; and they were received with honour.

787. Her nam Breohtric cining Offan dohter Eadburge. Ond on his dagum comon ærest iii scipu Norðmanna of Hereða lande. Ond þa se gerefa þærto rad, ond he wolde drifan to ðes cininges tune þy he nyste hwæt hi wæron. Ond hine man ofsloh þa. Ðæt wæron þa erestan scipu Deniscra manna þe Angel cynnes land gesohton.

788. ... *Karolus per Alemanniam uenit ad fines Bauuarie.*

789. Her Alfwold Norðanhymbra cining wæs ofslagan fram Sigan on ix kl Octobr. Ond heofenlic leoht wæs gelome seogen ðær þer he ofslagen wæs. Ond he wæs bebyrged on Hagust'dee innan þære cyrican... Ond Osred Alchredes sunu feng to rice æfter him, se wæs his nefa.

790. Her Ianbriht arcebiscop forðferde...

791. ...

792. Her Offa Myrcena cining het Æðelbrihte þæt heafod ofslean. Ond Osred þe wæs Norþanhymbra cining æfter wræc siðe ham cumenum gelæht wæs and ofslagen on xviii kl Octobr; ond his lic ligð æt Tinanmuþe. Ond Æðelred cining feng to niwan wife, seo wæs Ælfled gehaten, on iii k Octobr.

793. Her wæron reðe forebecna cumene ofer Norðanhymbra land, ond þæt folc earmlice bregdon; þæt wæron ormete lig ræscas ond wæron geseowene fyrene dracan on þam lyfte fleogende. Þam tacnum sona fyligde mycel hunger. Ond litel æfter þam þæs ilcan geares on ui id Ianr earmlice heðenra manna hergung adiligode Godes cyrican in Lindisfarena ee þurh reaflac ond mansleht...

794. Her Adrianus papa ond Offa cining forðferden. Ond Æðelred Norðanhymbra cining wæs ofslagan fram his agenre þeode on xiii k Mai... Ond Ecgferð feng to Myrcene rice, ond þy ilcan geare forðferde. Ond Eadbriht onfeng rice on Cent þam wæs oðer nama nemned Præn. Ond Æðelheard ealdorman forðferde on k Aug. Ond þa hæðenan on Norðhymbrum hergodon, ond Ecgferðes mynster æt Done muþe berefodon. Ond þær heora heretogena sum ofslægen wearð; ond eac heora scipu sume þurh ofer-weder wurdon tobrocene; ond heora feala þær adruncon. Ond sume cuce to þam stæðe common, ond þa man sona ofsloh æt ðære ea muðan.

795. ...

796. Her forðferde Offa Myrcena on iiii id Augusti. Se rixode xl wintra... Ond þy ilcan geare Ceolwulf Myrcena cining ofer hergode Cantware ond Merscware. Ond gefengon Præn heora cining, ond gebunden hine læddon on Myrce.

[789]. Here Beorhtric married King Offa's daughter Eadburh. And in his days there first came 3 ships of Northmen – from Hordaland – and then the reeve rode there and wanted to compel them to go to the king's town because he did not know what they were; and then they killed him. These were the first ships of the Danish men which sought out the land of the English race.

[787]. ... *Charles came through Germany to the borders of Bavaria.*

[788]. Here on 23 September Ælfwald, king of Northumbria, was killed by Sicga, and a heavenly light was frequently seen where he was killed; and he was buried in Hexham inside the church... And Osred, Alhred's son, succeeded to the kingdom after him – he was [Ælfwald's] nephew.

792. Here Archbishop Jænberht passed away...

791. ...

[794]. Here Offa, king of Mercia, ordered Æthelberht's head to be cut off. And Osred, who had been king of Northumbria, after coming home from a period of exile was seized and killed on 14 September; and his body lies at Tynemouth. And on 29 September King Æthelred married a new wife, who was called Ælflæd.

793. Here terrible portents came about over the land of Northumbria, and miserably frightened the people: these were immense flashes of lightning, and fiery dragons seen flying in the air.

A great famine immediately followed these signs; and a little after that in the same year on 8 January the raiding of heathen men miserably devastated God's church in Lindisfarne island by looting and slaughter...

[794]. Here Pope Adrian and King Offa passed away.[1] And Æthelred, king of Northumbria, was killed by his own nation on 19 April... And Ecgfrith succeeded to the Mercian kingdom, and passed away the same year. And Eadberht, who was by another name named Præn, succeeded to the kingdom in Kent. And [794] Ealdorman Æthelheard passed away on 1 August. And the heathen raided in Northumbria and looted Ecgfrith's minster at Jarrow; and there one of their commanders was killed, and also some of their ships were broken up by bad weather, and many of them drowned there; and some came to shore, and then were immediately killed at the river mouth.

[796]. ...

796. Here Offa of Mercia, passed away on 10 August; he ruled 40 years... And the same year [798] [Coenwulf], king of Mercia, ravaged over the inhabitants of Kent and the inhabitants of Romney Marsh, and captured Præn their king, and led him bound into Mercia.

---

[1] Adrian I on 25 December 795, and Offa 29 July 796.

Appendix B:

Widsith (lines 35-44)

Widsith is the name given by editors to one of the earliest pieces of English literature to survive. In a poem of 143 lines, a minstrel callling himself *widsið* ('widely-travelled') rehearses a catalogue of tales he may be called upon to perform. Few of the names mentioned are now known, but some, like Attila the Hun or Eormenric the Ostrogoth, were historical personalities. It survives only in the tenth-century anthology of vernacular poems: Exeter Cathedral MS 3501, ff. 84^v-87^r. Ed. B.J. Muir, *The Exeter Anthology of Old English Poetry*, Exeter, 1994, I, pp. 241-46, II, pp. 520-26; transl. S.A.J. Bradley, *Anglo-Saxon Poetry*, London, 1982, pp. 336-40.

Offa weold Ongle, Alewih Denum;   35
se wæs þara manna modgast ealra,
no hwæþre he ofer Offan eorlscype fremede,
ac Offa geslog ærest monna,
cnihtwesende, cynerica mæst;
nænig efeneald him eorlscipe maran   40
on orette – ane sweorde
merce gemærde wið Myrgingum
bi Fifeldore; heoldon forð siþþan
Engle ond Swæfe swa hit Offa geslog.

Widsith (lines 35-44)

Offa ruled Angeln, Alewih the Danes   35
– he was the most spirited of all those men
although he did not perform noble deeds
greater than Offa; but first among men Offa,
whilst a lad, won the greatest of kingdoms;
no one of the same age as him accomplished   40
a more noble deed – with a lone sword
fixed a frontier against the Myrgings
at the Monstrous Entrance, after which the Angles and
Swabians kept it as Offa established it.

Appendix C:

Beowulf (lines 1931-62)

Beowulf is the eponymous hero of an early English saga poem, some three thousand lines long, recounting incidents in the life of a Scandinavian Migration-Age hero. Drawing on early oral material, it probably achieved its present written form during the eighth century. The sole surviving manuscript is the late tenth- or early eleventh-century British Library, Cotton Vitellius xv, ff. 132^r-201^v. The poet's style is digressive. Ed. and transl. M. Swanton, *Beowulf*, Manchester, 1978.

                    Mod Þryðo wæg,
    fremu folces cwen, firen ondrysne.
    Nænig þæt dorste deor geneþan
    swæsra gesiða, nefne sinfrea,
    þæt hire an dæges eagum starede;   1935
    ac him wælbende weotode tealde,
    handgewriþene; hraþe seoþðan wæs
    æfter mundgripe mece geþinged,
    þæt hit sceadenmæl scyran moste,
    cwealmbealu cyðan. Ne bið swylc cwenlic þeaw   1940
    idese to efnanne, þeah ðe hio ænlicu sy,
    þætte freoðuwebbe feores onsæce
    æfter ligetorne leofne mannan.
    Huru þæt onhohsnode Hemminges mæg.
    Ealodrincende oðer sædan,   1945
    þæt hio leodbealewa læs gefremede,
    inwitniða, syððan ærest wearð
    gyfen goldhroden geongum cempan,
    æðelum diore, syððan hio Offan flet
    ofer fealone flod be fæder lare   1950
    siðe gesohte. Ðær hio syððan well
    in gumstole, gode mære,
    lifgesceafta lifigende breac,
    hiold heahlufan wið hæleþa brego,
    ealles moncynnes mine gefræge   1955
    þone selestan bi sæm tweonum,
    eormencynnes. Forðam Offa wæs
    geofum ond guðum, garcene man

Beowulf (lines 1931-62)

Thryth, imperious queen of the nation,
showed haughtiness, a terrible sin.
There was no brave man among the
dear companions, save for her overlord,
who by day dared venture to gaze at her with his eyes;   1935
but he might reckon deadly fetters,
twisted by hand, assured for him;
that after seizure, the sword would be prescribed,
the patterned blade should settle it,
make known a violent death. Such a thing is no queenly custom   1940
for a lady to practise, peerless though she may be,
that a peace-weaver should take the life
of a beloved man on account of a fancied insult.
However, Hemming's kinsman put a stop to that.
Those drinking ale told another tale –   1945
that she brought about fewer injuries to the people,
acts of malice, as soon as she was first
given, adorned with gold, to the young champion,
the dear prince, when she sought out Offa's hall
at her father's bidding in a journey across   1950
the yellowish flood. There she subsequently
occupied the throne well, famous for virtue,
whilst living made good use of the life destined for her,
maintained a profound love for the chief of heroes –
the best, as I have heard, of all mankind,   1955
of the entire race between the seas.
Indeed Offa, a spear-bold man,
was widely honoured for gifts and battles;

wide geweorðod; wisdome heold
eðel sinne. Þonon Eomer woc   1960
hæleðum to helpe, Heminges mæg,
nefa Garmundes, niða cræftig.

he held his homeland with wisdom.
Thence sprang Eomer,   1960
to be a help to heroes – a kinsman of Hemming,
grandson of Garmund, skilful in conflicts.

Appendix D:

Laȝamon's *Brut* (lines 14400-683)

An epic verse history, sixteen thousand lines long. Laȝamon tells us in the preface that he was living the pleasant life of a priest in Worcestershire when, impressed by the twelfth-century Wace's French *Roman de Brut*, he decided to compile a book on the origins of the English. What we are given in fact is two thousand years of British history climaxing with the reign of King Arthur – after which the country gradually slips into the hands of Germanic invaders: those various Anglo-Saxons who would all come to be known as 'the English'. Laȝamon's *Brut* survives in two thirteenth-century manuscripts: British Library Cotton Caligula Aix and, more briefly, Cotton Otho Cxiii. Ed. and transl. W.R.J. Barron and S.C. Weinberg, *Laȝamon: Brut*, London, 1995.

> Þa com an of his cunne, Carric wes ihaten,   14400
> and nom þisne kinedom, and mid seorȝen wunede þeron.
> Snel cniht wes Carric, ah he nes noht iseli;
> þat wes for unleoden spilden al his þeoden.
> Þeos king wes aðel Bruttisc mon; hux and hoker me warp him on!
> Heo forlætte Carriches and Kinric hine cleopede –
> and ȝet on feole bocken his nome me swa writeð.
> Folc hine gunnen hænen, folc hine gunne hatien
> and hoker loð sungen bi laðen þan kingen.
> Þa bigon weorre ouer al þissen arde;
> and Sexisce men sone seileden to londe   14410
> and herberȝe token aneouweste biȝeond þere Humbre.
> And þe king wæilien agon wide ȝeon þas þeoden;
> læð he wes al folke þa him on lokede.
>   Þa wes in Aufrike a king swiðe riche;
> he wes an Aufrican Anster ihaten.
> He hafde sonen tweien, snelle cnihtes beien;
> Gurmund hehte þe eldere, and Gerion hehte þe ȝeongere.
> Þe alde king deȝede – his daȝes weoren aȝeongen.
> He bitahte his sune Gurmunde selen his riche.
> Ah Gurmund hit forhoȝede and habbe he heo nolde,   14420
> and þohte al oðer, and ȝef heo his broðer,
> and seiden þat he nolde aȝen nane riche
> bute he heo biwunne mid wepnen and mid monnen;

Laʒamon's *Brut* (lines 14400-683)

Then came one of [British] race, who was called Carric   14400
and took this kingdom, and lived in it wretchedly.
Carric was a bold warrior, but he did not prosper;
that was because foreigners destroyed his whole realm.
This king was a noble British man; scorn and contempt were heaped
upon him! They forsook "Carric" and called him Kinric –
and in many books his name is still written thus.
People held him in contempt, people held him in disdain
and sang mocking songs about the despised king.
Then strife broke out all over this country,
and Saxon men soon sailed to the land   14410
and speedily took sanctuary beyond the Humber.
And the king wandered far and wide throughout this realm;
he was hateful to all people who saw him.
        There was in Africa a very powerful king;
he was an African called Anster.
He had two sons, both bold warriors;
the elder was called Wermund, the younger Werion.
The old king died - his days were ended.
He bequeathed his realm to his son Wermund.
But Wermund rejected it and would not take it,   14420
and thought quite differently, and gave it to his brother,
and said that he did not want to possess any kingdom
unless he had conquered it himself with men and arms;

ah mid compe he wolde   aȝen kineriche,
oðer nauermare   nolde he habbe nane.
       Gurmund was kempe   icostned on mæine,
and he wes þe strongeste mon   þæ æi mon lokede on.
He bigon to sende   ȝeond al þan londe,
into Babilonie,   into Macedonie,
in Turkie,   into Persie,   14430
into Nubie,   into Arrabie,
and bad alle þe ȝeonglinges   ȝeond þa hæðene londes
þat heo heom biȝeten   wurðliche wepnen,
and he heom forðrihtes   wolden makien cnihtes,
and seoððen mid heom wenden   and fonden whar he mihten
mid strongen kempen   biwinnen kineriche.
Hit halde touward Aufrike   of feole kuneriche;
monies riches monnes sune,   monie haðene gume
comen to Gurmunde,   þan hæðene þringe.
Þa þis ferde wes isomned   and his folc arimed,   14440
þa weoren þer italde   cnihtes swiðe balde
an hundred and sixti þusend,   freoliche iwapned,
wiðuten heore scutten   þa biuoren scolden scuuen,
wiðuten þan craftmonnen   þe comen to Gurmunde.
       Forð heo iuusden,   unimete uerden,
to þare se wenden;   þa heo wind hafden,
into scipe halden   haðene kempen.
Seouentene þer foren   þat kinges sunen weoren;
þer weoren twenti and æhten   of eorlene streone.
Suipten from londe seouen hundred scipene   14450
a formeste flocke,   wiðuten þa feoliende;
forð flet mid uðe   folc unimete.
Þa æitlondes allen   þa heo biforen funden,
alle heo eoden an honde   þan kinge Gurmunde.
Moniane kinge he faht wið,   and alle heo ȝirnden his grið;
and alle þe londes he biwon   þat he lokede on.
And þa a þan ende   he com to Irlonde.
And þat land he al biwon   and aqualden þa leoden,
and wes icleoped king þere   of þan kinelonde.
And seoððen he gon wende   into þissen londe;   14460
seil heo droȝen to hune   and comen to Suðhamtune.
       Þa wunede biȝeonde þere Hunbre   of Hengestes cunne
in þan norð ende   drenches sume sixe;
heo iherden tiðinde   of Gurmund þan kinge.

either he would gain a kingdom by warfare,
or he would never have one at all.

      Wermund was a warrior of proven might,
and he was the strongest man that anyone had ever seen.
He sent throughout all lands,
to Babylon, to Macedonia,   14430
to Turkey, to Persia,
to Nubia, to Arabia,
and bade all the young men throughout the heathen lands
to provide themselves with good weapons,
and he would quickly make warriors of them
and then set out with them and see where he could
win a kingdom with strong warriors.
They flocked to Africa from many realms,
the sons of many a powerful man, many a heathen youth
came to Wermund, the heathen chieftain.   14440
When this army was assembled and his forces numbered,
there were then present, all told,
one hundred and sixty thousand very bold warriors, splendidly armed,
not counting their archers who were to press forward in the van,
and not counting the artificers who had joined Wermund.

      They hastened forth, a countless force,
making their way to the sea; when the wind was favourable,
the heathen warrior took ship.
Seventeen who set out were sons of kings;
twenty-eight were the offspring of earls.   14450
Seven hundred ships sped from the shore
in the foremost squadron, not counting those following;
a countless host sailed forth over the waves.
All the islands which they came upon in their passage
came into the hands of Wermund the king.
He fought with many a king, and they all sued for peace with him;
and he conquered all the lands he set eyes on.
And then at last he came to Ireland.
And he conquered the whole of that land, and slaughtered the inhabitants,
and was declared king of that country there.   14460
And then he made his way to this country;
they hoisted sail and came to Southampton.

      At that time there lived in the northern region, beyond the
Humber, some six chieftains of Hengest's race;
they heard tidings of King Wermund.

Ofte heo heom biþohte   what heo don mihten,
hu heo mihten biswiken   Karic of his richen
and Bruttes alle aquellen   mid luðeren heore craften.
Sexisce men senden sonde   to Karic þan king,
and seiden þat heo wolden   wið hine grið iwurchen;
leofere heom weore   to here Karic   14470
þene Gurmunde,   þan uncuðe kinge,
ȝef he heom wolde griðien   þat heo mosten liuien,
and aȝeuen heom þat lond   þat while Uortigerne þe king
Hengeste bitahte   þa he nom his dohter leoue.
And heo him wolden senden   gauel of þan londe,
halden hine for hehne king,   Karic heore deorling;
and þis heo him toȝeornden   mid ȝislen to isoðien.
And Karic heom ilefde,   al heore leosinge,
and þis grið ȝette   and dai heom sette.
Þa wes Karic biswiken   al mid heore craften.   14480
Karic auer seoðen   Kineric he hehten;
al mid hoker-worden   þe king heo forhusten.
       Karic ileouede to soðe   Sexisce monne lare.
Under þan worden   heo letten writ makien
and senden heore sonden   to Gurmunt þen kinge;
and þus þa word seiden   þa a þan writ stoden:
'Hail seo þu, Gurgmund;   hal seo þu heðene king.
Heil seo þi duȝeðe;   hail þine drihtliche men.
We sunden men Sexisce,   selest of þan kunne
þa Hengest of Sexlande   hider mid him brohte;   14490
wunieð inne Brutaine   bi norðe þere Humbre.
Þu art heðene king,   we heðene kempen;
Karic is Cristine mon – he is us lað forðan.
And ȝif þu wult al þis lond   nimen to þire aȝere hond,
we wulleð mid þe uehten   mid fullere strenðen,
and Caric ofslæn   and alle his cnihtes flan,
and setten al þis kinelond   a þire aȝere hond.
Ȝif þu hit wult us aȝiuen,   we þe wulleð ȝelden
sixti hundred punden   to alches ȝeres firsten,
and we wulleð þine men bicumen,   to ȝislen sullen þe ure sunen. 14500
And ȝif hit þi wille weore   þat þu hider woldest wende,
þas forwarde makien   and þas spechen uæstnien,
we wulleð oueral   atlien to þe seluen,
a watere and a londe   halden þe uor kinge.'

They had often considered what they could do,
how they might deprive Carric of his kingdom
and kill all the Britons by their evil schemes.
The Saxon men sent messengers to King Carric,
and said that they wanted to make peace with him,
that they would rather serve Carric 14470
than Wermund, the foreign king,
if he would allow them to live in
peace, and give them the land which King Vortigern had at one
time granted to Hengest when he wed his beloved daughter.
And they would send him tribute from that land, regard
him, their beloved Carric, as sovereign; and this they urged
upon him, offering hostages as surety.
And Carric believed them, all their lies,
and agreed this truce and arranged a day with them.
Then Carric was deceived by all their trickery. 14480
Afterwards Carric was always called Kinric;
everyone derided the king with words of contempt.
      Carric believed the Saxon men's declarations to be true.
Under cover of these negotiations they had letters written
and sent their envoys to King Wermund;
and this is what the letters said:
'Good Health to you, Wermund; good health to you, heathen king.
Good Health to your retinue; good health to your noblemen.
We are Saxon men, the best of that race
which Hengest brought here with him from Saxony; 14490
we live in Britain, to the north of the Humber.
You are a heathen king, we are heathen warriors;
Carric is a Christian man, and therefore hateful to us.
And if you want to take this whole land into your hands,
we are willing to fight on your side with all our might,
and kill Carric and put all his warriors to flight,
and place this whole kingdom in your hand.
If you will entrust it to us, we will give you
each year six thousand pounds, and will
become your men, give you our sons as hostages. 14500
And if you be willing to come here
to make this agreement and confirm these proposals,
we will wholly commit ourselves to you, accept
you as sovereign by land and by sea.'

Þa bigon to spekene   Gurmund þe kene:
'Ʒarkieð mine scipen biliue;   forð ic wulle liðe.'
Seiles heo up droʒen,   forð heo gunnen siʒen,
luken rapes longe,   liðen forð mid uðen.
And swa heo gunnen wenden   to Norðhumbrelonde,
and speken wið Sexisce men   and sæhte iwurðen,   14510
and sworen þat heo wolden   heore forward halden.
Þa weoren heo al an,   Gurmund and Sexesce men.
Þa somneden heo uerde   unimete an ærde
and ferde touward Karriche,   þan kinge of þissere riche;
and æuere heo sungen mid hokere   of Kinriche þan kinge.
Caric his Bruttes gaderede   and beide heom tosomne,
and him to wende   al þat was on londe;
for rihtere neode   nusten heo red betere.
Caric muchel folc hafde   and ferde unimete,
and ofte he com to compe   to Gurmunde kinge,   14520
and ofte he him faht win   and neuere no ʒirde his grið.
And for heo hokerede him on   he iwarð swiðe kene mon,
and ʒif he hafde genge   efne wið Gurmunde,
Gurmund weore sone islaʒen,   his folc idon of lif-daʒen.
Ah æuere a þan ende   wæx Gurmundes genge,
and æuere a þan ende   feol Carriches genge.

    Gurmund draf Carriche   wide ʒeond þas riche;
and Carric at Cherinchestre   biclusde hine ful faste
(and moni dæi þer biuoren   he lette þider fusen
al þat he hafde ihalden   þat corn of þissen londe),   14530
and þa walles fastnede   wunder ane stronge.
Gurmund þet iherde   and þider he gon ride,
and bilæi Chirenchestre   wiðutene swiðe faste.
And Gurmund al þis kinelond   walde to his aʒere hond;
burʒes he forbarnde,   tunes he forswelde,
Bruttes he aqualde – balu wes on londe!
Munekes he forpinede   on mani are wise,
þa riche wif he lette his hired-men   makien to horen,
preostes he alle ofslæh,   alle þa chirchen he todroh,
clærkes he aqualde   alle þa he funde;   14540
eche child he lette seoðe,
alle þa cnihtes   he lette hon forðrihtes,
al þis lond forferde   a ueole cunne wise.
Wulc wræcche folc swa mihte   fleh ut of þeode;
sum to Wales wende,   sum to Cornwale,
sum into Neustrie   þe hatte nu Normandie.

Then the bold Wermund said:
'Prepare my ships quickly; I want to leave.'
They hoisted the sails; they got ready to leave;
heaving upon long ropes, set forth upon the waves.
And so they travelled to Northumberland,
and talked with the Saxon men and made   14510
a pact and swore that they would hold to their pledge.
Then they, Wermund and the Saxons, were at one.
Then they assembled a countless force in that region
and advanced upon Carric, the king of this country;
and they continually sang mocking songs about King Kinric.
Carric summoned his Britons and assembled them,
and all who were in the land flocked to him;
they knew no better course in such straits.
Carric had many followers and a countless army,
and he frequently engaged King Wermund in battle,   14520
frequently fought against him and never sued for peace.
And because they poured scorn upon him he became a very bold warrior,
and if he had had a force equal to Wermund's,
Wermund would quickly have been slain, his followers deprived of life.
But in the end Wermund's always had the upper hand,
and in the end, Carric's army was always defeated.
    Wermund drove Carric hither and thither throughout the kingdom;
and Carric shut himself up most securely in Cirencester
(and for many days beforehand he had had brought there
all the grain he had in this country),   14530
and fortified the walls very strongly.
Wermund learned of that and rode there
and besieged Cirencester very closely.
And Wermund had this whole kingdom in his hands;
he burned down cities, he set towns ablaze,
he slaughtered the Britons – there was chaos in the land!
He tortured monks in many ways,
he let his mercenaries make whores of the high-born women,
he slew all the priests, he pulled down all the churches,
he killed all the clerics he found;   14540
he had each child boiled,
had all the warriors promptly hanged, devastated
this whole land in many different ways.
Those wretched people who could fled from the country;
some went to Wales, some to Cornwall,
some to Neustria which is now called Normandy.

Sum fleh biȝeonden sæ into Bruttaine,
and gunnen wunien seoððe æn þet lond heht Armoriche.
And summe heo fluȝen to Irlonde for þan æie of Gurmunde,
and þer wuneden þeouwe inne þraldome, 14550
heo and al heore cun, and her ne come nauere aȝen.
And þus losede Bruttes al þas kinelondes.
And Gurmund bilæi Chirenchestre abuten swiðe uaste,
and Caric wes wiðinnen and moni of his monnen;
wa wæs þan leoden þe þa weoren on liuen.
    Hit was in ane dæie þat Gurmund mid his duȝeðe,
dringes heðene, riden a slatinge.
Þa com þer an gume riden to Gurmunde kingen;
he wes ihaten Isemberd – inne France wes his ærd;
he wes Louweises sune, þas kinges of þere þeode. 14560
His fader hine hafuede ut idriuen of al his kinerichen
þat no moste he neouwar wunie on al his onwalde,
and he fleh to þissen londe, to Gurmunde kinge.
He hafde to iueren twa þusend rideren,
and Gurmundes mon he bicom – ne mihte he na wurse don,
for Crist seolue he forsoc and to þan Wursen he tohc,
and þer forlete he Cristindom and heðescipe nom him on.
And swa heo uoren beien mid mucle heore uerde
and bileien Chirenchestre an elche halue wel faste.
Wel ofte Kariches men comen ut of burhȝen 14570
and ræsden an Gurmunde mid ræȝere strenðe,
and sloȝen of his folke feole þusende,
and senden heom to helle, heðene hundes alle.
Karic wes swiðe goud cniht and swiðe wel he heold his fiht,
and faste he heold Chirchestre mid strengðe þan mæste
þat ne mihte Gurmund næuere mæren his ferde
ar he lette heom mid ginnen biswiken wiðinnen.
Gurmund castles makede abuten Chirenchestre.
Þreo he bitahte þreom heðene cnihte;
himseoluen he heold þat ane, Isembard þat oðer. 14580
Gurmund makede ænne tur; þerinne he bulde ænne bur
þerinne he pleoȝede his plaȝen þa me luuede a þeon daȝen;
þerinne he hafde his maumet þa he heold for his god.
    Hit ilomp on ane dæiȝe þat Gurmund mid his duȝeðe
weoren swiðe bliðe and drunken of wine;
þa com þer an heðene mon – awaried wurðen he forþan! –
and askede tidende Gurmunde þe kinge:
'Seie me, lauerd Gurmund – þu art swiðe riche king –

Some fled across the sea to Brittany,
and thereafter lived in that land, called Armorica.
And some fled to Ireland because of Wermund's reign of terror,
and there lived in servitude as slaves,   14550
they and all their descendants, and never came back here.
And thus the Britons lost all these realms.
And Wermund besieged Cirencester very closely,
and Carric was inside with many of his men;
those still alive were in a wretched state.
     It happened one day that Wermund and his retinue,
heathen chieftains, rode out hunting.
Then a man came riding up to King Wermund;
he was called Isembard – his homeland was in France;
he was the son of Lewis, the king of that country.   14560
His father had driven him out from the whole of his kingdom
so that he could not live anywhere in his entire realm,
and he fled to this country, to King Wermund.
He had with him two thousand horsemen, and
he became a follower of Wermund – he could not have done worse,
for he abandoned Christ and turned to the Devil,
and so forsook Christianity and took to heathendom.
And then they both went to besiege Cirencester very closely on all sides
with their large army.
Carric's men very often sallied out from the town   14570
and attacked Wermund with furious might,
and slew many thousands of his followers,
despatching them, all heathen dogs, to hell.
Carric was a very fine warrior and conducted his defence very
successfully, and stoutly defended Cirencester with the greatest strength
so that Wermund was never able to defeat his forces until,
by a trick, he caused them to be destroyed from within.
Wermund set up strongholds around Cirencester.
Three of them he entrusted to three heathen chieftains;
he himself held one, Isembard another.   14580
Wermund built a tower; within it he made a chamber in which he
played all the games that men enjoyed in those days;
in it he kept his idol which he treated as his god.
     It happened on a certain day, when Wermund and his retinue
were in high spirits and drunk with wine,
there came there a heathen man - may he be damned for it! –
and enquired of King Wermund:
'Tell me, lord Wermund, you who are a most powerful king,

heou longe wult þu beoȝie   abuten þissere burȝe?
What wult þu ȝiuen me   ȝif ich þe burh ȝiuen þe   14590
and al þat is wiðinne   to don þine iwille
þat noht no bið to leue – al þu hit slat aȝe?'
Þa andswarede Gurmund,   þe riche heðene king:
'Ich ȝiue þe ane eorldom   auere to aȝe,
wið þat þu aneoste   þe burh me bitache.'
Þis forward wes imaked anan – lut men hit wuste.

     Þa þes heðene cniht   up aras forðrit,
and nettes bisohte   ibroiden swiðe narewe
and þa tolen þerto,   and tuht heom swiðe narewe;
þer biforen he gon ȝeoten   draf and chaf and aten.   14600
Þus he hit gon dihten,   and sparewen þerto liht,
and he a þan uorme drahte   swiðe monie he ilahte;
and he from þan grunde   nom heom mid isunde
þat alle heore whingen   noht awemmed neoren.
Þa bisohte he nute-scalen   and lette þe curneles ut draȝen,
and tinder nom   and lette i þan scalen don,
and foren to þære nihte   fur þeron brohte,
and to þan sparewen uoten   uaste heom icnutten.
Þeos he lette forð wenden,   swiðe ueole sparewen;
þa sparwen heore flut nomen   and fluȝen to heore innen   14610
ȝeond þare burȝen   þær heo ar wuneȝende weoren.
I þan eouesen he grupen,   swa heo duden in þen muȝen;
anan swa þet fur wes hat,   swa þe sparewe innere crap.
Þe wind com mid þere nihte   and þat fur awehte,
and þa burh a feole studen   gon hure to bernen;
an æst halue, an west halue,   wa wes Brutten þere.
Þenne heo wenden beon sikere   and fluȝen in ane ende,
þenne aras þat fur anan   biuoren and bihinden.
Gurmund lette blawen   hornes and bemen;
fiften þusende   þarsten to blase.   14620
Bruttes forburnen,   Bruttes gunnen irnen;
heo leopen ut of walle   and me heom sloh alle.
Nes hit nohwhar iseid,   no a bocken irad,
þat æi folc swa feire   swa forfare weore
swa wes Caric and his genge   þe king wes of Bruttene.
Þa burh born alle niht – þe brune wes unimete;
þat feht wes sone idon;   þat fur heom eoden ouenon,
and Carrich king him isah   þat he ouercume wæs.

how long do you want to be about this town?
What will you give me if I give you the town 14590
and everything inside to do with as you wish,
so that nothing of it remains – it shall all be yours?'
Then Wermund, the mighty heathen king, answered:
'I will give you an earldom to be yours for ever,
if you deliver the town to me without delay.'
This bargain was made at once – not many knew about it.
   Then this heathen warrior immediately set to and found
closely woven nets and the tackle for them,
and stretched them out very tightly;
in front he scattered husks and chaff and oats. 14600
He arranged it so that sparrows alit upon it,
and in the first haul he caught a large number;
and he picked them up uninjured
so that their wings were not damaged at all.
Then he got nut shells and removed the kernels,
and took tinder and put it inside the shells
and, just before nightfall set fire to them,
knotting them firmly on the feet of the sparrows.
These sparrows he let go in large numbers;
the sparrows took flight and flew to their perches 14610
throughout the town where they were formerly dwelling.
They perched on the eaves as they did on hay-stacks;
as the fire was hot, the sparrows crept further in.
With night the wind came and fanned the fire,
and the town caught fire in many places;
to east and west Britons were in distress.
When, hoping for safety, they fled in one direction,
the fire suddenly sprang up in front and behind.
Wermund had horns and trumpets sounded;
at the blast fifteen thousand men thronged forward. 14620
Britons were ablaze, Britons took flight;
they leapt down from the walls and were all slain.
It is nowhere said, nor to be read in any book,
that men as fine as Carric, the king of the Britons, and his followers
were ever destroyed in such a way.
The town burned all night – the heat was intense;
that combat soon finished; the fire overwhelmed them,
and King Carric realised that he was defeated.

Þe king him gon crepen   an heonden and a futen
swulc he mid unsunde,   al uorwunded weore;   14630
and swa he swiðe stille   bistal from his duʒeðe,
and west him gon wenden   into þe Walsce londen.
And þas waiʒes he wende   ut of þisse londe;
and nuste nauere na man   whar Karic him bicom,
buten ænes an ane tide   an cniht þer com ride
and seide Gurmunde   of Kariche tidende,
þat he in Irlonde   somnede genge
and wolde mid fehte   æft faren hidere.
Ah nuste nauere na man   to whan þe þret him bicom.
And þus wes Chirenchestre   and his londes aweste,   14640
and Gurmund ihouen to kinge   of al þisse kinelonde.
For þenne þe burh wes biwunnen   mid swulches cunnes ginnen,
mid sparewen þat beren þat fur;   and sparewen heo forbarnden!
And feole wintere seoððen   þat folc þa þer wunede
cleopeden heo Sparewenchestre   in heore leod-spellen,
and ʒet hit dude summe men   to imuʒen þe alde deden.
And þus wes þa riche burh   mid reouðen fordemed,
and Gurmund wes on londe   iheouen her to kinge.

    And Gurmund wes an heðene mon,   and fordude þane Cristindom;
þa þis wes al þus ifare,   þæ wes her sorʒe and muchel care: 14650
Gurmund falde þa munstres   and anheng alle þa munkes;
of cnihten he carf þe lippes,   of madenen þa tittes,
preostes he blende.   Al þis folc he scende,
ælcne bilefued mon   he lette bilimien,
and þus he gon to taken on   and fordude al þisne Cristindom.
And seoððen he uor to Lundene,   to ane muchele hustinge;
þider gunnen siʒe   alle Sex-leode
þa wuneden i þissen londe   mid Gurmunde kinge,
and his men bicome,   monie and uniuoʒe,
heom heold forward   and aʒef heom sone al þis ærd   14660
of him to heoldenne,   and habben hine for kinge.
And þe king hehte   al þat hine lufede
þat wharswa heo mihten finde   Bruttes i þissen londe,
þat hine anan sloʒen   oðer mid horsen todroʒen,
buten he libben wolden   his lif in þraldome,
and forsaken Godes mæsse   and luuien hæðenesse;
þenne moste he libben   þeou a þisse londe.

    Bisiden Allemaine is a lond   Angles ihaten;
þer weoren iborne   þa ilke þe weorn icorne,
þa Gurmund an hond   bitahte al þis kinelond,   14670

The king crept away on hands and knees
as if he were injured, all wounded;   14630
and so he very stealthily stole away from his retinue,
and made his way westwards into the land of the Welsh.
And by these means he left this country;
and no one ever knew what became of Carric,
except that on one occasion there came riding a warrior
who gave Wermund news of Carric,
that he was gathering an army in Ireland
and intended to return here by force.
But no one ever learned what became of the threat.
And in this way Cirencester and its environs were laid waste,   14640
and Wermund was raised to be king of this whole realm.
And so by a trick of this kind the town was taken,
by sparrows who carried the fire there; and sparrows burned it down!
And for many years afterwards the people there
called it in their native tongue Sparrowchester,
and some people still do in memory of past events.
And so that prosperous town was sadly destroyed,
and Wermund was raised to the kingship in the country here.

And Wermund was a heathen, and destroyed Christianity;
when all this came to pass there was great sorrow and misery here: 14650
Wermund tore down the monasteries and hanged all the monks;
he cut off the lips of warriors, the breasts off young women,
he blinded priests. He grievously afflicted this whole nation,
mutilating every devout man,
and, acting in this way, completely destroyed Christianity here.
And then he went to London, to a great assembly;
where there were gathered all the Saxon people
living in this country, together with King Wermund,
and became his men in large numbers,
kept their agreement with him and at once gave him this whole country
to possess, accepting him as king.   14661
And the king ordered all who supported him
that, wherever they came upon any Briton in this country,
they should immediately slay him or have him torn apart by horses,
unless he would live his life in servitude
and, abandoning the divine sacrament, honour the heathen religion;
when he might live in this country as a slave.

Next to Germany is a country called Angeln,
where were born those who had been singled out,
into whose hands Wermund gave this whole kingdom,   14670

alse he heom a forward hædde   ȝif he hit biwunne.
Al his biheste   he heom bilaste.
Of Englen heo comen,   and þerof heo nomen nomen,
and letten heom cleopien fuliwis   þat folc þat wes Ænglis;
and þis lond heo cleopeden Ænglelond,   for hit wes al on heore honde.
Seoððe ærest Bruttes   bæhȝen to þissen londe
Brutaine hit wes ihaten,   of Brutten nom taken,
a þat þis folc com   þa þisne nome him binom.
And moniee of þan burȝen   and monie of þan tunen
and monie of þan londen   and of þan hamen   14680
heo binomen heore namen,   al for Bruttene sceome,
and nomen al þis lond   and setten hit al an heore hond;
for Gurmund hit heom al ȝette;   and himseolf aȝein wende.

as he had agreed with them if he should conquer it.
He did everything he had promised them.
They came from Angeln, and they took their name from there
and, indeed, called themselves the English nation;
and they called this country England because it was wholly in their hands.
After the Britons first came to this country
it was called Britain, taking its name from the Britons,
until this people came who deprived it of that name.
And from many of the towns and many of the cities
and many of the regions and the homesteads   14680
they removed their names, all due to the Britons' downfall,
and took the whole land all into their own hands;
for Wermund granted it all to them; and he himself departed.

Appendix E:

The Welsh *Brut y Tywysogyon*, AD 776-96.

The *Brut y Tywysogyon* (*Chronicle of the Princes*) represents the Welsh translation of a now lost Latin original. Apparently intended as a continuation of William of Monmouth's *History of the Kings of the Britons*, it was produced during the thirteenth century probably by a Welsh cleric living at the Cistercian abbey of Strata Florida in mid-Wales. Starting where William's largely fantastic story ends, with the death of Cadwaladr, supposedly in 682, it provides for this period a relatively pedestrian series of brief annals recording events such as battles, earthquakes or the deaths of kings. Its manuscript history is complicated and a variety of post-medieval elaborations exist. Significant early versions are that in National Library of Wales, Peniarth MS. 20, ed. T. Jones, *Brut y Tywysogyon*, Cardiff, 1941, and transl. 1952, and that in the 'Red Book' found at Hergest Court, now Bodleian Library Oxford, Jesus College MS. 111, ed. and transl. T. Jones, *Brut y Tywysogyon*, Cardiff, 1955.

776-77. Ac yna y bu distryw y Deheubarthwyr gan Offa vrenhin.[1]

780-83. Petwar ugein mlyned a seith cant oed oet Crist pan diffeithawd Offa vrenhin y Brytanyeit yn amser haf.[2]

790-95. Deg mlyned a phetwar ugein a seith cant oed oet Crist [pan] doeth y Paganyeit yn gyntaf y Iwerdon.

795-96. Ac y bu varw Offa vrenhin a Maredud, brenhin Dyfet. Ac y bu vrwydyr yn Rudlan.

---

[1] A transcript by the fifteenth-century poet Gutun Owain, National Library of Wales, MS. 7006D, prefers: 'gwyr Deheubarth Kymre a diffeithassant yr ynys hyd ar Offa, brenhin Mers'.

[2] Gutun Owain reads: 'yr haf y diffeithws y Kymre kyuoeth Offa, ac yna y peris Offa gwneuthur clawd yn deruyn ryngthaw a Chymre val y bei haws ydaw gwrthnebu y ruthyr y elyion, a hwnnw a elwit glawd Offa yr hynny hyd hedyw. Ac ef y sydd yn estynnv or ar gogledd gorvwch y Fflint y rwng mynachloc ddinas Basing a mynydd y Glo.'

The Welsh *Chronicle of the Princes*, AD 776-96.

776-77 And then was the harrying of the men of Deheubarth by King Offa.[1]

780-83 It was *Anno Domini* seven hundred and eighty when King Offa ravaged the Britons in the summer season.[2]

790-95 It was *Anno Domini* seven hundred and ninety when the Heathens first came to Ireland.

795-96 And King Offa and Meredith, king of Dyfed, died. And there was a battle at Rhuddlan.

---

[1] Gutun Owain's transcript prefers: 'the men of south Wales harried the island as far as Offa, king of Mercia'.

[2] Gutun Owain reads: 'in the summer the Welsh harried the kingdom of Offa, and then Offa had a dyke made as a frontier between him and Wales so that he could withstand the attack of his enemies more easily, and it is called Offa's Dyke from that time to this day. And it extends from one sea to the other, from the south near Bristol to the north above Flint between the monastery of Basingwerk and Coleshill.'

Appendix F:

Extracts from the Danish *Annales Ryenses*

The *Annales Ryenses* consists of an outline chronicle, written in rough Latin, of the Danish people from their legendary origins until the thirteenth century. The version we have, which reveals a decidedly anti-German view, was compiled at the Cistercian Ryd Abbey on Flensburg Fjord in Schlesvig. Ed. J.M. Lappenberg, *Annales Ryenses*, *Monumenta Germaniae Historica, Scriptores rerum Germanicarum*, 16, Hanover, 1859, pp. 386-410.

> [28] Wermundus Blinde. Hic uir bellicosus erat. Huius tempore Keto et Wiggo, filii Frewini, praefecti Sleswicensis, occiderunt Athislum regem Sueciae in ultionem patris sui. Huic successit Uffo Starke filius eius.
>
> [29] Uffo Starke. Iste a septimo anno aetatis usque ad trigesimum noluit loqui, quousque in loco, qui adhuc Kunengikamp dicitur, super Eydoram cum filio regis Teutonicorum atque meliore pugile totius Teutoniae solus certans, ambos occidit, atque sic conditione utriusque gentis, Teutonia Danis iam quarto tributaria facta est. Huic successit Olaf filius eius.

Annals of Ryd

[28] Wermund the Blind. This man was warlike. In his time Keto and Wiggo, the sons of Earl Frowinus of Schleswig, killed King Eadgils of Sweden in vengeance for their father. Then [Wermund's] son Offa the Strong succeeded.

[29] Offa the Strong. From seven years old until thirty this man had refused to speak, until – in a place on the Eider which is still called 'Kings-combat' – fighting alone against the son of the king of the Teutons together with the best champion among all the Teutons, he killed them both; and in this manner it came about that a quarter of the Teutons were now subject to the Danes. Then his son Olaf succeeded.

Appendix G:

Sweyn Aageson, *Brevis Historia Regum Dacie*, 2-3

One of the first to write a connected history of Denmark, Sweyn Aageson was born somewhere around 1140-1150 into a wealthy family descending from the Danish chieftain Palnatoke, who some two centuries earlier in 986 had persuaded Sweyn Forkbeard to wage war on his father King Harald Bluetooth, and had himself killed the king. The family also included notable ecclesiastics like Asser, the first Archbishop of Lund (1104-1137). Like his predecessors, Sweyn Aageson became part of the royal household, joining war-expeditions carried out by Valdemar I and Canute VI. There remains evidence of administrative writings: military laws (*Lex Castrensis*), and a genealogy of Danish kings (*Genealogia Regum Dacie*). However, his best-known work is *Brevis Historia Regum Dacie*, an outline of Danish history from *c.* 300 AD to 1186.

[2] Huius filius et hreres regni extitit Wermundus, qui adeo prudentire pollebat uirtute, ut in de nomen consequeretur. Unde et 'Prudens' dictus est. Hic filium genuit, Uffi nomine, qui usque ad tricesimum aetatis suae annum fandi possibilitatem cohibuit, propter enormitatem opprobrii, quod tunc temporis Danis ingruerat, eo quod in ultionem patris duo Dani in Sueciam profecti, patricidam suum una interemerunt. Nam et tunc temporis ignominiosum extitit improperium, si solum duo iugularent; presertim cum soli strenuitati tunc superstitiosa gentilitas operam satagebat impendere.

Prefatus itaque Wermundus usque ad senium regni sui gubernabat imperium; adeo tandem aetate consumptus, ut oculi eius pre senio caligarent. Cuius debilitatis fama cum apud transal[b]inas partes percrebuisset, elationis turgiditate Teotonica intumuit superbia, utpote suis nunquam contenta terminis. Hinc furoris sui rabiem in Danos exacuit Imperator, se iam Danorum regno conquisito sceptrum nancisci augustius conspicatus. Delegantur itaque spiculatores, qui turgidi principis iussa reportent prefato Danorum regi, scilicet Wermundo, duarum rerum prefigentes electionem, quarum pars tamen neutra extitit eligenda. Aut enim regnum iussit Romano resignare imperio, et tributum soluere, aut athletam inuestigare, qui cum imperatoris campione monomachiam committere auderet.

Sweyn Aageson, *Brief History of the Kings of Denmark*, 2-3

The Latin might be rough compared with that of his younger contemporary Saxo[1], but, given the Classical knowledge displayed, he also probably received a comprehensive education in Paris or elsewhere. He speaks of Saxo as his associate in the ménage of the powerful Archbishop Absalon of Lund (1178-1201), but how well he knew Saxo, twenty years his junior, is uncertain. The term he uses is *contubernalis*, which was open to a wide range of meanings, both practical and metaphorical, at this time. Ed. M.C. Gertz, *Scriptores Minores Historiae Danicae*, Copenhagen, 1917-20, I, pp. 94-174 (pp. 98-105); transl. E. Christiansen, *The Works of Sven Aggesen*, London, 1992, pp. 50-54.

[2] Wermund, the son and heir of the king [Frothi the Bold], who succeeded to the kingdom, was so outstanding for the virtue of prudence that he got his nickname from it: for this reason was called 'the Prudent'. He had a son named Offa, who suppressed his faculty of speech until the thirtieth year of his life because of the great disgrace which had fallen upon the Danes at that time, due to the fact that two Danes who had gone to Sweden to avenge their father slew the father's killer by attacking him both at once. For at that time it was reckoned a shameful and dishonourable deed if two men slew one who was alone; especially when the superstitious pagans of those days tried to devote their energy solely to deeds of valour.

Therefore the aforesaid Wermund governed the kingdom until his old age, by when he was so stricken in years that his eyes had grown dim with age. When news of this infirmity reached the regions beyond the Elbe, the pride of the Teuton began to swell and grow puffed up, since he was never content with his own boundaries. Now the emperor wreaked his fury on the Danes, seeing himself as having already conquered the Danish kingdom and won the sceptre. Therefore emissaries were sent who carried the orders of this puffed-up prince to the aforesaid king of the Danes, that is, Wermund; they set before him a choice of two courses, neither of which, however, was fit to choose. For it was ordered that he either resign his kingdom to the Roman Empire and pay tribute, or find a contestant who dared engage with the emperor's champion in single combat.

[1] See below pp. 173-4.

Quo audito, regis extitit mens consternata; totiusque regni procerum legione corrogata, quid facto opus sit, diligenti inquisitione percontabatur. Perplexam se namque regis autumabat autoritas, utpote cui et ius incumbebat decertandi, et qui regno patrocinari tenebatur. Uultum cecitas obnubilauerat, et regni heres elinguis factus, desidia torpuerat, ita ut in eo, communi assertione, nulla prorsus species salutis existeret.

Nam ab infantia prefatus Uffo uentris indulgebat ingluuiei, et Epicureorum more, coquine et cellario alternum officiose impendebat obsequium. Corrogato itaque cetu procerum, totiusque regni placito celebrato, Alamannorum regis ambitionem explicuit, quid in hac optione haud eligenda facturus sit, indagatione cumulata senior sciscitatur.

Et dum uniuersorum mens consternaretur angustia, cunctique indulgerent silentio, prefatus Uffo in media concione surrexit. Quem cum cohors uniuersa conspexisset, satis nequibat admirari, utquid elinguis uelut orationi gestus informaret. Et quia omne rarum dignum nouimus admiratione, omnium in se duxit intuitum. Tandem sic orsus cepit: 'Non nos mine moueant lacessentium, cum ea Teotonice turgiditati innata sit conditio, ut uerborum ampullositate glorientur, minarumque uentositate pusillanimes et imbecilles calleant comminatione consternare. Me etenim unicum et uerum regni natura produxit heredem, cui profecto nouistis incumbere, ut monomachie me discrimini audacter obiiciam, quatenus uel pro regno solus occumbam uel pro patria solus uictoriam obtineam. Ut ergo minarum cassetur ampullositas, hec imperatori referant mandata, ut imperatoris filius et heres imperii, cum athleta prestantissimo, mihi soli non formidet occurrere.'

Dixit, et hec verba dictauit voce superba. Qui dum orationem complesset, a collateralibus senior sciscitabatur, cuiusnam hec fuisset oratio. Cum autem a circumstantibus intellexisset, quod filius suus, prius ueluti mutus, hunc effudisset sermonem, palpandum eum iussit accersiri. Et cum humeros lacertosque, et clunes, suras atque tibias, ceteraque membra organica crebro palpasset: 'Talem,' ait, 'me memini in flore extitisse iuuentutis.' Quid multa? Terminus pugne constituitur et locus. Talique responso percepto ad propria legati repedabant.

Hearing which, the king was dismayed; but, gathering together leading men from out of the whole kingdom, he urgently questioned them as to what should be done. For the king declared himself perplexed as to on whom fell the duty of settling the matter by battle, and who would undertake the defence of the realm. Blindness veiled his own face, and the heir to the kingdom, being turned mute, sank in idleness, so that it was generally agreed that there was no hope of salvation from him.

For from childhood the aforesaid Offa had indulged the gluttony of his belly, and in the manner of the Epicureans studiously cultivated the pleasures of both kitchen and cellar. Therefore [the king] had gathered them together to an Assembly from far and wide from the whole kingdom, and explained the ambition of the German king; the old man asked them, with repeated questions, what should be done about a choice which was scarcely a choice at all.

And while the minds of all were full of dismay at these dire straits, and sunk in silence, the aforesaid Offa arose in the midst of the conclave. When the whole host caught sight of him, they could scarcely have been more amazed, that a speechless man should make as if with the gestures of oratory. And because every fresh oddity deserves admiration, he drew everyone's attention to himself. At last he began to speak thus: 'Let's not be worried by these threats, when it is the inbred character of the puffed-up Teutons to glory in bombastic words and have long known how to dismay sissies and imbeciles with empty wind and threatenings. I, indeed, am the one true heir to the kingdom produced by nature, upon whom, as you know, falls the duty of defending it; I therefore boldly offer myself for single combat at this crisis, seeing that either I alone will fall for the kingdom, or alone gain victory for the homeland. Thus, so that this threatening bombast may cease, let them take back this message to the Emperor, that the Emperor's son and heir to empire – along with their most outstanding contestant – must not fear to face me alone.'

He spoke, and pronounced these words with a magnificent voice. When the oration was over, the old man asked his neighbours who had made this oration. However, when he understood from those standing around that it was his son, formerly as if dumb, who had poured out these words, he ordered that he should be sent for so as to touch him. And when he had repeatedly touched shoulders and arms, and haunches, calves and shins, and other bodily limbs, he said: 'I remember that I was like that in the flower of my youth.' What more? The time and place for the combat were settled. And the messengers returned to their own people with the reply they had received.

[3] Superest ergo, ut arma nouo militi congrua corrogentur. Allatisque ensibus, quos in regno prestantiores rex poterat inuestigare, Uffo singulos dextra uibrans, in partes confregit minutissimas. 'Hæccine arma sunt,' inquit, 'quibus et uitam et regni tuebor honorem?'

Cuius cum pater uiuidam experiretur uirtutem: 'Unicum adhuc,' ait, 'et regni et uite nostre superest asylum.' Ad tumulum itaque ducatum postulauit, in quo prius mucronem experientissimum occultauerat. Et mox intersigniis per petrarum notas edoctus, gladium iussit effodi prestantissimum. Quem illico dextra corripiens, 'Hic est,' ait, 'fili, quo numerose triumphaui, et qui mihi infallibile semper tutamen extitit.' Et hec dicens, eundem filio contradidit.

Nec mora; terminus ecce congressioni prefixus arctius instabat. Tandem, confluentibus undique phalangis innumerabilibus, in Egdore fluminis mediamne locus pugne constituitur; ut ita pugnatores ab utriusque cetus adminiculo segregati nullius opitulatione fungerentur. Teotonicis ergo ultra fluminis ripam in Holsatia considentibus, Danis uero citra amnem dispositis, rex pontis in medio sedem elegit, quatenus, si unigenitus occumberet, in fluminis se gurgitem precipitaret, ne pariter nato orbatus et regno cum dolore superstes canos deduceret ad inferos.

Deinde emissis utrinque pugilibus, in medio amne conuenerunt. Ast ubi miles noster egregius Uffo, duos sibi conspexit occurrere, tanquam leo pectore robusto infremuit, animoque constanti duobus electis audacter se opponere non detrectauit; illo cinctus mucrone, quem patrem supra meminimus occuluisse, et alterum dextra strictum gestans. Quos cum primum obuios habuisset, sic singillatim utrumque alloquitur; et, quod raro legitur accidisse, athleta noster elegantissimus, cuius memoria in eternum non delebitur, ita aduersarios animabat ad pugnam: 'Si te,' inquit, 'regni nostri stimulat ambitio, ut nostre opis, potentieque, opumque capessere uelis opulentias, comminus te clientem decet precedere, ut et regni tui terminos amplifices, et militibus tuis conspicientibus, strenuitatis nomen nanciscaris.' Campionem uero hunc in modum alloquitur: 'Uirtutis tue experientiam iam locus est propagare, si comminus accesseris, et eam, quam pridem Alamannis gloriam ostendisti, Danis quoque propalare non cuncteris. Nunc ergo famam tue strenuitatis poteris ampliare, et egregie munificentie dono ditari, si et dominum precedas, et clypeo defensionis eum tuearis. Studeat, queso, Teotonicis experta strenuitas uariis artis pugillatorire modis Danos instruere, ut tandem optata potitus uictoria, cum triumphi ualeas exultatione ad propria remeare.'

[3] So all that remains is to gather appropriate weapons for the new warrior. The king ordered the best swords in the kingdom to be brought to try out, but Offa, wielding them one by one in his right hand shattered them into the smallest pieces. 'Are these the weapons' he asked, 'with which I am to defend my life and the honour of the kingdom?'

When the father had proof of this vigorous strength, he said: 'There still remains one safeguard for our kingdom and life.' So he ordered to be led to a burial-mound in which he had formerly hidden a well-tried blade. And soon, guided by marks among indications on the stones, he ordered that this most remarkable sword be dug up. Grasping which straightway in his right hand, he said: 'Here it is, my son, with which I triumphed many a time, and which always proved an unfailing protection for me.' And so saying, he handed it to the son.

No delay! See, the time appointed for the encounter swiftly drew near! At length, when countless platoons had gathered from all sides, the place of combat was decided upon – an islet in the middle of the river Eider; thus in this way the combatants, cut off from all aid from either side, should receive no assistance. So the Teutons seated themselves on the further bank of the river, in Holstein, the Danes took up their positions on this side of the stream, whilst the king chose a seat in the middle of a bridge, so that if his only son should die he might throw himself into the depths of the river, and not survive, deprived at once of offspring and kingdom, to take his grey hairs in sorrow to the grave.

Thereupon, the fighters sent from either side met in the middle of the stream. But when our noble warrior Offa saw that two men were coming against him, he growled from his mighty chest like a lion, and with steadfast heart did not shrink from boldly confronting the two chosen men; at his belt the blade which his father had kept hidden, as we mentioned above, and carrying another, drawn, in his right hand. As soon as they were face to face, he addressed them both, one by one; and, what is seldom read of happening, this most handsome champion of ours – whose memory will never be effaced – encouraged his adversary to the fight. He said: 'If ambition to win our kingdom incites you, so that you long to seize our riches, power and plenty, you ought by rights to go in front of your retainer in close combat, so that you extend the boundaries of your kingdom and win a name for valour in the sight of your warriors.' But the champion he addressed in this fashion: 'Here is the place for further proof of your courage, if you will come near for close combat, and not delay in exhibiting to the Danes that glory which you showed the Germans long ago. Now, therefore, you will be able to increase your reputation for vigour, and grow rich with generous gifts, if you go in front of your lord and safeguard him with your protecting shield. I beg you, let him endeavour to teach the Danes the vigour in the various arts of war at which Teutons are expert, so that finally you may win the longed-for victory and go back to your own people exulting in triumph.'

Quam cum complesset exhortationem, pugilis cassidem toto percussit conamine, ita ut, quo feriebat, gladius in duo dissiliret. Cuius fragor per uniuersum intonuit exercitum. Unde cohors Teotonicorum exultatione perstrepebat; sed contra Dani desperationis consternati tristitia, gemebundi murmurabant. Rex uero, ut audiuit, quod filii ensis dissiliuisset, in margine se pontis jussit locari. Uerum Uffo, subito exempto, quo cinctus erat, gladio, pugilis illico coxam cruentauit, nec mora, et caput pariter amputauit. Sic ergo ludus fortune ad instar lune uarius, nunc his, nunc illis successibus illudebat, et quibus iamiam exultatione fauebat ingenti, eos nouercali mox uultu, toruoque conspexit intuitu. Hoc cognito, senior iam confidentius priori se iussit sede locari. Nec iam anceps diu extitit uictoria. Siquidem Uffo ualide instans, ad ripam amnis pepulit heredem imperii, ibique eum haud difficulter gladio iugulauit. Sicque duorum solus uictor existens, Danis irrogatam multis retro temporibus infamiam gloriosa uirtute magnifice satis aboleuit. Atque ita Alamannis cum improperii uerecundia, cassatisque minarum ampullositatibus, cum probris ad propria remeantibus, postmodum in pacis tranquillitate precluis Uffo regni sui regebat imperium.

[4] ....

When he had finished this exhortation, he struck the champion's helmet with all his strength, in such a way that the sword split in two. The sound of its breaking rang out over the whole army. At which the host of Teutons shouted aloud with exultation; but on the other hand the Danes, desperate and dismayed, uttered a great groan of grief. In fact when the king heard that his son's sword had split, he ordered them to place him on the edge of the bridge. But Offa suddenly drew the blade which he had at his belt, immediately drew blood from the champion's hip, and without delay cut off the head as well. Thus, therefore, the game of Fortune, as variable as the moon, mocking now these, now those that follow them, those to whom her favours even now brought great exultation, she soon looks on with a stepmother's countenance and grim gaze. Learning of this [and] more confident, the old man ordered them to place him in his former seat. Nor did victory remain in doubt for long. Indeed, Offa, pressing hard, drove the Emperor's heir back to the river bank, and there, with little trouble, slew him with the sword. In this manner, by being the victor alone against two others, he wholly erased by his magnificent and glorious courage that infamy the Danes incurred in times long past. And in this way, when the Germans had gone back to their own people, disgraced, ashamed and their bombastic threats proved empty, Offa reigned over his kingdom henceforth in peace and tranquillity.

[4] He begot a son to whom he gave the name of Dan.

Appendix H:

Saxo Grammaticus, *Gesta Danorum*, Book IV extract

Sweyn Aageson[1] speaks of Saxo as an associate (*contubernalis*) in the ménage of the powerful Archbishop Absalon of Lund, (1178-1201), active Baltic crusader and statesman, to whom Saxo's work paid attention. The archbishop's will forgives a certain *clericus* named Saxo a small financial debt but urges him to return two books borrowed from the library.

Saxo tells us in the preface to his *Gesta Danorum* that both his father and grandfather had served in the army under the Danish king Valdemar I (1157-82), and that he himself would be happy to serve Valdemar II (1202-41) if in a more spiritual way. His sophisticated Latin learning perhaps reflects education in Paris, and by 1342 he was being called *grammaticus* (master of letters).

> Cui filius Wermundus succedit. Hic, prolixis tranquillitatis otiis felicissima temporum quiete decursis, diutinam domesticae pacis constantiam inconcussa rerum securitate tractabat. Idem prolis expers iuuentam exegit; senior uero filium Uffonem sero fortunae munere suscitauit, cum nullam ei sobolem elapsa tot annorum curricula peperissent. Hic Uffo coaeuos quosque corporis habitu supergressus, adeo hebetis ineptique animi principio iuuentae existimatus est, ut priuatis ac publicis rebus inutilis uideretur. Siquidem ab ineunte aetate nunquam lusus aut ioci consuetudinem praebuit; adeoque humanae delectationis uacuus fuit, ut labiorum continentiam iugi silentio premeret, et seueritatem oris a ridendi prorsus officio temperaret. Uerum ut incunabula stoliditatis opinione referta habuit, ita post modum conditionis contemptum claritate mutauit; et quantum inertiae spectaculum fuit, tantum prudentiae et fortitudinis exemplum euasit. Cuius pater socordiam contemplatus filiam ei Sleswicensium praefecti Frowini in matrimonium ascescit, illustrissimi uiri affinitate utilissimum gerendi regni subsidium recepturo.

[Digression regarding the dishonourable slaying of the Swedish king, Athisl, two-against-one, by Offa's brothers-in-law Keto and Wigo.]

---

[1] See above, pp. 165-6.

Saxo Grammaticus, *Deeds of the Danes*, Book IV extract

Written at the suggestion of the archbishop, the *Gesta Danorum* describes the history of Denmark, and in part Scandinavia in general, from the legendary past to the twelfth-century present, including stories such as that of Hamlet, prince of Denmark, similar to the one on which William Shakespeare (1564-1616) based his play. Stories of Scandinavian heroes are arranged in a series of biographies, passing into history in the tenth century with the reign of Gorm the Old, and finishing in 1186, with the subjection of eastern Germany by Canute VI.

Only very small fragments of manuscripts presently survive, but an early printed copy (1514) was made from a manuscript in the possession of the then archbishopric of Lund. Ed. J. Olrik and H. Ræder, *Gesta Danorum*, Copenhagen, 1931-57; transl. H.E. Davidson and P. Fisher, *History of the Danes*, Cambridge, 1979-80.

> [Viglet's] son Wermund succeeded him. As this lengthy period of peace and prosperity ran on, he maintained a prolonged and steady peace at home in undisturbed security. In the prime of life he was devoid of offspring; but despite all the years which had passed him by with no issue, as an older man, by a late gift of fortune, he begot a son, Offa. This Offa surpassed all those of his age in bodily size, but as a youngster was considered so dull and foolish in spirit as to appear useless for business, public or private. Indeed, from early years he never spent time in play or merriment, and was so devoid of human pleasure that he kept his lips sealed in continual silence, and wholly inhibited his grim countenance from laughter. But although supposed stupid from the cradle onwards, what happened afterwards changed contempt to high esteem; and just as he had been the picture of lethargy, so he turned into the model of wisdom and bravery. His father, seeing a simpleton, married him to a daughter of Frowin, the governor of the men of Schleswig – so that by a relationship with so illustrious a man he might receive practical help in administering the kingdom.

[Digression regarding the dishonourable slaying of the Swedish king, Athisl, two-against-one, by Offa's brothers-in-law Keto and Wigo.]

Cumque Wermundus aetatis uitio oculis orbaretur, Saxoniae rex, Daniam duce uacuam ratus, ei per legatos mandat, regnum, quod praeter aetatis debitum teneat, sibi procurandum committat, ne nimis longa imperii auiditate patriam legibus armisque deficiat. Qualiter enim regem censeri posse, cui senectus animum, caecitas oculum pari caliginis horrore fuscauerit? Quod si abnuat, filiumque habeat, qui cum suo ex prouocatione confligere audeat, uictorem regno potiri permittat. Si neutrum probet, armis secum, non monitis agendum cognoscat, ut tandem inuitus praebeat, quod ultroneus exhibere contemnat.

Ad haec Wermundus, altioribus suspiriis fractus, impudentius se aetatis exprobratione lacerari respondit, quem non ideo huc infelicitatis senectus prouexerit, quod pugnae parcus timidius iuuentam exegerit. Nec aptius sibi caecitatis uitium obiectari, quod plerumque talem aetatis habitum talis iactura consequi soleat, potiusque condolendum calamitati quam insultandum uideatur. Iustius autem Saxoniae regi impatientiae notam afferri posse, quem potius senis fatum opperiri, quam imperium poscere decuisset, quod aliquanto praestet defuncto succedere, quam uiuum spoliare. Se tamen, ne tamquam delirus priscae libertatis titulos externo uideatur mancipare dominio, propria manu prouocationi pariturum. Ad haec legati, scire se inquiunt, regem suum conserendae cum caeco manus ludibrium perhorrere, quod tam ridiculum decernendi genus rubori quam honestati propinquius habeatur. Aptius uero per utriusque pignus et sanguinem amborum negotio consuli.

Ad haec obstupefactis animo Danis, subitaque responsi ignorantia perculsis. Uffo, qui forte cum ceteris aderat, responsionis a patre licentiam flagitabat, subitoque uelut ex muto uocalis euasit. Cumque Wermundus, quisnam talem a se loquendi copiam postularet, inquireret, ministrique eum ab Uffone rogari dixissent, satis esse perhibuit, ut infelicitatis suae uulneribus alienorum fastus illuderet, ne etiam a domesticis simili insultationis petulantia uexaretur. Sed satellitibus Uffonem hunc esse pertinaci affirmatione testantibus, 'Liberum ei sit,' inquit, 'quisquis est, cogitata profari.'

When Wermund had lost his sight due to the infirmity of old age, the king of the Saxons, thinking the Danes lacked an accepted leader, ordered him through envoys to commit into his charge the kingdom which he held beyond due span; unless, greedy for power too long, he strip the fatherland of laws and defence. For how could he be reckoned a king, whose spirit was darkened with age, and his eyes with a blindness no less gloomy and awful? If he refused, but had a son who would dare accept a challenge and fight with his own son, he should allow the victor to possess the kingdom. If he agreed to neither, let him understand that it was a matter of weapons not warnings, so that at length he must unwillingly surrender what he scorned to yield voluntarily.

At this, Wermund, shaken with heavy sighs, answered that it was insolent to reproach him with taunts as to his years; for he had passed no timid youth, nor shrunk from battle, that age should bring him to this misery. Neither was it fitting to censure the infirmity of his blindness, for it was common for such a loss to accompany such a time of life, and might seem a calamity fitter for condolences than insults. In fact he himself could more justly charge the king of the Saxons with impatience, for it would have been seemlier to wait for the old man's death than demand his realm; because it was preferable to succeed to the dead than despoil the living. However, rather than be thought to hand over the honour of ancient freedom, like a madman, to a foreign power, he would accept the challenge with his own hand. At this the envoys affirmed that they knew their king would shrink from the mockery of fighting with a blind man, because such a ridiculous kind of combat was thought more shameful than honourable. It would surely be more appropriate to settle the affair by means of blood-relations on either side.

At this the Danes were astonished, and suddenly at a loss for a reply. Offa, who happened to be there with the rest, demanded permission from his father to reply, and suddenly it was as if a voice came from the dumb. And when Wermund enquired who had thus begged leave to speak, and servants with him said it was Offa, he declared that it was quite enough for the insolent foreigner to jeer at his misererable pains, without being vexed by similar impudent insults from the household. But as those around continued to aver that this really was Offa, he said: 'Whoever he is, he's free to say what he thinks.'

Tum Uffo, frustra ab eorum rege regnum appeti, inquit, quod tam proprii rectoris officio quam fortissimorum procerum armis industriaque niteretur. Praeterea nec regi filium nec regno successorem deesse, sciantque, se non solum regis eorum filium, sed etiam quemcumque ex gentis suae fortissimis secum adsciuerit, simul pugna aggredi constituisse. Quo audito legati risere, uanam dicti animositatem existimantes. Nec mora, condicitur pugnae locus, eidemque stata temporis meta praefigitur. Tantum autem stuporis Uffo loquendi ac prouocandi nouitate praesentibus iniecit, ut, utrum uoci eius an fiduciae plus admirationis tributum sit, incertum extiterit.

Abeuntibus autem legatis, Wermundus, responsionis auctore laudato, quod uirtutis fiduciam non in unius, sed duorum prouocatione statuerit, potius se ei, quicumque sit, quam superbo hosti regno cessurum perhibuit. Uniuersis autem filium eius esse testantibus, qui legatorum fastum fiduciae sublimitate contempserit, propius eum accedere iubet, quod oculis nequeat, manibus experturus. Corpore deinde eius curiosius contrectato, cum ex artuum granditate lineamentisque filium esse cognosset, fidem assertoribus habere coepit, percontarique eum, cur suauissimum uocis habitum summo dissimulationis studio tegendum curauerit, tantoque aetatis spatio sine uoce et cunctis loquendi commerciis degere sustinuerit, ut se linguae prorsus officio defectum natiuaeque taciturnitatis uitio obsitum credi permitteret? Qui respondit, se paterna hactenus defensione contentum, non prius uocis officio opus habuisse, quam domesticam prudentiam externa loquacitate pressam animaduerteret. Rogatus item ab eo, cur duos quam unum prouocare maluerit, hunc idcirco dimicationis modum a se exoptatum respondit, ut Athisli regis oppressio, quae, quod a duobus gesta fuerat, Danis opprobrio extabat, unius facinore pensaretur, nouumque uirtutis specimen prisca ruboris monumenta conuelleret. Ita antiquae crimen infamiae recentis famae litura respergendum dicebat.

Then said Offa, that it was idle for their king to crave a kingdom which could rely on the diligence of its ruler and on the arms and wisdom of the strongest noblemen. Besides which, the king did not lack a son, nor the kingdom an heir; and they should know that he was prepared to fight not only their king's son, but at the same time any one of their people's strongest men with him. Having heard which, the envoys laughed, considering the vehement words empty. Without delay the place for the fight was agreed on and a deadline fixed. However, the bystanders were so surprised by the unexpectedness of Offa's oration and challenge, that one can scarcely say if they were more astonished at his words or his confidence.

But on the departure of the envoys Wermund praised him who had made the response, because he had shown confidence in his courage by challenging not only one, but two; and said he would rather resign his kingdom to him, whoever he was, than to a proud foe. But when everyone averred that it was his own son who had spurned the arrogance of the envoys with lofty self-confidence, he told him come nearer, to test with hands what he could not by eye. After carefully feeling his body, he recognized him to be his son by the size of his limbs and by his features; and began to believe their assertions and ask him why he had taken pains to conceal the sweet sound of his voice with such careful dissembling, and had endured living so long a span of life without voice or any conversation, so as to let men believe him utterly incapable of speech, and born dumb? He replied that until now being satisfied with the protection of his father, he had not needed the use of his voice until he saw their native good sense hard pressed by the babble of foreigners. Asked also why he had chosen to challenge two instead of one, he replied that he wanted this mode of combat so that the death of King Athisl which, having been caused by two men, was a standing reproach to the Danes, might be offset by a single-handed exploit, and a new example of valour expunge the old memory of embarrassment. New honour would thus wipe out the offence of old dishonour he said.

Quem Wermundus iustam omnium aestimationem fecisse testatus, armorum usum, quod iis parum assueuisset, praediscere iubet. Quibus Uffo oblatis, magnitudine pectoris angustos loricarum nexus explicuit; nec erat ullam reperire, quae eum iusto capacitatis spatio contineret. Maiore siquidem corpore erat, quam ut alienis armis uti posset. Ad ultimum, cum paternam quoque loricam uiolenta corporis astrictione dissolueret, Wermundus eam a laeuo latere dissecari, fibulaque sarciri praecepit, partem, quae clipei praesidio muniatur, ferro patere parui existimans. Sed et gladium, quo tuto uti possit, summa ab eo cura conscisci iussit. Oblatis compluribus, Uffo manu capulum stringens, frustatim singulos agitando comminuit; nec erat quisquam ex iis tanti rigoris gladius, quem non ad primae concussionis motum crebra partium fractione dissolueret.

Erat autem regi inusitati acuminis gladius, Skrep dictus, qui quodlibet obstaculi genus uno ferientis ictu medium penetrando diffinderet, nec adeo quicquam praedurum foret, ut adactam eius aciem remorari potuisset. Quem ne posteris fruendum relinqueret, per summam alienae commoditatis inuidiam in profunda defoderat, utilitatem ferri, quod filii incrementis diffideret, ceteris negaturus. Interrogatus autem, an dignum Uffonis robore ferrum haberet, habere se dixit, quod, si pridem a se terrae traditum recognito locorum habitu reperire potuisset, aptum corporis eius uiribus exhiberet. In campum deinde perduci se iubens, cum, interrogatis per omnia comitibus, defossionis locum acceptis signorum indiciis comperisset, extractum cauo gladium filio porrigit. Quem Uffo nimia uetustate fragilem exesumque conspiciens, feriendi diffidentia percontatur, an hunc quoque priorum exemplo probare debeat, prius habitum eius, quam rem ferro geri oporteat, explorandum testatus. Refert Wermundus, si praesens ferrum ab ipso uentilando collideretur, non superesse, quod uirium eius habitui responderet. Abstinendum itaque facto, cuius in dubio exitus maneat.

Igitur ex pacto pugnae locus expetitur. Hunc fluuius Eidorus ita aquarum ambitu uallat, ut earum interstitio repugnante, nauigiis dumtaxat aditus pateat. Quem Uffone sine comite petente, Saxoniae regis filium insignis uiribus athleta consequitur, crebris utrimque turbis alternos riparum anfractus spectandi auiditate complentibus. Cunctis igitur huic spectaculo oculos inserentibus, Wermundus in extrema pontis parte se collocat, si filium uinci contigisset, flumine periturus. Maluit enim sanguinis sui ruinam comitari, quam patriae interitum plenis doloris sensibus intueri.

Having affirmed that it was a correct judgement of everything, Wermund ordered there to be preliminary instruction in the use of arms, since there had been little acquaintance with them. The size of his chest split the links of breastplates when Offa tried, nor was any found large enough to hold him properly. In fact he was too big in body to be able to use the arms of anyone else. Eventually, when his father's breastplate also broke by the violent constriction, Wermund had it split on the left side and patched with a clasp, thinking it mattered little if the side guarded by the shield were exposed to a weapon. He also told him to take great care in choosing a sword which he could use safely. A number were offered, but Offa, grasping the hilts in his hand, one by one shattered them into pieces by shaking, none of which was so hard-tempered as not to break into many pieces at the first blow.

However, there was a sword of the king's of extraordinary sharpness, called 'Skrep', which at a single stroke would cleave any obstacle whatsoever; nothing would be hard enough to parry the edge driven at it. Loth to leave this for the enjoyment of posterity, greatly grudging others the benefit of it, he had buried it deep, intending, since he despaired of his son's improvement, to deny it to others. But asked whether he had a weapon worthy of Offa's strength, he said that he had one which, if he could recognize the lie of the land and locate what he had consigned to the earth long ago, he could offer appropriate to the bodily strength he showed. Then, telling them to lead him into open country where, questioning his companions through all of it, recognized from the signs the place where the sword was buried, took it from its hole and handed it to his son. Seeing that it was fragile with great age and corroded, Offa, hesitating to strike with it, asked whether he might prove this one also like the rest, declaring that he must try the blade before the battle was to be fought. Wermund replied that if this blade shattered from brandishing, there was nothing left which would answer his strength. He must therefore refrain from an act, the outcome of which remained uncertain.

So they went to the place of combat as agreed. It is encircled by the waters of the River Eider, which roll between, and bar any approach save by boat. Offa made for it without companion, whilst the son of the king of Saxons was attended by a champion famous for his strength. On either side, dense crowds of eager spectators thronged the winding banks. When all bent their eyes upon this scene, Wermund placed himself at the end of a bridge, meaning to perish in the flood if his son were defeated. For he would prefer to share in the ruin of his own flesh and blood than behold, with heart full of grief, the downfall of his own country.

Uerum Uffo, geminis iuuenum congressibus lacessitus, gladii diffidentia amborum ictus umbone uitabat, patientius experiri constituens, quem e duobus attentius cauere debuisset, ut hunc saltem uno ferri impulsu contingeret. Quem Wermundus imbecillitatis uitio tantam recipiendorum ictuum patientiam praestare existimans, paulatim in occiduam pontis oram mortis cupiditate se protrahit, si de filio actum foret, fatum praecipitio petiturus. Tanta sanguinis caritate flagrantem senem fortuna protexit. Uffo siquidem filium regis ad secum auidius decernendum hortatus, claritatem generis ab ipso conspicuo fortitudinis opere aequari iubet, ne rege ortum plebeius comes uirtute praestare uideatur. Athletam deinde, explorandae eius fortitudinis gratia, ne domini sui terga timidius subsequeretur, admonitum fiduciam a regis filio in se repositam egregiis dimicationis operibus pensare praecepit, cuius delectu unicus pugnae comes ascitus fuerit. Obtemperantem illum propiusque congredi rubore compulsum, primo ferri ictu medium dissecat. Quo sono recreatus Wermundus, filii ferrum audire se dixit, rogatque, cui potissimum parti ictum inflixerit. Referentibus deinde ministris, eum non unam corporis partem, sed totam hominis transegisse compagem, abstractum praecipitio corpus ponti restituit, eodem studio lucem expetens, quo fatum optauerat. Tum Uffo, reliquum hostem prioris exemplo consumere cupiens, regis filium ad ultionem interfecti pro se satellitis manibus parentationis loco erogandam impensioribus uerbis sollicitat. Quem propius accedere sua adhortatione coactum, infligendi ictus loco curiosius denotato, gladioque, quod tenuem eius laminam suis imparem uiribus formidaret, in aciem alteram uerso, penetrabili corporis sectione transuerberat. Quo audito Wermundus Screp gladii sonum secundo suis auribus incessisse perhibuit. Affirmantibus deinde arbitris, utrumque hostem ab eius filio consumptum, nimietate gaudii uultum fletu soluit. Ita genas, quas dolor madidare non poterat, laetitia rigauit. Saxonibus igitur pudore maestis, pugilumque funus summa cum ruboris acerbitate ducentibus, Uffonem Dani iucundis excepere tripudiis. Quieuit tum Athislanae caedis infamia, Saxonumque opprobriis exspirauit.

In fact, assaulted by both the young men together, Offa, distrusting his sword, parried the blows with his shield, determined to be patient and see which of the two he must beware of more carefully, so that he might reach at least that one by a single stroke of the blade. Wermund, assuming that he took the blows so patiently because of his feebleness, edged slowly forward to the western end of the bridge, meaning to fling himself down and perish, that his longing for death should all be over with his son. Fortune protected the old man who loved his flesh and blood with such passion. For Offa urged the king's son to engage with him more eagerly, to do some spectacular deed of prowess worthy of his great birth, lest the low-born companion should seem superior to the prince. Then, in order to test the bravery of the champion, he admonished him not to skulk timidly behind his master, but justify by noble deeds of combat the trust put on him by the king's son who had chosen him to be his sole companion in the fight. He complied, and when shame drove him to fight at close quarters, the first stroke of the blade clove through the middle. The sound revived Wermund, who said that he heard his son's blade, and asked on what particular part the stroke was delivered. Then when the retainers answered that no one part but the man's whole frame was sliced through, he drew back from the precipice, came again on to the bridge, hoping as passionately now for life as he had just wished for death. Then Offa, wanting to despatch his remaining foe in the fashion of the first, incited the king's son with stronger words to wreak vengeance, offer some sacrifice for the soul of the servant slain in his cause. Drawing him near by these exhortations, and carefully noting the spot to place his stroke, he turned the other edge of his sword to the front, fearing the thin side to be too fragile for the impact, and pierced the body through with a penetrating stroke. Hearing this, Wermund declared that the sound of the sword Skrep had reached his ears a second time. Then, when the judges announced that both foes were killed by his son, his face dissolved in tears from an excess of joy. Thus gladness watered the cheeks which sorrow could not moisten. So the Saxons, miserable with the disgrace, bore the fighters to burial with bitter shame, the Danes receive Offa with leaps of joy. Then the disgrace of Athisl's murder was laid to rest, and the Saxons' taunts came to an end.

Appendix H

Ita Saxoniae regnum ad Danos translatum, post patrem Uffo regendum suscepit, utriusque imperii procurator effectus, qui ne unum quidem rite moderaturus credebatur. Hic a compluribus Olauus est dictus, atque ob animi moderationem Mansueti cognomine donatus. Cuius sequentes actus uetustatis uitio sollemnem fefellere notitiam. Sed credi potest, gloriosos eorum processus exstitisse, quorum tam plena laudis principia fuerint. Tam breui factorum eius prosecutione animaduerto, quod illustrium gentis nostrae uirorum splendorem scriptorum penuria laudi memoriaeque subtraxerit. Quod si patriam hanc fortuna Latino quondam sermone donasset, innumera Danicorum operum uolumina tererentur.

Uffoni Dan filius succedit...

Thus the kingdom of Saxons passed to the Danes; Offa, after his father, undertook its rule; and he, who had not been thought up to administering a single kingdom properly, was now appointed to govern both. Here he was called Olaf by the majority, and was given the by-name of 'the Mild' for his spirit of moderation. Through the ravages of time, his subsequent deeds have lacked formal record. But it can be supposed from such praiseworthy beginnings that their sequel was glorious. I give such a brief account of his actions, because the lustre of the famous men of our race has been lost to memory and praise by the lack of writings. Because if by good luck the fatherland had in olden times been endowed with the Latin language, there would have been countless volumes about of the deeds of the Danes.

Offa's son Dan came afterwards...

BIBLIOGRAPHY

Abels, R., *Lordship and Military Obligation in Anglo-Saxon England*, London, 1988.

~ 'Alfred and his biographers: images and imagination', in *Writing Medieval Biography*, ed. Bates, *et al.*, pp. 61-75.

Acta Sanctorum, ed. J. Bolland, Antwerp, 1707.

Adam of Bremen, *Gesta Hammaburgensis Ecclesiae Pontificum*, ed. B. Schmeidler, *Monumenta Germaniae Historica, Scriptores rerum Germanicarum*, Hanover, 1917.

~ transl. F.J. Tschan, *History of the Archbishops of Hamburg-Bremen*, New York, revd edn, 2002.

Ælfric, *Catholic Homilies*, ed. P. Clemoes, Early English Text Society, Suppl. Series 17 (1997).

Æthelweard, *The Chronicle*, ed. A. Campbell, London, 1962.

Alcuin, *Letters*, ed. E. Dümmler, *Epistolae Karolini Aevi*, II, *Monumenta Germaniae Historica*, Berlin, 1895.

~ transl. S. Allott, *Alcuin of York*, York, 1974.

Alfano, C., 'The issue of feminine monstrosity: a re-evaluation of Grendel's mother', *Comitatus*, 23 (1992), 1-16.

Amaya-Jackson, L. and J.S. March, 'Posttraumatic Stress Disorder', in *Anxiety Disorders in Children*, ed. March, pp. 276-300.

Ammianus Marcellinus, *Rerum Gestarum Historia*, ed. J.C. Rolfe, London, 1935-40.

Ancient Laws and Institutes of England, ed. B. Thorpe, Rolls Series, 28, London, 1840.

Andersen, H.H., H.J. Madsen and O. Voss, *Danevirke*, Copenhagen, 1976.

Andersen, J., *The Witch on the Wall: Medieval erotic sculpture in the British Isles*, Copenhagen, 1977.

Anglo-Saxon Chronicles, ed. J. Earle and C. Plummer, Oxford, 1892-99.

~ transl. M. Swanton, revd edn, London, 2000.

Anglo-Saxon Wills, ed. D. Whitelock, Cambridge, 1930.

Anglo-Saxon Writs, ed. F.E. Harmer, Manchester, 1952.

Annales Fuldenses, ed. F. Kurze, *Monumenta Germaniae Historica, Scriptores rerum Germanicarum*, Hanover, 1891.

~ transl. T. Reuter, Manchester, 1992.

Annales Regni Francorum, ed. F. Kurze, *Monumenta Germaniae Historica, Scriptores rerum Germanicarum*, Hanover, 1895.

Annales Ryenses, ed. J.M. Lappenberg, *Monumenta Germaniae Historica, Scriptores rerum Germanicarum*, 16, Hanover, 1859, pp. 386-410.

Annals of St Neots, ed. D.N. Dumville and M. Lapidge, Cambridge, 1984.

Anthony, I.E., 'Excavations in Verulam Hills Field, St Albans, 1963-4', *Hertfordshire Archaeology*, 1 (1968), 9-50.

Ashdown, M., 'The single combat in certain cycles of English and Scandinavian tradition and romance', *Modern Language Review*, 17 (1922), 113-30.

Asser, *Life of King Alfred*, ed. W.H. Stevenson, revd. D. Whitelock, Oxford, 1959.

~ transl. S. Keynes and M. Lapidge, *Alfred the Great*, Harmondsworth, 1983.

Augustine, Aurelius, *Opera Omnia*, ed. J.P. Migne, *Patrologia Latina*, 32-77, Paris, 1845-87.

Ball, W., *Rome in the East*, London, 2000.

Barron, W.R.J., *English Medieval Romance*, London, 1987.

Bartlett, R., *Trial by Fire and Water: The Medieval Judicial Ordeal*, Oxford, 1986.

Bassett, S.R., 'A probable Mercian royal mausoleum at Winchcombe, Gloucestershire', *Antiquaries Journal*, 65 (1985), 82-100.

~ 'How the west was won: the Anglo-Saxon takeover of the west midlands', *Anglo-Saxon Studies in Archaeology and History*, 11 (2000), 107-18.

Bates, D., J. Crick and S. Hamilton, ed. *Writing Medieval Biography 750-1250*, Woodbridge, 2006.

Battiscombe, C.F., ed. *The Relics of St Cuthbert*, Durham, 1956.

Battle of Maldon, ed. D.G. Scragg, Oxford, 1981.

Bax, M., 'Rules for ritual challenges: a speech convention among medieval knights', *Journal of Pragmatics*, 5 (1981), 423-44.

Beddie, J.S., 'The ancient classics in the mediaeval libraries', *Speculum*, 5 (1930), 3-20.

Bede, *Ecclesiastical History of the English People*, ed. and transl. B. Colgrave and R.A.B. Mynors, Oxford, 1969.

Bede, *Opera Historica*, ed. C. Plummer, Oxford, 1896.

Beowulf, ed. and transl. M. Swanton, Manchester, 1978.

Bibliotheca Historica, ed. C.H. Oldfather *et al.*, London, 1933-67.

Biddle, M. and B. Kjølbye-Biddle, 'St Albans', *Current Archaeology*, 11 (1990-93), 412-3.

~ 'The origins of St Albans Abbey: Romano-British cemetery and Anglo-Saxon monastery', in *Alban and St Albans*, ed. Henig and Lindley, pp. 45-77.

Birkeland, H., *Nordens historie i middelalderen etter arabiske kilder*, Oslo, 1954.

Bjork, R.E. and J.D. Niles, ed. *A Beowulf Handbook*, Exeter, 1997.

Bloomfield, M.W., 'Beowulf, Byrhtnoth, and the judgment of God: trial by combat in Anglo-Saxon England', *Speculum*, 44 (1969), 545-59.

Blunt, C.E., 'The coinage of Offa', in *Anglo-Saxon Coins*, ed. R.H.M. Dolley, London, 1961, pp. 39-62.

Boberg, I.M., 'Die Sage von Vermund und Uffe', *Acta Philologica Scandinavica*, 16 (1942), 129-57.

Bökönyi, S., 'Data on Iron Age horses of Central and Eastern Europe', *Bulletin of The American School of Prehistoric Research*, 25 (1968), 1-71.

Bosworth, J. and T.N. Toller, *An Anglo-Saxon Dictionary*, Oxford, 1898.

Bradley, S.A.J., *Anglo-Saxon Poetry*, 2nd edn, London, 1995.

Bragg, L., 'Telling silence: alingualism in Old Icelandic myth, legend, and saga', *Journal of Indo-European Studies*, 32 (2004), 267-98.

Bredsdorff, P., *Kortlægning og historiske Studier*, Copenhagen, 1973.

Breeze, D.J., 'The Antonine Wall', in *Glasgow, the Antonine Wall and Argyll*, ed. H. Swain and P. Ottaway, London, 2007, pp. 11-18.

Brook, D., 'The Early Christian church east and west of Offa's Dyke', in *The Early Church in Wales and the West*, ed. N. Edwards and A. Lane, Oxford, 1992, pp. 77-89.

Brown, M. and S. Seaton, *Christmas Truce*, London, 1984.

Brown, M.P. and C.A. Farr, ed. *Mercia: an Anglo-Saxon Kingdom in Europe*, London, 2001.

Bruce-Mitford, R.L.S., *The Sutton Hoo Ship-Burial*, London, 1975-83.

Brut or Hystoria Brutonum, ed. W.R.J. Barron and S.C. Weinberg, London, 1995.

Brut y Tywysogyon: Peniarth MS 20, ed. T. Jones, Cardiff, 1941, transl., Cardiff, 1952.

Brut y Tywysogyon: Red Book of Hergest, ed. and transl. T. Jones, Cardiff, 1955.

Bullough, D.A. and R.L. Storey, eds, *The Study of Medieval Records*, Oxford, 1971.

Bu'Lock, J.D., 'Vortigern and the Pillar of Eliseg', *Antiquity*, 34 (1960), 49-53.

Burgess, J.T., 'Saxon remains at Offchurch', *Journal of the British Archaeological Association*, 32 (1876), 464-67.

Byrne, M.E., 'On the punishment of sending adrift', *Eriu*, 11 (1932), 97-102.

Cadogan, M. and D. Schutte eds, *The William Companion*, London, 1990.

Caesar, *The Gallic War*, ed. H.J. Edwards, London, 1917.

Camden, William, *Britannia*, London, 1586.

Campbell, J., *The Hero with a Thousand Faces*, Princeton, NJ., 1949.

~   'Some twelfth-century views of the Anglo-Saxon past', in *Essays in Anglo-Saxon History*, ed. J. Campbell, London, 1986, pp. 209-28.

Carisella, J. and J.W. Ryan, *Who Killed the Red Baron: the final answer*, London, 1969.

Cartularium Saxonicum, ed. W.G. Birch, London, 1885-99.

Cassius Dio, *Roman History*, ed. H.B. Foster, transl. E. Cary, London, 1914-27.

Cessford, C., 'Exogamous marriages between Anglo-Saxons and Britons in seventh century northern Britain', *Anglo-Saxon Studies in Archaeology and History*, 9 (1996), 49-52.

Chambers, E.K., *The Mediaeval Stage*, Oxford, 1903.

Chambers, R.W., *Six thirteenth century drawings illustrating the story of Offa and of Thryth (Drida)*, London, 1912.

~   *Widsith: a Study in Old English Heroic Legend*, Cambridge, 1912.

Chance, J., *Woman as Hero in Old English Literature*, Syracuse, NY, 1986.

Chancellor's Roll, ed. D.M. Stenton, The Pipe Roll Society, 45 (1930).

Charles, B.G., *Non-Celtic Place-Names in Wales*, London, 1938.

Charles-Edwards, T.M., 'Wales and Mercia, 613-918', in *Mercia: an Anglo-Saxon Kingdom in Europe*, ed. Brown and Farr, pp. 89-105.

Chaucer, G., *The Canterbury Tales*, ed. F.N. Robinson, Oxford, 1986.

Chick, D., 'The coinage of Offa in the light of recent discoveries', in *Æthelbald and Offa*, ed. Hill and Worthington, pp. 111-22.

Chronicon de Abingdon, ed. R.S. Stevenson, Rolls Series, 2, London, 1858.

Cleasby, R. and G. Vigfusson, *An Icelandic-English Dictionary*, 2nd edn, Oxford, 1957.

Clover, C.J., 'Maiden warriors and other sons', *Journal of English and Germanic Philology*, 85 (1986), 35-49.

~ 'Regardless of sex: men, women, and power in early Northern Europe', *Speculum*, 68 (1993), 363-87.

Colgrave, B., 'Pilgrimages to Rome in the seventh and eighth centuries', in *Studies in Language, Literature, and Culture of the Middle Ages and Later*, ed. E.B. Atwood and A.A. Hill, Austin, Texas, 1969, pp. 156-72.

Constantius, *Vita Germani*, ed. B. Krusch and W. Levison, *Passiones Vitaeque Sanctorum Aevi Merovingici*, Hanover, 1919, pp. 225-83.

Corolla Sancti Eadmundi, ed. F. Hervey, London, 1907.

Costanzo, P. *et al.*, 'Social Development', in *Anxiety Disorders in Children*, ed. March, pp. 82-108.

Councils and Ecclesiastical Documents, ed. A.W. Haddan and W. Stubbs, Oxford, 1869-78.

Cox, J.C., 'Ecclesiastical History' in *The Victoria History of the County of Nottingham*, London, 1906-10, II, pp. 37-177.

Crick, J., 'Offa, Ælfric and the refoundation of St Albans', in *Alban and St Albans*, ed. Henig and Lindley, pp. 78-84.

~ ed., *Charters of St Albans*, Oxford, 2007.

Crumlin-Pedersen, O., 'Ship types and sizes AD 800-1400', in *Aspects of Maritime Scandinavia AD 200-1200*, ed. O. Crumlin-Pedersen, Roskilde, 1991, pp. 69-82.

Cubitt, C., *Anglo-Saxon Church Councils, c. 650-c. 850*, Leicester, 1995.

~ 'Sites and sanctity: revising the cult of murdered and martyred Anglo-Saxon royal saints', *Early Medieval Europe*, 9 (2000), 53-83.

Cumont, F. 'Les noms des planètes', *L'Antiquité Classique*, 4 (1935), 5-43.

Dainton, M. 'The myths and misconceptions of the stepmother identity', *Family Relations*, 42 (1993), 93-98.

Damico, H., 'The valkyrie reflex in Old English literature', in *New Readings on Women in Old English Literature*, ed. H. Damico and A.H. Olsen, Bloomington, Indiana, 1990, pp. 176-90.

Davidson, H.E., *The Sword in Anglo-Saxon England*, Oxford, 1962.

~ 'The hero as a fool: the northern Hamlet', in *The Hero in Tradition and Folklore*, ed. H.E. Davidson, London, 1984, pp. 30-45.

Davies, W., *Patterns of Power in Early Wales*, Oxford, 1990.

Davies W. and H. Vierck, 'The contexts of Tribal Hidage: social aggregates and settlement patterns', *Frühmittelalterliche Studien*, 8 (1974), 223-93.

Davis, R.H.C., 'Did the Anglo-Saxons have warhorses?', in *Weapons and Warfare*, ed. Hawkes, pp. 141-44.

Davison, G.C. *et al.*, *Abnormal Psychology*, 9th edn, New York, 2004.

Deeds of Hereward the Wake, see *Hereward*.

Delehaye, H., *Sanctus*, Brussels, 1927.

Denholm-Young, N., *Handwriting in England and Wales*, Cardiff, 1954.

Dobbie, E. v. K., *The Anglo-Saxon Minor Poems*, New York, 1942.

Dockray-Miller, M., 'The masculine queen of *Beowulf*', *Women and Language*, 21 (1998), 31-8.

Dolley, R.H.M.,'The so-called piedforts of Alfred the Great', *Numismatic Chronicle*, 6th S. 14 (1954), 76-92.

Dümmler, E.L., *Geschichte des ostfränkischen Reiches*, Leipzig, 1887-88.

Dumville, D.N., 'The Anglian collection of royal genealogies and regnal lists', *Anglo-Saxon England*, 5 (1976), 23-50.

Earle, John, 'Beowulf, II,' *The Times*, 29th October, 1885, 3.

Early Welsh Genealogical Tracts, ed. P.C. Bartrum, Cardiff, 1966.

Edda: die Lieder des Codex Regius, ed. G. Neckel, rev. H. Kuhn, Heidelberg, 1962.

~   transl. H.A. Bellows, *The Poetic Edda*, New York, 1923.

~   ed. and transl. U. Dronke, *The Poetic Edda*, Oxford, 1969-97.

Edwards, H., *The Charters of the Early West Saxon Kingdom*, Oxford, 1988.

Edwards, N., 'Rethinking the Pillar of Eliseg', *Antiquaries Journal*, 89 (2009), 143-77.

Egger, C., 'The canon regular', in *Adrian IV, The English Pope (1154-1159)*, ed. B. Bolton and A.J. Duggan, Aldershot, 2003, pp. 15-28.

Einhard, *Vita Karoli Magni*, ed. O. Holder-Egger, *Monumenta Germaniae Historica, Scriptores rerum Germanicarum*, Hanover, 1911.

~   transl. L. Thorpe, *Two Lives of Charlemagne*, Harmondsworth, 1969.

Ekwall, E., *English River-Names*, Oxford, 1928.

~   'Tribal names in English place-names', *Namn och Bygd*, 41 (1953), 129-77.

Eliason, N.E., 'The "Thryth-Offa Digression" in *Beowulf* ', in *Medieval and Linguistic Studies*, ed. J.B. Bessinger and R.P. Creed, London, 1965, pp. 124-38.

Ellmers, D., 'Die Shiffe der Angelsachsen', in *Sachsen und Angelsachsen*, ed. C. Ahrens, Hamburg, 1978, pp. 495-509.

English Historical Documents, ed. and transl. D. Whitelock, London, 2nd edn, 1979.

English Mediaeval Lapidaries, ed. J. Evans and M.S. Sergeantson, Early English Text Society, Old Series 190, London, 1933.

Enright, M.J., *Lady with a Mead Cup*, Dublin, 1996.

Epistolae Merowingici et Karolini Aevi, ed. E. Dümmler, *Monumenta Germaniae Historica*, Berlin, 1892-95.

Erckert, R. von, ed. *Wanderung und Siedelungen der Germanischen Stämme in Mittel-Europa von der ältesten Zeit bis auf Karl den Grossen*, Berlin, 1901.

Erlenkeuser, H., 'Neue C14-datierungen zum Danewerk', in H.H. Andersen, *Danevirke og Kovirke*, Aarhus, 1998, pp. 189-201.

Evison, V.I., *The Fifth-Century Invasions South of the Thames*, London, 1965.

~   'The Dover ring-sword and other ring-swords and beads', *Archaeologia*, 101 (1967), 63-118.

Fasciculus Morum: a Fourteenth-century Preacher's Handbook, ed. and transl., S. Wenzel, Pennsylvania, 1989.

Faull, M.L., 'The semantic development of Old English *wealh*', *Leeds Studies in English*, NS 8 (1975), 20-44.

Fee, C., '*Beag & beaghroden*: women, treasure and the language of social structure in *Beowulf* ', *Neuphilologische Mitteilungen*, 97 (1996), 285-94.

Ferrante, J., 'Public postures and private maneuvers: roles medieval women play', in *Women and Power in the Middle Ages*, ed. M. Erler and M. Kowaleski, Athens, Georgia, 1988, pp. 213-29.

Finberg, H.R.P., *The Early Charters of the West Midlands*, Leicester, 1961.

Fisher, E.A., *The Greater Anglo-Saxon Churches*, London, 1962.

Fleischman, S., 'On the representation of history and fiction in the Middle Ages', *History and Theory*, 22 (1983), 278-310.

Förstemann, E., *Altdeutsches Namenbuch*, Bonn, 1900-16.

Fox, A. and C., 'Wansdyke reconsidered', *The Archaeological Journal*, 115 (1958), 1-45.

Fox, C., 'Dykes', *Antiquity*, 3 (1929), 135-54.

~   *The Personality of Britain; its influence on inhabitant and invader in prehistoric and early historic times*, Cardiff, 1932.

~   *Offa's Dyke. A Field Survey of the Western Frontier-Works of Mercia in the Seventh and Eighth Centuries A.D.*, London, 2nd edn, 1955.

Fox, R., *Kinship and Marriage*, Harmondsworth, 1967.

France-Lanord, A., 'La fabrication des épées damassées aux époques mérovingienne et carolingienne', *Le Pays Gaumais*, 10 (1949), 19-45.

Fredegar, *The fourth book of the Chronicle: with its continuations*, ed. J.M. Wallace-Hadrill, London, 1960.

Furnivall, F.J. *et al.*, eds, *Originals and Analogues of some of Chaucer's Canterbury Tales*, London, 1872-88.

Galbraith, V.H., *Roger of Wendover and Matthew Paris*, Glasgow, 1944.

Gale, D.A., 'The seax', in Hawkes ed., *Weapons and Warfare*, pp. 71-83.

Gannon, A., *The Iconography of Early Anglo-Saxon Coinage*, Oxford, 2003.

Gebühr, M., 'Angulus desertus?', *Studien zur Sachsenforschung*, 11 (1998), 43-85.

Gelling, M., *The Place-Names of Oxfordshire*, English Place-Name Society, 23-24, Cambridge, 1953-54.

~   *Signposts to the Past*, London, 1978.

~   'Why aren't we speaking Welsh?', *Anglo-Saxon Studies in Archaeology and History*, 6 (1993), 51-56.

Geoffrey Gaimar, *L'Estoire des Engleis*, ed. A. Bell, Oxford, 1960.

Gerould, G.H., 'Offa and Labhraidh Maen', *Modern Language Notes*, 17 (1902), 201-3.

Gesetze der Angelsachsen, ed. F. Liebermann, Halle, 1898-1916.

Gesta Abbatum Monasterii Sancti Albani, ed. H.T. Riley, Rolls Series, 28, London, 1867-69.

Ghidini, A. and L. Lynch, 'Prenatal diagnosis and significance of fetal infections', *Western Journal of Medicine*, 159 (1993), 366-73.

Giles, J.A., *English History from the Year 1235-1273*, London, 1852-54.

Giraldus Cambrensis, *Opera*, ed. J.S. Brewer *et al.*, Rolls Series, 21, London, 1861-91.

Gough, A.B, *The Constance Saga*, Berlin, 1902.

Goulstone, J., *An Introduction to English Royal Descents*, Bexleyheath, 1993.

Gover, J.E.B. *et al.*, *The Place-Names of Warwickshire*, English Place-Name Society, 13, Cambridge, 1936.

~   *The Place-Names of Hertfordshire*, English Place-Name Society, 15, Cambridge, 1938.

Gransden, A., *Historical Writing in England*, London, 1974-82.

Gräslund, A-S., 'Is there any evidence of powerful women in Late Iron Age Svealand?', in *Völker an Nord- und Ostsee und die Franken* , ed. U. von Freeden *et al.*, Bonn, 1999, pp. 91-98.

Gregory of Tours, *Historiae Francorum*, ed. W. Arndt and B. Krusch, *Monumenta Germaniae Historica, Scriptores rerum Merovingicarum*, I, Hanover, 1885.

~   transl. L. Thorpe, *The History of the Franks*, Harmondsworth, 1974.

Grierson, P., 'Some aspects of the coinage of Offa', *Numismatic Circular*, 71 (1963), 223-25.

~   'Carolingian Europe and the Arabs: the myth of the mancus', *Revue Belge de Philologie et d'Histoire*, 32 (1954), 1059-74.

~   'Money and coinage under Charlemagne', in *Karl der Grosse, Lebenswerk und Nachleben*, ed. W. Braunfels, Düsseldorf, 1965-8, I, pp. 501-36.

Grierson, P. and M. Blackburn, *Medieval European Coinage*, I, Cambridge, 1986.

Grimm, J., *Deutsche Mythologie*, Göttingen, 1844.

Guillaume Durand, *Le Pontifical*, ed. M. Andrieu, *Studi e Testi*, 88, 3, (1940).

Haddan, A.W. and W. Stubbs, *Councils and Ecclesiastical Documents*, Oxford, 1869-78.

Hahn, C., 'The limits of text and image?: Matthew Paris's final project, the Vitae duorum Offarum, as historical romance', in *Excavating the Medieval Image*, ed. D.S. Areford and N.A. Rowe, Aldershot, 2005, pp. 37-58.

Hamerow, H., 'Migration theory and the Migration period', in *Building on the Past*, ed. B. Vyner, London, 1994, pp. 164-77.

~   'Wanderungstheorien und die angelsächsische "Identitätskrise"', *Studien zur Sachsenforschung*, 11 (1998), 121-34.

Hankinson, R. and A. Caseldine, 'Short dykes in Powys and their origins', *Archaeological Journal*, 163 (2006), 264-69.

Hannaford, H.R., *Archaeological Excavations on Wat's Dyke* , Shrewsbury, 1998.

~   'An excavation on Wat's Dyke at Mile Oak, Oswestry, Shropshire,' *Transactions of the Shropshire Archaeological and Historical Society*, 73 (1998), 1-7.

Hardy, T. D., *Descriptive Catalogue of Materials relating to the History of Great Britain and Ireland*, Rolls Series, 26, London, 1862-71.

Härke, H., '"Warrior graves"? The background of the Anglo-Saxon weapon burial rite', *Past and Present*, 126 (1990), 22-43.

Harrison, S., 'The thirteenth-century west front of St Albans Abbey', in *Alban and St Albans*, ed. Henig and Lindley, pp. 176-81.

Hart, C., *The Danelaw*, London, 1992.

Haslam, J., 'Market and fortress in England in the reign of Offa', *World Archaeology*, 19 (1987-8), 76-93.

Hawkes, S.C., ed., *Weapons and Warfare in Anglo-Saxon England*, Oxford, 1989.

Hawkes, S.C. and R.I. Page, 'Swords and runes in south-east England', *Antiquaries Journal*, 47 (1967), 1-26.

Henig, M., 'Religion and art in St Alban's city', in *Alban and St Albans*, ed. Henig and Lindley, pp. 13-29.

Henig, M. and P. Lindley, ed. *Alban and St Albans*, Leeds, 2001.

Henry of Huntingdon, *Historia Anglorum*, ed. and transl. D. Greenway, Oxford, 1996.

Hereward, Deeds of in Gaimar, *Lestorie des Engles*, ed. T.D. Hardy and C.T. Martin, Rolls Series, 91, London, 1888-89, I, pp. 339-404.

~ transl. M. Swanton in *Medieval Outlaws*, ed. T.H. Ohlgren, Stroud, 1998, pp. 12-60.

Herodotus, *Histories, English and Greek*, ed. A.D. Godley, London, 1920-25.

Hill, D.H., 'Offa's and Wat's Dykes – some exploratory work on the frontier between Celt and Saxon', in *Anglo-Saxon Settlement and Landscape*, ed. T. Rowley, Oxford, 1974, pp. 102-07.

~ 'The construction of Offa's Dyke', *Antiquaries Journal*, 65 (1985), 140-42.

Hill, D. and M. Worthington, *Offa's Dyke: History and Guide*, Stroud, 2003.

~ ed. *Æthelbald and Offa, two Eighth-century kings of Mercia*, Oxford, 2005.

Hill, P. and L. Thompson, 'The swords of the Saxon cemetery at Mitcham', *Surrey Archaeological Collections*, 90 (2003), 147-61.

Hines, J., *The Scandinavian Character of Anglian England in the Pre-Viking Period*, Oxford, 1984.

~ 'The becoming of the English', *Anglo-Saxon Studies in Archaeology and History*, 7 (1994), 49-59.

~ 'Cultural change and social organisation in early Anglo-Saxon England', in *After Empire. Towards an Ethnology of Europe's Barbarians*, ed. G. Ausenda, Woodbridge, 1995, pp. 75-93.

~ 'The conversion of the Old Saxons', in *The Continental Saxons from the Migration Period to the Tenth Century*, ed. D.H. Green and F. Siegmund, Woodbridge, 2003, pp. 299-328.

Hoare, F.R., *The Western Fathers*, London, 1954.

Hofmeister, A., 'Puer, iuvenis, senex', in *Papsttum und Kaisertum*, ed. A. Brackmann, Munich, 1926, pp. 287-316.

Holthausen, F., 'Kleinere altenglischen Dichtungen', *Anglia*, 41 (1917), 400-04.

Hooke, D., *Kingdom of the Hwicce*, Manchester, 1985.

Hope, W. St J., 'The loss of King John's baggage train', *Archaeologia*, 60 (1907), 93-110.

Howorth, H.H., 'The Ethnology of Germany, IV. The Saxons of Nether Saxony', *Journal of the Anthropological Institute*, 9 (1880), 406-36.

Hull, M.G.R., *et al.*, 'Population study of causes, treatment, and outcome of infertility', *British Medical Journal*, 291 (1985), 1693-97.

Hutton, R., *The Stations of the Sun: a history of the ritual year in Britain*, Oxford, 1996.

Hvass, S., 'Fem års udgravninger i Vorbasse', *Mark og Montre*, 15 (1979), 27-39.

Ingelmark, B.E., 'The skeletons', in *Armour from the Battle of Wisby, 1361*, ed. B. Thordeman *et al.*, Stockholm, 1939-40, I, pp. 149-209.

Jacob, G., *Arabische Berichte von Gesandten an germanische Fürstenhöfe aus dem 9. und 10. Jahrhundert*, Berlin, 1927.

Jacobs, N., 'Anglo-Danish relations, poetic archaism and the date of *Beowulf*', *Poetica* (Tokyo), 8 (1977), 23-43.

James, M.R., 'Two Lives of St. Ethelbert, king and martyr', *English Historical Review*, 32 (1917), 214-44.

~   'The drawings of Matthew Paris', *Walpole Society*, 14 (1925-26), 1-26.

Jankuhn, H., *Die Wehranlagen der Wikingerzeit zwischen Schlei und Treene*, Neumünster, 1937.

~   'The Continental home of the English', *Antiquity*, 26 (1952), 14-24.

~   *Haithabu. Ein Handelsplatz der Wikingerzeit*, Neumünster, 8th edn 1986.

~   'Terra... silvis horrida', *Archaeologia Geographica*, 10-11 (1961-63), 19-38.

~   'Archäologische Bemerkungen zur Glaubwürdigkeit des Tacitus in der Germania', *Nachrichten der Akademie der Wissenschaften in Göttingen: Philol.-hist. Klasse*, 10 (1966), 409-26.

~   'Karl der Grosse und der Norden', in *Karl der Grosse, Lebenswerk und Nachleben*, ed. W. Braunfels, Düsseldorf, 1965-8, I, pp. 699-707.

Jenkins, C., *The Monastic Chronicler and the Early School of St. Albans*, London, 1922.

Jensen, S., 'Stengården: the problem of settlement continuity in Later Iron Age Denmark', *Journal of Danish Archaeology*, 1 (1982), 119-25.

John of Antioch, *Fragmenta Historicorum Græcorum*, ed. C. Müller, Paris, 1841-74.

John of Glastonbury, *The Chronicle of Glastonbury Abbey*, ed. J.P. Carley, Woodbridge, 1985.

John of Salisbury, *Policraticus*, ed. C.C.J. Webb, Oxford, 1909.

~   transl. C.J. Nederman, *The Frivolities of Courtiers*, Cambridge, 1990.

John of Wallingford, *Chronicle attributed to*, ed. R. Vaughan, Camden Miscellany, 3rd S. 90, 1958.

John (*alias* Florence) of Worcester, *The Chronicle*, ed. and transl. R.R. Darlington *et al.*, Oxford, 1995-98.

John, E., 'The point of Woden', *Anglo-Saxon Studies in Archaeology and History*, 5 (1992), 127-34.

Jordanes, *Getica*, ed. T. Mommsen, *Monumenta Germaniae Historica, Auctores Antiquissimi*, 5 (1), Berlin, 1882.

~   transl. C.C. Mierow, *The Gothic History*, Cambridge, 1915.

Jørgensen, A.N., 'Sea defence in Denmark AD 200-1300', in *Military Aspects of Scandinavian Society in a European Perspective, AD 1-1300*, ed. A.N. Jørgensen and B.L. Clausen, Copenhagen, 1997, pp. 200-09.

Judith, ed. M. Griffith, Exeter, 1997.

Jürgs, M., *Der kleine Frieden im Grossen Krieg*, Munich, 2003.

Kalendre of the Newe Legende of Englande, ed. M. Görlach, Heidelberg, 1994.

Kannner, L., 'Autistic disturbances of affective contact', *Nervous Child*, 2 (1943), 217-50.

Ker, N.R., *Catalogue of Manuscripts containing Anglo-Saxon*, Oxford, 1957.

~   *Medieval Libraries of Great Britain*, 2nd edn, London, 1964.

Keynes, S., 'A lost cartulary of St Albans Abbey', *Anglo-Saxon England*, 22 (1993), 255-79.

~   'The kingdom of the Mercians in the eighth century', in *Æthelbald and Offa*, ed. Hill and Worthington, pp. 1-26.

King, P.D., *Charlemagne: Translated Sources*, Kendal, 1987.

King Alfred's West Saxon Version of Gregory's Pastoral Care, ed. H. Sweet, Early English Text Society, Old Series, 45, 50, London, 1871-72.

Kirby, I.J., 'Angles and Saxons in Laȝamon's Brut', *Studia Neophilologica*, 36 (1964), 51-62.

Knight, J.K., 'Britain's other martyrs', in *Alban and St Albans*, ed. Henig and Lindley, pp. 38-44.

Knowles, D. *et al.*, *The Heads of Religious Houses, England and Wales: I, 940-1216*, Cambridge, 1972.

Kormáks Saga, ed. E.Ó. Sveinsson, *Íslenzk Fornrit*, VIII, Reykjavík, 1939.

~   transl. W.G. Collingwood, *The Life and Death of Cormac the Skald*, Ulverston, 1902.

Krappe, A.H., 'The Offa-Constance Legend', *Anglia*, 61 (1937), 361-9.

Lamb, J.W., *The Archbishopric of Lichfield (787-803)*, London, 1964.

Lanfranc, *Chronicon Beccensis abbatiae*, *Patrologia Latina*, 150, cols. 639-90.

Last, C.G. *et al.*, 'Anxiety disorders in children and their families', *Archives of General Psychiatry*, 48 (10) (1991), 928-34.

Latouche, R., *Les Origines de L'Économie Occidentale (IVe-XIe siécle)*, Paris, 1956.

Laur, W., 'Angeln und die Angeln in namenkundlicher Sicht', *Jahrbuch Heimatvereins der Landschaft Angeln*, 22 (1958), 46-9.

~   'Der Flussname Eider', *Zeitschrift der Gesellschaft für Schleswig-Holsteinische Geschichte*, 87 (1962), 263-71.

Laws of Early Iceland, ed. A. Dennis, P. Foote and R. Perkins, Winnipeg, Manitoba, 2000.

Laȝamon, *Brut*, ed. and transl. W.R.J. Barron and S.C. Weinberg, London, 1995.

Le Saux, F., *Laȝamon's Brut: the Poem and its Sources*, Woodbridge, 1989.

Legge, M.D., *Anglo-Norman Literature and its Background*, Oxford, 1963.

Leonard, H. and S. Dow, 'Selective Mutism', in *Anxiety Disorders in Children and Adolescents*, ed. March, pp. 235-50.

Lethbridge, T.C., 'The riddle of the Dykes', *Proceedings of the Cambridge Antiquarian Society*, 51 (1958), 1-5.

Levison, W., 'St. Alban and St. Albans', *Antiquity*, 15 (1941), 337-59.

~   *England and the Continent in the Eighth Century*, Oxford, 1946.

Lewis, S., *The Art of Matthew Paris in the Chronica Majora*, Aldershot, 1987.

Liber Diurnus Romanorum Pontificum, ed. T. von Sickel, Vienna, 1889.

Liber Eliensis, ed. E.O. Blake, London, 1962.

Liebermann, F., ed. *Ungedruckte Anglo-Normannische Geschichtsquellen*, Strassburg, 1879.

Lindahl, C. *et al.*, ed. *Medieval Folklore*, Oxford, 2002.

Lintzel, M., 'Myrgingas und Mauringa', in *Beiträge zur Kulturgeographie*, ed. I. Siedentop, Gotha, 1932, pp. 113-22.

Lloyd, J.E., 'The personal name-system in Old Welsh', *Y Cymrodor*, 9 (1888), 39-55.

~   *A History of Wales*, 3rd edn, London, 1939.

Lucan, *The Civil War*, ed. and transl. J.D. Duff, London, 1928.

Lucy, S., 'Housewives, warriors and slaves? Sex and gender in Anglo-Saxon burials', in *Invisible People and Processes*, ed. J. Moore and E. Scott, London, 1997, pp. 150-68.

~   *The Anglo-Saxon Way of Death*, Stroud, 2000.

Lunt, W.E., *Financial relations of the Papacy with England to 1327*, Cambridge, Mass., 1939.

Lydgate, *The Minor Poems*, ed. H.N. MacCracken, Early English Text Society, Extra Series, 107, Oxford, 1911.

Magennis, H., '"No sex please, we're Anglo-Saxons"? Attitudes to sexuality in Old English prose and poetry', *Leeds Studies in English*, NS 26 (1995), 1-27.

Magoun, F.P., 'Fifeldor and the name of the Eider', *Namn och Bygd*, 28 (1940), 94-114.

~   '*Annales Domitiani Latini*, an edition', *Mediaeval Studies* (Toronto), 9 (1947), 235-95.

Malone, K., 'Ealhhild', *Anglia*, 55 (1931), 266-72.

~   ed. *Widsith*, London, 1936.

~   'The Myrgingas of *Widsith*', *Modern Language Notes*, 55 (1940), 141-42.

~   'Hygd', *Modern Language Notes*, 56 (1941), 356-58.

Mansi, J.D. *et al.*, ed. *Sacrorum Conciliorum, Nova Collectio*, Florence, 1767.

Marcellinus Comes, *Chronicon*, ed. J.P. Migne, *Patrologia Latina*, 51, Paris, 1844-64.

March, J.S., ed. *Anxiety Disorders in Children and Adolescents*, New York, 1995.

Martin, R., '*The Lives of the Offas*: the posthumous reputation of Offa, king of the Mercians', in *Æthelbald and Offa*, ed. Hill and Worthington, pp. 49-54.

Matthew Paris, *Chronica Majora*, ed. H.R. Luard, Rolls Series, 57, London, 1872-83.

~   transl. J.A. Giles, *English History from the Year 1235-1273*, London, 1852-54.

Matthews, S., 'Legends of Offa: the journey to Rome', in *Æthelbald and Offa*, ed. Hill and Worthington, pp. 55-58.

Maurer, K., *Altisländisches Strafrecht und Gerichtwesen*, Leipzig, 1910.

Mawer, A. and F.M. Stenton, *The Place-Names of Bedfordshire and Huntingdonshire*, English Place-Name Society, 3, Cambridge, 1926.

McKitterick, R., 'The illusion of royal power in the Carolingian Annals', *English Historical Review*, 115 (2000), 1-20.

McLeod, W., 'Alban and Amphibal: some extant Lives and a lost Life', *Mediaeval Studies*, 42 (1980), 407-30.

McNeill, J.T. and H.M. Gamer, *Medieval Handbooks of Penance*, New York, 1938.

Memorials of Saint Dunstan, ed. W. Stubbs, Rolls Series, 63, London, 1874.

Middle English Dictionary, ed. H. Kurath, S.M. Kuhn *et al.*, Ann Arbor, Michigan, 1952-2001.

Mommsen, T., *Inscriptiones Britanniae Latinarum*, Berlin, 1873.

Moore, W.J., *The Saxon Pilgrims to Rome and the Schola Saxonum*, Fribourg, 1937.

Morgan, N., *Early Gothic Manuscripts, I, 1190-1250*, London, 1982.

Morris, J., 'The date of Saint Alban', *Hertfordshire Archaeology*, 1 (1968), 1-8.

Much, R., 'Widsith: Beiträge zu einem Commentar', *Zeitschrift für deutsches Altertum*, 62 (1925), 113-50.

Muir, B.J., ed. *The Exeter Anthology of Old English Poetry*, 2nd edn, Exeter, 2000.

Müller-Wille, W., 'Siedlungs-, Wirtschafts- und Bevölkerungsräume im westlichen Mitteleuropa um 500 n. Chr.', *Westfälische Forschungen*, 9 (1956), 5-25.

Museum of London, *The Prittlewell Prince*, London, 2004.

Myres, J.N.L., 'Wansdyke and the origin of Wessex', in *Essays in British History*, ed. H.R. Trevor-Roper, London, 1964, pp. 1-27.

~   *Anglo-Saxon Pottery and the Settlement of England*, Oxford, 1969.

~   *The English Settlements*, Oxford, 1986.

Nash-Williams, V.E., *The Early Christian Monuments of Wales*, Cardiff, 1950.

Nelson, J.L., 'Queens as Jezebels: the careers of Brunhild and Balthild in Merovingian history', in *Medieval Women*, ed. D. Baker, Oxford, 1978, pp. 31-77.

~   'Carolingian contacts', in *Mercia: an Anglo-Saxon Kingdom in Europe*, ed. Brown and Farr, pp. 126-43.

~   'Did Charlemagne have a private life?', in *Writing Medieval Biography*, ed. Bates, et al., pp. 15-28.

Nennius, *Historia Brittonum*, ed. F. Lot, Paris, 1934.

Niblett, R., *Verulamium, the Roman City of St Albans*, Stroud, 2001.

Niblett, R. and I. Thompson, *Alban's Buried Towns*, Oxford, 2005.

Nova Legenda Anglie, ed. C. Horstman, Oxford, 1901.

Noy, D., 'Wicked stepmothers in Roman society and imagination', *Journal of Family History*, 16 (1991), 345-61.

Nurse, K., 'New dating for Wat's Dyke', *History Today*, 49.8 (1999), 3-4.

Ogier de Danemarche, *La Chevalerie*, ed. M. Eusebi, Milan, 1963.

Old English Apollonius of Tyre, ed. P. Goolden, Oxford, 1958.

Orosius, *The Old English Orosius*, ed. J. Bately, Early English Text Society, Supplementary Series, 6 (1980).

Osborne, M., *Defending Britain: Twentieth-century Military Structures in the Landscape*, Stroud, 2004.

Otter, M., *Inventiones: fiction and referentiality in twelfth-century historical writing*, London, 1996.

Overing, G.R., *Language, Sign, and Gender in Beowulf*, Carbondale, Illinois, 1990.

Ovid, *Metamorphoses*, ed. F.J. Miller, London, 1916.

Pächt, O., *The Rise of Pictorial Narrative in Twelfth-Century England*, Oxford, 1962.

Pächt, O., C.R. Dodwell and F. Wormald, *The St. Albans Psalter*, London, 1960.

Page, R.I., 'Anglo-Saxon episcopal lists', *Nottingham Mediaeval Studies*, 9 (1965), 71-95; 10 (1966), 2-24.

Pappe, I., *A History of Modern Palestine: One Land, Two Peoples*, Cambridge, 2004.

Parks, W., *Verbal Dueling in Heroic Narrative*, Princeton, NJ, 1990.

Passerini, L., 'Mythbiography in oral history', in *The Myths We Live By*, ed. R. Samuel and P. Thompson, London, 1990, pp. 49-60.

Paulus Diaconus, *Historia Langobardorum*, ed. L. Bethmann and G. Waitz, *Monumenta Germaniae Historica, Scriptores rerum Langobardicarum*, Hanover, 1878.

~   transl. W.D. Foulke, *History of the Langobards*, Philadelphia, 1907.

Payton, P., *A.L. Rowse and Cornwall*, Exeter, 2005.

Perkins, D.R.J. and S.C. Hawkes, 'The Thanet gas pipeline phases I and II, 1982', *Archaeologia Cantiana*, 101 (1984), 83-114.

Picasso, *Woman with Stiletto*, Musée Picasso, Paris, nos. 136, 1135, *Picasso's Picassos*, London, 1981, pp. 23, 89.

Pohl, W. 'Ethnic names and identities in the British Isles', in *The Anglo-Saxons from the Migration Period to the Eighth Century*, ed. J. Hines, Woodbridge, 1997, pp. 7-40.

Powicke, F.M., 'The compilation of the "Chronica Majora" of Matthew Paris', *Modern Philology*, 38 (1941), 305-17.

Procopius, *History of the Wars*, ed. H.B. Dewing, London, 1914-40.

Ptolemy, *Die Geographie*, ed. O. Cuntz, Berlin, 1923.

~   transl. E.L. Stevenson, *Geography of Claudius Ptolemy*, New York, 1932.

~   *Tetrabiblos*, ed. and transl. F.E. Robbins, Cambridge, Mass., 1940.

Radford, C.A.R., 'The archaeological background on the Continent', in *Christianity in Britain 300-700*, ed. M.W. Barley and R.P.C. Hanson, Leicester, 1968, pp. 19-36.

Ramsey, L.C., *Chivalric Romances: Popular Literature in Medieval England*, Bloomington, Indiana, 1983.

Reaney, P.H., *The Place-Names of Cambridgeshire and the Isle of Ely*, English Place-Name Society, 19, Cambridge, 1943.

Reuter, T., 'The recruitment of armies in the early Middle Ages: what can we know?', in *Military Aspects of Scandinavian Society*, ed. Jørgensen and Clausen, pp. 32-37.

Reynolds, R.L., 'Reconsideration of the history of the Suevi', *Revue Belge de Philologie et d'Histoire*, 35 (1957), 19-47.

Richard of Cirencester, *Speculum Historiale*, ed. J.E.B. Mayor, Rolls Series, 30 (1863-69).

Rickert, E., 'The Old English Offa Saga', *Modern Philology*, 2 (1904-5), 29-76, 321-76.

Rickert, M., *Painting in Britain: the Middle Ages*, 2nd edn, Harmondsworth, 1965.

Riddle, M.A. *et al.*, 'Obsessive compulsive disorder in children and adolescents: phenomenology and family history', *Journal of the American Academy of Child and Adolescent Psychiatry*, 29 (1990), 766-72.

Robinson, F.C., 'The prescient woman in Old English literature', in *Philologia Anglica*, ed. K. Oshitari *et al.*, Tokyo, 1988, pp. 241-50.

Rodwell, W. *et al.*, 'The Lichfield angel', *Antiquaries Journal*, 88 (2008), 48-108.

Roger of Wendover, *Chronica sive Flores Historiarum*, ed. H.O. Coxe, London, 1841-44.

~   transl. Giles, J.A., *Flowers of History*, London, 1849.

Rollason, D.W., 'Lists of saints' resting-places in Anglo-Saxon England', *Anglo-Saxon England*, 7 (1978), 61-93.

Roman de Brut, ed. J. Weiss, Exeter, 1999.

Ross, D.J.A., 'Old French', in *The Traditions of Heroic and Epic Poetry*, ed. A.T. Hatto, London, 1980-89, I, pp. 79-133.

Rowse, A.L., *An Elizabethan Garland*, London, 1954.

Royal Commission on the Ancient and Historical Monuments of Scotland, *Eastern Dumfriesshire*, Edinburgh, 1997.

Royal Commission on Historical Manuscripts, *Twelfth Report*, London, 1891.

~   *Guide to the Location of Collections described in the Reports and Calendars Series, 1870-1980*, London, 1982.

Royal Commission on Historical Monuments (England), *An Inventory of the Historical Monuments in Hertfordshire*, London, 1911.

Saga of the Volsungs, ed. R.G. Finch, London, 1965.

Salwen, L.V., 'The myth of the Wicked Stepmother', *Women and Therapy*, 10 (1990), 117-25.

Sawyer, P.H., *Anglo-Saxon Charters: an Annotated List*, London, 1968.

Saxo Grammaticus, *Gesta Danorum*, ed. J. Olrik and H. Ræder, Copenhagen, 1931-57.

~   transl. H.E. Davidson and P. Fisher, *History of the Danes*, Cambridge, 1979-80.

Sayers, J.E., 'Papal privileges for St. Albans abbey and its dependencies', in *Study of Medieval Records*, ed. Bullough and Storey, pp. 57-84.

Scharer, A., 'Die Intitulationes der angelsächsischen Könige im 7. und 8. Jahrhundert', in *Intitulatio III*, ed. H. Wolfram and A. Scharer, Vienna, 1988, pp. 9-74.

Schick, J., 'Die Urquelle der Offa-Konstanze-Sage', in *Britannica, Max Förster, zum...*, Leipzig, 1929, pp. 31-56.

Schlauch, M., *Chaucer's Constance and Accused Queens*, New York, 1927.

Scholz, B.W., 'Sulcard of Westminster: Prologus...', *Traditio*, 20 (1964), 59-91.

~   *Carolingian Chronicles*, Ann Arbor, 1970, pp. 88-89.

Scull, C.J., 'Approaches to material culture and social dynamics of the Migration Period in eastern England', in *Europe between Late Antiquity and the Middle Ages*, ed. J. Bintliff and H. Hamerow, Oxford, 1995, pp. 71-83.

Searle, W.G., *Onomasticon Anglo-Saxonicum*, Cambridge, 1897.

~   *Anglo-Saxon Bishops, Kings and Nobles*, Cambridge, 1899.

Sharp, S., 'Æthelberht, king and martyr: the development of a legend', in *Æthelbald and Offa*, ed. Hill and Worthington, pp. 59-63.

Sharpe, R. *et al.*, ed. *English Benedictine Libraries, the Shorter Catalogues*, London, 1996.

Shepherd, D.J. 'The elusive warrior maiden tradition: bearing weapons in Anglo-Saxon society', in *Ancient Warfare*, ed. J. Carman and A. Harding, Stroud, 1999, pp. 219-43.

Simeon of Durham, *Historia Regum*, ed. T. Arnold, Rolls Series, 75, London, 1882-85.

Sims-Williams, P., *Religion and Literature in Western England, 600-800*, Cambridge, 1990.

Sklute, L.J., 'Freoðuwebbe in Old English poetry', in *New Readings on Women in Old English Literature*, ed. H. Damico and A.H. Olsen, Bloomington, Indiana, 1990, pp. 204-10.

Smith, A.H., *English Place-Name Elements*, English Place-Name Society, 25-26, Cambridge, 1956.

~   The Place-Names of Gloucestershire, English Place-Name Society,   38-41, Cambridge, 1964-65.

~   'The Hwicce', in Medieval and Linguistic Studies in Honor of Francis Peabody Magoun, ed. J.B. Bessinger and R.P. Creed, London, 1965, pp. 56-65.

Smith D.M. and V.C.M. London, The Heads of Religious Houses, England and Wales: II, 1216-1377, Cambridge, 2001.

Smith, T.P., The Anglo-Saxon Churches of Hertfordshire, Chichester, 1973.

~   'Early recycling: the Anglo-Saxon and Norman re-use of Roman bricks', in Alban and St Albans, ed. Henig and Lindley, pp. 111-17.

Snorri Sturluson, Heimskringla, ed. B. Athalbjarnarson, Reykjvík, 1941-45.

~   transl. E. Monsen and A.H. Smith, Cambridge, 1932.

Solberg, B., 'Weapon export from the Continent to the Nordic countries in the Carolingian period', Studien zur Sachsenforschung, 7 (1991), 241-59.

Somerset, F.R. (Lord Raglan), The Hero, London, 1936.

Song of Roland, ed. G.J. Brault, London, 1978.

Southern, R.W., 'Aspects of the European tradition of historical writing: 4, The sense of the past', Transactions of the Royal Historical Society, Fifth Series, 23 (1973), 243-63.

Spiegel, G., Romancing the Past, Berkeley, California, 1993.

Squatriti, P., 'Digging ditches in Early Medieval Europe', Past and Present, 176 (2002), 11-65.

Stafford, P., 'Political women in Mercia, eighth to early tenth centuries', in Mercia: an Anglo-Saxon Kingdom in Europe, ed. Brown and Farr, pp. 35-49.

Stanford, S.C., The Archaeology of the Welsh Marches, London, 1980.

Stenton, F.M., Anglo-Saxon England, 3rd edn, Oxford, 1971.

Stefanović, S., 'Zur Offa-Thryðo-Episode im Beowulf', Englische Studien, 69 (1934), 15-31.

Stephens, G.R., 'A note on the martyrdom of St Alban', Hertfordshire Archaeology, 9 (1983-6), 20-21.

Stevenson, J., The Church Historians of England, London, 1854.

Stoodley, N., The Spindle and the Spear, Oxford, 1999.

Story, J., Carolingian Connections: Anglo-Saxon England and Carolingian Francia, Aldershot, 2003.

Suchier, H., 'Ueber die Sage von Offa und Þryðo', Beiträge zur Geschichte der deutschen Sprache und Literatur, 4 (1877), 500-21.

Swanton, M.J., 'Heroes, heroism and heroic literature', Essays and Studies, NS 30 (1977), 1-21.

~   Crisis and Development in Germanic Society, Göppingen, 1982.

~   St. Sidwell: an Exeter Legend, Exeter, 1986.

~   'Die altenglische Judith: Weiblicher Held oder frauliche Heldin', in Heldensage und Heldendichtung im Germanischen, ed. H. Beck, Berlin, 1988, pp. 289-304.

~   Anglo-Saxon Prose, revd edn, London, 1993.

~   'Gobelen iz Baio: Epicheskoe skazanie ne v stikhakh, no v vyshivke', Mirovoe Drevo, 4 (1996), 47-62.

~   *English Poetry before Chaucer*, Exeter, 2002.

Sweyn Aageson, *Chronicle*, in *Scriptores Minores Historiae Danicae*, ed. M.C. Gertz, Copenhagen, 1917-20, I, pp. 94-174.

~   transl. E. Christiansen, *Works*, London, 1992.

Sympson, E.M., 'Where was Sidnacester?', *Reports and Papers of the Associated Architectural and Archaeological Societies*, 28 (1905), 87-94.

Tacitus, *Annals*, ed. J. Jackson, Cambridge, Mass., 1951.

~   *Germania*, ed. M. Winterbottom and R.M. Ogilvie, *Opera Minora*, Oxford, 1975.

~   transl. J.B. Rives, Oxford, 1999.

Tatlock, J.S.P., 'St. Amphibalus', *Essays in Criticism* (California), 2S, 4 (1934), 249-57, 268-70.

Tatton-Brown, T., 'The medieval building stones of St Albans Abbey', in *Alban and St Albans*, ed. Henig and Lindley, pp. 118-23.

Taylor, P., 'The early St. Albans endowment and its chroniclers', *Historical Research*, 68 (1995), 119-42.

Thacker, A.T., 'Some terms for noblemen in Anglo-Saxon England, c. 650-900', *Anglo-Saxon Studies in Archaeology and History*, 2 (1981), 201-36.

~   'Kings, saints and monasteries in pre-Viking Mercia', *Midland History*, 10 (1985), 1-25.

Theopold, L., *Kritische Untersuchungen über die Quellen zur angelsæchsischen Geschichte des achten Jahrhunderts*, Lemgo, 1872.

Thiébaux, M., *The Stag of Love: the Chase in Medieval Literature*, Ithaca, New York, 1974.

Thompson, E.A., *Saint Germanus of Auxerre and the end of Roman Britain*, Woodbridge, 1984.

Thompson, S., *Motif-Index of Folk-Literature*, revd edn, Bloomington, Indiana, 1966.

Thomson, R.M., *Manuscripts from St Albans Abbey, 1066-1235*, Woodbridge, 1982.

Thorpe, L., *Two Lives of Charlemagne*, Harmondsworth, 1969.

Þorsteins Þáttr Stangarhǫggs, ed. J. Jóhannesson, *Austfirðinga Sǫgur*, Reykjavík, 1950.

~   transl. E. Magnússon and W. Morris, *Tale of Thorstein Staff-smitten*, Cambridge, Ont., 2000.

Three Eleventh-Century Anglo-Latin Saints' Lives, ed. R.C. Love, Oxford, 1996.

Tillmann, H., *Die päpstlichen Legaten in England bis... 1218*, Bonn, 1926.

Turner, R.H. and L.M. Killian, *Collective Behavior*, Englewood Cliffs, New Jersey, 1972.

Tyler, D.J., 'Orchestrated violence and the "supremacy of the Mercian kings"', in *Æthelbald and Offa*, ed. Hill and Worthington, pp. 27-33.

Unverhau, H., *Untersuchungen zur historischen Entwicklung des Landes zwischen Schlei und Eider im Mittelalter*, Neumünster, 1990.

Vaughan, R., 'The handwriting of Matthew Paris', *Transactions of the Cambridge Bibliographical Society*, 1 (1949-53), 376-94.

~   *Matthew Paris*, Cambridge, 1958.

Vegetius, *Epitoma Rei Militaris*, ed. M.D. Reeve, Oxford, 2004.

Victoria County History of Hertfordshire, II, ed. W. Page, London, 1908.

Virgil, *Aeneid*, ed. H.R. Fairclough, revd., London, 1934-35.

Vita Alcuini, ed. W. Arndt, *Monumenta Germaniae Historica, Scriptores*, 15, Hanover, 1887, pp. 182-97.

Vitae Sancti Bonifatii, ed. W. Levison, *Monumenta Germaniae Historica, Scriptores rerum Germanicarum*, 57, Hanover, 1905.

Vries, J. de, *Altnordisches Etymologisches Wörterbuch*, Leiden, 1962.

~   *Heroic Song and Heroic Legend*, London, 1963.

Wace, *Roman de Brut*, ed. J. Weiss, Exeter, 1999.

Wacher, J., *The Towns of Roman Britain*, 2nd edn, London, 1995.

Wagner, F., 'L'organisation du combat singulier au moyen âge dans les états Scandinaves', *Revue de Synthèse Historique*, 56 (1936), 41-60.

Wainwright, F.T., 'Æthelflæd Lady of the Mercians', in *The Anglo-Saxons*, ed. P. Clemoes, London, 1959, pp. 53-69.

Waldere, ed. F. Norman, London, 1933.

Wallace-Hadrill, J.M., 'Charlemagne and England', in *Karl der Grosse, Lebenswerk und Nachleben*, ed. W. Braunfels, Düsseldorf, 1965-8, I, pp. 683-98.

Walter Map, *De Nugis Curialium*, ed. M.R. James, revd C.N.L. Brooke and R.A.B. Mynors, Oxford, 1983.

Watts, W., ed. *Vitæ duorum Offarum... Et uiginti trium abbatum Sancti Albani*, London, 1639.

Weaver, C.P., *The Hermit in English Literature from the Beginnings to 1660*, Nashville, Tennessee, 1924.

Wedel, T.O., *The Mediæval Attitude towards Astrology, particularly in England*, Oxford, 1920.

Weir, A. and J. Jerman, *Images of Lust*, London, 1986.

Wenham, S.J., 'Anatomical interpretation of Anglo-Saxon weapon injuries', in *Weapons and Warfare*, ed. Hawkes, pp. 123-39.

Werner, J., 'Frankish royal tombs in the cathedrals of Cologne and Saint-Denis', *Antiquity*, 38 (1964), 201-16.

William of Malmesbury, *Gesta Regum Anglorum*, ed. and transl. R.A.B. Mynors *et al.*, Oxford, 1998-99.

~   *Gesta Pontificum Anglorum*, ed. and transl. M. Winterbottom, Oxford, 2007.

William of Newburgh, *The History of English Affairs*, ed. and transl. P.G. Walsh and M.J. Kennedy, Warminster, 1988.

William Worcestre, *Itineraries*, ed. J.H. Harvey, Oxford, 1969.

Williams, G., 'Mercian coinage and authority', in *Mercia: an Anglo-Saxon Kingdom in Europe*, ed. Brown and Farr, pp. 210-28.

Williams, L.F.R., 'William the Chamberlain and Luton Church', *English Historical Review*, 28 (1913), 719-30.

~   *History of the Abbey of St. Alban*, London, 1917.

Willroth, K-H., *Untersuchungen zur Besiedlungsgeschichte der Landschaften Angeln und Schwansen*, Neumünster, 1992.

Wilson, R.M., *The Lost Literature of Medieval England*, London, 1952.

Woolf, H.B., *The Old Germanic Principles of Name-giving*, Baltimore, 1939.

Woolliscroft, D.J., *Roman Military Signalling*, Stroud, 2001.

Wormald, P., *Legal Culture in the Early Medieval West: Law as Text, Image and Experience*, London, 1999.

Worthington, M., 'The Offa's Dyke project', *Archaeology in Wales*, 25 (1985), 9-10.

Wrenn, C.L., 'Two Anglo-Saxon harps', in *Studies in Old English Literature in Honor of Arthur G. Brodeur*, ed. S.B. Greenfield, Portland, 1963, pp. 118-28.

Wright, C.E., *The Cultivation of Saga in Anglo-Saxon England*, Edinburgh, 1939.

Yorke, B.A.E., 'The vocabulary of Anglo-Saxon overlordship', *Anglo-Saxon Studies in Archaeology and History*, 2 (1981), 171-200.

~ 'Joint kingship in Kent c. 560 to 785', *Archaeologia Cantiana*, 99 (1983), 1-19.

~ *Nunneries and the Anglo-Saxon Royal Houses*, London, 2003.

Zipperer, S., 'Coins and Currency – Offa of Mercia and his Frankish neighbours', in *Völker an Nord- und Ostsee und die Franken*, ed. U. von Freeden *et al.*, Bonn, 1999, pp. 121-27.

INDEX